THE ATOM BOMB AND THE FUTURE OF MAN

KARL JASPERS

THE ATOM BOMB AND THE FUTURE OF MAN

TRANSLATED BY E. B. ASHTON

The University of Chicago Press
Chicago and London

This book was originally published in 1958 by R. Piper & Co.,
Munich, under the title, *Die Atombombe und die Zukunft
des Menschen*. An earlier edition of this translation appeared
under the title, *The Future of Mankind*.

Library of Congress Catalog Card Number: 60-7237
ISBN: 0-226-39482-4
The University of Chicago Press, Chicago 60637
The University of Chicago Press, Ltd., London

TRANSLATOR'S
NOTE

The Atom Bomb and the Future of Man was written to elaborate a lecture which Karl Jaspers broadcast in the fall of 1956. Deluged with letters, he asked his correspondents in a prefatory note to "take this book for an answer to their objections, questions, and imprecations." The book was published in 1958 and evoked reactions ranging from the Peace Prize of the German book trade to savage attacks from opponents of German rearmament and of the Western alliance.

In 1960 Professor Jaspers came under fire from all sides. In a television interview he spoke of the illusive quest for German reunification, and instead of bowing to the inevitable protests, he earnestly took up his pen to demolish that fetish of German political life. At the core of both storms lay a philosopher's inability to put the label of truth on the fictions men live by. The pace at which facts are now catching up with these fictions makes the *The Atom Bomb and the Future of Man* seem even closer to home.

In English, it was initially planned to shorten the book so as to give only the essence of the original. This proved impossible. Hardly a page turned out to be not of the essence. By and large, therefore, only editorial cuts were made in the translation. If illustrations from European history or German literature would have required explanation, they were omitted. Omitted, too, were the author's detailed positions on specifically German controversies unknown abroad. The "excursions" of the German text — digressions in small type, on subjects not directly related to the main theme — could have been fully rendered only in long footnotes; wherever possible, they were fitted into the text. Finally, having made a point, posed a question, developed an argument, or stated a thesis in simple language, Jaspers likes to elaborate in terms which in German add depth but would hinder rather than aid in following the train of thought in English. These elaborations were pruned — but all the points, questions, arguments, or theses of the original are in the English version. This book is not an abridgment.

One more word on the problems of a translator. I had rendered Jaspers' German terms "chiffre" and "chiffre-writing" — used not in the dictionary sense, but for the concepts and terminologies we apply to the inconceivable, to transcendental reality — as "symbol" and "symbolic language." One day, I chanced to read an interview with Jaspers in an American art magazine. "The symbol is less than the chiffre," he had told the interviewer. "The step is from the symbol to the chiffre. The artist creates symbols as visible appearances and re-creates them to achieve the chiffre."

I was just about to turn all "symbols" in this book into "chiffres" when I started thinking. *The Atom Bomb and the Future of Man* does not deal with art. The "chiffre-writing" mentioned in it is religious; the difference from what we call "religious symbolism" seemed too subtle to warrant distracting the general reader with words of unorthodox meaning. In this book, after all, Jaspers speaks to the general reader. It is "those everywhere who do their own thinking" whom he hopes to reach and to bring to "a more conscious recognition of what they already know."

I let "symbols" stand — and if Karl Jaspers reads this, may he forgive me.

E. B. Ashton

FOREWORD

An altogether novel situation has been created by the atom bomb. Either all mankind will physically perish or there will be a change in the moral-political condition of man. This book is an attempt to clarify what strikes us as a choice between two fantasies.

Despite the apparent calm of our daily lives, the progress of the dread menace seems now irresistible. Topical aspects change quickly, but the over-all aspect remains the same: either the sudden outbreak of nuclear war in a matter of years or decades, or the establishment of world peace without atom bombs, with a new life on the economic basis of nuclear power. Political and legal operations alone will not take us in this direction, nor will unanimous abhorrence of the bomb. We realize today that actually no start has yet been made toward achieving world peace. Do we know what is to be done?

Prophets might save us if they could cast their spell on high and low alike, convincing everyone by their example, their strong faith, their call to penance. They would bring about the change in man, without which he seems doomed. But there are no prophets nowadays, nor could we believe them. My book should not be taken for a prophetic call; it carries no authority but that of rational thought which is given to all human beings. It appeals from reason to reason — but to the grand reason, not to the mere intellect. I should like it to reach those everywhere who do their own thinking.

Let us not deceive ourselves about the intellectual likelihood that all rescue efforts will fail — but even less about the fact that this need not dash our great, inspiring hope. If we grow sure of our freedom, and thus of our responsibility, there is a chance for the change, and thus for salvation.

The point of this book is, first, to take note of the facts, to visualize the world situation, to test all viewpoints, one by one, and to get our bearings in the entirety of realities and possibilities. The book will take patience. To be understood, it will have to be read to the end. It approaches every idea from a point of view which is subsequently transcended. The reader should not be trapped by statements made en route; they will lead to dead ends. Their visualization does not imply a change, although it may stimulate one.

The change itself involves a new way of thinking. If we admire the ingenious products of human skill and hard work, and if we share in these achievements, this need not result in the way of thinking that prevails today. Our time thinks in terms of "knowing how to do it," even where there is nothing to be done. We want to find salvation in a technological conquest of technology — as if the human use of technology might itself be subject to technological direction. Hence, we are optimistic about planning for the specific purpose of peace without changing the rest of our lives. On the other hand, many of us see through the illusion and despair, perceiving only the abyss — for blind activity, wrapped in purposes and immensely intensified, leads nowhere. The turn in our destinies will come from the realization that technology, know-how, achievements, are not enough. The science and technology of man must become parts of an encompassing whole. Our thinking is not wholly serious until we come to the end of our know-how. Our age must learn that some things are beyond "doing."

We draw attention to the turning point — the transformation, or change, or jump — from outwardly productive to inwardly active thinking, from intellect to reason. Our objective, rationalistic thinking need not stray into dark fantasies when it fails; it can turn back to luminous, encompassing thinking. The reader who is accustomed to present ways of thinking may resent not being handed a key with instructions how to unlock the door to salvation with it. Or he may come along willingly, feeling encouraged in what he already knows: in the rational thought that opens all views and leads to creative decisions.

This book wants to aid in bringing the political consciousness of our time into an encompassing "suprapolitical" whole. For as a mere line of human endeavor — a department, so to speak — politics cannot solve the question whether or not mankind will survive.

Philosophical thought should also help the individual achieve a rational state of mind in our total peril. I want to know what I should like to live for and to work for; I want to know what is, so as to do what I can — but also so as to be ready for what may come. We shall have to live with manifest peril.

Yet a teacher of philosophy must know his limits. He can point out; he can induce reflection in a frequently heedless world, by trying to say the simple, essential things. But reflection is not action. Those who think along with us can do no more than spadework in "inner action"; the decisions are made in practice.

Profound thought and concrete action ought to coincide in one and the same individual: in the statesman. In fact, they are usually separate. The philosopher is responsible for the truth of his thought, whose effects are incalculable; but he is not tied to the situations of the day. The statesman, on the other hand, is responsible for the effect of his actions and bound by the effect of his words at the moment, in a particular situation. Both have their weaknesses: the philosopher does not act, and the statesman limits his thinking to close quarters. But philosophy and politics should get together.

KARL JASPERS

CONTENTS

PART ONE

1

THE
NEW
FACT

New weapons of destruction have always been called criminal, the first cannon as well as the recent unrestricted submarine warfare of World War I; yet habit soon made them unquestioned facts of life. The atom bomb of today is a fact novel in essence, for it leads mankind to the brink of self-destruction.

Experts say definitely that it is now possible for life on earth to be wiped out by human action. The scientists who brought the new fact into being have also publicized it. Neither they nor we laymen know how far atomic weapons manufacture has progressed, though each of us can apprehend that America and Russia, trailed by England, keep bending every effort to pile up more such bombs and to increase their destructiveness. The facts are shrouded in official secrecy. It is not publicly known whether — if all bombs in stock were dropped — the radioactive poisoning of the atmosphere would suffice to end life on this planet. One may be right in doubting that the day has come when all life on earth can be annihilated. But in ten years or less the day will come. This slight difference in time does not diminish the urgent need for reflection.

We may assume that the leaders of the two superpowers are informed — though nobody knows the extent to which secrets are guarded and compartmentalized, even among the leaders. Their plans are probably not clear to themselves. Not knowing what to do, they temporize, at the same time preparing for actions that seem inconceivable to all of them. The public is told nothing — except in such monstrous threats as Khrushchev's, which sound fantastic and contain no concrete data either. It is as if silence were imposed upon statesmen, not, as of old, by military secrecy alone, but by the very risk of speaking. There is a tendency abroad, fostered by governments, not to let matters alarm their people.

Alarm keeps growing, nonetheless, though perhaps in the wrong directions. There are protests against hydrogen bomb tests. There is concern about increased radioactivity everywhere. There is local opposition to the construction of atomic piles, lest they explode. Of course, the observation and publication of actually or potentially harmful phenomena is sensible and justified, but we must distinguish between three types of danger:

First, there are dangers inherent in the peaceful use of atomic energy, as well as in hydrogen bomb tests in peacetime. The dangers seem to be substantial; disease and mutations may result from the steady absorbtion of initially slight doses of radioactivity. But those are special problems and can be studied and met like other dangers. Though hundreds of thousands should succumb to the resulting injuries, the harm is limited, and constant efforts will probably limit it further.

Second, in case of war there are dangers of unprecedented destruction. The superbombs, whether delivered by plane or rocket, immediately exterminate all life in a large area. In a larger surrounding area the victims die slowly. In time, survivors in this vaguely circumscribed zone will note diseases and abnormalities in their offspring. Since this disaster will befall big cities and entire countries, there is now unanimous agreement that a new world war would destroy civilization. "I do not know what weapons will be used in the next war," Einstein said years ago, "but the one after that will be fought with bows and arrows."

The third danger, due to cumulative effects that may extend to lethal contamination of the whole atmosphere, is the destruction of mankind, of life itself.

All three dangers have this in common: we do not know to what extent they exist. But the concepts differ both in kind and in degree, progressing from local and special disasters to the end of civilization, and then to the end of mankind. Against the first, there are technological safeguards. From the second, remnants of humanity can be saved by protective measures, by straining the resources of technology to succeed, perhaps, in benefiting an infinitesimal fraction. Against the third, essentially new, danger there is no protection. What can be done in the face of it will be the theme of this book.

This third danger is intensified by dissembling. Attention is drawn from the genuinely new, unprecedented, overriding fact to other great but relatively superficial dangers. Overstatements of the present effect of the bomb tests, speculations about their possible effect — these are refutable; and when fears prove unfounded, a false calm results. There is at present no recognizable chance for a chain reaction to spread from its proper substance to matter at large, thus disintegrating the globe. The idea of one man pushing a button to explode the planet remains as illusory as ever. Another distraction is the fearful excitement about the perils of peaceful production and use of atomic energy. There are no "foolproof machines," nor can accidents be excluded, but credible reports tell us that a high safety rate can be achieved by the proper controls and that the dangerous atomic waste need not be feared either, since it can be buried and rendered harmless.

The refutation of these erroneous notions is deceptive. It tends to make the fact itself seem questionable, to shift an already real possibility into the realm of fantasy, to let our mood vacillate between misplaced exaggeration and a sense of calm where we should be profoundly alarmed.

We can rely on the natural scientists' judgment of facts. What they tell us is reality, not speculation. An intelligent person cannot read their statements without a sense of enormity; they have put the handwriting onto the wall for all to see. Until now an individual could take his own life, could kill or be killed in battle, and nations could be exterminated. Now, mankind as a whole can be wiped out by men. It has not merely become possible for this to happen; on purely rational reflection it is probable that it will happen.

This statement seems rash. We hesitate. We must examine it.

On the assumption that the scientists are right in their expert opinions — and we can scarcely doubt this — we mean to show here that this oppressive intellectual prognosis is indeed compelling, but also that it is not the last word. For probability is not certainty, and above all, we are dealing not only with recognizable, inexorable necessities of nature but with the future acts of men, with the potential of their freedom.

An effective awareness of the probability of total perdition is the only way by which the presently probable might become finally improbable, if not impossible. To this end we must make proper use of our factual knowledge. I may know something but insulate the knowledge, as it were: deny its validity, live as if it were not there. If knowledge is to bear fruit in us, we must think of it daily. Today the terrible threat of the hydrogen bomb seems not yet acute. It does not affect me bodily, here and now. I know of it, to be sure, when I am asked; but I think there is time. No, there is not much time. At most, it is a matter of decades, and perhaps the time is shorter. Perhaps the decisive moment is close at hand.

The atom bomb is today the greatest of all menaces to the future of mankind. In the past there have been imaginative notions of the world's end; its imminent expectation for their generation was the ethically and religiously effective error of John the Baptist, Jesus, and the first Christians. But now we face the real possibility of such an end. The possible reality which we must henceforth reckon with — and reckon with, at the increasing pace of developments, in the near future — is no longer a fictitious end of the world. It is no world's end at all, but the extinction of life on the surface of the planet.

A small thing, in this situation, yet a prerequisite of everything else, is to *think*: to look around us; to observe what is going on; to visualize the possibilities, the consequences of events and actions; to clarify the situation in the directions that emerge — until we feel the brutal new fact push our thinking to the very roots of human existence, where the question arises what man is and can be.

The basic human situation is to be in the world and not to know whence or whither. The possibility of total self-destruction makes us newly, differently conscious of this situation; it shows us a side of which no one has thought before. We must make sure of ourselves, in this new situation. True, our reason cannot plumb ultimate depths, but it can clarify what exists for us and what we want of it.

The atom bomb, as the problem of mankind's very existence, is equaled by only one other problem: the threat of totalitarian rule (not simply dictatorship, Marxism, or racial theory), with its terroristic structure that obliterates all liberty and human dignity. By one, we lose life; by the other, a life that is worth living. Both extreme possibilities bring us today to an awareness of what we want, how we would wish to live, what we must be prepared for.

The two problems seem fatefully linked. In practice, at least, they are inseparable. Neither one can be solved without the other, and the solution of both calls for forces in man to well up from such depths as to transform him in his moral, rational, political aspects — a transformation so extensive that it would become the turning point of history.

It is astonishing to find the obvious new fact not really acknowledged by people the world over, least of all in Russia and America. Thus the revolution in our way of thinking, which reflection upon the fact would seem to make inescapable, has not yet occurred. Our attention is distracted, drawn to side issues that are grave but not of absolute moment. Our vision is narrowed as we regard the fact in isolation, though it receives its full weight only in connection with the entirety of human existence, and with man's questions about himself. We tend to forget, preoccupied as we are with the momentary well-being of economic prosperity.

These distracting, narrowing, oblivious factors work involuntarily. They could be overcome only by total reflection and the ensuing change in, first, the individual. This inner change could spread through mankind like a wave — not just of alarm, not just of outrage at all agents of perdition, but of rational will. This will would lead to a re-examination of the whole of our humanity, of our lives, our motives. The eternal source could yield a new beginning of what we should be, to be worthy of life. It is only if consciousness of the new fact came to influence our lives that conventional politics, its interests and objectives, could be transformed into a new politics that might cope with the threat of extinction.

No book can bring this about. But if many tread parallel paths, the mere communication of thought can give notice and prepare the way.

To restate the present situation: we talk as if we knew and sound as if we did not want to know. What cannot but shock us in print is soon swamped by other sensations; what we may not doubt at the moment seems still too appalling to be given access to our hearts. We catch ourselves looking upon certainty as, after all, not quite certain. But then we are still ignorant of the fact. For knowledge, in this case, means conviction that we are dealing with the ultimate fact — with the point, so to speak, from which all that we are and can be would have to be put onto a different plane.

One is tempted to ask a question. If the first Christians believed in the end of the world, if they were sure of it even though they did not know, even though they were, in fact, mistaken — do we today, who know the fact, have to believe it as well, to accept its reality, and to make it a factor in our way of life?

We let it stand as if it did not concern us, since at this moment, here and now, it is not yet acute. As the sick man forgets his cancer, the healthy man his mortality, the bankrupt his plight — is this how we react to the atom bomb, covering up the horizon of our existence and muddling through, unthinkingly, a while longer?

We would prefer to know nothing of the atomic menace. We explain that neither politics nor planning is possible under the threat of total disaster; we want to live, not to die — but this catastrophe would finish everything, so there is no point in thinking of it. It seems to be one of these things which decency forbids mentioning, lest it make life unbearable. And yet, nothing but this very unbearableness can cause the event that might change it.

What a purposely blind state of life! Disregarding the possible controverts reason. Whoever is himself wants to know all there is to be known. And what poor politics! Today we find ourselves inescapably overshadowed by the cataclysm. Only the ostrich will, before thinking it through, treat a real possibility as if it would disappear if he ignored it.

Today the constant presence of the cataclysm as a possibility — indeed, a probability — offers a signal opportunity for reflection as such, and at the same time the one chance for the political rebirth that would avert the cataclysm. The stakes of the game should be part of everyone's life, as a call for reflection. There lies the horizon of reality in which we must stand. A refusal to know is already part of the disaster.

We hope that all men will know, and that this knowledge will be pervasive and consequential. For pervasive knowledge alone can prevent calamity. It not only enables individuals to act to a purpose; it enables man to change himself and his life, to recast his basic mold.

The threat of total extinction points to thoughts about the meaning of our existence. The atom bomb cannot be adequately comprehended as a special problem; man can prove equal to it only if his true self responds to the chance at hand. If he treats the matter as one among other difficulties, he will not master it.

It is the purpose of this book, therefore, to range to the best of my ability through all the fields in which the bomb poses questions. I want my words to convey a sense beyond their content, a sense of what truly counts. I want to bring my readers to a more conscious recognition of what they already know, to its re-examination, and, perhaps, to a view of it that may be clearer than mine.

Only by questioning in all directions can truth become manifest. I should like to approach the challenge of the bomb from every possible angle, each time in its own way, and to try out every road. I should like to give voice to all moods: the outraged, the aggressive, the hopeless, the despairing, the nonchalant, the trustful. I want to detach the arguments, insofar as they are objectively valid, from the moods. I should like to state the case for fundamentally different ways of thinking. As not all the questions and answers lie on the same level, they cannot be treated alike, as of the same kind; I want to test the ways of thinking on their own levels and to let each reveal its limits.

I am aiming at the whole of the politico-philosophical consciousness that can today become reality and truth. I know that if one man ventures to do so he will, at first, surely miss much and go wrong often; but the principle of thinking through the whole is vital. This is what mattered to me. One man's attempt to realize this aim is bound to fall short, but the important thing, to my mind, is to make the attempt, not just to state the aim in general terms. The idea of entirety must be at work in the background, whatever particulars are under investigation.

I hope that others traveling the same road will do better, without forgetting what this book touches upon. Such entire awareness, with its tensions, must become general if we are to reason with each other, to prepare our decisions with full clarity, and to reach them in the broadest scope.

Of all-encompassing importance is the distinction between two ways of thinking. *Intellectual thought* is the inventor and maker. Its precepts can be carried out and can multiply the making by infinite repetition. The result is a world in which a few minds devise the mechanics, creating, as it were, a second world in which the masses then assume the operative function. *Rational thought*, on the other hand, does not provide for the carrying-out of mass directives but requires each individual to do his own thinking, original thinking. Here, truth is not found by a machine reproducible at will, but by decision, resolve, and action whose self-willed performance, by each on his own, is what creates a common spirit.

What grows out of the free acts of countless men and comes upon us like an overwhelming tide of events is no mere tide of events. Every individual acts in it as a free agent. However powerless he may feel, no one is wholly powerless. We may quail before the course of history as before a relentlessly rising tidal wave, and we may be swept along. But we join in building dikes, and men have been able to stand fast. History differs from the tides of the sea. Those tides are mute. History speaks, and we answer. The very union of men is no mere natural phenomenon but an event animated by their freedom. However minute a quantity the individual may be among the factors that make history, he is a factor. He cannot attribute it all to a tide of events of which none is his doing.

The self-awareness of man is founded in the inner change that is incomprehensible, unreal even, to the intellect. If I base my awareness of existence on the mental attitude of the intellect, on its know-all and know-how, I sink into nothingness. Searching for myself along this road is futile; I shall have forgotten myself in mere intellectual thought. Reason brings me back to myself.

After the inner change, intellect and reason remain linked. Whatever is objectively, intellectually thinkable must be thought through to its limits, to be retained, conversely, in the realm of reason. The bounds of cognition are met and surpassed at the same time.

Everything along the way of presentation, taken by itself, will justify objections. Because it must first become clear by itself, it tempts us into a premature fixation on the question and answer of the moment; we get caught in discussions that made sense only along the way, from a limited point of view. It sounds final, so we allow ourselves to be trapped, so to speak, and lose ourselves in it.

In fact, however, nothing exists by itself. It is only after passing through all the perspectives with their emerging aspects that we can visualize the whole so as to serve our purpose. What we attain is not a system of the whole but an orderly discussion of the perspectives. Our aim is to make sure, within the scope of data and conceivabilities, of the ultimate motives from which our judgments and trends of action spring.

The parts of this book, therefore, complement one another. None seems to be dispensable. They can be understood only in the whole, and yet the whole itself is not visible. This corresponds to our human situation, which limits us to directions and ascertainments, and to an awareness of the foundations on which we live in history.

Not everything is solved, and the whole is never completed. If we beware of many premature, intellectually facile but unnecessary alternatives, we will the more decisively encounter the few alternatives that are true — because in our situation they are unbridgeable. They face us with the great historic decisions which in our temporal existence we cannot dodge. They seem inexorable, although we cannot sufficiently define them in rational form; if we could, the decisions would become mere arithmetical problems from a point of view outside the alternatives

— but we stand within the alternatives. We want to surmount them, and in truth we cannot see beyond them.

In complementary thinking, as well as in touching on our final alternatives, we can do no more than reach the space that seems to await us, limitless and beyond all perspective. There we find the resolution for what we do on our way of life — which is still not the way of all men. So, general suggestions must not be taken for ultimate truth, only for the medium in which — ever unsure of the whole — we know what we want here and now, in this situation, in the face of unsettled history.

The purpose of this book is not to take a "departmental" position — as, for example, from the viewpoint of philosophy as an academic discipline. I mean to address that part of man which is above departments. This intention is vulnerable, because it seems to involve bringing up anything and everything; but it is necessary because in no other way can we approach what matters. The problem is basic, and solving it takes all of man.

True, every task calls for a division of labor. We have special fields in science, organized departments in administration, a diversity of specialists in politics; we defer to the authority of expert knowledge, of professional standing, of official position, of membership in groups, nations, states. But all division presupposes the unity of the whole. Departments have a limited meaning. The whole which unites them also limits their realm of validity; it is their source and their guidepost. The whole, on the other hand, is common to all and belongs to no one or everyone — but only insofar as he realizes the whole, as he is a complete human being. Departmentalization ceases where all departments must be directed so that each can thrive. But the whole, or the source, or the final goal — these cannot in turn become matters for a department, or be departments themselves. It is from there, rather, that all the departments derive their meaning.

This same problem recurs in every sphere of our existence as thinking creatures. It encompasses the problem of intellect and reason, of specialized science and philosophy. Science is objectively compelling intellectual cognition; philosophy is rational self-enlightenment. Both are distinct and inseparable. Science becomes bottomless without philosophy; philosophy can take no step without the intellect, that is, without science.

A way of thinking that belongs to no department and does not surrender to any — this is a kind of philosophy we may expect of everyone.

It may be dormant, but in the true human being it can be raised to bright consciousness and critical assurance. "Philosophy is too high for me. . . . I'm no expert in philosophy. . . . I've never cared for philosophy. . . ." Such phrases serve to reject what everyone does unwittingly and, therefore, as a rule, poorly. This constant philosophy in all of us stamps our consciousness, determines our motivations, and is the bearer of all that we publicly take for granted.

It is the philosophers' fault — and in particular the fault of us professors of philosophy — if, instead of searching for the human language, we permit our thinking to limit itself and to degenerate into a department, into academic philosophy. We do not have mass incomprehension to complain about, but our own unseriousness and ineptitude.

This book is philosophical in intent. It makes no suggestions, performs no political act, offers no over-all solution. It belongs to no "department" and does not claim to be authorized by one. In the atom bomb question today, the typical procedure is for each expert in turn to state his case — physicist, biologist, military man, politician, theologian — and then to declare himself incompetent outside his special field. Yet all of them in so doing appeal to a listener or reader who is supposed to understand them all, to check their statements understandingly as best he can, to gain an over-all insight and to judge them, in his turn, on an over-all basis. Where is this complete man? He is every individual, including the lecturing specialists. We are too ready today to accede to such disclaimers as "I am not competent there" or "This is not my field." They may be true in regard to specialized knowledge and skills, but they become untrue if applied to concepts, decisions, and resolutions that concern the issue as a whole and thus the whole human being.

The limit of departmental thinking is the existence of issues that concern the whole and are up to everyone. This limit shows up in the question of the atom bomb. It is not a particular problem which experts might solve by special measures. It is today not one question among others; it is the one vital question: to be or not to be. Its shadow falls on whatever else we may do or inquire. Its solution lies at a depth of human existence which man achieves by no special knowledge, by no special activity, only by himself. Here he faces a task that he cannot meet with a "task force." It is vain to view the problem in isolation, as a particular threat that might be answered particularly and surmounted singly. The issue, rather, involves all of man and requires him to commit all his life to coping with it — in peacetime by his entire manner of living and in the crisis by courage and sacrifice. He has opportunities for which his intellect cannot plan, but which must be seized if he is to master the situation. Here, departmentalized thinking comes to a standstill. Truth, here, not only concerns everybody but must be grasped, created, realized by everybody from the depths of his existence. We are entering a zone where conventions fade, where departmental manners grow meaningless, where the foreground of respect for taboos, for silence, for mutual untouchability is breached.

Since we possess the power of total destruction, but not yet the power of controlling it with calculating certainty, everyone asks: What can be done? Where is the way out?

One wants an unequivocal, definitive answer. One wants concrete proposals: for actions, for institutions, for treaties, for gradual developments that would put everything right. One demands the impossible.

For a concrete moment, of course, stressing a particular idea or insisting upon a particular demand makes sense. These are political acts and can have meaning only in concrete situations, from the standpoint of the actor. They become true only insofar as all perspectives remain present in their own horizons.

These horizons can be shown. We can think and feel them through — we can, so to speak, experimentally place ourselves within them, thus realizing the inner condition from which proposals and actions spring at the concrete moment and can be examined. Thought sets the stage; clears up the premises; purveys the knowable data, the ground on which the way must be found. It is not easy to understand that, while our insight can develop only in a multiplicity of aspects and ways of thinking, the real action remains the plunge into the tide of history — and that is not deducible. It follows neither from general rules, like the solution of an arithmetical problem, nor from the manifest view of facts, of the state of the world.

In the nature of the case, therefore, a book like this should not be approached with false expectations. I do not show how to do things. I unveil no theory of what will happen. I take no definitive stand. I have no consoling final answer. I will indeed mention proposals, discuss projects for the future, assume occasional positions — but all this is by the way. I will try to survey our situation, but this, too, only in the possible perspectives. It will all remain in suspense. I will show that for thought alone there is no solution that might be worked out according to instructions.

Such thinking — which is granted to man without giving him the rest of a conclusion — takes stamina. It calls for endurance in the tensions of insolubility. It requires the candor of seeking fulfilment only from the ultimate source.

Yet in the end all suspense, all candor, all boundlessness of questioning is not skepticism but a will to make a resolute existence possible by thought. Existence itself is left free, left to its own responsibility which nothing can alleviate. Thinking helps to attain purity. Such thinking is the enthusiasm of reason.

A problem that has no lasting solution seems all the more formidable for being inescapable. It appears as soon as we see through the false intellectual premise that all problems are soluble — and that the insoluble ones are so because we ask the wrong questions. The intellect starts with the erroneous assumption that man can manage his affairs in the world; disappointed, it jumps to the erroneous conclusion that all is in vain and the world will surely perish.

Pronouncements by scientists, men of letters, philosophers, theologians, are all to the good insofar as they tell facts. If they go further, they are political in the narrow sense of the word, serving parties and states, whether or not they intend to — or else they would be prophetic proclamations, postulates by virtue of higher authority. One should hear them, read them, look at the speakers to see whether, in this sense, they merit credence. The present book wants to serve only for orientation, for clarification, and as a reminder. Action, not thought, will bring the solution of the mystery — the innumerable actions of innumerable people who have prepared themselves for this by thinking it through.

As for my thoughts about the consequences of the atom bomb, I have arranged them in three parts: first, general discussions that lead to dead ends; second, a review of the present world situation; third, a clarification of the human essence. In the first part, principles will be developed along the lines of the realities of our time, to show us that, while indispensable to our insight, they provide no solution but arrive at limits where they fail. The second part will show the concrete facts which no one in quest of reality can ignore. The third part will try, on the basis of the theoretical and concrete knowledge of the first two, to bring encompassing reason to the fore. Our new situation should revive our sense of what we are — our sense, as Kant put it, of what it means to be human.

The third part is the most extensive. It deals with the questions that came up most frequently, all but exclusively, in letters from my radio audience. It brings us to the philosophy that is not merely a matter of academic teaching but a reality in man as a truly human, as a rational creature.

In this tripartite arrangement, the end of the book should, from the beginning, play a part in our examination of particulars — and conversely, particular views should be kept in mind until the end. The basic ideas should keep recurring in variations. It will be seen from the outset that all politics depends on something above politics, but also that this suprapolitical element is not unequivocal. We may call it ethics, self-sacrifice, reason — yet each of these three is dependent upon the others, or at one with them. Distinction is only a way to make them communicable. It should help to make us aware of the mission of man; to lift our eyes beyond the world, to the source of our strength to fulfil our reality in the world.

2

INITIAL POLITICAL THINKING ABOUT THE NEW FACT

If a new world war comes, atom bombs are sure to fall. If an atomic holocaust is to be averted, no world war must break out. Every little war threatens to set off a world war. So there must be no more war.

Concretely, today the logic is as follows: Nuclear warfare is actually double suicide for the antagonists. They will not commit it, for their fear of the consequences will overcome their ill will.

But then the reasoning goes on: Because atomic war has become impossible, all war between the atomic superpowers has become impossible. Since at some stage of a world war for survival the nuclear threat would materialize, no great power will any longer risk starting a war. Since it would be a war of annihilation for all, it can no longer happen. Total peril engenders total deliverance. An extreme emergency compels forms of political existence which make not only the bomb but war itself impossible.

Yet this general idea does not dispel our worries. Fear alone is not enough to rely upon in the long run. Something must be done to assure permanence. As a result we are hearing two demands: first, the atom bomb must be abolished; second, world peace must be established not on fear alone, but on law.

The prevalent notion today is that we should stop testing atom bombs, forbid their manufacture, and destroy the ones on hand. This seems the simplest way. It could be done by agreement. A condition of the agreement would be mutual controls, which alone can guarantee observance.

This would be the act of salvation. But it would immediately do more than abolish the nuclear threat, for mutual controls would necessarily involve a transformation of political existence — a change from the status of nations facing each other like beasts in a state of nature to an international community founded on legal agreements guaranteed by common institutions. It would be the transition from a status of mere co-existence, unilaterally changeable to war at any moment by an act of violence, to a status of co-operation, with the freedom of all dependent upon their subordination to agreements jointly arrived at and put into effect by executive organs. It would be the beginning of world peace.

Such controls would, in the first place, entail a complete mutual privity, in itself a form of the mutual candor that would in turn produce the common spirit indispensable for peace. The resulting ubiquity of information would be the first act of making peace. The second result of controls would be the voluntary restriction of the sovereignty of all, by *de facto* recognition of the validity of treaties above sovereignty — treaties which, like all treaties, must rest not only on faith but on effective control agencies. The treaty powers would have to place such agencies above themselves. Only then would brute force no longer be free to tear up agreements.

The establishment of mutual controls would be the first and decisive step toward world peace. The rest of its realization would be incomparably easier. However, abolition of the atom bomb and establishment of an effective control agency do not seem possible as isolated, independent fruits of intelligent political planning, for several reasons.

First, any judgment of the reliability of controls presupposes the technical knowledge reached at the time. A conference of Russian, American, English, and, perhaps, other physicists — not politicians — would have to clarify the possible and necessary procedures for reliable controls. No such conference has done so at the time of this writing.

Second, no controls can function with absolute reliability in areas as vast as the American and Asian continents; even huge stores and factories can always be hidden underground. Even successful controls would be assured only in peacetime; all states in possession of the construction secrets could manufacture the bombs in case of war and use the peace to prepare their industrial plant for rapid manufacture. Finally, the difficulties of control would rise with the growing facility of atom bomb production and with the number of countries acquiring the bomb.

Third, the requisite scope of controls is apparent from the American Baruch Plan, dating from the time when Russia did not have the bomb as yet. All atomic energy on earth would have to be placed under an international authority which would not only control but own and administer all the uranium deposits on earth and all the industries producing and using atomic energy. Its officials were to be granted extraterritorial rights, like diplomatic envoys, and to be free to inspect and photograph anything they liked, anywhere in the world. In the directing councils of this authority there was to be majority rule without veto.

This plan — which America then offered to accept, while Russia hesitated — had one condition attached: it could only be carried out simultaneously with general disarmament. It was for this reason, too, that the existing bombs (then exclusively American) were to be destroyed only after the control machinery had started functioning.

We conclude: Controls are impossible without general disarmament. Not until world peace will be secured can they be adequate. The mere idea and attempt to establish controls cannot achieve their purpose.

There is no solution without eliminating war from the course of human events. War, which has existed as long as man, would have to cease. What used to be settled by war would have to find other ways of settlement; whatever courage and self-sacrifice or adventurous recklessness, wanton savagery, destructive hatred used to be released in war would have to find other outlets. Without world peace there is no preventing the extinction of mankind in an atomic holocaust.

In practice, however, controls are rejected today not only because no nation, not even the Western ones, will accept the premises of world peace. The decisive reason now is that controls and the totalitarian form of government are mutually exclusive. For totalitarianism to permit controls would be to abandon itself, to abdicate; for this form of government rests upon secrecy and state direction of all information. It can tolerate neither the free circulation of news nor the unlimited publication of ideas. To make known what the state itself does not make known counts as espionage or treason. Totalitarianism and its carriers, the leaders and the machine, must resist controls as long as they identify themselves with their form of government. Their minds must necessarily be set against controls as a matter of self-preservation: *principiis obsta*. And this attitude in turn must be disguised; they must talk as if, in principle,

prediction + prophecy)

they were prepared to accept controls. They must constantly negotiate about them, but so as to strangle them at birth. They must invent controls that are ineffective and yet will serve to deceive those who are taken in by appearances.

In other words, the acceptance of controls presupposes a readiness for their infallible effect of assuring peace. By the very fact of their establishment, controls imply the solidarity they would create.

World peace will be achieved only by a new politics. Let us outline its principles, deducing them from its nature without asking now about the possibility of its realization — not dreaming up a fantasy of a utopian realm of immaculate spirits, but proceeding from the realities of human nature and freedom. This will gives us a yardstick to measure what we want and what already exists.

World peace rests on two premises: First, on *free will* — right and justice are to rule instead of force. Second, on *reality* — the human world is not and will never be one of right and perfect justice, but man can strive to make progress on the road to justice.

Nothing but the maintenance of this free pursuit of justice is definitive in existence. Everything is subject to revision: new realities appear; new questions are raised; tests are prepared in public discussion and carried out in legal forms that are revisable in their turn, but held inviolate for the duration of their validity. The one mortal foe of this freedom is a resort to violence.

As our condition can never be one of perfect justice, it can only be a condition of law that still includes some injustice — a condition of nonviolence that still includes a minimum of force to maintain itself. The mortal enemy of this condition is indifference to wrong and to violence. Its survival depends on constant sensitivity to wrong and injustice, and on the energy to correct them.

On these two premises, the principles of this condition within and between states can be expressed as follows:

1. *To restrain violence, there must be binding commitments.*

a) All must be bound to recognize legality. Treaties must be acknowledged as legally in force as long as they are not altered by new negotiations.

b) All must be bound to renounce arbitrary action. Supremacy of law entails a renunciation of absolute sovereignty, as well as a renunciation of the veto power over decisions of any legally established authority.

c) There is always a remnant of force. It is an illusion that the right could be relied upon to prevail. As truth needs exponents, the right needs power — a power that is not inherent in it. War can be eliminated only if there is a supreme legal authority that can replace violence with law and arbitrate the gravest conflicts of opinion and interest. But this authority must dispose of effective means to enforce and maintain its decisions. A state cannot abolish the police, and states that bind themselves by treaty cannot abolish the force required to secure the treaties made under their guarantee. The creation of supranational authorities, which the nations would have to set up and to equip with unprecedented powers — the realization of the form in which the remaining force would, as a common force, be placed at the disposal of the legal authority — that is the great problem.

d) All must be bound to recognize the ballot, majority rule, and the determination of the popular will of the moment by free, secret elections. Let him who would act politically inform the people, use thought to persuade them, and reasons, points of view, and his own example to educate them. Truth must be able, in the long run, to win confirmation from the people. Only thus do men grow to partake in knowledge, to comprehend, and to resolve to make the change that is incumbent on mankind.

Those whom indignation at mass stupidity turns against free elections are forgetting that in the course of history — with some accidental exceptions — rulers have been no wiser, no more truthful, no better, no more responsible than a majority of the governed, and vice versa. They are forgetting also that, the greater the task, the more important is the education and co-operation of all.

We have no other means of inquiry than the ballot. To make it yield the best possible results is the responsibility of everyone, above all of those who seek power. Free secret elections are the only tangible means of political freedom as well as of peace — for only insofar as they follow the idea of democracy and recognize its commitments are the nations capable of peace.

2. *The establishment, maintenance, and development of binding commitments requires unrestricted communication.*

a) Freedom without violence is possible only if information is exchanged, if peoples mingle, and if discussion is public — and only when all this happens without restriction. The first act of peacemaking, therefore, is to permit the communication of news and the publicity of debate throughout the world, free from censorship and without risk for the individual. Real, world-wide, unlimited publicity is a premise of freedom and peace.

b) The principle of truthfulness demands that facts be admitted, that people put themselves in other people's shoes, that they see different interests, and voice their own true motives.

c) The community of peace exists only on the strength of a public communal spirit: a sensitive consciousness of right, which in most cases makes everyone co-responsible when any wrong is done. This alone will keep the wrong from attaining proportions that make violent rebellion irresistible and end the state of peace.

Ever since the time of the Seven Greek Sages, one rule has held for every citizen of a free state: The wrong that is done to another citizen is done to me. And what applies to the citizens of a state is true, in a peaceful world situation, among the citizens of all states. This world condition demands that we, through the community of nations, intervene to protect people anywhere who are deprived of their human rights. The internal tasks of each state are inseparable from its concern with the internal conduct of all other states — not, however, manifested by direct intervention, but by way of intervention on the part of supranational authorities.

3. *To keep the unjust results of changing conditions from causing violence, the way for peaceful revision of all relationships must be left open.*

That men and nations have a claim to equal rights is a recognized principle, but this claim conflicts with the actual inequality of nations as well as men. Their native endowments — never finally determinable — differ as much as their strength, their talents, their visible accomplishments, their actions and the consequences of their actions, and their numbers. There can only be equality of opportunity within the external possibilities, no actual equality of all. If an external equality were established today, it would be changed by tomorrow into obvious inequality by the differences between men; in fact, their equalization beyond equality of opportunity would be the height of injustice. If there is to be peace, ineradicable inequalities must, as a matter of principle, be respected and allowed to grow non-violently into levels of rank.

But inequalities, and thus actual orders of rank, are constantly changing. Vested inequality is unjust. True, there is a historical continuity due to the actions and achievements of parents and ancestors; they have broken ground that remains fertile, bearing privileges of origin and inception — but only insofar as these credibly represent and prove themselves in the present. There are no definitive, permanently valid realities of rank by birth, descent, tradition, or property.

The principle of peace, therefore, is both to recognize inequalities and to be ready to revise the realities of rank on the basis of changes in fact — but only legally and after due reflection.

Likewise, political boundaries and treaties that have become unjust must be legally revisable. Subject peoples, or those evolving toward particularity, are to be freed on demand by a supranational authority.

It is easy to outline such principles of political peace, but thinking them out and proving them right does not make them real. Of course, it is still easier to smile at them and point to realities, to call them utopian and boast of one's own shrewd realism. Kant has given the answer to this attitude: "A constitution of the greatest possible human freedom, under laws which enable the freedom of each to endure together with that of all others, is at least a necessary idea. . . . Nothing can be more noxious and unworthy of a philosopher than the vulgar appeal to allegedly contrary experience — which, after all, would not exist if those measures had been taken in good time, in line with their ideas."

This is why those outlines are not utopian as long as they are understood in the ideal sense. They unfold the pattern of the idea whose realization remains an infinite task, and as such they are the standards for our critique and judgment of reality, and our guidelines for the efficacy of the idea within us.

In fact, to be sure, the principles of world peace are still rejected. Politics still runs in the same channels as ever, uses the same means and the same sophistry of argument. It is easy to show that the very opposite of the principles outlined above is in effect today — that within states they apply only partially and unreliably, while internationally they are either wholly ignored or slightly observed by only a few of the Western or Westernized nations. And they are not merely ignored in fact; as most men want peace, statesmen pronounce "principles of peace" — but theirs run diametrically counter to a truly peaceful world order.

What are the taboos? Absolute national sovereignty — hence, the demand for mutual non-interference and a veto right in common councils; equal rights for all to act arbitrarily; finally, peaceful coexistence of governmental and social systems based on concepts of law so utterly different as to be mutually exclusive, with mutual intercourse barred by iron curtains.

Let us examine these principles one by one.

Absolute sovereignty and non-interference are needed today to prevent the inevitable abuse of interference and to delay the outbreak of war; in a truly peaceful state of the world they would be unbearable. From a legal point of view, asking for absolute sovereignty and non-interference amounts to asking for the freedom, in a concrete situation, to decide alone and arbitrarily what is right — which means, in fact, the freedom to do wrong. It implies a readiness to break agreements and to make war if one has the power and if circumstances seem auspicious.

The holding of a veto on decision-making bodies thwarts any subordination of states to a rule of law.

Non-interference keeps the spirit of law from developing jointly in the mutual intercourse of nations. As every citizen should feel the wrong done to another as a wrong done to himself, every state should react to injustice suffered by citizens of another state as if its own had suffered it. Neither a nation nor an international community can long endure if its people remain indifferent to injustice practiced against people elsewhere. Governments ruling their subjects by terror constitute the antithesis of peace; they are a threat to world peace, being always ready to carry their violence from their own countries to the rest of mankind.

Equal rights thwart peace if they mean equal rights of arbitrary action, not just the same right to defend one's interests by legal means.

Failure to permit the free flow of news, to allow free public discussion, to tolerate the contest of parties in free elections — this bespeaks the determination of a power apparatus to retain the features it cannot risk showing in public. The need for concealment proves that wrong is being done. Concealment, stealth, and mendacity amount to potential violence. He who lacks power, or an opportune moment to use it, may for the time being resort to the fraud called "peaceful coexistence." By "peacefully" weakening his antagonist wherever possible, he will prepare for the final act of violence. Warding it off takes publicity. Not only the rulers but the peoples must talk to each other. Iron curtains mean violence and impairment of freedom.

The principles of absolute sovereignty, of veto powers, of equal rights for every state, including the right to maintain a reign of terror and refuse full public information — these principles are but a seemingly moral smoke screen, behind which everyone does as he pleases to safe-guard his power. Besides, they are a dam built in the public conscious-ness to delay the disaster, but a dam that may give way at any moment. On the one hand, these principles leave room for the use of force; on the other, they are available for the manipulation of a wavering public opinion that is easily taken in by them, even at the very moment of their violation.

Peace never comes from coexistence, only from co-operation. To gain a breathing spell and at least to postpone war, one takes coexistence into the bargain. In the present situation, even what is known to be adverse to peace cannot be rejected — for to put the principles of peace under law into practice unilaterally, without delay or limitations, would be suicidal. The principles of world peace and the stated principles of the present situation are poles apart. What then is to be done?

If we keep thinking politically, we should plan to make the peace-promoting principles prevail, in time, over the ones now dominant. Since humanity does not want to perish, nations would have to agree to limit their sovereign power. What was done on a small scale when governments were first instituted might be repeated with an inter-national confederation. What scientific intelligence produced in the atom bomb — the possibility of utter disaster — might be surmounted by the same intelligence, by institutional techniques that would make treaties effective.

If this effort succeeded, man would not need to change. By means of intelligently conceived institutions, the will of all would restrain every individual from further yielding to the basic human drives: the drive to use force; the delight in violence and its risks; the urge to sacrifice one-self in violent action, to conquer or die; the love of high adventure as a release from the tedium of our existence. Jointly imposed curbs would now channel these drives into forms that would not menace the community.

So far, however, this process fails to take place. What looks like it turns out to be not progress but procrastination. Behind the veil of ap-pearances, we rather find power positions being reinforced and prep-arations being made for extremity. True, the political arguments favor-ing an institutional improvement of the situation are plausible, and at-tempts along this way should never be abandoned. But they can never suffice.

The way of politics itself needs another guidance. No man who has left a lasting mark in politics has ever acted from purely political motives. No politics fit for man has ever been self-sufficient. There are fortunate incidents in history, as in the English, Swiss, Dutch, and American struggles for freedom, when a truer ethos permeated the competence, the astuteness, the methods of politics — distinguished from great political achievements that are due to the superior skill of individuals and, as mere displays of skill, are ephemeral because they effect no political education.

Thus the continuation of political thinking brings us to the frontier where mere politics fails and a resolve is needed — the resolve of the human being in whom a change is wrought by extremity. There is, to be sure, an old, recurrent, and still widespread view that human nature is immutably the same we have always seen in practical politics, that wars are ineradicable, and so is the unscrupulous course of political action with its lies, betrayals, and trickery. This fact of nature should indeed not be forgotten, but neither should another fact: that one of the driving forces in politics is something above politics.

This is why purely political thinking, confined to political rules, is at a loss in extremities. Such thinking, supposedly realistic, is a smoke screen in which the human self is forgotten — just as the illusions of some other ways of thinking would have us forget the realities of human nature. Something above politics must guide political institutions, legislations, designs — if they are to endure. This is the font of the spirit that must pervade their reality in concrete situations, if they are to be trusted.

To us, the *suprapolitical* element is manifested in the ethical idea and in the valor of sacrifice. They can provide the conditions for the achievement of world peace — conditions impossible to create by treaties and institutions, but growing, rather, out of man's other side which the observer of tangible reality never perceives.

3

THE POWER
OF THE
ETHICAL IDEA

In the past, folly and wickedness had limited consequences; today they draw all mankind to perdition. Now, unless all of us live with and for one another, we shall all be destroyed together. This new situation demands a corresponding answer. It is not enough to find new institutions; we must change ourselves, our characters, our moral-political wills. What used to distinguish individuals, to be effective in small groups but impotent in society at large, has now become a condition for the continued existence of mankind.

I do not think I am exaggerating. Whoever goes on living as before has not grasped the menace. Mere intellectual speculation about it does not mean absorption into the reality of one's life — and the life of man is lost without a change. Man must change if he wants to go on living. If he thinks only of today, a day will come when the outbreak of nuclear war is apt to finish everything.

Now, what are the facts of today? Political motivation does not reach far enough, but as yet we see no change in ethical motives either. Man is still the same as ever. We see the same violence, ruthlessness, belligerent recklessness, coupled with the same indolence and indifference, the same desire for quiet and lack of provident concern in those who happen to be well off at the moment — a condition in which bold adventurers always found them easy prey. We see the same brazen blackmail and the submission to it, the same general hiding behind a fictitious authority which some secretly despise, others regard as a guarantee of their comfort, and all will forsake at the decisive moment.

The change can come only in every man's manner of living. Every little act, every word, every attitude in millions and billions of people matter. What happens on a large scale is but a symptom of what is done in the privacy of many lives. The man who cannot live in peace with his neighbor, the mischief-maker or secret ill-wisher or slanderer or liar, the adulterer or undutiful son or negligent parent or lawbreaker — by his conduct, which even behind locked doors is never wholly private — keeps peace from the world. He does, in miniature, what on a larger scale makes mankind destroy itself. Nothing that man is and does is quite without political significance.

The actions of statesmen also need the ethical illumination that is our premise for the survival of mankind. A man may have delivered the most eloquent moral-political speeches at the conference table; if he is faithless at home, he shares the blame for the continuing evil. If he is so tolerant of human failings as to allow loose-living individuals in his official domain, he undermines the trustworthiness of the whole. If he wants the miracle to happen, if he wants an ethical change, and still puts his mind to letting the world carry on unthinkingly, he makes ethics itself suspect. And so it goes: talking, negotiating, enterprising, organizing, until the day when everything will be erased.

We may ask how "private" conduct can affect political action, when obviously one has nothing to do with the other. The question rightly points to the absence of a direct causal link, but it fails to recognize that a man's private life is a symptom of his personality, which is the same in whatever sphere he may move. It is opportunism which, in one sphere, lets him obey rules he may flout in others. A stockbroker keeps his word because one failure to do so would finish him in his profession. The politician follows the rules of an international community because the consequences of violating them under normal conditions would be too unpleasant. But the dictates of opportunism and convention do not hold in matters of life or death. The motivations of men at such times cannot be special ones, kept in abeyance for the day of need. They will work only if they have been working for a lifetime, in politically harmless circumstances and in the entire life of the individual. The moral idea is one and indivisible.

If politics depends on the suprapolitical element, this element itself must be independent of politics. An absolute politics will fail even before political tasks; a politics not dependent on something above it can plunge headlong into ruin. The visible embodiment of this relationship in the constitutions of free states is the subordination of political organs and acts to a constitutional tribunal. A "politicized" judiciary is not only destructive of the suprapolitical element but ruinous to politics as well. Unlike all things political, *the moral idea cannot be planned.* We would be wrong to think of moral earnestness not for its own sake but as a means to the preservation of human life. It is the other way around. The salvation of human life can be the consequence of the unconditional, suprapolitical ethos, but not its goal. A resort to ethics as a lifesaver is futile, because the very purpose would void the ethics.

As everything that can be planned becomes political, we may think that we need something we cannot plan. And indeed, there is no concrete answer to the question, "What should we do?" — there are only the ancient prophets to remind us of potentialities now dormant. What we need now, in the face of extremity, is more than a better insight: it is a change of heart. But this change cannot be forced.

We can point out realities and sound the call of thousands of years ago. Both the possibilities of the future and the demands of that prophetic voice should permeate our schools, though even among the young the results, if any, are left to the freedom of every individual. If the basic facts of our political existence are laid bare and the consequences of varying conduct set forth, the answer must come from the individual — not in an opinion but in his life.

Is it possible for man to change? Was he not always the same in the thirty or fifty centuries of his known history and, by inference, in those that went before? History teaches that anything great made by men was soon destroyed by men. History is a field of rubble. On grounds of experience we can expect no change.

This thesis is true enough for the natural makeup of man as one living creature among others. But it ignores the phenomenon that makes man truly human, more than a zoölogical species: unaltered in his psychophysical constitution, man does, in recurrent changes, transform his historical appearance. All that is great, luminous, inspiring, has risen — against all experience, over all that keeps dragging us down — from a different source. Historically, in spite of what biology and psychology can comprehend, a change in man is possible. It happened with the Hebrew prophets, with the Greek poets and philosophers, with the Hellenistic and Christian regenerations of the first centuries A.D., with the biblically grounded ethics of the Protestant world. Each of these transformations, while withering soon, has remained a challenging memory.

The ethical idea becomes "moral" when it exhausts itself in commands and prohibitions. There is truth left in this morality, but only as an element of something more inclusive. As the substance of Kant's categorical imperative it is indeed inescapable and absolutely valid; but its concrete embodiment in a particular situation is incalculable. The form of the absolute is no help in deducing the content.

Morality has a place of honor in the speeches of politicians. They like to use it in conclusions, as a kind of ornament, to send the audience home in good humor and with their chests thrust out. I recently read a speech whose closing paragraph contained these three sentences: "Morality, too, can be power. . . . In the atomic age, no policy will get us anywhere if it is not deeply rooted in the moral sense of the people. . . . In matters of morality you have to start with yourself." The truth of these three sentences would show if the thought unfolded — if by his actions it were proved in the person of the orator and became visible, convincing, and thus exemplary.

Ethos is diluted to mere morality when it is detached from the self-sacrifice that underlies our reality and from the human reason that transcends mere intellect. Reason must control both ethics and self-sacrifice, although all three spring from an absolute source. In the course of this book we shall attempt to clarify what must be supplemented in self-sacrifice and ethics, and how their illumination will more deeply justify them both.

4

SACRIFICE

The fact of the atom bomb is monstrous enough to put politics into a different state of aggregation. It is from this fact that all political action — whose old motivations remain at work even though subordinated to a new and different authority — will now take its bearings.

Our initial picture of present political thinking has shown that the threat of the atom bomb cannot be met by removing the bomb alone. It can only be met by removing war, by establishing world peace. The idea that in the long run wars might be waged without atom bombs, but with intimidation by the atom bomb, is an illusion.

Yet the stated principles of world peace had one great shortcoming. The very opposite not only happens but is still expressly recognized today. The principles failed to provide for what is necessary as long as the secret privilege of venting its ill will, whenever possible, is claimed not only by the exceptional, criminal, element but by the average majority. How are law and order to prevail on the premise that man is evil?

Evidently there is a limit to pure politics. To succeed where it fails, to keep from lapsing into the anarchy of techniques and foundering in crisis, it requires a suprapolitical guidance. Since world peace cannot be realized in purely political fashion, we came to an inescapable conclusion: Man is lost unless the pressure of the situation moves him freely to change. This change cannot be the object of a new politics, but it must be its premise.

The political way looked meaningful but futile, by itself, while the moral way, since it cannot be planned, strikes the political realist as unreal. Pointing to human nature, as it has always been and always will be, the realist is absolutely pessimistic in the long run (which can quickly become a short one). His politics is for the moment. The moralist, on the other hand, derives impossible demands from his conception of a reborn, moral humanity, and because his thinking misses the present reality, he remains unheard. The course of history, considered realistically, seems hopeless, and a moral rebirth seems utopian.

Have we perhaps been thinking too unequivocally both in our political thought and in our moral appeal? The facts of reality and the justice of ethics are undeniable, but they become truth only if they take their bearings from something that encompasses both realism and moralism. Is there something beyond, something that makes both of them effective?

In political and moral thinking we forget what it means to risk our lives, to die, to sacrifice. We talk about it, but we do not realize it inwardly. We know it, but our political and moral thought does not focus attention upon it.

The political ethics of national leaders is not grounded in the awareness that any moment may jeopardize their necks. They become civil servants, lawyers, functionaries. They listen to laws and wait for orders or decisions from other authorities, in order to be secure in doing what in the nature of the things has an element of radical insecurity and, therefore, inescapable responsibility.

If the task of politics is the securing of life, this task calls at the crucial moment for the sacrifice of life.

Unlimited self-sacrificing courage is a political reality. It shows in the way whole nations have defied force with force — in the Dutch and Swiss struggles for independence, in the French Revolution, and in today's Hungarian fight for freedom. These examples differ markedly. The Swiss and the Dutch underwent a long process of fighting their way through to freedom. In the French Revolution enthusiasm spent itself in total planning, shortly producing the opposite of its initial intent. In Hungary, we saw an elemental revolt against foreign oppression and exploitation, and we cannot yet say what ethical-political forces in it will remain permanently active. In each case, huge sacrifices were made with the greatest daring.

The world's reaction to such events manifests the moral-political fiber of man, his will to freedom and justice. The valiant breaking of chains re-echoes in those who take no part but are moved by the spectacle to store up impulses for their own future action. Hence the convulsion that spread suddenly through Europe and America after the Hungarian revolt, the all but unprecedented unanimity in the awakening conscious-

ness of human dignity and the experience of its total peril! Such an experience is like a hurricane sweeping the minds, irresistibly subduing
even the restive. Conscience stirs the world over, though politically and
militarily the world is just looking on. Independently of religions, classes,
and interests, man responds to the event as a human being. "There is no
forgetting such things," Kant wrote after the French Revolution.

Politics is proved right only by success and disproved by failure, while
the suprapolitical element which can pervade politics has an inherent
meaning and value. Self-sacrifice is not a political instrument, but it has
decisive political consequences. It is the fire which, once alight, glows
in the embers and may flare up again.

These events differ in kind from Alexander's conquest of Asia, or
Caesar's of Gaul, which had such extraordinary historical consequences
— positive ones, from our viewpoint today, for the spiritual development
of Europe and Asia — but were ethically and politically meaningless.
Struggles for independence become exemplary for political ethics, deeds
of Alexander's or Caesar's type only for later conquerors and for the
impulses of violence. Admiration for them by frenzied enthusiasts or
powerless malcontents prepares for blind participation in political evil.

However terrible, the failure of suprapolitically based struggles for
freedom does not lessen their significance. The French Revolution soon
turned into the Terror, and then into a condition of new servitude,
military dictatorship, and suppression of thought; but its inception had
another meaning, which was so perverted only by later circumstances.
This is why Kant, in spite of everything, never lost his original faith in
that revolution.

Not so Burke, who thought of the consequences apt to emerge in the
context of political realities and predicted them correctly from the start:
he rejected the very inception of that revolution, because of its irresponsible surrender of all historical substance. Therein lies the truth
and the limitation of Burke's judgment. Kant truly saw the suprapolitical
source of the revolution in the ethical self-sacrifice of man; Burke truly
saw its suprapolitical qualification in the already historical state of the
English mind; and both are opposed by the false concept of an absolute
politics, denying the suprapolitical element and demanding compliance
with eternal laws of political nature. Decisive, then, is nothing but success, the success of maintaining and increasing power, regardless of the
content of what is maintained. The means have always been the same:
force, cunning, deception, lies. Such politics is immoral in itself, such

power in itself evil. But the sphere of evil has its own laws; it is a thesis of *Realpolitik* that he who enters it without obeying these laws is lost, besides acting outside the specifically political ethics of evil. This is the political doctrine taught unconditionally, for the sole end of gaining power, in India (*Kautilyas Arthashastra*) and with some qualifications — an ultimate goal of political freedom and national independence — by Machiavelli.

Politics is the association with force. But force itself, man's attitude toward it, and his realization that he cannot go beyond this attitude — these are suprapolitical. From this direction come the motivations of political ideology. In this light, the meaning of the will to non-violence, the meaning of sacrifice, of political responsibility, of soldierly virtue, are manifested. We have seen that the elimination of force in favor of law and justice is a principle of world peace; but the whole seriousness of force as an ineluctable boundary situation of human existence is usually lost sight of in political discussion.

The basic situation of all living things — that they devour one another, defend themselves, and escape; that within a species there is contention for mates, for food, for power; that the Hindu "law of the fish" prevails and the big ones eat the little ones — all this recurs in the case of man. But man builds a dam against force. He tries, in the interest of all, to channelize it. To the extent of his success there is public order. Force cannot be eliminated from human existence; it would be absent only from a kingdom of angels. Men can only regulate it successfully under a government of laws, but only by placing a police force at the government's disposal. Police action is the minimum of force, the force that protects from force.

Men will always either use force (and be termed criminals under a government of laws) or suffer what they deem injustice. Not every decision and not every law need be just under a government of laws; men can keep striving for greater justice, but they cannot achieve perfect justice. Police action has the law on its side, but it can actually perpetrate injustice. Under a government of laws I suffer such injustice, either because I realize that the legal form of even injustice is preferable to the arbitrary power of doing what one thinks is right, or, failing this insight, I submit to the constraint of the situation, to the total power of the state, which makes resistance hopeless and fraught with even worse consequences for me.

Yet public order is broken not only by criminals but also by the force which states use against one another and by civil warfare. The extremity of boundless violence occurs again and again. Man first brought force under the control of law, but in every catastrophe he has to do it all over.

If peace seems the natural condition, we may state that war — the exception — is the continuation of politics by other means. If the condition of violence seems natural, we may call politics the continuation of war by other means. This has so far been the case, and in today's "cold war" it has become more consciously apparent than ever.

In its reality, though not in its aim, the existence of every human order is founded on force. States maintain themselves by force or by the threat of force. If at all possible, we like to disguise the facts of this basic situation; we should like to take it for the exception, for the abnormal, unhealthy aspect of certain conditions and to regard peace, quiet, and non-violence as normal. To see through this disguise does not mean to glorify force or to sympathize with its use; it merely means to be honest enough to admit the hard fact and strip away the self-deceptions that result in general hypocrisy. It is the hypocrisy that makes for situations in which the most unscrupulous use of force brings men to the top. Those who live in, and profit by, the comfortable faith in safety by non-violent legality are easily taken in by deception and trickery, because they have qualms, if no consciences, and do not think it possible that violence could be so unscrupulous.

Physical force between states (war) could be excluded if law came to prevail among them, as it does among the citizens of a state. The idea is to subordinate force to the law and thus to legalize it. As within the state, there would remain only a minimum of illegal force — that of one state rebelling against the community of all others — but this impotent force would be subdued, like the criminal's within the state, by the power of the common order. War would be replaced by police action.

This seemingly simple thought is self-deception as long as there are great powers — powers against which a "police action" would be no police action at all, but war. The name would mask the reality. True, there is power in the idea of law; there is power in conviction, in intellectual mastery, in the example. But this power can be relied upon only if at the decisive point it is secured by force.

We must not forget, first, that a state of law has come into being only if force was risked in founding it; and, second, that law is effective only if the decisions of the legal authority must be enforced over all possible resistance. True, the idea of an objective, universally valid law is persuasive, but it can be realized only if opposing parties, convinced of being in the right and unable to agree, submit to superior authority because — in international as in domestic affairs — the loser admits that legality is better than force even in case of a miscarriage of justice. If the parties do not recognize the authority and think — between states — that they have adequate power, the result is war. It does not help to differentiate between aggressive and defensive wars, or to speak of just wars or holy wars. These judgments are not pronounced by superior authority; they are partisan judgments even if the parties are not identical with states but cut across them.

As long as war is possible, our party divisions differ from the partisan struggle in a state of regulated force — that is, of peace. The difference between the totalitarian and the politically free world is that one excludes this peaceful conflict, whereas in the other, though constantly menaced, it is largely possible. Arguing from the injustice of the social order, totalitarianism, backed by blind masses, upsets this order to establish one that is not only more unjust but unfree in principle. In the free world one senses the abyss when the counterpart does not hear, does not think, does not reflect, and is merely poised for violent action. As long as war is possible, as long as there is no agency to secure peace by effective decisions, man's claim to be the absolute authority is presumptuous. He can only preserve himself by fighting force with force. That peacemaking agency would not be absolute, either, for its decisions could be wrong. But it would, in due course, be possible to correct them by legal means. What decides in war is force, not law.

It is only in peace and political freedom that man can implement and defend in rational argument what he believes to be right and what may legally come to prevail. The idea of law has incalculable effects. Conscience is not a fiction. Politicians, despots, and criminals still pay homage to it in denying misdeeds and disguising the wrong they do as right. But that the basic ideas of law can be securely effective in our lives only if force is available for their realization — this is a basic situation which dreamers have to keep impressing upon their memories. The idea of law as such can only prevail by allying itself with force. The law is morally based, but real owing to force.

The ideas of law are themselves in historic evolution. The concept of mankind has existed since the time of the Sophists and grown in power since the "natural law" of the Stoics and, finally, since the advent of biblical religion. Since the eighteenth century, "rights of man" have been stated and men have tried — unfortunately in vain — to give them historical reality. When the French Revolution proclaimed them, Burke promptly protested: no rights of man — the rights of an Englishman were to him the foundation of political life. Sure of his historical consciousness, aware that "rights," in fact, can only make secure if they command force, he drew the grand conclusion that frightens us; but he has been right to this day. It is clearer than ever that each individual can rely only on the rights he possesses by virtue of his nationality — in other words, by virtue of a power that commands force. He who would rely on the rights of man and tries to do so as a stateless person — forcibly turned into one, perhaps, by his own state that took away his citizenship — will find out that he has actually no rights at all, fewer than a man. I have never seen a clearer, more compelling, more relentless exposition of this reality of our contemporary world than in Hannah Arendt's *Origins of Totalitarianism*.

Hannah Arendt has shown that the rights of man, now counting for less than ever, have at the same time become more urgent than ever. When all historical ties are broken in fact, when the mass of the uprooted who feel superfluous and belong nowhere keeps growing, when the abandonment of countless human beings becomes unbearably clear, we must seek a new foundation, a new ground to bear them all. When all the nations on earth, all cultures and states, meet on the path of a common fate, the fate of humanity, they need something by which to understand each other. When mankind becomes one by being threatened as one, and able, in the long run, to save itself only as one — when every nation's survival depends on all other nations — then the rights of man become the premise of this deliverance, because nothing else can create mutual confidence. The necessary basis of each individual's existence is also that of the existence of mankind — which, after all, is made one only by one common, inviolate ground.

This conflicts today with the fact that the rights of man are still despised in practice by the overwhelming majority of men, that even Marx disavowed them as a bourgeois-capitalist ideology. We must admit that the philosophical statement of these rights has not yet had any political effect. Magnificent aid and care is extended, indeed, by individuals to individuals, and occasionally even by states to carefully limited numbers of the stateless who have lost their rights. But the appeal to the rights of man is politically ineffective. It could become effective only if a great nation were to adopt the rights of man (not only human rights for its own citizens) as part of its constitution and to proclaim them as rights of all men. For without power to insure it there can be no right.

But as no country is big enough to open its doors to all refugees, malcontents, and immigrants without endangering its own existence, the rights of man will have a chance only if many and finally all states guarantee them to their citizens — so that flight and emigration would become unnecessary, expulsion impossible because of the inviolability of original nationality, and all other countries would have opened their doors to the exceptional case. Such developments presuppose that a majority of mankind will be unanimous in recognizing human rights and will be clearly conscious of these rights. Only what men really want will have the needed power at its disposal.

Today the unity of mankind is an idea imposed upon us by reality itself. It can be wrought only by unanimity about the rights of man. This is another premise of the salvation of mankind.

Human rights cannot be effective as abstract ideas. Their significance can be grasped only if they are experienced from the root of human existence. They are grounded in the creation of man. They antedate the rationality which puts them into words but does not invent them. They face men with a challenge of encompassing authority: Live up to us, or all of you are doomed.

The real situation is still one of violent struggle governed by the self-assertion of our particular, timebound, historically conditioned existence. Politics is still the sum total of the methods of such self-preservation, constantly eyeing the force from which, and by which, it protects itself. In the concrete situation, then, we ask: whose self-preservation? That of an individual in power? Of a group, an oath-bound community, a nation, a way of life, a tradition, a state apparatus, an army as such? Of a conception of freedom as reality? Of an abstract idea? Of a historical basis or ideology? Of love of house and home, of wife and children, of native soil? Of such ideas as "the West," "Europe," "Christianity"? Of the existence of people accidentally gathered, organized, and fed on fictions — people who, if fictions collapse along with the power that bore them, are left as a lost, bewildered crowd?

Since the essence of politics is association with force employed for self-preservation, we come to an absurd requirement: The renunciation of force would involve the renunciation of self-preservation. Then all politics would cease. This has actually happened in the lives of the saints who followed the Word from the Sermon on the Mount: "Resist not evil; but whosoever shall smite thee on thy right check, turn to him the other also." Where such a life remains consistent it has its own dignity, however undignified it may be politically. It is a life that is heedless of either living or not living, a life indifferent to itself, existing because of chance and circumstance, entirely absorbed by something outside this world, to which the world does not matter.

But now the idea of non-violence has itself been turned into politics. I do not mean the method of the Russian revolutionaries before they came to power, the method of all underground movements: to refrain from open combat with superior power, to stay in hiding, to strike only by terrorism, assassination, sabotage, and then to vanish again. These are the methods of temporary impotence in quest of power; once in possession of power, it will use it all the more effectively against any hidden resistance, because familiar with its methods. What I mean is the *political principle of non-violence* followed by men who show themselves openly, radically reject force on their part, but are ready to suffer it and confident of conquering it in this fashion.

The nations want peace; peace is possible only if we renounce force. This renunciation, into which pacifists would like to coax the nations, is born of fear and the lassitude of wanting just to be happy. It is not an inner renunciation of violence as such, only of its hazards. In this state of mind we think, blindly, that if only our country would not use force, would not arm, would express its will to peace and demonstrate it by making itself impotent — besides giving its citizens a materially better life by reducing the arms burden — everything would be well. This state of mind is usually associated with an aggressiveness, indignation, and a tendency to riskless violence. No suprapolitical power is here at work, but a subpolitical illusory intellectualism and self-deceit.

Only once has non-violence had suprapolitical roots and succeeded. Gandhi, this extraordinary figure of our time, baffles us: his life and actions show the self-sacrificing valor that counts in dealing with force — not only if it is mixed with force, as usual, but precisely if non-violence is attempted. Does Gandhi show us the way?

Gandhi freed India from British rule, not with soldiers, but by a non-violent appeal to justice. He acted politically, for he dealt with force, but in unheard-of fashion. In a world claiming to live by the ideas of law and ethics (and actually living by them, to a small but essential extent) — in a world upheld by the power of the British Empire, that would use force only in extreme cases but then with extreme brutality — in this "civilized" world, which had pushed military force into the background of consciousness, Gandhi lifted the screen. He unveiled the rule of force not only in theory (this had long been done) but in practice, by exposing himself to violence and suffering it in view of the whole world. He did not go from the world into solitude, like the saints. He did not act alone either, but jointly with the masses he had convinced. His activity was not force, but a challenge to the rule of force.

This non-violent action consisted in non-co-operation with the British, and in civil disobedience to British laws which the Indians considered unjust — such as the refusal to pay certain taxes or the production of salt in violation of the salt monopoly. Criminal prosecutions, the first consequence, bogged down in the mass of offenders. There were not enough courts or jails. Gandhi's decisive strength lay in his readiness to suffer any consequences imposed by the ruling force and in his ability to arouse the same readiness in the Indian masses. He claimed that opponents should be convinced, not conquered. Instead of building a dividing wall against them, one should prepare for the right co-operation with them by exposing actual injustice. Thus Gandhi stunned the world as he fought force with non-violence, methodically and so as to inspire his people.

Gandhi succeeded. Eventually, after decades of this non-violent struggle, India was freed by the British. Gandhi, at first a strange curiosity with his theory and way of life, more an object of smiles than of serious concern, won world-wide respect scarcely equaled by any statesman of his times — for nothing succeeds like success. But was he a statesman? Did he create something politically valid and exemplary? Did he found a political way of life? What can we learn from him?

Gandhi developed the theory of his action. He based his politics on religious, suprapolitical grounds, on the inner activity of *satyagraha*, the firm adherence to existence and truth. Gandhi begins with himself. Outward resistance is to flow from the active power of love, of faith, and of sacrifice. The *satyagrahi*, is no passively vegetating individual but "a worrier of truth." Gandhi may remind us of the Hindu ascetics of many centuries, but he differs from them in his refusal to leave the world: he accepted responsibility within the world. He renounced violence but not politics. He wanted the impossible: politics by non-violence. He had the greatest possible success: the liberation of India. Is the impossible possible, after all?

The crucial point, decisive for the understanding of Gandhi's achievement, is to see in what sense it is a unique, highly peculiar event. Briefly put, it resulted far more from the British political state of mind than from Gandhi's — indeed, he seems almost like a tool in the course of English history.

Gandhi could speak in public. He was allowed to be active even in jail. British liberal views and legal concepts gave Gandhi his scope. Why did the British government look more and more helpless before massive passive resistance? Because it said: We can't arrest them all. To some Englishmen, to be sure, it had occurred that everything depended on the ruthlessness of terror. Those said: We must kill, not arrest; abolish publicity and kill a hundred thousand Indians, and three hundred millions will keep quiet. History teaches that men can be made to obey if you risk exterminating them and leaving a desert. The Athenians did it in Samos, the Romans in Palestine, the medieval church in Provence, Cromwell in Ireland. Absolute rule is possible whenever it does away with restrictions and qualms, whether in naïve political action or by referring to a revealed deity. Such terror makes for submission, in which proud nations that value their freedom will perish. Nations do not react alike.

How far is a ruling power prepared to go if its rule is threatened? Faced with this great question, the British decided that the end of their rule was better than radical terror.

It was only under the British, and only under their attempt at liberal rule which is unique in the history of empires, that Gandhi could succeed. Never before would such non-violent policies have led to the same outcome, and in the future they could lead to it only under conditions analogous to British liberalism, freedom of speech, and legality. The liberation of India is far more a matter of British politics, far more the consequence of England's struggle with herself, than it is an Indian feat.

Unique, however, is the great fact which no one expected: that a man who clearly knew what he was doing and demonstrated it by his life engaged in politics on a suprapolitical basis. Sacrificing his own person, he turned the suprapolitical into a valid political force in our time. He did not divorce politics from ethics and religion but anchored them there, unconditionally: better to die, better to "wipe the whole nation off the map," than to surrender the purity of the spirit.

Gandhi seems never to have lied. He always said openly what he wanted and what he meant. The principle of the lie, which plays so decisive a role in all other politics, he gave up altogether. Self-education and self-purification, the personal life of the individual who issues the suprapolitical challenge to all, was his premise of true politics. Politics became religion. Politics without religion kills the soul, he said; it is a "trap for man."

Today we face the question of how to escape from physical force and from war, lest we all perish by the atom bomb. Gandhi, in word and deed, gives the true answer: Only a suprapolitical force can bring political salvation. It may be inspiring that this answer, in our time, comes from an Asian. His example, however great in its suprapolitical seriousness, is impossible as a signpost for our political action. We cannot follow even the form of this seriousness, whose content touches us strangely (and occasionally surprises us by vulgar Hindu superstitions). We cannot follow the concrete method of a kind of politics that could succeed only in the atmosphere of British rule and for the limited purpose of Indian liberation. For the extremity of present world-wide realities Gandhi gives us no answer.

In the struggles against totalitarianism, Gandhi's procedure would not be a political way but a way to certain doom. Every sacrifice would be secret, rendered without publicity, untouchable in its metaphysical substance, to be sure, but unknown to men. Because no echoes would reach the public, no political consequences would result. Against a terror that knows no restriction by legal or conscientious qualms, sacrifice is futile insofar as it remains outside the communication of human activities.

On the other hand, Gandhi's non-violent doctrine perfectly suits politicians who lack his suprapolitical grounding and use it only to deceive the world. How fatal it would be for men to yield in good faith, to dispense with force, because they believe in non-violence! They would be so much more radically conquered by the force hiding under the shroud of the fraudulent doctrine. Gandhi's enthusiasm for truth would become deception, surrender, and self-destruction. We can no longer doubt that unlimited terror will destroy all resistance that does not consist of equal physical force. The subjection of Hungary has shown to the dullest eye that the totalitarian Russian terror would have preferred

Hungary as a desert to Hungary free. Against total violence there is no help in less violence, nor in non-violence. Only one limit is conceivable: the destructive engine would cease to obey if the human being in it were touched by the power of conscience. That this is a hope and not an impossibility, but that it is contingent upon the unfolding of suprapolitical reasons in every individual, will be discussed in the third part of this book. Gandhi demonstrated the power of the suprapolitical in the situation in which he was active, but the contents and methods are neither transferable nor exemplary.

Western pacifism is nothing like Gandhi's non-violent politics. It does not present us with the personal ethos of the man whose whole life is an open book, but with mere demands, mere judgment, and theory. The action of pacifism is the protest; but in fact it is protesting against human life. It will not see the boundary: if we want the human world to exist, to keep building, to continue its unpredictable historical course, we cannot evade the fact that in the face of force nothing remains but force or submission to force — eventually totalitarian force. The pacifist says that force is unable to make peace and to make life secure. This is quite true, but the unconditional renunciation of force would have consequences only for those who renounce it, not for the over-all condition of mankind.

The realistic will to do everything possible to prevent war is not pacifism. But the idea of non-violent politics is either serious, as for Gandhi, or it is confused, unrealistic pacifist thinking. Einstein, who called himself a pacifist, was not one when he advised Roosevelt to make the atom bomb; at that moment he honored the need of force in view of Hitler's Germany. Born calls Einstein free of blame, "except from the point of view of extreme pacifism, which teaches that force should never be used, not even against the greatest evil" — but this non-extreme pacifism, which the overwhelming majority of men agree upon, is no pacifism at all. Whenever force against force is recognized as inevitable, we enter a boundary situation of human existence, and he who then keeps calling himself a pacifist has not thought through the consequences. At what stage men make the decision to use force (as distinct from the countless compromises of differing material interests which can be peacefully settled) is up to their freedom; freedom can surrender all material particulars, but not itself. We shall see where the situation under the threat of the atom bomb can lead.

Today there is widespread realization that the atom bomb can be abolished only by the abolition of war, but many still think the bomb alone might be put out of action. Their wrath is not aimed at war but at the bomb. They protest only against the bomb, as the pacifists do against war. But just as peace societies have contributed nothing to the prevention of wars, all present efforts to abolish the bomb only, without seeing it in the context of the real actions of nations and the evident motives of most men, are futile. They cling to symptoms and fail to get at the root of the human calamity. Pacifists or not, they go on behind the façade of opinions and emotions to live, day in, day out, in the manner of living and thinking that is the rotten soil of human reality on which these horrors thrive. Effective truth requires that we should not fool with symptoms but should see the basic problem in the evil's source.

Our reality is, on the one hand, the atom bomb, on the other, the present ethical-political state of mankind. What truth is "in league" with these realities? It is only in the presence of all the arguments yet to be considered that the answer may be sensed like a vague glow of dawn, without being unequivocally expressible.

In violent situations there may arise a primordial phenomenon that is incomprehensible in terms of our rational, objective thinking — a phenomenon which, furthermore, depresses our absolute will to live and tends, therefore, to be talked away. For example, when the inhabitants of an Indonesian island, or rather its princes and nobles, were to be forced to meet the requirements of European expediency, they allowed themselves, one and all, to be shot by the Dutch. They did not fight back but walked solemnly in their ceremonial robes toward the firing squad. The Dutch were quite disconcerted. Thus many Indians died during the conquest of America, and many natives of Siberia at the hands of the Russians. Herodotus already tells of similar events.

This kind of sacrifice is the core, if not the broad aspect, of such struggles for freedom. We have seen it in 1956, in Hungary. The agony of exploitation and economic distress, the accumulated despair of years, the unbearable loss of freedom, the enforced untruthfulness of life as a whole — all this brings matters to a point where a nation will dare all, will dare the impossible.

The truth and reality at the core of such happenings must not be spoiled for us by the ambiguity of the broader scene. The suprapolitical sacrifice offered by the moving spirits seems to vanish in the contagion of a mass movement, in the obliviousness of an overwhelmingly subjective atmosphere. It was thus in the Middle Ages, with the flagellants and the Crusades. The creative force does not lie in the passing flareup.

Not the purpose of sacrifice, but its possible consequence in the world — whose failure does not void its meaning — is to be remembered by survivors who will some day repeat what had failed. Martyrs double the strength of those who emulate them.

Yet in reality the hard boundary remains: it is only by leadership and organization that any lasting political reality can be achieved. The crafty terror of superior power can kill all freedom, and then the fight of the free can but enhance their misery. Sheer force has no limit, for it can destroy all life. But there is *one* limit: that destruction may manifest something more real than life and all force.

Force bars the door to a definitive, rational order of human relations. Where there is force — where men kill and are killed — there is struggle which demands the sacrifice of life. And elsewhere, where life goes on in an orderly way guaranteed by force, there is the "peaceful" struggle for material existence, as relentless as physical conflict. Sacrifice belongs to life, whether as an instantaneous taking of life or its constant attrition in the loss of opportunities.

As a mere fact, this would be common to all creatures. Essential to man is the *conscious* sacrifice, the risking of his life: conscious risk in the world which is not adequately comprehensible in terms of the world. The foundation of everything sublime in man is sacrifice. Even in failure, the sacrifice as such is a fulfilment of infinite significance. Man does not know his humanity until he proves it by courage and by contempt of death. These have a different basis from mere life. There is more to man than life. And though self-denial, if we go on living, is but a partial sacrifice, this too can be experienced like the destruction from which another life arises. We like to disguise sacrifice and its meaning because we cannot bear it. Or we seek to compensate for it by renunciation supposed to take its place. We do not face it, because we do not want to make the sacrifice; we should like to be happy without it. But it is a vain attempt to wrest happiness from a sacrifice we have evaded. Without sacrifice, there is a rift in our existence; it dims itself in self-delusions.

Sacrifice has two aspects: withdrawal from the world, and activity in the world.

An unworldly sacrifice is the wanton waste of life in battle, proudly conscious only of one's own contempt of death or yielding to blind obedience in obscure expectation. Ascetics and saints who are ready to die at any time, without a worldly will or responsibility, also make unworldly sacrifices. So do conscientious objectors who are not trying to save their lives but will bear every pain and humiliation, who would rather be killed by their state than take part in killing — in short, who make things harder on themselves, not easier, than the rest do. For they shift the sacrifice where they will be despised as well, while the others make theirs with the support and admiration of the community.

To risk death with a will to live in the world is quite a different matter. Out of this risk alone grows real earnestness. Only those live constructively who are prepared to give their lives and will sacrifice them in the constant wear of service to their task. This sacrifice, if not consummated in death, works creatively, builds in the world, provides fulfilment. Should it call for death, though, man can believe in himself if — having pondered and exercised prudence and considered the relative values — he is able to die calmly and to bear the failure of his cause.

But, we asked, if life is sacrificed for life: for which life? In whose self-preservation? What is worth the sacrifice?

Here lies the inescapable paradox. Made for something in the world, the sacrifice retains its meaning even if everything for which it happened in the world miscarries. In other words: its worldly purpose is no adequate explanation of the sacrifice. To interpret a soldier's death as a means to an end is to traduce the soldier. To say he died in vain if the objective is not reached deprives his sacrifice of substance. The eternal meaning of sacrifice is independent of the success of its worldly purpose, and yet it is substantial only in conjunction with the will to a worldly realization.

The purpose is an object of struggle that makes life seem not worth living if the sacrifice is not risked. But bound up with the sacrifice is something timeless, hypersensory, and unconditional. Even if "useless," it is not "senseless."

Sacrifice reveals the secret at the frontier of all human affairs. The awareness of this goes back to primordial ages, when it was voiced in the myth of the god who sacrifices himself.

A glow of the all-embracing, all-encompassing sacrifice is reflected in daring force and challenging force. Let us examine the situation of force first in indirect (political) and then in direct (physical) conflict.

Politics relates to the possible use of physical violence. Its actual use is a matter for the soldier.

There are two extremes: politics as such, which seeks nothing but power, and the suprapolitical element searching for spiritual purity in another world. The extremes can mutually promote each other; they can even occur in one and the same person, but they cannot turn into one — for then the soul splits and man ceases to be himself.

Great politics, on the other hand, has a suprapolitical direction. This appeared first in the ethical demand for the elimination of war, in keeping with the commandment "Thou shalt not kill." It gave meaning to the regulation of force by a government of laws. But then the suprapolitical element gave meaning to sacrifice, to the risk of life for a life that is worth living — so that failure, uselessness to its purpose, would not make it senseless. The way in which the suprapolitical takes effect is the determining force in politics.

A responsible political decision can violate moral commandments such as to tell the truth or not to kill; it can break laws; it can break treaties. But a man whose ethics oblige him to take responsibility for his actions can never justify such violations as right or as permissible. He knows what he is doing and he makes of it neither a standard nor an example. The integrity of his action would be jeopardized if he tried to legitimize it. He takes the blame he cannot shift, neither to orders issued to him nor to general laws; if he does shift the blame, he is denying the only ground on which his act can be an exception, unjustifiable and singular, an exception with which the actor identifies himself in time and eternity — in time by answering personally for all the consequences, in eternity by taking the act upon himself. For the rest of his life he will be subject to an ineradicable memory, guilt-laden, humiliated. If he was not acting under an irrevocably felt necessity beyond human comprehension — since the world is no mathematical equation — he was yielding to the nullity of his urges and his conventional rationalism and making an irresponsible political blunder to boot. The 1914 "scrap of paper" of Bethmann-Hollweg, that vainly self-justifying, honest but politically helpless bureaucrat, may serve as an example.

In this unmanageable world the statesman stands on the frontier of cognoscibility, acting on perpetually insufficient knowledge, in a historical medium that he believes in and whose self-preservation is at stake. What he is to take upon himself seems beyond human strength.

At such a point it is untruthful to seek vindications. They would be not only untrue but dangerous, for an irresponsibility beneath the moral pale would like to legitimize itself with misused slogans from an "ethics of responsibility."

The mortal sins of politics are the self-preservation of vacuous unsubstantiality (e.g., National Socialism); comfortable avoidance of responsibility by illusory expectations and complacent self-deception (e.g., the policy of appeasing totalitarianism); the vanity drunk with the overrated appearance of power, which heedlessly betrays the requirements of politics and the interests of state and nation (e.g., Kaiser Wilhelm and his retinue).

The responsible statesman's idea can be realized only if it finds an echo in a nation able and willing to see and accept its share of responsibility. The idea is lost if a nation puts the sole responsibility upon its leaders in the belief that they must know better what to do. It is only if the tension spreads to the nations themselves that man can rise to the monstrous situation in which he finds himself today.

Fighting   risking one's life so as either to meet force with force or else to use force to win power and booty — is a primordial phenomenon of human life. The primordial element is the fierce fighting spirit. Unleashed, it engenders the self-transcending lust of flinging one's life away and the savagery that rates other lives no higher, vents itself in pillage and rape after victory, and finally abates in the climactic feeling of power: to spare the conquered and let him serve as a slave.

This abatement led Hegel to interpret the productive meaning of life-and-death struggles. The warrior is a human type, but not everyone is a warrior. One man facing a life-or-death struggle will choose to risk his life for a chance to live in freedom and to gain power, the other will choose to insure his life and live in slavery. In Hegel's interpretation, the first, the fearless one, views the risk of his life as the only test of his freedom, whereas the other, who wants life at any cost, feels "the fear of death, the absolute master." The warrior wins the mastery, the only use of which to him is to be served, or he dies and leaves the spectacle of his victory for others. The one who submits, on the other hand, is as good as dead, for his life is consumed by labor: but in this labor he actually gains a new life with its own fulfilment. The warrior, whether he dies or dominates, stays empty, while the subject's work brings him to himself and to real development. The course of human affairs requires both warriors and subjects, masters and thralls, but the road to the evolution of creative life leads through thralldom.

The fierce fighting spirit becomes soldierly if it is curbed for orderly commitment in a military unit. It is disciplined; it breaks out only at the will of those in command. The soldier does not fight when he wants to but when he is told to. He is in service. He lives in comradeship with others linked with him in the risk of life. He lives in loyalty to his leader. He fights with arms he must learn to use, in joint operations that have to be practiced. Commanding soldiers becomes one of many tasks in the realm of human existence; the officer makes it his life's work. His business is to kill in combat, at the risk of being killed. The profession consists in preparing all the means and all the skills for the moment when the task confronts him in reality. The execution of the task takes soldiers — today including every able-bodied citizen — who must, for a limited training period and then for the duration of hostilities, adopt as their common trade what others practice as a life-long profession.

Apart from the comradeship of common risk and the soldier's sworn loyalty, the specific professional ethics is the discipline of service in the reliable execution of orders. This ethics, calling for the personal qualities of self-control and courage, goes back through the ages, amplified by a consciousness of specific masculinity — as if we had here a mystery uniting men and separating them from women (a concept realized in the communal dwellings of men in primitive societies, and in a sublime form still casting its deep shadow on the glory of Athens). "We men" is a phrase of pride, of courage, and of power, today indeed outmoded and absurd but still resonant for romanticists. We tend to forget that in the crises of history women frequently stepped into the breach. When a nation's life hung in the balance, they fought too. They are the physically weaker but no less heroic sex, and no less astute in the decisive moments.

In dealing with the enemy as well as with the helpless, the soldier's ethics has sometimes produced "chivalry." For soldierly combat has indeed evolved from fierce martial instincts, but by their regulation and control. Thus there arose an ethical way of fighting. Battles are not waged among beasts but among men; they are subjected to rules that make them chivalrous. Men want to be heroes fighting heroes. They want a foe of equal strength; else the contest is ignoble. Certain weapons are barred.

Today all this sounds like a fairy tale, incredible in view of the realities of World War II, to say nothing of the military outlook for the future. Our most recent experiences of war — although in exceptional cases without practical effect the old soldierly qualities of chivalrous encounter may still have appeared — were such that nearly all reports agree in horror. After the First World War there were still war books sensing a pseudo-mythical greatness even in the inhuman battle of machines. After the Second, there was nothing of the kind. War had assumed dimensions beyond the power of men to grasp, to shape, to direct — it had become a chaos of human abasement.

The development of weapons technology since the latest war has now once more so radically changed all military possibilities that we are on the threshold of a new era — one in which the concept of the soldier, dominant throughout recorded history, can play hardly any, certainly no essential, role in any of its old forms. What began with the immensely intensified mechanization of war has reached its goal and its conclusion in the atom bomb. The decisive borderline is this: combat has ceased to be combat when you push a button to launch an engine of death against which there is no defense. The killer stops being a soldier, so does his victim. The mechanization of combat has long been moving toward this borderline, but it has reached it only with the superbomb.

Within itself, the evolution of weapons technology has taken the further, fundamentally new, step to the potential destruction of all mankind. Even the Hiroshima bomb and the hydrogen bomb differ not only quantitatively but qualitatively in destructive power. The new factor is lost from view when attention is focused on the limited effect of atomic weapons: which of them will be used? In what sequence and combination? Is there a limit, or do we soon go all out, according to the law of war — or do we start with the worst?

More and more, war has changed from combat to technological extermination. In the age of technology, violence itself has taken on a basically new form, first in part and now completely.

Yet everything is still in flux. Weapons technology, operational possibilities, strategy — all are constantly being transformed by inventions and combinations, so rapidly that the conceptions of a few years ago are now obsolete. But the obsolete still has meaning. Soldierly combat still exists alongside atomic technology. We distinguish between conventional weapons and atomic weapons, local wars and world war. Traditional warfare has been eclipsed in the sense of the basic transformation of war, but as a subordinate instrument of politics it is by no means finished.

A situation in which everything keeps changing so fast causes obvious bewilderment. We no longer know what to want. Intensified thinking and planning along new ways only make us feel inadequate to the scope of the possibilities. In comparison, the manifold techniques of war and aspects of soldiering in all past history are one, for the transformation of warfare by the new technology of violence has brought with it a transformation of the entire military profession. "The soldier" is becoming a romantic figure. It is easy to show the disintegration of the old concept, but difficult or impossible to say what new form could rise to the height of the soldierly idea. Let us analyze the disintegration:

1. The old-type soldier did not simply meet force with physical force. It has been said, to be sure, that "God is with the greater number of battalions," and when the pope was mentioned, Stalin asked, "How many divisions has he?" But if there is something to that attitude — because at some point resistance to overwhelming power is suicide — it is still false, because the point is indeterminable. The greatest number is not always decisive; courage, imperturbability, presence of mind amidst confusion, a quick grasp of the essentials of a new situation, firmness born of clarity and self-sacrifice, loyalty and reliability have done much. Small groups have not infrequently conquered vast hordes. In many a battle, a few resolute men have magically communicated their courage to others. But somewhere, of course, is a limit where the bravest succumb, crushed by mass or annihilated by technology.

What agility of mind can do against mass stolidity, what technical cunning can do against the power of technical apparatus, as David killed Goliath and a giant of Hindu mythology was killed by a mouse — this we cannot foresee. But neither can we build on it, and somewhere is the limit to all possibilities. Today this limit is the total, mechanically accomplished annihilation at one blow.

2. About to vanish is the soldierly spirit, the ethos of an independent profession where many a German youth might still seek refuge in the first years of Nazism, mistaking the present for the past and vainly expecting still to find there truthfulness and decency and personal freedom. That army changed apace; a standardized life became impossible when machinery replaced the standards. Soldierly integration in an impersonal framework changed when the impersonal factor turned from the substance of a cause into an automatic debasement of man. Self-

discipline became empty when it was purposeless. Self-sacrifice became pointless when the sacrifice lacked an aim. The whole became a mere mechanism of obedience and discipline without the freedom of soldierly ethics, a total inhumanity cloaked in hollow words.

3. In mass armies, the soldier no longer fights because he is freely resolved to risk his life in solidarity with his countrymen, with common political freedom, with his native soil. On the contrary: it is to save his life, which would be forfeit if he refused, that he allows himself to be pressed into the army. Daring and sacrifice change places when the state is no longer political substance but a nihilistic machine. Where there is no sacrifice, where men obey out of fear for their lives, it is mendacious to drape their actions in heroic glory. And where there are still true sacrifices, they are branded crimes against the state and disposed of, quietly stifled, by superior power. Remains there, then, neither daring nor sacrifice, the progeny of freedom — only the machinery? Is apparent daring more and more often just inertia and thoughtlessness?

4. The specific peril of the combatant has given way to the peril of the whole population. This, not the soldier, takes the risk. Indeed, the soldier is safer now, due to the maximum protection of all military activities. The combat situation in the old sense has spread to the whole population, which suffers most and is most liable to be exterminated.

5. Surprise is the best ally of technological warfare. Therefore, war is no longer declared. Since it would be much too risky to delay mobilization until after a declaration of war, and earlier mobilization would be obvious to foreign agents, everything depends on the suddenness and the magnitude of the first "act of war" — which is intended to be too vast to leave a chance for significant counteraction. Thus the formal act disappears which used to give notice and allow preparations for war in all spheres of life, and a constant state of potential war comes to be felt at the same time. The possibility of the worst is always with us. From the start, the intent of military action aims at totality in the sense of extermination. There is no more room to develop a soldierly spirit.

This picture of the disintegration of the soldier is extreme, although in a coming world war it would certainly become reality. Yet the traditional element is far from expired. It still plays a considerable part, first, in the distinction between conventional and nuclear arms, and second, in that between local and world war.

As distinct from nuclear arms, all those used up to now are called conventional. Most states have only such arms, and the three atomic powers have by no means abolished them. What remains of the soldier concept is associated with conventional arms.

The Western powers are inclined to shelve conventional weapons in favor of nuclear ones. One reason is economic: the cost of both armaments lowers the standard of living. In Russia this lowering is enforced, on the ground of cold political calculation; Russia is vastly superior to the whole world in conventional armaments.

A second reason for preferring nuclear arms is the wish to lessen the soldierly sacrifice, the risk of life for one's own citizens who do not like to submit even to the personal restrictions of military service in peacetime. Since Korea, the American people have been decidedly averse to sending troops abroad. They mean to shift war from the personal risk of each able-bodied man to the field of technology, to let the more and more perfect and destructive atomic weapons replace the soldier. Mass annihilation of the enemy is to save lives at home. One would like to exchange the seriousness of self-sacrificing combat for a single, total, technical operation that requires no more soldiers. One would like to reduce all armaments and concentrate on the one of total technical annihilation — and this on the ground that then there would be no more war.

The idea had a terrible, demoralizing allure when America alone had the atom bomb. Now — since Russia has the same weapons, since no one knows any more who is superior in the field, since the American continent is within range of well-aimed Russian missiles — the idea has fallen flat, for the American people are in the same danger of mass annihilation which they had intended for their enemies alone. Russia can dispose of her masses. Over the years she has equipped them with the best arms and given them military training, and a prodigious effort aided by outstanding physicists and engineers has now brought her nuclear weapons also to the level of the American ones. A revolution must be taking place in the American military mind. America wants no war that requires men, and now she fears for herself in the nuclear war she did everything to prepare for.

Conventional weapons have obtained a new significance. Perhaps there will be no total extinction; perhaps nine-tenths of humanity will be wiped out, but the nation that will prevail, the state that will conquer in the end, will be the last to fight with the old heroic courage. Those with an unsoldierly turn of mind would then be destroyed, and the spirit of self-sacrificing valor would be re-established.

Only the two or three atomic powers — the only great powers — have the problem of weighing nuclear against conventional weapons. All others, so far, have only conventional weapons. As a result, the local wars of small nations are still waged with these, and only a world war between the great powers would undoubtedly be an atomic war

Present military thinking lies therefore on two levels. There is a strategy of local wars and a strategy of world war. The two are interdependent; the possibilities of local war are overshadowed by the world strategy of the great powers. Small nations ask themselves either: How are we to take part in world strategy as followers of a great power on which we depend for our self-preservation? Or: how can we hold aloof from world strategy and yet protect ourselves in our situation — exposed to the conventional weapons of others, but left to ourselves by the great powers as long as we are not essential to them? None can avoid the global thoughts of world strategy, since all are inescapably drawn into the whirlpool; but the small ones retain some incalculable elbowroom in their place within the whirlpool, and there they must prepare for their self-preservation — up to the point where a great power forces them into the context of its own global strategy.

It is not that the small armies could be abolished just because they would not prevail against atom bombs and missiles, or that small countries must subordinate themselves to the strategy of the great powers (even though they take their lead from it). Israel, for example, would not exist and could not survive without its small army.

In the interstitial existence of the small nations and until the moment when everything will be settled by a "push-button war" of global mass extermination, the concept of the soldier still has its place. But even there it cannot remain the same. The inner attitude is fundamentally altered if every skirmish is fought under the threat of the last trumpet, which has not yet sounded but may sound any day, extinguishing everything soldierly along with everything else — and if, moreover, one's own fight may set off the holocaust and would thus bear a responsibility beyond that of combat. It is not "heaven," as formerly, that presides over battles and makes the ordeal by combat truly decisive; it is the possessors of the atom bomb who can intervene at any moment, reverse any outcome, and erase the whole.

The end is either the extermination of life or the transformation of man and the human condition, so that physical combat ceases. We are still in a period of transition. The actors in the different situations and places on earth will have to experience, to know, to want, and to decide in relativity — or, in chaotic helplessness, they will not know what they want and will be mere objects of disaster.

The situation is both so obscure and so monstrous that passivity is tempting: there is nothing we *can* do. If a world war comes, think a a good many, all is in vain anyway. There is no defense against atom bombs. In the age of these bombs military armaments have lost their value. Armaments and military service have become superfluous; even civil defense is impossible. The soldier feels debased by the overwhelming power of technology; romantic glorification of the battle of matériel has become utterly implausible. Resentfully, but resignedly, we give up all hope and would like to ignore the fact that will one day draw everything into the whirlpool of destruction.

But this resignation is untrue and cowardly. In view of a supposedly inevitable development it actually fosters the conditions that will bring about the self-destruction of mankind. While the shadow of the atom bomb confronts man with the supreme challenge to examine all his actions in relation to the goal of world peace, and while this challenge ought to raise life to its highest tension, many react in the opposite way. They would like to elude war by disarming and letting others arm. Unwilling to experience any more horror, they thoughtlessly put themselves at the mercy of a future that will deliver them to coercion, to pillage, to pauperization by forced labor under terrorism, at whatever moment the possessor of arms finds convenient. They want to get rid of the military question by refusing to take it seriously. They want to reduce life's burden instead of adding to it. But if I hide reality from myself and do not look into its fearful face, I am shirking the human task.

Instead, we succumb to notions of horror. We condemn the terrible suffering of atom bomb victims by humanitarian standards. Rightly so — but to see anything new in this would be an error. Violent killing has always been pitiless and inhumane. Sudden death by bombs, poisons, gases may even seem "more humane" than the agony of slowly bleeding to death on the battlefield, helpless, ignored, racked by fever and thirst and pain. Now as ever, the forms of death and disablement are manifold but identical in essence. The difference is quantitative: whether a few or millions or all men perish miserably. The new inhumanity lies in this prospect: once combat is replaced by machinery, the victim cannot fight back, and the killer kills mechanically, without endangering himself in the moment of execution and without perceiving the act of killing as such, whether he is launching missiles that gut cities and will kill millions over thousands of miles or turning a handle to let gas stream into the chambers where hundreds are to die.

We may ask how, in spite of everything, a new type of soldier might arise in this transition period.

What is happening now is obvious: officers are turning into professional military engineers, and enlisted men into mechanics. Both need long training in knowledge and technical skill. They are no longer mere military technicians of a locally circumscribed field of battle, as in the First World War; for from the start of the third, the battlefield would be the entire global land area along with air space and sea, above and under the water — a single theater of war between the sky and the depths of the ocean.

How the eternal concept of the soldier can be realized in such situations, assuming new forms in such new, unprecedented circumstances, we cannot imagine or predict. If we try to discuss it, we can only do so in the ideas and forms of the past and will stray into dreams like the following:

The individual is no more than a technical functionary of military action; once the evil starts, he is helpless wherever he may be, protected only in the chains of command, while they last. There are unpredictable, unusual situations in which opportunities can be seen and seized by an individual who may thus come to determine the course of events. Might a new soldierly honor possibly lie in becoming a perfect technician? In a sense of being and operating in space, detached from the soil? Even apart from the politics of totalitarianism and freedom, could the power of a way of life lead here to a professional ethos of technology that would be the same everywhere and call for technical precision, improvement, and superiority? Would this ethos of technical perfection turn the servants of technology into its masters and give them an inner distance from it?

Further, could there be a new dignity for the soldier who takes part in world strategy and finds his meaning in it? Would he be entering a dimension in which, because the planet is at issue, man would be at issue — a dimension giving rise to a world citizenry that would be at home everywhere, whose country would be Earth, to whom home, fatherland, ancestry in our sense would be unforgotten but no longer determining the ultimate decisions by any political and military power of their own? (Many people, millions of them, have had the fate of historic rootlessness imposed upon them by deportations or forced migrations; but where this historic soil is still real and beloved, it needs protection by an encompassing order in which it is not the determining factor any more.) Would the human being, rather than a geographical fatherland, fight for its self-preservation? Would a world war become ideological in Nietzsche's sense, as were the wars of religion? Will for a common and uniting technological ethos the future issue still lie between freedom and totalitarian death? Will the fight be not for a state but for humanity? Such ideas cannot be put into concrete form. They no sooner seem to touch essentials in us than they will lure us into crusading notions that do not belong here at all.

Should a new truth arise for the soldier if he himself became political, instead of letting himself be misused as a tool? Would he find out that a monopoly in arms leads to world rule by despotism and that the freedom of all depends, first, on a balance of forces, and then on the further development of this vast machinery of violence? A development based upon a common will that was aware of its unity in technological perfection and would now like to realize itself in the mutual, non-violent communication of everything human? This might be the decision to come, or rather, the premise or core of all decisions.

The new technology of war involves a new, unprecedented distribution of danger. Immediately, the soldier is perhaps the least endangered. Because his act itself would be total destruction, he may perhaps show an unprecedented kind of courage. He may feel a responsibility not to plunge himself and mankind blindly into the doom he is to bring about.

Will the new soldier bring about what seems impossible now: that a global, unorganized fraternity of those controlling the means of destruction, strengthened by their new honor, dignity, and truth, might balk at the employment of those weapons? Might they refuse to obey the politicians' order, with the assurance of previous understanding that the soldiers on the other side would do the same?

These are fantastic notions, but to dream of them is not senseless, although to rely on them would be absurd.

In this breathing spell we live in, more and more eyes may be opened, conceptions and ways of action may arise whose spread would open the way to salvation, and finally they may take hold of the men who operate the machine of technological annihilation, who would refrain, then, from letting it take effect. We are still far from that; one cannot start at the end of the road. The premise of an effective change in the new technological soldier is a community of man that cuts through all iron curtains. Salvation does not come to mankind as a gift, and men are not to pursue their trivial happiness by the valor of others. Dreams can open possibilities.

Let us go on dreaming: Is there something enduring in man, usually asleep and sometimes awake? With the warfare of the past, the soldier of the past is at an end. The threat of nuclear war could produce a new soldier — one who, in possession of the means of war, would prevent war. And if thus, on the very brink of total perdition, the way were found to a state of world peace — however unstable it would necessarily be — then this new soldiery would serve a new world. Even if mankind is lucky enough to survive, life will be no paradise despite the magnificent gifts of technology. The soldierly qualities — self-sacrifice, reliability, chivalry in whatever forms of combat may then exist, a courageous approach to life, the freedom and independence of one who does not want to live at any cost — these will remain, but their appearance will change. Our imagination would like to anticipate the unknown, but it cannot be done. Evidently we are to do our part in the dark rather than with a deceptive sense of total foresight.

A general exposition of the suprapolitical sacrifice leads only to dead ends. In general terms it had no justifying meaning. It is concrete and historical. Except in the inaccessible metaphysical sense, no sacrifice as such is true and great; if man, for example, seeks to prove himself to himself by rising above his life, risking it and daring all, no matter why or when, such sacrifice looks like an irreverent revolt against Transcendence, which demands life in this world. Nor is the purpose of sacrifice ever an adequate meaning. The general idea of sacrifice can only point to the non-general, the unique in the transcendent foundation of a reality impervious to objective knowledge.

But sacrifice is the inescapable foundation of true humanity. If its soldierly form disappears, it will assume others. What renunciations, self-denials, ventures, lie on the road to a new reason cannot be specified in advance. Only this much is certain: without sacrifice we are not truly human. The great renunciations are not only necessary to save a free world but also to bring man back from a life lost in an empty consumer's existence after a few hours of unrelished work. Sacrifice would not only make peace possible; it would fulfil it.

A lasting peace could only be achieved if the greatness, the strength, and the valor of the sacrifice hitherto shown in history by the soldier would now materialize in no lesser form.

PART TWO

5

THE
MILITARY
SITUATION

If in view of the threatened annihilation of mankind, knowing that only world peace can avert the threat, we ask what might be done, we must think not only generally about legal principles and moral attitudes and sacrifice, but realistically about the present state of the world. Let us begin with a glance at the military situation and the instability of our position.

Both Russia and America, the two great powers with large stocks of atom bombs, can destroy each other's cities and industrial centers with hydrogen bomb-carrying guided missiles — each from her own territory or bases, without military action, simply by the use of technological machinery. But they cannot thus win a war, for each would expose herself to the same destruction by an instantaneous counterblow.

The physicists have made it clear: formerly, strengthened attack would be met by a strengthened defense, but now there is no more defense, only retaliation. According to Baron Manfred von Ardenne, a German physicist working for the Russians, an atomic blitzkrieg can never prevent retaliation but is bound to bring it about. Hans Bethe put the situation thus: "If two opponents armed with hand grenades face each other in a six-by-nine-foot cellar room, how great is the temptation to throw first?" Max Born stated the prevailing view: "We believe that a war between great powers has become impossible, or will at least become impossible in the near future."

A unique factor appears to compel no mere mitigation, but elimination of violent combat: what would destroy both antagonists at once seems unemployable. No one, it seems clear, would dare to use atom bombs if his opponent has them. If there is no defense, but instant retaliation, both sides are paralyzed. If New York were leveled and all its inhabitants killed, the same would happen to Moscow within the hour.

However plausible this idea may seem, it cannot be relied upon. Desperate men may go to senseless extremes; fear of their own destruction may prevent their use of the bomb for a long time, but not forever. If we expect anything from the simple intellectual thoughts commonly called reason, we are concealing the terminal situation from ourselves. We believe in a reason that would be no more than purposive intellect. But the human intellect is untrustworthy in practice, especially in extremity. The use of existing weapons will not be dependably confined by the workings of mere intellect.

In fact — and in spite of the thought that atomic war, and thus any large-scale war, is impossible — all nations are arming. The scope of armaments is more vast than ever. Military expenditures around the world have been calculated at about a quarter of a billion dollars daily.

For a short time, America alone had atom bombs, and Churchill said then that only American bombs were checking Stalin's conquest of all Europe. But now Russia has the bomb, and the result has not been world war, although both are arming at full speed for atomic warfare, spending huge sums to produce what they never wish to employ, and bending every effort to achieve superiority in this weapon. Nuclear war is considered impossible — the more impossible, the stronger the nuclear weapons — and yet, paradoxically, this actual armament race prepares just what the participants want to avoid.

Today, however, there is an important difference between America and Russia. Russia has made the bomb only one of her main weapons. She has retained and improved the old weapons to such an extent that they, and her masses of trained personnel, leave her vastly superior to all other countries, even after a reduction of her standing army. America, on the other hand, is concentrating on nuclear armament, tending to relegate ground troops and all the old weapons to secondary rank. Russia maintains her whole military potential; America would like to rely on deterrence by the bomb. Russia, though she does not seem to want a world war any more than America does, keeps using force wherever she can. She does not want the world to calm down. She exploits every instance of unrest, either to promote her "peaceful" world conquest or to extend her starting positions for a future world war;

besides, a calm world would mean the development of freedom. So, Russia lets small nations wage war and supplies them with arms and technicians, without going to war herself. And America answers by shipping arms to the small nations attacked, or threatened with attack, by Russia.

The evolution of weapons technology brings constant innovations. We quickly hear, then, that the past has been made obsolete — conventional arms by nuclear arms, bombers by guided missiles, bases by launching pads that can be stationed anywhere. But in the framework of world armaments, the obsolete still plays a considerable part. And the oldest of all, the man with a weapon in his hand, will play the last act of any war in which men survive. Yet we do observe some basic "re-equipments" and see the constantly changing tasks evoke understandable restlessness in military circles.

About 1900, "thinking in continents" was the new world-political fashion — an imperialistic rather than strategic concept, save for the establishment of naval supply bases. Now, in consequence of the new armament techniques, world strategy has turned to "global thinking," in which all of Earth becomes one battlefield. We can only guess at what is going on in the strategic brains of Russia and America; but in the West it looks as if bafflement were the source of isolated actions, new planning attempts, confusions, and partial contradictions. There is no unity even in Europe, nor between Europe and America, nor among the American services. In the East, on the other hand, there seems to be central direction, over-all planning, and a consistent transformation of the whole.

We see facts resulting from geography. Europe and America have more to fear from atomic war than Russia, because of the greater concentration of their population in big cities and their dense industrial areas. A surprise attack by Russia would succeed more easily than one in the other direction.

The preparatory world-strategical acts differ in the East and the West. Russia sets up satellite states that actually are in her power and obey her commands; being held by force, however, they carry germs of resistance and sabotage in wartime. America tries to ally herself by treaties, not by force, with free sovereign states. With their agreement she sets up aviation and missile bases and supply depots, but if a country so desires, she will evacuate these positions at the expiration of a treaty. She gives economic aid and military guarantees. But with the other country's politics controlling in each case, this method, by which the Russian world is presently ringed with bases, has succeeded only partially, most reliably among the Western nations.

It is a consequence of world strategy that all military planning of small nations, while locally to the point, depends upon the actions of the great powers. Whether they take sides or attempt to stay neutral, the small nations get their orientation from the great powers. They have some leeway left to them — in case of war only if their conquest or destruction would be too costly, measured by the total purpose — but they are part of the one global battlefield.

So far, we have seen, the threat of atomic war has not ended war. Wars can be waged without atom bombs, though in the shadow of the possibility of atom bombs. Compared with world war, these are small, local, yet terribly devastating wars. The statement, "There will be no wars, because there are atom bombs," must be rephrased: "Today there are wars without atom bombs."

Should warfare, then, become a terrible prerogative of small nations? They commit acts of violence to change their situation. They threaten their small opponents in order to conquer by force, as of old, and in so doing they also threaten the great powers with triggering off a world war. This threat has an intimidating effect. If small nations break treaties by force, the great powers dare not use force to induce respect for law. But this privilege of the small sovereign nations is possible only because the powers are not united in defense of law and treaties — because, on the contrary, they use the acts of the small ones to extend or maintain their own respective power positions.

The two superpowers play according to old political rules, but under the tacit compulsion of the atom bomb which has so far prevented their clashing directly. Their motives and political purposes are unchanged, but they stand under pressure. Thus, with brief intervals, the world keeps getting into situations which used to lead immediately to war, while threats, humiliations, and intimidations are tolerated today as never before.

What can happen now? The great powers take pains to pacify the small ones, but not without mental reservations. They take sides, nearly always against each other — a grotesque exception was America's joint intervention with Russia against England, France, and Israel, via the United Nations. So, as the small countries fight with their permission and aid, and under their partial protection, the great powers themselves run the risk of a world war starting between them. Without the sense of a common order to hold them together, they are always merely putting off a world war. Since each small war is a great-power war in disguise, each involves the danger of world conflagration.

Today, therefore, politics has two sources: the two superpowers and the special interests of the many small nations. The latter, as in the past, use all means to get what they want by the old methods, acting on the most varied national, social, religious motives. They want status, independence, more power, a chance to form new states. Yet none of these wars is like earlier ones. The difference is that all ventures are undertaken with a glance at the two superpowers, with their help or permission, and with the idea of gaining advantages from them and playing one against the other. And the interest of both great powers is involved in all wars. They have a hand in every one. Neither of them wants to see its influence in the world decline; each wants to extend it.

The present situation is governed by the tension between the "impossibility" of an atomic world war and the danger, constantly kindled by small wars, that the impossible will happen. For the time being, the age of a "new politics" manifests itself in the fact that since 1945 all small wars and conflicts have ended not in decisions but in armistices. When Russia herself, in the Berlin blockade, risked an attempt to use force beyond the limits of her territorially secured power, America beat it off peacefully, at immense cost, with the unexpected airlift. When the Israelis, abandoned by the British withdrawal, rose in 1948 to defend their new state against the attacks that were launched from all sides to destroy them, the conclusion of the struggle — which would have been the wholly unexpected, hard-earned, but overwhelming victory of Israel — was cut short by the British threat of aerial bombardment; the result was not a peace such as used to follow upon a victorious war, but an armistice. In the Korean and Indonesian wars the outcome was similar: an armistice, not peace. "Armistices" are the hallmark of this new politics in our world. Each time, world war threatens; each time, the possibility is nipped in the bud at the expense of some small nation. Again and again, the actions, the events, the words are such that world war should be expected at once, by all previous standards. The tension of such moments is repeated, and one is never quite sure that there will be no total disaster. But when world war really seems imminent, both superpowers have so far called a halt.

Thus the extremes of atomic war and world peace are parted by a wide range of wars with conventional weapons. What matters here is to bring the scale of realities, of contemporary facts, into proper perspective. We must not fail to prepare for dangers near at hand because we see only the extreme danger. The extreme may happen any day, but it need never happen. It is a limit to all possibilities of action, but within this limit lie the concrete tasks we must perform.

Small nations — and today all are small, except for the two superpowers — must reckon with wars. Political changes can be brought about by small wars if the great powers do not interfere, or if they want the changes. Those who wish to preserve themselves, their way of life, their identity as a people, their form of the principle of political freedom, must be ready for small wars — small in comparison with total atomic wars, but as terrible as ever for whole nations. Those who cannot maintain themselves in small wars are lost in this transitional period which determines what nations and territorial boundaries will survive in a totally different future. Hence the general apprehension of being totally menaced by the shadow of the bomb, even if it is not used. Politics has not replaced war by any means, and stocks of "old weapons" and soldierly valor in "small wars" are by no means immaterial.

Let me restate the present military situation. America and the West are far inferior to Russia in conventional arms; Russia is catching up with America in nuclear arms, and in missiles to deliver them she is at the moment superior. The total war potential of the West would today — given time to bring it into play in case of war — still exceed Russia's considerably. If Russia should start the war — by crossing her western boundaries, for example — her immense armies could quickly conquer Europe with conventional weapons and would probably be met at once with atomic weapons. America would thus commit the first act with such weapons but would suffer retaliation within the hour. Russian politicians have said that they would never be the first to use the bomb, but would use it only in retaliation — statements which carry scarcely more weight than their pledges of peace, long refuted by actual deeds of violence. American politicans have made no such pronouncements, saying only that they would never use atomic weapons except as a last resort; but American military men have declared that these weapons would come into play at once against a Russian attack on Europe. Such statements do carry weight, for they would scarcely be made if they were not meant seriously.

It would be self-deception to distinguish between tactical and strategic bombs, or generally between types of nuclear weapons. The use of "atomic artillery" would instantly result in total atomic war. This has been expressly stated by the Russians and has the same weight as the American statement; it would not be said if it were not meant seriously.

In this presently world-wide confusion, the power of leadership appears to be declining everywhere. More and more of the men we see coming to the top seem to be merely drifting. If no leader follows a simple line derived from his thinking, from the logic of his position — whether in totalitarian fashion, like Stalin, or by means of reasons convincing to his people and by the power of his personality, as in Churchill's or Roosevelt's case — we get an ersatz leadership by a phantom, a pseudo-leadership.

The result is helplessness in a collective leadership that hides from the public. A world war might be decided upon because no one dares any longer to say no, because all agree, although they are against it. Each fears the others, and each thinks the other wants what he himself does not want but must agree to, if he is to keep his miserable bit of power. If no one dares any more, on his own responsibility, against the welter of opinions, prevailing or otherwise, to carry all others along on the path of righteousness, the disaster will come — with all disclaiming responsibility. But their evasion makes all of them jointly guilty. There could be, in intensified form, a repetition of 1914, when a war which nobody wanted came, and in which no one, or all, shared the guilt.

Matters are becoming less and less predictable. We used to have Stalin and Truman, and although one employed pitiless terror while the other was anxious but firm in defense, both were acting from a rationale: a reasoning attitude that knows what it sees and what it wants. You could figure out their intentions, whether reprehensible or desirable. There was then still something like leadership in the world, but at the time of this writing it appears more leaderless than ever. We no longer seem to see anything but doctrinaire notions on one side and momentary moves, skilful or blundering, on the other; we sense nothing simple and constant. Thus begins the drifting and the rule of accident, which will no longer serve a flexible leadership as an eminently history-making force.

The political aspects of the present situation, what is happening and what is possible, will be considered here, in Part Two of this book, under three aspects.

First: constructive political action must always start from proximity and find its way on the basis of facts, with a view to the world as a whole. Political action becomes bottomless if confined to the narrow horizons of single nations and states; it becomes equally bottomless in general abstractions, from which the goals of an infinite future are expected to materialize at once. Politics depends upon historically founded steps here and now, in the real, imperfectible course of events.

Second: to escape annihilation we must prevent war. The United Nations has the task of achieving world peace by legal means. But in the actual proceedings of the UN, the palm seems to go to the untruthfulness that has been revealed in the world press for all these years.

Third: lest we lose human freedom, we must not conceal the possibility that at some moment to come a choice may have to be made between totalitarian rule and the atom bomb — between the destruction of a life worthy of man and the possible destruction of all men. A refusal to envision this possible alternative implies the loss of the courage of sacrifice. But sacrifice remains the foundation of true humanity.

Inevitably, in these chapters, the negative features of contemporary politics will appear. We must not let that deceive us. If we stick to the concrete facts of the present situation, we can take the saving steps — by a radical renunciation of colonialism, we can come to a new way of Western self-preservation and thus to a new world order. Also, the concept of law, however untruthfully represented, has a chance as long as free men live; even in its mendacious form it helps to prolong the breathing spell. Lastly, the possible sacrifice of all mankind reminds us of our deepest roots. Such recollection gives us courage to do in fact what we can. Only sacrifice can keep that choice from ever becoming reality.

If we keep our eyes on the goal of world peace, we may see each silver lining and seize the faintest possible hope. But above all, we must never forget that the course of events is no observable, causally necessary process but the outcome of free human decisions. The negative may yet turn positive.

6

THE

END OF

COLONIALISM

The present world situation is the result of four centuries of European expansion, which has united mankind as a factual unit of communication. Today hardly anything can happen anywhere without concerning everybody. In the papers we read every day of events the world over.

This unity of communication, technologically based and now intensified to the highest degree by airplanes and radio waves, is the premise of mutual knowledge, of understanding and participation, of revulsion and hatred, or of co-operation. Whether it will grow into a world communion of the human spirit, and how this might look, is an unanswered question. It depends on a spiritual and moral choice: whether mutually exclusive human possibilities are divided by a gulf that must lead to mutual rejection and a desire to destroy what is foreign, or whether men are united by a rational spirit in which all can meet without having to surrender the differences of their ways of life and faith. The question will not be answered by experience; it will be decided by the human beings who will work for one or the other. There is an uneasy readiness for unity in all nations. It has been demonstrated; it has also been denied. That mankind has one root and one goal, that true human beings are linked by something that transcends even mortal conflicts — this is a faith which can indeed be buried only along with rational humanity itself.

Since 1914, the flow of emigration has come to an abrupt stop. The event crept up on us, at first without attracting attention. The world is no longer open; all at once, everything has been jarred within bounds.

There is no more running away. There are no distant opportunities either for the individual or for the overflow of populations. At first, this damming-up causes confusion everywhere, as water recoils in eddies if it cannot flow on.

The time is past when men knew themselves surrounded by a wide world — which most of them dreaded, but which meant liberty because it beckoned to the daring. Now, Earth has been distributed. There is no more freedom to move.

Globally speaking, this freedom of movement had been a Western prerogative. Even America soon banned the immigration of Chinese and Japanese, when she had too many of them. Now such bans are common. All countries, large and small, select and choose in each case whom they will allow to immigrate.

Since the globe has been divided up, all men must make do in the space they are born with. If there is to be peace, the territorial status quo must be respected. The slogan of a "nation without space" confers no right; it simply means war. If the division of Earth is not acknowledged, there seems to be no alternative but war — wars of extermination or forced migration.

The present division of territories is the result of past history and largely accidental. Some nations have vast land masses with rich resources — America, Russia, China; others have little room. With the jolt that put an end to expansion, the situation of that moment proved highly favorable to some and most unfavorable to others. Each insists on the possession of his own territory. External population pressures due to unequal increase justify no claim to land in less populated areas. Australia did not admit any Japanese; Russia closes her Asian border against immigration from China. Any seizure of land means war.

How did the age of European expansion differ from all previous conquests, migrations, and colonial movements? Western expansion spread to *all* non-Western peoples; it was a conquest of the globe. But this entire globe was held to be fair prey, as beyond the pale of European laws and mores. An abyss lay between Europe and the world: in Europe there was a common ethos, a community in biblical religion, a legal order fixed in a host of treaties and partitions; outside Europe were unoccupied lands that belonged to no one — to no European, that is — and thus invited pillage, occupation, settlement, and exploitation by anyone who wished and dared.

This expansion could succeed because resistance to the superior weapons of European technology was impossible, even for the highly civilized nations of Asia. These nations lived in their large but, in global terms, limited spaces, regarding their world as the world of mankind, utterly ignorant of the violence that was unleashed against them. And the superiority of the Europeans was further enhanced by the sum of their rational skills.

This colonization ushered in an age of horror for all the peoples on Earth. A spirit of greed, ruthlessness, and tyranny became general. If Europeans happened to meet in this no man's land of the whole non-European Earth, they started fighting as fiercely over the booty as they had fought the original inhabitants. They were at peace in Europe, but abroad they waged an informal war without beginning or end, often in such obscurity that no news of it reached Europe. On Spitsbergen, for example, many graves still testify to nameless battles fought by the Dutch and the British while their countries were at peace — symbols in a far-off place of the atmosphere of lawlessness and rapacity which the Europeans spread around the globe. This colonial process was perhaps most pitiless in North America, where the native population was exterminated over the centuries. Today, a few Indian remnants are kept there on reservations, as in a game preserve; and masses of Negro slaves were imported.

Decisive for this colonial age was the fact that Europeans did not regard non-Europeans as human beings like themselves. The biblical view of the unity of the race held good in theory, but in practice the foreign peoples were not only not equal, they were without any rights whatever. Only Christians had the rights of men. The others, the savages, were, at best, human beings whose conversion to the Christian faith — that is, to one of the contending Christian sects — and consequent salvation was a Christian duty. Otherwise, if not wiped out, they were objects of exploitation. No authority with political power kept the Europeans from forcing these people to do their bidding, or from killing them outright.

Later, the non-Europeans became objects of research. A distinction was made between "savages" and "semicivilized nations." But all of them and their products, including the glorious art of China, were objects of knowledge; their place, as late as the beginning of this century, was in ethnological museums. They were degraded. And correspondingly, world history was seen as the continuous history of the West.

The consequence of this colonial process of four centuries was a hatred of Europeans by all other nations on Earth. It was inevitable, since they were deemed inferior races, since the spirit of their native cultures was slighted, since their exposure to ruinous technology kept them for a long time in humiliating impotence. For generations this hatred has been bred into them. They have become rightly sensitive, so much so that today the slightest reminder of their past will rekindle their indignation. A basic reality of mankind's present existence is this open or hidden hate of Westerners — both Europeans and Americans — in all who are not Westerners.

People wonder why in Asia, for instance, "nationalism" is a much stronger force than in Europe. But there the same word "nationalism" has quite a different meaning. The nationalism of the great Asian nations is based on a real racial difference between them and the Westerners, all of whom are akin, from the Americans to the Russians. It is rooted, further, in their entire culture, essentially different in its age-old heritage; the Indian, Chinese, and Japanese worlds are spiritually much closer to each other, linked by historical events, mainly by the spread of Buddhism, than all of them are to the West. Finally, this nationalism derives from feelings of inferiority in the reluctant acquisition of Western technology and thought, combined with feelings of superiority in their own religiously and philosophically grounded way of life.

These people have been awakened from the comparative quiet of many centuries of misery and many centuries of beautiful and joyous living. They have been swept into the movement of a technological age which they feel to be foreign to themselves. They may seem happy as children over their technical successes, but they are deeply unhappy at the same time. And this evil, too, is due to the West that indirectly forced them to turn to technology as a condition of their self-preservation. In the end, the West also taught them the nationalist way of thinking. They use Western concepts to justify its application to their own very different reality. Thus their nationalism has something inappropriate and brittle about it, but unlike its Western counterpart it is bound up with dark, elemental drives.

Now, after centuries in which it seemed impossible for non-European nations to have any importance of their own, this era has all but abruptly ended. As recently as 1900, the British Empire seemed unshakable. Other nations had their colonies in its shadow. After a German diplomat was murdered in Peking by the secret society of the Boxers,

England, Germany, Russia, America, and other countries intervened with a joint expeditionary force under British leadership — a military operation without any risk to themselves. Kaiser Wilhelm II dispatched his troops from Germany with orders to "give no quarter and take no prisoners." The British field commander's order, "The Germans into the line!" caused rejoicing in Germany. It was the last demonstration of a fundamental colonialism spawned by the arrogance of Western powers.

But the tide had already begun to turn. One had been obliged to ask Japan to join in that act of violence against China. In 1895, in her war against China, Japan had surprised the Westerners; she was the first foreign power to prove herself by the adoption of European military and organizational techniques. In 1904–5, this same Japan inflicted a disastrous defeat on Russia. A mighty empire of the white race, half-European, one of the world's great powers, succumbed to an Asian nation, which had to be recognized now as a great power itself.

What had happened? At first, the whites were like gods, because they possessed the miracle of technology. Or else they seemed — to the Chinese, for example — barbarians without an inkling of the depth, truth, and beauty of human culture and joy of living. But the prestige of their invincibility paralyzed nations even where only glimpses of it appeared. British world dominion was a bluff, says Liddell Hart, a Briton. But if it was a bluff, it ceased working when England and France brought millions of Indians and Africans to Europe, as soldiers in their war against Germany. The result was a tremendous increase in the self-assurance of the non-Europeans. "We can do this, too," they were bound to think, especially in view of the war of whites against whites.

For the peoples of the globe, subjected to European technology, the question was whether to go down as impotent objects of oppression or to adopt this technology for their own self-preservation. Today, they have all more or less gone the way of Japan. They have claimed their freedom from the West and, with some exceptions, have achieved it. But the independence they won is still in the process of consolidation. In the areas of the so-called underdeveloped countries, European technology and production methods are yet to be established.

The age of colonialism is at an end. Europe's rule of the world is shattered, her world position in ruins, her pre-eminence a thing of the past, her own future gravely imperiled. What will happen? If the world's population grows from two billion to three billion and more; if the Westerners, already outnumbered, continue to fall behind; if the vast colored masses, possessing most of the world's area and the bulk of its resources, become the technological equals of the West — will this human majority, not yet free from the hatred begotten by four centuries, not turn against the West? Is there a chance for a community of all nations?

With the collapse of colonial rule, technology has conquered the world and made history, for the first time, world history. Is this a triumph of the European mind — not only in science and technology but in its thinking processes, in Anglo-Saxon enlightenment, in Marxism, in nationalist oratory, in the whole rationale of organization, of planning, of calculating? A common knowledge and know-how covers the world. Whether received with the delight of children who suddenly discover an undreamed-of skill or with the reluctance of one who adopts what he feels will lead to his destruction — it is always the same irresistible development of the technological age.

It is no European triumph. What came into the world by means of Europe, historically speaking, is valid in itself, independently of its origin. It is not a unique culture but the property of man as such, of man as a rational being. It is identically transferable. Where it has once been acquired, it can, with more or less talent, be cultivated — whether for mere use, for participation in further scientific research, or for technical inventions. The necessary talent is no basic trait or permanent condition of nations. For example, the number of patent applications is today a sort of yardstick of national inventiveness, and it varies enormously. In the nineteenth century, France marched in the van of progress, but today new French patents are scarce, and we find the highest number in America. Among the men active in the immensely difficult construction of the American atom bomb were a large number of European immigrants from Germany, Italy, and Hungary. What we have in common is the technological age of history; the talent for it is scattered at random and attracted by challenges and opportunities. It no longer belongs to a few privileged nations. In Russia and Japan, for instance, discoveries and inventions have reached the universal level of human ability.

But this common element does not unite. Science and technology are equally well understood and practiced, but they are employed no less as weapons than as bonds. A common, identical understanding of the atom bomb does not prevent us from making these bombs for the purpose of destroying one another. Peace can come only from bonds that link, not only intellect with intellect, but man with man.

Peaceful union presupposes understanding. The possibilities of such universal understanding must grow, the more all human kinds can meet in reality. The image of man changes where it is no longer harnessed in narrow blinders and deprived of means of comparison. The unity of mankind can come to clear and steady consciousness only by the actual experience of diversity.

We have so far neglected this aspect in our description of the colonial age, because in past centuries it has been almost ineffective. But though futile in the process at large, things that bespoke the good will of individual Westerners, at least, happened even in the course of colonization. Not a few were moved by the humanity of the "natives," by their moral and religious depth — especially in China and India. In dealing with them, they came to a loving, thorough understanding of the spiritual life of these nations. They turned to scientific investigation of their languages, their creations, their lives, much as humanism had once taken up the study of Antiquity. They not only fought the injustices done to these nations but opened ways of communication for human heritages meeting on the same level, and thus they brought new wealth to the West as well. Their reports and translations of foreign works taught Europeans to know these extraordinary phenomena. The Jesuits in China, for example, acquired their understanding of Chinese thought and faith in order to infuse the natives with biblical thought; but this understanding led to their great achievement of communicating the Chinese reality to the West. Their aim was to make possible a new source of religious life in China, but their reports became the basis of European thinking about China by such men as Leibniz, Voltaire, and Hegel. The consequences over the centuries and the needs of today both follow this line of love and understanding. For communication does not begin until understanding goes beyond the insipidity of average rational thought, to the historic essence.

We cannot say that such communication is now taking place the world over. For today the substance of great traditions is steadily dwindling here as well as in Asia. The age of technology makes questionable what we live by; it uproots us, and it does so all around the globe. And to the great Asian cultures it does it more violently, since they lack the transitional period in which the West was producing the technological world — a world that now, finished and overpowering, engulfs people whom their past culture has neither prepared for nor disposed toward it.

We human beings meet each other less and less on the ground of our respective faiths, more and more in the common uprooting vortex of our existence. Technology with its consequences is initially ruinous for all age-old traditional ways of life.

A common concern, therefore, unites the nations today: can technology be subordinated as a tool? As yet no one knows how. Will the deeper source, dried up at first, well up again with new vigor, in new forms; will it master technology and convert it into the mere management of life? We see no sign of this, but we must expect it if we are conscious of our human roots. Or will technology become absolute and destroy man — a notion easy to throw out but impossible to think through?

We are looking for outlines of political thought that would aim, in the breathing spell before the threatening end, at two inseparable objectives: true humanity and the preservation of existence. Let us try to draft such a kind of new politics for our situation at the end of the colonial age. It will be governed by two basic, closely related problems.

One concerns *liberation and self-preservation*. Peace can be served only by truth, not by lies in points of principle. From the Western point of view, honesty requires, first, the actual and unqualified liberation of all colonial areas, and second, in view of the dangers arising therefrom, the accompanying defensive self-preservation of the West.

As to the first, there is no more stopping the non-European peoples' march to freedom. It is futile to maintain domination anywhere, in any past forms, with no matter how many concessions. The withdrawal from all colonial areas demands a simultaneous reversal of the colonial idea into its opposite, a will to leave the existence of others to their own responsibility.

As to the second, the vast dangers arising from racial hatred; from shortsighted, confused actions of the liberated; from their frequent incompetence in making their way in the technological age; from the incalculable consequences of the violence they employ toward each other — these dangers can be met only by a defensive union of the West. This calls for substantial economic sacrifices, for giving up ingrained feelings of national power, and for a transformation of technological, economic, and social ways of life. Only thus can we preserve ourselves reliably and non-aggressively.

The second problem concerns the direction *toward a world order*. In liberation and self-preservation, the prevailing mood is still one of hostility. The final stage of peace cannot be mere juxtaposition, cannot involve constant threats and the constant danger of explosions. The grand objective of politics must be a world order — starting out, to be sure, from the given states, territories, and power relationships. We must envision possible ways, as well as seemingly insuperable obstacles, to such an order.

Both aspects of the new politics are problems of mankind. They outrank all special national problems and pervade all politics not thoughtlessly confined to local interests of the moment. Yet both, today, differ from the analogous conceptions of past ages. They are not to be imagined after the pattern of the former European community; they must come into being in the framework of the one, globe-wide humanity, not in the framework of a European world. We cannot seek order by means of the communion of any single faith, only by means of a future communion of reason. Therefore, this new world order cannot be symbolized either by an idea of empire or by the idea of a universal church. These could only be deceptive stage props of a global despotism. If freedom is to be saved — that is to say, if man is to be saved — he will have to keep struggling for himself in a process of self-education that can never end. What remains — in constant danger, based on historical premises, never lastingly terminable — will be an unstable situation that must always be realized and secured again.

A fundamental fact is that the conflict between the West and its former colonies cuts across another conflict: between Russia and the West, between totalitarianism and freedom. Both Russia and America support anticolonialism. Russia foments hatred and offers herself and her communism as useful allies, but America also offers herself and her freedom. Neither is acting unselfishly, for they vie for influence abroad. Each stresses her anticolonialism and accuses the other of colonialism; each wants to increase her own power and to contain the other's. It is in the shadow of this struggle over the vast formerly colonial areas that we must see the possibilities of liberation and self-preservation. On the one hand, the interplay of the two conflicts — West versus former colonies, and America versus Russia — promotes the rapid but still quite external liberation of all colored nations; but, on the other hand, it beclouds the liberation issue that might otherwise be clear.

Descriptions of the colonial age sound either like indictments or like vindications. In view of this whole four-hundred-year process that made the European technological era a global era, and thus made the world one and let history become world history, indictments and vindications seem rather inappropriate, unless we speak in terms of original sin. Still, it was we of the West who wrought this evil.

Particular indictments and vindications always bear on common human traits. Terrible, merciless, treacherous actions mark the history of China and India no less than ours. Indeed, it is to the credit of Europe that in her case self-criticism of colonial activities set in early and persisted. Nor was it quite ineffective. The motives of the Europeans active in colonialism were varied: adventure; love of danger and violence, of discovery and exploration; missionary zeal; self-sacrifice in the service of God; greed; the search, on foreign soil, for a freedom suppressed at home; or the will to create new political forms. This great process was a terrible outbreak of human passions. But its greatness lies on the dreadful side of world history, beyond good and evil. No one intended this dreadful greatness; no one may cite it either for vindication or complaint.

We may doubt the desirability of freeing peoples who have never known inner political freedom. Their liberation has thrown mankind into chaos. Were not all nations happier — as far as men can be happy — before the end of colonial rule? Was the world peace about 1900, the world communion under British dominance, not a great and singular moment in world history? Yet we are deceiving ourselves if we give in to this idea. If the Westerners' political wisdom and moral purity had entitled them to rule and educate mankind until their guidance, respecting the spiritual roots of others, would have nurtured the slow growth of world-wide political freedom — then such colonial rule would have been preferable. But the West, in its actual conduct, has been no better or politically wiser than the great Asian civilizations, even though individual thinkers and statesmen realized what was happening and tried to do better — as the British, at times, did in India. In fact, the combination of common human cruelty, of negligence and sloth, of the enjoyment of fruits reaped by adventurers, of ambiguous administration and imperialistic ambition — the combination of these blazed a trail unfit to be the high road of humanity. For a moment, the West had a task. It failed. The results are final.

Yet the non-Westerners are no better. Those who have obtained freedom from us are men, not angels. The freedom that all but fell into their laps in the technological age — thanks, above all, to Anglo-Saxon initiative — confronts them with a task which they must now solve for themselves. No one can guide or teach them. They have forgotten their own traditional wisdom — and again it is frightening how much they seem like the natural prey of totalitarian rule. But not inevitably.

As yet, no one blames us for our most dubious achievement: having dragged down all mankind to a technological fate. What is resented is not technology but dependence upon the white man; his technological world, and all that it implies, is exactly what all seem to want. On grounds of religious tradition, some nations were initially averse and later reluctant, but now all accept with enthusiasm. It is like a conquest — not by human beings, not by a foreign culture, not by Europeans, but by the thing itself which belongs to man as an intellectual being, to all men alike, challenging all to make of it what they can.

The liberation of nations from colonial rule is governed not only by an elemental urge for independence but by ideas introduced by colonization itself. In liberating themselves, they continue what colonial rule began. Without England, for example, there would today be no large, unified India with rudiments of common education, of a common law, and of industrial development. Everywhere intellectuals educated in or by the West are leading the way. The nations themselves are still largely in the dreamlike hold of newly questioned traditions. But no country seeks to return to its condition before colonial rule. China and India deal with their historic substance — the very thing that so greatly distinguishes them in our eyes — as if it were of no account.

To achieve world peace, to reduce the hatred which more than half of mankind harbors against the West, it is essential for the West to acknowledge honestly and unreservedly that colonialism is finished. We must think through the consequences of this situation and outline the principles of the resulting political actions. That is easy to say, but for Westerners, and for all others, it is hard to find the right and effective way to peace in the world chaos left behind by colonialism — and this world peace alone can save us from the atom bomb.

The first step is a great renunciation. The Western powers must withdraw to their own territories. They must grant others the full independence they seek. In large measure this has already been done. Where it has not yet been done, there is constant unrest — in the Near East, in North Africa, in the African territories. The renunciation must be simultaneously political and economic, to establish political and economic relations on a new basis of free reciprocity. Why and to what end is this renunciation necessary for world peace?

First: expansion has come to an end because the world has been distributed. As the globe at large has no more free space, the self-restriction of all to their own territories must follow.

Second: people resent not only the political power of the West but its economic power. Their experience with this strikes them, often justly, as exploitation, oppression, fraud. Taxation seems like tribute to them, the procurement of raw materials from their territories, with the help of freely hired and paid native labor, like robbery and enslavement. Economic thinking, tied to legal warrants and calculable sureties, is foreign to them. This attitude is fostered by transferring Marxist notions of the entrepreneur-worker relationship to that of colonial powers and natives. The existence of this attitude is a powerful fact, a fact surmountable only if the liberated will have their own experience of freedom, and if the economic ethics of a technologically unified world will draw upon a new source for the binding force of equality.

Third: granting that all achievements of the colonial powers — of the British in India, the Dutch in Indonesia, the Germans in their former African colonies and in Chinese Kiao-Chou — testified to technological skill and economic efficiency and benefited the natives, they still were not motivated by the natives' interest, even if this was subsequently considered. The motives were self-interest and delight in achievement as such, and these have no absolute value that would justify placing them above everything else. We must restore the true hierarchy of values, which technological and economic progress has obscured for both colonial powers and natives.

Withdrawal to one's own territory has taken economic sacrifices and will take more. Moreover, its inescapable consequence is a change in the principle of the industrial age. In this age industry lived by expansion, by the extension of markets, by the steadily increased procurement of raw materials wherever they were made cheapest by organized Western exploitation, and by the export of capital for the establishment of enterprises abroad. The result of all this was direct or indirect economic expropriation, secured by the power of governments assuming the protection of business transactions and agreements. Now, external expansion must yield to inner intensification.

If this alone can pave the way to world peace, the greatest sacrifices would be minor in comparison with the alternative. The new principle, which seems absurd to our economic and technological thinking, must at least be thought through. This is a matter for the energies of economic analysis — which is not my field — in conjunction with a new moral will.

It takes free will to keep the inevitable from taking a ruinous course; it cannot be done in the framework of past economic thought alone. If European expansion conditioned nineteenth-century economic life, the end of this expansion requires a change in economic life. If economic development must turn about, from expansion to intensification, we need a new economic ethics.

Domestically, we must not regard problems such as economic balance and world peace as soluble by institutions, by certain laws, by any contrived nostrum; the reform of a non-expansive, internally intensified economy will probably be very radical. And in foreign policy the renunciation of colonialism calls for private enterprise abroad to be controlled by the renouncing nations; they can no longer allow their citizens to contract freely for the uncontrolled exploitation of the natural resources of formerly colonial areas. In fact, economics can no longer be separated from politics. The method of winning global economic success without accepting political responsibility, of economic domination and political "neutrality" — "dollar imperialism" — has become illusory. The actual way of uniting politics and economics is daily being settled in practice, but still in rather murky fashion. Full clarity about this basic problem of both politics and economics remains to be achieved in intellectual conflict.

It is an illusion to consider foreign raw materials as vital to the free world. There is no doubt, in view of present dependence, that serious economic crises would result from the failure of this supply; but although the present tendency is to identify special interests with requisites of life, even grave impediments to our economic existence do not affect the absolute necessities. The end of expansion is the destiny and turning point of our economy. Whether the limit is the globe or half the globe, the principle is the same.

True, it is foolish and imprudent to let raw materials lie unused. Men are understandably reluctant to renounce anything under pressure of unreasonable political forces; they are right in considering the whole business absurd. But world peace comes first. And if we prepare for it and do not violate its temporary and permanent conditions, renunciation need not at all mean a rupture of relations and a permanent loss of the use of the raw materials. We cannot tell what will be possible under conditions of world peace and a new political ethics. If business interests were tempered and controlled instead of being absolute, our relations with the formerly colonial world could freely develop once more, without expansion, and mutual access to raw materials would be re-established around the world.

We in the free world must not be deceived any longer by allegedly inviolable economic demands. From Germany's World War I claim that "the German economy could not exist without the Briey Basin" (a claim then backed by many leading economists), to Eden's proclamation of the Suez Canal as "Britain's life-line," or the present thesis that "Europe absolutely needs Middle Eastern oil" — the kernel of truth in these and similar statements is always only a need to solve a serious economic problem or, perhaps, to surmount a seemingly disastrous situation. We have surmounted worse situations. We must find the will and the way in the co-operation of all nations of the free world. This co-operation, and great sacrifices — of glory, of prestige, of sovereignty, of material comfort, of privilege — are premises of survival. If they are forced upon us by events, the situation will be far more disastrous than if we reflect calmly, in time, and muster the *élan* of doing freely, in time, what we recognize as unavoidable.

We now condemn in public what has always been done and is still being done: capital investment abroad, in risky but lucrative ventures under the protection of the home government; dealing with natives ignorant of the mechanism of economic calculation; employing native labor, paying them wages, and raising their standards of living, but so as to make their lives empty and their pleasures meaningless because the substance of their tradition succumbs to the deceptive glamor of technological civilization. We thought we could educate the nations, as the British — often with the best intentions — did in India on a large scale. But essentially they could bring only book learning, techniques, organization, administration, law — the things whereby, thanks to England, an Indian empire can now, for the time being, do without England. But nations want to teach themselves; they do not want to be taught. They want to deal with the new technology and economy on their own initiative, out of their inherited substance.

Even with colonialism at an end, those nations can never return to their previous state. Along with Western technology they have come to know Western thought — usually in garbled or misunderstood form —

and to take up Western amusements on their lowest level. Men molded by the new civilizing patterns run to a basic agnosticism — unconsciously due, in Asians, to Buddhist and Hinduist attitudes which the intellectuals among them deny as substantive beliefs. They cling to traditional rites and modes of conduct but like to accept nihilistic ways of thinking as truth. This means, however, that the modern intellectual struggle for the meaning of life, for the image of man, for insight into Transcendence, has become world-wide. It is just beginning, and it takes freedom of communication to carry it on.

It is false to take Western civilization for the only true one, to regard technological progress, material prosperity, and a high standard of living by themselves as happiness. Abandonment of the colonialist spirit means tolerance for other possibilities of life. There is really no need to bring the whole world to our technological civilization, as supposedly the only one. This is what happens now and will probably go on happening, owing as much to its universal appeal — for all want to be part of it — as to the greed of private or public enterprise everywhere, among all races and nations.

International trade in the technological age requires observance of generally recognized rules. Everyone wants this trade, even the totalitarians who will lift their iron curtains for this purpose, under state control. The reduction of colonialism and the great renunciation, the West's withdrawal to its own territories, means neither a break in relations nor a refusal to trade; but the first requirement of pure and honest relations is the freedom of the former subjects of colonial rule. Even if we know that material hardship, perhaps a misery greater than ever, will be the first consequence of their desire for freedom, this is no reason to force ourselves upon them. It seems that the natives everywhere must gather their own experiences; they cannot believe what they have not experienced themselves, and not until then will they seek co-operation on their own initiative.

After the reduction of colonialism, therefore, the great question is how international trade can be carried on. The old way — now to treat others as people like ourselves, now to despise and suppress and trick them — can no longer be taken for granted. But the idea of their meeting us in a generally human business spirit, measured by the standards of the honest trader and engineer, is as false today as the notion that the West had, in most instances, met them in this spirit.

Put more precisely, the great question is what conditions would permit agreements to be made in good faith and equally well understood by both parties, so that the benefit would be equal not only in fact but in purpose.

Agreements require the same spirit in both partners. Both must know what they are doing and must have the will to keep their promises. Agreements made in any other spirit are not really agreements; they are disguises to conceal either superior power or an impotence that yields but seeks to gain by cunning. He who does not know, or does not want, real agreement is abusing the form; he secretly takes it for an act of violence or fraud and is subsequently ready to break the agreement. Without a common spirit of contractual fidelity, there can be no real agreements and no trade relations, least of all in the technological age. If there is to be trade, it cannot rest only on trust in the business spirit. It needs guarantees envisioning compulsion or other safeguards; but the weaker side feels that this constitutes coercion and enslavement. The native populations have not entered into commerce on their own initiative; it has come over them. They are rightly distrustful, feeling fettered without knowing how. The West distrusts them as well — and just as rightly, having found out that agreements are not kept.

In consequence of the nations' desire for freedom, previous treaties — which such native powers as Egypt, Indonesia, Iran, etc., break or cancel at will, anyway — are now either liquidated or freely re-established on new, consciously phrased premises. The rejection of violence as a means for their enforcement presupposes a spiritual and moral-political development of the natives. There is no telling how it will come about — except for this: peace has no chance if we maintain the old fictions. Reality tells us that agreements can be made only with exact guarantees of reciprocity, without deceit, for mutual benefit. The premise of mutual reliability means — if faith is genuine — a simultaneous stipulation of the consequences of a breach of faith. If this is not possible, neither is honest trade; but it is better for peace to have no trade than to have dishonest agreements. Nations are right to call for freedom, but only if they can freely help themselves and can turn license into freedom under law. Else the call would mean: "You must free us — but you must also keep giving us the means to use our freedom as we please, without sharing in the hard work and orderly life of the technological age."

At the outset, reality puts quite a different face on the nations' high and just claim to independence and self-education. The terrible misery, malnutrition, and starvation in many parts of the world cry out for help, but the immediate material help from the West, rendered in Christian charity, is never more than a drop in the bucket. It is most admirable and often gives the few beneficiaries a chance to live; it bespeaks a helpful turn of mind; it is good that it exists — but it does not change the total misery anywhere. Nor is the cry of people's acute distress the cry of their governments, which would like to treat the distress as their own business and feel humiliated by outside help.

What the governments demand is not less; it is more. They want economic help with their development as a whole, in line with the free-world principle of "aid to underdeveloped countries."

Gifts have also been made to "developed" countries. In the postwar emergency, America helped Europe through the Marshall Plan. This was "pump priming" to get the economy started again; the point was to help the recipients to help themselves. Such aid worked wonders in some cases, but the effects varied greatly, even among the nations of Europe.

Aid to "underdeveloped" countries is another matter. It is supposed to push them into the age of technology, although their way of life has not prepared them for the thinking and working style of this age. Economic help is futile if the premises of its use are lacking. It is not only pernicious for competing Western oil companies to lavish millions of dollars on Oriental despots, just because the oil they can do nothing with happens to lie beneath their soil; it is pernicious also to render "economic aid" where it remains a mere gift and is not transformed into spontaneous work. Such aid falls into a bottomless pit and serves only to make the recipient nations greedier. Material help to the "underdeveloped" is senseless if they do not want it as a spark for self-help. We must leave them room to live in their own way, to starve, to be born in masses, and to perish. They have the right to be free, but they do not have the right to expand beyond their borders. The abolition of colonialism cuts both ways, and the distribution of the globe has drawn the lines.

The present world situation often shows both the "underdeveloped" and the "helpers" in a strange light. The underdeveloped demand independence, sovereignty, and freedom in disposing of the help given to them. They want no strings attached to it. But they demand it as their right — credit, capital investments, supplies of arms and machinery, help for their hungry. When it is forthcoming, they are not thankful but suspicious of encroachments upon their independence; and if it is not forthcoming, they are indignant — it is a denial of their due, a hostile act. As for the nationalization — that is, expropriation — of capital investments, this is their sovereign right. They feel that what Western technology has produced, with enormous effort, is theirs even though they have taken no part in the effort. Being wooed by the two superpowers of the free and totalitarian worlds, they want thanks for their willingness to accept gifts.

Of course, the underdeveloped are not all alike; this general description is unfair to each single one of them. But they have this in common: they cannot help themselves in the new technological world they are coming to know; they are familiar with the problems of hunger and over-population; they more or less lack the Westerners' working ethics and initiative; and they have neither experience with nor a will to domestic political freedom.

Nor do the "helpers" present a better picture. They are self-serving; their help is not primarily meant to help at all. They give it to win sympathy for themselves, to influence the recipients against the other great power. They want to create economic dependencies for their own economic benefit — to assure themselves of oil, for example. Or, in regard to the natives' political development, they think that all men could become instantly democratic and manage their affairs by majority vote. Deluding themselves about the vast problems of their own democracy, without an inkling of the hand-to-mouth existence of the masses, they presume all men to be naturally fit for immediate political freedom and the modern life of skilled workers in highly developed industries. And if their expectations are disappointed, they consider violence justified.

Let us restate the implications of the required renunciation. We must give up all forms of struggle, whether political, military, or economic, for territories which are not at one with the West historically and by the will of their people. This retreat must be unconditional. But the free world, despite its constant losses, has not yet managed this fundamental decision to confine itself to what clearly belongs to it.

We must permit others to live in ways that differ from ours but have meaning to them. For the sake of world peace, we must put up with any way of life that stays within a nation's borders. If a nation is incompetent and lazy, tends to idleness and playful self-indulgence, we must let it be as one possibly true form of humanity. We must not seek to rule, to exploit, or to destroy it. Everyone has a right to be materially wretched; things may grow in him that competence can never understand. But those who live in misery must bear the consequences.

We do not segregate them. Though prudence compels us to start from the solidarity of free nations rather than from the abstraction of an entirety of all human bodies politic, this solidarity is open to all. Yet it is bound to premises grown and obtained in history. The solidarity of a part of mankind, united for self-preservation but not for conquest, can be reliable only if every member lives contractually and truly in a community of mutual trust. No one may join who has not proved himself; no one is forced to join against his will.

Freedom is the most-used word of our time. What it is seems obvious to all. Every country, every people, every individual wants to be free; the whole world seems as one in claiming and asserting freedom. Yet there is nothing more obscure, more ambiguous, more abused.

A few words on political freedom:

It is historically manifold, and nowhere quite reliable. We find it in ancient English liberty, in Dutch and Swiss liberty, in the liberty of the French Revolution, in that of the Scandinavian states, even in that of Bismarck's pseudo-constitutional Germany, and in American liberty. There is no such thing as universal freedom; there are only its historical metamorphoses. It is not yet freedom when a so-called democratic structure is imposed, as a matter of form, on a population that knows nothing of freedom and is merely ruled in its name by despotic, if not totalitarian, methods in our technological age.

Political freedom is not identical with, but essential to, Western freedom. Where political freedom is forsaken, we feel that freedom as such, Europe, and the West are forsaken as well. Europe is rooted in the idea of freedom. Europe is where the reality of the present rests upon the inner voice of thirty centuries, where men, despite all divergencies, are linked by this age-old common past.

We may object: How is world peace to come if so many nations are still unable to create their own free political life? We may ask: What is to become of the millions without substance, of the victims of the technological age, while we of the West are about to lose our own substance? The answer is that neither we nor any others have the world in hand. We must see what the formally liberated want and will do. We cannot coerce them, because freedom cannot be coerced. We must wait to see what responsibilities they will encounter and accept.

All this would be simple and unequivocal if there were no totalitarian Russia. The free world is dealing with the former colonies under pressure of the Russian menace, and we must reckon with the possibility that the non-Western peoples may throw themselves into the Russians' arms.

But we can successfully fight this only by not fighting, by being ready for a free partnership, if anyone meets us in freedom, good will, and veracity.

The great mass of former colonial subjects are now objects of competition. The great powers vie for permission to give presents to the small ones, and the small ones let them, expecting to remain free. Even the tiniest of them plays Russia against America; we do not hear about the reverse, but it may well be going on in secret. The situation becomes a menace to all.

America rightly fears that the former colonies will fall to Russia if their wishes are not met. So she keeps yielding. Mighty America bows to the most brazen challenges as if she were weaker than any Oriental puppet; and indeed, the combination of warlike acts and peaceful gestures on the part of totalitarianism is steadily reducing the possessions and prestige of the free world. Treaties are broken on a vast scale, and the West acquiesces, at America's urging, so as not to risk a world war. The totalitarians, on the other hand, insist on the letter of their agreements wherever they have set foot, and they do not shrink from extreme terrorism.

The nations of the free world give up positions and grant sovereignty where they used to rule — always expecting thus to gain a more loyal allegiance. The opposite usually happens. The method seems proper, as an inescapable reversal of past colonialist conduct; but it becomes illusory if Russia — in other forms, under other names, and by stirring up the anticolonialist hatred of the colored — seeks a rule that will be more terrible than any past colonial one. The nations knew the old colonialism for four hundred years; it is a ghost now, but they still see it as reality. Russian rule is unknown except in areas living under Russian terror. England withdrew from Jordan when the Jordanian government demanded it, but what happened in Hungary in October, 1956, seems to have made no impression outside the Western world. What has not been felt does not work on the imagination.

Colonialism has by no means given way to universal national independence and freedom. The former colonies are still largely incapable of freedom. We see them sink into chaos, as in Indonesia; and it is possible and may be probable that India — still a unit, thanks to British patterns — will follow up its original partition with Pakistan by disintegrating into the many senselessly and aimlessly embroiled dominions of her previous history. Colonial memories backed by the Marxist rejection of the capitalist world make the method of free communication and free enterprise seem like oppression to most nations. To them, the new form of rule which threatens to replace colonialism is not an experience but a welcomed paradise, a utopian order which will turn out to be terror only in reality. The totalitarians cloak their ambitions in charges of colonialism and use "liberation" to make the colored peoples gradually but wholly dependent upon themselves. The charge of imperialism cloaks their own new way of pursuing world domination. It is curious that today it does not help to speak of Russian imperialism or Russian colonialism; the world outside the West simply does not believe it.

We talk of a struggle for the "vacuum" between Russia and America — a vacuum that includes the bulk of the globe. The question arises: What risks must the Western world run of Asian, African, and American nations turning to Russia if their demands are refused?

1. The world situation may look as if the globe-wide colonial struggles of the Western powers were continuing by different methods, such as "aid to underdeveloped countries." In this, the West is at an obvious disadvantage. Its propaganda of freedom is felt to be propaganda for the well-known old colonialist attitudes, while the totalitarian Marxist propaganda appears to be a confidence-inspiring promise. The West can have a chance only if its traditional colonialist motivations are really and completely given up, if its renunciation of colonialism is sincere enough to be convincing. In deceit and coercion Russia is superior, not only because she has no scruples, but chiefly because of her unified political leadership, in contrast to the lack of solidarity among the Western powers.

The Western notion of keeping totalitarianism out of Asia and Africa by economic aid, given under free-enterprise ethics, may be a political mistake. For these economic ethics will always make the recipients feel that they are taken advantage of, while communism attracts them as a vague paradise, unknown and blindly desired. If this is the case, all aid would in the long run strengthen them only for further progress toward communism, until they succumb to totalitarian rule and the jail door slams shut. The West, deceived by short-term curbs on Russian influence, would be actually arming its enemies. Totalitarian gains cannot be halted by means of aid that is not given in a common spirit — least of all by subsidizing political adventurers and princes who in a crisis will not hesitate to sell out to the Russians, or whose people, in league with the Russians, will kick them out.

2. The question, in every case, is whether states and nations that are still free have an honest desire to be protected from totalitarian conquest by Western powers that have honestly renounced colonialism. The only weapon against Russian interference is non-interference. Only if honest Western readiness meets with an equally honest will to mutual protection — as apparently in Turkey's case — can aid really be helpful, and then only should arms be supplied. The readiness must be free from any trace of imposing oneself. The risk that the bulk of mankind will join the totalitarian terror against the free world is inescapable.

3. The freedom of wavering between East and West, playing one side against the other, is a fiction that has a certain reality only at this moment of transition. The seesaw politics found all over the world today is the cunning of the unscrupulous, with Tito as its seemingly successful model. In the long run, this very wavering means the beginning of totalitarianism.

4. The danger cannot be averted by continuous concessions on the part of the West. Nations cannot be spared the experience of Russian oppression by submission to their blackmail, but only by their own insight that would lead to true co-operation with the insight of the free West. What matters is the freedom of relations between the West and the former colonies. Where this has been achieved by nations aware of the Russian menace, no anxious opportunism should consider yielding, at the expense of such nations, to the demands of other, ambiguous nations.

5. The "struggle" can succeed only without a struggle — that is to say, by the example of free communication. First, the West would have to change; only our credible, non-aggressive will to co-operate rather than dominate can be convincing. Our success is questionable, but unquestionably we have reason to fear the billions of others — especially as we Westerners, until we have become what we should be, cannot deal with them as we should.

6. Political freedom as a form of government is of European origin, founded in Greek and Roman reality and thought, and in the German concept of co-operation. This form of government has means and forms that seem translatable like science and technology — the parliamentary system, for example, the separation of powers, and so on. If so, they would not be bound to the West but accessible to all men. It is not enough, however, to translate them intellectually, like technology; they need a deeper grounding in man himself, a basis which to us seems

generally human but may not be that at all. We must wait and see what the non-Westerners will do. They can develop their freedom only by self-education in view of the free world; we cannot educate them except by making ourselves into an example. We can only be ready for them, if they want us.

Must the liberated be caught in the snare of totalitarianism? Must they experience what they will then for a long time — forever, perhaps — be unable to throw off? Is it certain that they will travel this road? No, although for many it is probable.

Although the risk of Russian expansion is today inevitable, it is reduced by reliable and unequivocal ties with the nations whose own free will prompts them to seek solidarity with the West. It is further reduced by our readiness for mutual economic reinforcement, by free agreements based on respect for the sanctity of agreements, wherever there is a clear will to that end. The risk of Russian expansion is reduced, finally, by the attraction of the free Western way of life, provided it becomes purer, more honest, and more homogeneous among the Western nations than it is now.

Some day, perhaps, when they have experienced Russian oppression, the spirit of the Asians will turn against it. A day may come when the Russians appear to them as Westerners worse than any they have ever known. Then the Chinese threat might finally cause Russia to seek an alliance with the West. But all this is still far from the realm of real political reflection.

We conclude: in the nations' own interest, in the course of our self-preservation, in view of the world peace that is our responsibility — under all these aspects — there is no avoiding the risk that the liberated will be caught up in Russia's totalitarian machinery, used and consumed like Russia's own population. This risk is a necessary concomitant to the honest reversal of colonialism. But the demand is and remains the same: Liberate! If the totalitarians seem to the peoples in question to be doing this, while obviously doing nothing of the kind, only the freedom of the affected can decide which view they wish to take.

How can we cope with the risk? Only in the solidarity of self-preservation. The risk is justifiable on one condition only: the West must realize its determination to preserve itself by standing firmly together. We shall either fail to achieve solidarity and be destroyed, or we shall run the essentially inevitable risk together. Our self-preservation can be successful only if the nations of the West — Europe, America, and all the rest that are free not as a mere matter of form but in the moral-political consciousness of their population — join voluntarily, firmly, and in time.

Solidarity must now pervade all political motivations. It can be kept firm by the terrible threat to us all; this uncomfortable knowledge, compelling foresight and sacrifice, must not be concealed. Wishful thinking, neutralism — whose blindness and lack of convictions make it as contemptible as treachery — and fatalism are destructive of solidarity.

For us Westerners, there is no way but radical renunciation of world dominion and simultaneous, absolutely reliable unity. Unless we take this road, the world will go down in chaos and totalitarianism or else it will perish by the bomb.

As yet, solidarity has not been achieved. It is disturbing — in fact, in view of the world situation, it is almost incredible — that it seems still so distant. Everyone talks about it, but the slightest demand for sacrifice is enough to thwart any attempt. We have no right to spoil solidarity in fact by clinging to remnants of old domination — as Great Britain and France, above all, are still doing. Half-measures, in old-style politics and in calling for a new kind, plunge the West into the political and intellectual confusion which the Russians exploit with great success. In short, we seem to be rushing headlong toward self-annihilation — in the activities of traditional diplomacy, in dissident politics, in indecision, and in the irresponsibility of a decaying democracy, where every self-will, every opinion, every interest and privilege claims its absolute right, at home as well as in the democracies' dealings with one another. If they want to save their freedom, they must make themselves responsible for it. Only thus can democracy become real and worth saving.

Let us examine some phenomena which indicate that this has not happened yet.

The fact that totalitarianism kills freedom has by no means entered the minds of all. Many Western intellectuals go in for fuzzy, neutralist thinking. The presence of totalitarian influences, rudiments, and trail blazers in the Western world shows that the loss of freedom in totalitarianism is a generally human possibility apart from the Russian blueprint.

Further: nationalism has a right to survive in Europe only in distinct ways of life, in traditional views, in language, spirit, and education; as a power principle of states it has not only lost its reason for being but works against Western unity. European frontiers ought to turn more and more into boundaries of Europe's administrative areas. There are some great individual "Europeans," but their field is thought, not politics. Our hopes still rest in personalities only, notably from the small nations; in the larger European countries the old nationalism appears indestructible. The nation, its interests, its position in the world are foremost in everyone's mind, and Europe comes later. There are countless examples. Churchill, for instance, when he resumed as Prime Minister, seemed to have forgotten his marvelous Zurich speech of 1946, ending in the call, "Europe arise!" And after Eden's political and military failure in the Suez crisis revealed the British position and power as they really are, the new Prime Minister, Harold Macmillan, could say, "Great Britain has been great, is great, and will remain great." Nor were the statesmen alone led by national pride: in the summer of 1956, after Nasser's coup, enthusiastic crowds in British ports watched the fleet sail for the Mediterranean.

Finally: political unification can be secured only by a mutual limitation of sovereignty among all Western nations. This alone would make their position impregnable to any possible attack, totalitarian or otherwise. But their solidarity is still feeble. It is frightening to observe Russia's success in increasing her power by the ancient maxim of "divide and rule," used by every unscrupulous conqueror. The present success of this policy is purely the fault of the West, of the free nations' pursuit of their own selfish interests — eventually to the grotesque extent of America, because of Egypt, teaming up with Russia, ordering Britain and France to withdraw from Suez, allowing Bulganin to threaten their capitals with atom bombs, and thus making them yield. A Russo-American alliance prevailed over free nations, and Eisenhower proudly declared that America, for the first time, had made herself independent of British and French Asian policies! Let us admit: it was the most foolish and the most disgraceful moment of contemporary Western politics.

True, Britain and France, in their political confusion and imprudence, were at least as much to blame for the rupture of solidarity, for they ignored the tacit, morally and politically justified hegemonic position which the greatest power in the free world inevitably holds in regard to foreign policy decisions. Solidarity requires that no one act in foreign affairs without a previous understanding with America, and America has an analogous obligation to the smaller powers: she must consider the real, non-fictitious interests of the several free nations but subordinate them to the total interest of common self-preservation. Global policy cannot be made by majority votes. Solidarity demands compliance. In case of disagreement at any given moment, America must prevail even if she is wrong. Yet such hegemonic solidarity can endure only in a relationship of mutual loyalty among unequal partners — realized by consulting, reasoning together, pointing out, listening to arguments, visualizing the over-all situation, and assessing special motives and wishes. Without such loyalty — which at some time will exact hard renunciations from everyone — freedom must fail and prove inferior to the centrally directed will of the great totalitarian power.

The centralization of terror that is possible in the technological age stands against the league of free nations. In the free world, therefore, all depends on faith in the mutual alliance, while in the totalitarian world the suspicions of all against all are forced to co-operate by iron bonds. But faith, as a premise of free-world survival, demands — without being able to enforce it — that no government conspire on behalf of its own interests with powers outside the alliance. Their utterly invulnerable solidarity should be the cardinal principle of the free nations. Individually they ought to shun no sacrifice; any sacrifice is better than the loss of everyone's freedom — which otherwise would in the end be shown up as a freedom not worth protecting and preserving. The people whose freedom has grown from their history, and they alone, are responsible for the consequences to all of mankind if this freedom should be lost.

To sum up: unless Europe and all of the West can be firmly united in time, Europe will be overrun and America lost in short order. At the right moment we ought to see something as radical as Churchill proposed in 1940 for a part of Europe: all Englishmen and all Frenchmen were at one stroke to be citizens of one state, with equal rights, to preserve themselves against the totalitarian Germany of Hitler. We need not extend this particular proposal to the entire West, but some such union must be deemed urgent by anyone who does not blink the facts. With weapons technology as it is, there will be no time after the outbreak of hostilities to make up for previous neglect — as the Anglo-Saxon countries used to do in the past, at sacrifices far exceeding those that would have been advisable beforehand. Today these sacrifices would be futile. We shall only be saved by foresight and by acting upon it. The democracies will have lost the moral right to their freedom if they waste its use on ephemera.

History shows us a great example of foresight in Themistocles. He advised the Athenians to use all income from their mines at Laurium to build a fleet on a par with the Persian colossus in the East, which would surely attack Greece one day. His simple foresight, and the material sacrifice made by the prudent Athenians, saved Greece and Western freedom ten years later, when the attack was launched with all the might of the huge empire.

How shall we preserve ourselves in the rising tide of chaos? Today a single totalitarian power has built up an immense war machine and is strengthening it daily, exploiting its whole population according to plans which a few men can make in a totalitarian state and force upon the ignorant remainder. Against this, nations can remain free only if their freedom enables them, out of prudence, to make the sacrifices of material goods, living standards, cheap pleasures, which terror can compel elsewhere — if the statesman, under much more complex conditions, can emulate Themistocles and convince the people themselves.

World peace is now threatened only by totalitarianism. Hitler, aware of his superiority in armaments, recklessly unleashed war in 1939; Russia raped the Baltic countries, Poland, Hungary, and others, and provoked the Korean and Indochinese wars. If men are not blackmailed into choosing slavery, peace can be saved only by a sufficiently vigorous self-defense of the free world, to deter totalitarian attack and initiate developments that may end in a natural world peace. Self-defense involves risks; we cannot foresee the reaction of the others, whom we now call "the vacuum." But their reactions will also depend on our actions. We must reckon with the possibility that almost all of them may topple into totalitarianism. We cannot prevent this by force, only by persuasion. In this sphere, our only weapon is non-violence, combined with readiness to co-operate in the common spirit of freedom and veracity for our objectives as free men.

The West, like all mankind, has the only non-violent weapon at its disposal: the truth. The conflict of the two worlds is one between falsehood and truth — but while totalitarianism rests upon the principle of falsehood and thus grows mighty, the free world is not truthful enough and thus grows weak.

The power of truth is incalculable, but between freedom and totalitarianism it will be decisive. To preserve itself, the free world must make itself more truthful by ceaseless self-education — a hard task that cannot be planned. Easier, but equally necessary, is a much more active public enlightenment about facts and right thinking. Today the energy behind planned totalitarian lies still exceeds the energy devoted by the intellectuals of the West to the constant, clear exposition of facts. In daily newscasts, in the papers, in other writings, the untruthfulness of the totalitarian world, its deception of others and its self-entanglement in its own lies, should not be unmasked only now and then — which is done — but shown up time and again, in ever new instances, and more simply manifested to all. Even the Eastern literary defenders of Marxist thought draw more strength from the heritage of philosophy than their Western opponents — who believe they know it all, ignore the power of philosophical thinking, and refuse to bother.

Non-violence presupposes the strongest possible armament against possible aggression by the totalitarian war machine. The maxim, "Attack is the best defense," does not apply to the battle for the vacuum, or to the case of an opponent armed to the teeth and seemingly about to strike. Today's maxim says: Reliable unity, solidarity in arming for defense and in dealing with both the totalitarians and the nations of the vacuum, and community in sacrifice — these alone can make up a body that will be capable of self-preservation, though even the biggest of its parts would be lost if it would depend upon itself.

Self-preservation in our own realm forbids even the slightest offensive action to enlarge this realm. It is only in case of attack — including totalitarian violence against the very smallest allied nation — that it would rebound as a powerful offense by all means. This peaceful attitude, aimed only at self-preservation and truly not at expansion, does not permit a shift from "containment" to "rolling back" — except by agreements that would bring about an understanding between totalitarian Russia and the free world about nations of Western character and origin, such as Hungary, Poland, East Germany. If the free nations are true to their own selves, they will not wish to be guilty of using the atom bomb and initiating the annihilation of mankind — which means that they will go in for powerful conventional rearmament, inevitably lowering their standards of living. The next question — whether the self-preservation of freedom also requires readiness for the total sacrifice in which mankind might perish — will be discussed in a later chapter.

7

FREEDOM
AND
TOTALITARIANISM

Liberation and self-preservation is not enough. It is not peace. How can relations between essentially different states be so conducted as to achieve world peace?

About 1900, world peace seemed to be guaranteed by an Anglo-European world order. The colonial period had led, for the first time in history, to such a global order — which in retrospect looks like a fairy tale. Wars were local and regarded as abnormal relapses into an obsolete past. The year 1914 revealed that the century of world peace was a sham; since there was in fact no world order, the European war became a world war and let loose all the powers and populations on earth. The question of a world order is a new one and can be really put now for the first time.

Any idea of a future world order must start from the actual state of the world today. Therefore, the premise of reflection on it is information about the present condition of nations all over the inhabited globe. Such information reaches us, always in limited measure, in communications from those with firsthand experience. From people who have earned their living abroad — businessmen, engineers, diplomats, missionaries, soldiers, colonial officials, travelers, journalists — we get descriptions, experiences, current opinions, and judgments in writings of unequal value. Besides, there are collections of materials, economic and statistical data, political and legal documents. We read accounts of the events of our time, how they came to pass and how they unfolded and how they looked on the spot.

No thought of a world order can become concrete except on the basis of such information. But even the best-informed cannot know "reality" itself — only an inexhaustible field of facts and unfathomable causal and conceptual relations. Also, our knowledge of these realities is always apt to be distorted. Pictures deceive us by their visibility and vividness, and reality itself is changing fast: a comparison of travel accounts from the past century shows that what was real yesterday is no longer real today. Yet misconceptions themselves are an effective reality. The purpose of any action based upon them does not coincide with its actual effect; but as purposes and effects will hardly ever tally, misconceptions and deficient knowledge play a part in all action.

I cannot even outline the present notions of the reality of the human world — chiefly because my own knowledge is deficient. I can only try to discuss some areas of fact and ideas from the point of view of progress toward a world order. I want to find the tendencies that can point to such an order, and the great conflicts that stand in its path.

The fundamental mistake is to think in terms of a world government. Today, as a matter of course, people think along these lines: all men are equal; all nations are of a kind; all countries have the same right to their frontiers; men everywhere have the same desire to be free. Thus the realities on earth are covered with an abstraction, and this abstraction has engendered ways of speaking, arguments, and claims.

In the Europe of the past, for all its conflicts, the common ground of Antiquity and the Bible produced a certain community of cohesive and constructive ideas and laws. Today there is no world community in that old European sense; there is only the abstraction. This can be sophistically utilized, but not for the building of peace.

The idea of world government is founded upon the untruthfulness of the abstraction. A world order is said to require the establishment of a world parliament, a world police, a world currency, and so forth. No progress is made, because reality is not only ignored but violated.

In reality a world government could be established only by conquest. If this happened, there would indeed be peace, but also the most frightful despotism. A victorious totalitarian world would stabilize its terrorism as the only means of quieting the constant desperate discontent of men. But even if the free world were to prevail in a last conflict — and if a part of mankind should survive — the result would be almost the same terrorism. For, in the course of that war, the all-embracing power organization required to fight the dragon would have made a dragon of the very champion of freedom.

Even the abstract illusion of a world government set up by treaty, with a central police force to keep the peace, could not fail at some time to lead to the tyranny of those in power. Whatever combines all force in one hand will soon crush freedom. Political freedom can be preserved only by a separation of powers, by the system of checks and balances that has been conceived and realized in variously modified form ever since Antiquity. Men, being human, need control and restraint. In reality this can succeed only if potential force is curbed by other potential forces — in our case, if there are many police forces on earth. To be reliably confined — that is to say, legally directed — force must remain plural, since only decentralized force, governed by law at every step, provides a chance for imminent lawlessness to be nipped in the bud by the joint action of other forces if one force should show despotic inclinations. But this chance is bound up with the permanence of danger.

Peace lies in the freedom of confederation. A free world order can only take the form of a confederation in a lastingly unstable state. It cannot begin as a world confederation designed to bring essentially different elements into apparent union without regard for basic laws and ways of life. Confederation can be made effective only by treaties between nations living under free constitutions, with unlimited freedom of speech and the desire to preserve that freedom jointly.

Thus far, and as far as we can see ahead, the confederation of free states cannot be world-wide. Outside the circle of international law established within the confederation, there is accordingly another law for the rest of the world, which Kant termed "world citizenship," without elaborating upon it. There are two steps to be distinguished: the confederation of free states, and the association of all states in a world citizenship for the maintenance of peace. The provisional non-universality of the confederation results from the premise that only free nations are capable of joining it.

Such a confederation is today not only the aim of a political ethos; it is necessitated by the twin threats to liberty, from totalitarianism and from the substantially still undirected revolt of the huge masses of men in the former colonial areas. Free nations that firmly renounce the principles of colonialism can, even though they used to be great powers, preserve themselves now only as small powers within the confederation. The withdrawal to their own territories involves the renunciation not only of conquest, but of the maintenance of former power. The league of the resigned is their only form of self-preservation.

Today we have the politics of the free nations, of totalitarianism, and of the great mass of nations on earth that are neither totalitarian nor free. The free would like to live politically so that their form of government and their conduct might attract the others to the confederation and eventually make it world-wide. Totalitarianism, on the other hand, wants to coerce. It seeks world peace by conquest — not a league of free nations but total rule by terroristic subjection. The remaining nations constitute the arena in which the two great principles of freedom and totalitarianism contend.

Freedom and totalitarianism are mutually exclusive. Besides, the free world stands under the real threat of totalitarian expansion, while totalitarianism feels threatened by the mere existence of freedom. But since, in view of the consequences of the atom bomb, neither wants to go to war against the other, they have invented "coexistence" as a minimum of peaceful world order.

Pure coexistence, which would end all conflict by ending all contact, can occur only in radical isolation. The global surface, which is physically one, and mankind, which grows from a single root, would be split in two. Only a single agreement would then be required: to have no crossings of the border. It would be as if there were two worlds, with each knowing only that the other exists. Just as the planet is in fact a closed surface, its surface might consist of two closed parts. And each, then, would face the problem which has come to confront mankind as a whole on the one, now known and partitioned, Earth: how to live without expansion? Only now it would have to be solved twice, independently.

The idea of such coexistence of two isolated areas need only be thought through to be found impossible. The actual interest of men in what is happening on the other side, what is to be learned or bought there; the desire to know, to find out what exists wherever men can go; finally, the original unity of human nature, man's basic power to communicate in speech — all exclude this path. But if coexistence is not complete, there is either co-operation or, in case of discord, conflict — for all communication is the beginning of either one or the other. True, before there was world travel and trade, the nations of the Earth were coexisting, but travel and trade have brought both co-operation and conflict. Since a return to pure coexistence is impossible, the concept can have only a special meaning.

There is something equivocal about the desire for coexistence or the proposal to coexist rather than fight. It may mean either temporary toleration of the other political way of life, so as to come gradually, by co-operation in specific areas, to a cessation of mere coexistence and to over-all co-operation. Or it may mean co-operation in specific areas in the breathing spell before total war — so as to prepare more effectively for that war which one does not want to risk. In short, "political coexistence" is a notion with which the world is now deceiving itself. We want to deal with one another, to co-operate economically, culturally, even politically, in particular about those vast regions that are neither totalitarian nor free. But in the two private, essentially different forms of government, in the principles of the totalitarian and free worlds, there is to be pure coexistence. This sphere is to be taboo. But it cannot be. If there are contacts and mutual concerns anywhere, they will, in fact, be everywhere. Where we concern one another, we do not merely exist side by side.

Under the formula of coexistence, one side is hiding its will to eventual world conquest by coercion, the other its will to world conquest by persuasion. The former must fear, above all, the effect of this persuasive power once its own peoples learn what freedom is. The latter must fear the total force that will erupt from concealment at the first promising opportunity.

Readiness for coexistence as the only present possibility of peace serves to conceal what both sides expect from the future. Totalitarianism, in accordance with Marxist thought, is waiting for the inevitable collapse of the capitalist world; it expects this world to develop automatically so as to fall prey to totalitarianism without military conflict. The free world, on the other hand, feels that totalitarianism conflicts with human nature and is accordingly bound, in the course of generations, to soften up and dissolve. Man's innate freedom will shatter it; we need only wait, and the whole world will be free, with men unfolding in fraternal diversity on common premises of political freedom.

These expectations have been shaken on both sides. They fluctuate with the events of the day. Thus the conflict — still without world war — takes the form of each side trying to protect itself by hastening the expected development.

This struggle — without war, and yet with a constant eye to war — is carried on only in part by the age-old political methods. Essentially new ones, differing on both sides, have been added. If we glance only at the intellectual battle for the ideas and motives of men in both camps, we note, in essence, that one camp insulates its people from information, ideas, and discussions of the free world, while the other demands precisely the removal of all obstacles to communication. The battle becomes one for communication itself. Totalitarianism wants no free press, no universality of public communication, because the very perception of the liberty of others by its own population would encourage them to rebel against totalitarian rule. The free world, on the other hand, wants to broaden communication so as to publish world events and human thought to the limits of human habitation.

Because the life of the free world depends upon unlimited communication, it cannot close its borders to the intellectual activities of totalitarianism, which has no qualms about using the freedom it has killed in its own realm for the most deceitful propaganda on behalf of the justice, greatness, and truth of its road. It can do so, with frightening success, for two main reasons. First, life under totalitarianism looks entirely different to those who seek to achieve it while living in a free world, and to those inside who suffer it. The imagination of most people does not suffice to picture it, although it actually exists elsewhere in the world.

Second, in the free world, discontent, rootlessness, misfortune, indignation, or a sense of superfluity make many ready to press for a world situation that strikes them as a redemption. Even in the free world, totalitarianism is a dangerous spiritual and political disease. In fact, it is only in this world that a moral-political battle takes place, for in the other world it is forbidden. For the time being, the truly responsible decision must be made entirely within the free world; this alone is the arena. It would give itself up if it were to use force against the intellect, even the lying intellect. It must trust in itself, in the final emergence of truth from liberty, for it would have lost its justification if it turned dogmatic and chose to rely upon force rather than free thought. But all totalitarians and neutralists, though no harm befalls them in the free world, are traitors to this world on whose terms they live and think.

In the totalitarian world, where people experience it in the last fiber of their being — even though most are too numbed by mendacious propaganda to be clearly aware of it — there would be an explosion if information were unrestricted. Without the blockade of intellectual communication between the two worlds, today's great, all-befogging lies would be impossible. Hence, today, the "coexistents" can wage their battle in the most violent forms of the Cold War, which permits everything in order to avoid one thing: total war itself. But it would be a mistake to think that coexistence in this limited and untruthful sense could be a permanent state of affairs. Totalitarianism, unable to bear the menacing presence of freedom, must strive for world conquest by all possible means, and because of this constant threat of violence the free world cannot silently acquiesce in the presence of totalitarianism.

The present state of affairs, which is no world order but keeps the peace for the moment, takes three forms: hegemony, subjection, and spheres of influence. Hegemonic relations exist today in the free world by virtue of American pre-eminence. Subject satellite states exist all around Russia. Spheres of influence are vaguely delimited, claimed by both sides in the rest of the world, and a source of constant unrest.

Hegemonic relations are indispensable in the league of free nations. They are not a matter of formal treaties but of political confidence, political loyalty, and political tact. They bear only on foreign policy — that is to say, on policy toward totalitarianism and the great fluctuating mass of nations that do not yet wield any political power of their own. Nowhere do these hegemonic relations need to infringe upon the inner freedom of states and peoples. The small ones have the right to consult and advise, but not the right to act independently without the consent of the dominant power or against it. Every Westerner has, in a sense, two countries: the country of his heart, his origin, his language, his ancestors, and one that is the sure foundation of his political reality. Those fatherlands are many, but this foundation is today only one: the United States of America.

The free nations are constantly weakened in their hegemonic relations by selfishness and disloyalty. Thus far, in these relations, freedom is inadequate for joint self-preservation, because it keeps lapsing into license. One cannot compel an awareness of the whole and its requirements, whose fulfilment is the condition for the survival of every individual. Freedom can live only by intelligent freedom.

By contrast, rule over satellite states differs in essence. The voluntary common foreign policy is demoted to a mechanism of obedience, and domestic liberty is abolished in favor of a totalitarian constitution. Hungary showed how obedience is enforced by the employment of foreign military power against a whole people. In every nation one can find some traitors to impose the foreign will by terror, with foreign help.

Because of an utter unfreedom mislabeled independence, satellite states are marked by an unproductive unrest that can only be stifled by force or break out by force. The interrelation of states in the various spheres of influence, on the other hand, has no principle. These spheres no longer exist on nineteenth-century lines, set by treaties between the great colonial powers. The present factual, unrecognized, and unacknowledged spheres of influence are a field for contention and competition, resulting in the illusion that these states are very independent.

These three types of international relations have very different implications for world peace. Relations of hegemony are necessary as free acts only while the existence of the free states is threatened from outside. Satellite relations exist by force as long as the force is applied. The claim to spheres of influence, which both sides raise without admitting it, is linked with the global conflict of the great powers and would vanish with it. And all three relationships are based upon the threat of war.

The forced subjection of people who wish to be free exists only in the totalitarian sphere. The free world puts up with it, for the time being, because the alternative would be world war. It was dishonest of the Republican party in the first Eisenhower campaign to trump Truman's "containment" with a promise of "rolling back." This irresponsible encouragement to the satellite states led to a cruel disillusionment when the Hungarian people heard Eisenhower's words, "We did not encourage the Hungarians to rebel."

The co-operation of free states in relations of hegemony and the obedience of satellites are both called "forming blocs." But a bloc of free states formed for non-aggressive self-preservation is something quite different from a bloc created by actual conquest, by foreign military power acting under the disguise of treaties. It is part of the confusions of current usage that things essentially different and even contradictory are called by the same name.

Human life is always in a state of transition, and today this has become a crisis with the possibility of total doom. If the transitional stage with its attendant wars is overcome, world peace (if it is not the peace of a totalitarian graveyard) will still be established only so as to leave a constant, if peripheral, danger of war — as a possible threat but also as an incentive to serious action. Peace can never be absolutely secure.

Peace in freedom is tied to the danger of war, but today war dooms mankind. We may ask: Does freedom then belong only to the historic interval between prehistory and the end of the human race? Do we have to choose between man's destruction of his own existence and a terminal state of peace under total rule, in which human existence in the sense of our age-old history is no longer possible? It may seem so to the mere intellect. But the human will to freedom, by which alone man knows his true humanity, will never accept this choice as compelling. Man will always prefer instability with its danger of war and its chance of destruction — a condition appropriate to human nature in its interminable flux. If he should ever prefer the absolute calm of an endlessly peaceful existence, he would cease to be human and would pass into a functionalized, unexistential reiteration of life.

The issue of total rule against political freedom strikes us today as a real clash of principles, not of nations. In the issue of anticolonial hatred against stubbornly retained remnants of colonial domination, we see historically founded, deeply rooted hostile feelings. But issues such as capitalism versus socialism, liberal versus Marxist thought, seem obsolete as adequate expressions of a real struggle. They are now mere slogans in a fight for something else.

All issues are encompassed in that of the actual great powers with military potential. Today these are Russia and America, but this need not long remain the case; once China has been organized, for example, things may look quite different in thirty years. Where the great powers meet in reality, the lines are seldom clearly drawn. They are real in the organization of power, but so ambiguous in content that men may be fighting against their stated opinion and betraying their chosen goal. In fact, the struggle proceeds in a welter of opinions guided only by actual force and its effects.

To this extent, the global divisions of opinion, of interest, of hatred leading to a vast variety of possible conflicts, are mere side issues to organized force. Force may take advantage of such conflicts, adding fuel to them if their effect benefits its power. Or it may try to settle them, if their effect is to its disadvantage. While the decision rests with the interest in the maintenance of power, there is no true and halfway reliable confederation striving for a just solution of conflicts in the interest of universal peace and freedom.

The great powers are still the reality of force in our time, utilizing all divisions in their own struggle. But even though they are side issues to force today, these divisions may really contain the deeper element that will outlive the great powers and indeed utilize them, in a sense, as changing forms. We see such a deep, comprehensive, and historically decisive division today in the issue of political freedom and totalitarian rule. The nature of total rule has been brilliantly analyzed by Hannah Arendt, and I am following her exposition in these pages.

Total rule allows no parties. It is based upon a single party which retains its name from the time when it was fighting for power in the free world. The party remains a minority, selected from the population and constantly controlling and purging itself. It claims to be so fully identified with the workers and the peasants and the whole people that every move against it is a move against the workers and the peasants and the people. Thus the workers lose the right to strike, for as, through the state, they are the owners of industry, they would be striking against themselves, which would be criminal nonsense. Or we hear, "The leader is the people." To think and act against the leader is to act against the people and commit high treason.

The rule of the party knows no legal opposition, only opponents who must be "liquidated" because they are either ill-natured, owing to their origin or native character, or ill-disposed. Hence, the terrorism — which as a form of government maintains the fiction of the existence of dangerous enemies under various names, used to disparage the actual opposition of the basic human will to freedom: counterrevolutionaries, fascists, capitalists, nationalists, imperialists.

Sociologically, the new situation appears in the unity of state and society. Any division of power is abolished in favor of the one guiding power of the party, from which the government arises. "Class" distinctions — characterized under capitalism by private ownership of the means of production — are replaced by distinctions of rank among the functionaries. Private property is replaced by the control over the work of all and over the means of production, which the state exercises in the form of small ruling strata. These become the exploiters. The differences in income, living standards, and luxuries are greater, in fact, than in "capitalist" countries. The workers and peasants have lost their freedom in the name of a co-ownership of all property which fails to affect their actual state of helpless exploitation.

This is only one aspect. "Dictatorship," "rule of a new class" — these categories are not incorrect, but they are insufficient. Amazed, aghast, despairing, we face a condition in which imprisonment, deportation, execution by governmental and police action is possible at any time, without public trial, even without stated cause. All life is functionalized, every person put to work according to plan. Everyone is replaceable. This functionalization embraces even the leadership; it involves every individual under total rule.

The form of totalitarian rule is terror as such, requiring constant purges and the persecution of alternating groups, new power concentrations or class structures — in the army, in the police, in industrial management, in the peasantry, in the party machine itself. But who or what is it that leads, that purges, that protects itself? The will to power of individuals or groups? Again, this is not an incorrect answer, but it seizes only on one factor, a factor recurring in history. Is it something called the party line, the true doctrine? That is not enough, either, for party line and doctrine are constantly and unpredictably transformed — against "revisionists," "dogmatists," "right" and "left deviationists" — in each ephemeral stage of the ceaseless struggle. What we have here is the mystery of an effective center which, once the terror of total rule exists, forces everyone, even the dictator, into the human will to power and self-protection. When all are suspicious of all, when every power is threatened by another, when it is impossible for any lasting government to establish itself in an atmosphere of trust, a self-destructive process is set in motion, together with the process of building up vast military and industrial power.

This is an automatic occurrence, as it were, distinguished from machinery only by the fact that no man conceived it and none can direct it. All who enter are drawn into this total monstrosity that entwines with unbreakable threads of steel, pulverizes in merciless grinders, builds towers of Babel by ostensibly purposeful mass consumption. It can only be smashed as a whole or break down and stop running like a machine clogged with sand.

Yet it is men who produce this automatism. It reveals a constant potential of man in a new, destructive form. This form of rule can be realized only by means of technology, but technology as such does not bring it about. The common features of all great technical enterprises are present in total rule, but they do not mark it specifically. What does mark it is *the principle of the lie*. Truth and falsehood, reality and fiction, are so blended that the outcome is not illumination but the reality of the radical lie. Let us consider this phenomenon in some of its aspects.

The leadership has more than absolute power. Whatever its form, it claims to be so wise, so free from error, as to monopolize truth. On principle, the population, the average man, must not be exposed to all knowledge. True knowledge is reserved for the political leadership and entitles it to exclusive control of education and schooling in basic views, to exclusive propaganda, to censorship of all intellectual activity, and to the erection of iron curtains around its territory, to block all inroads of free thought and undesired information.

Moreover, since all truth rests with the state leadership, its supremacy in power becomes at the same time a supremacy in justice. Legal controls are as superfluous as an examination of basic doctrine in critical discussion. Any criticism of the leadership, or the doctrine, is an act of war, and thus a crime against the state that calls for the destruction of the criminal. Whenever the leaders, disquieted by the disquiet among their people, try to allow the slightest criticism, the slightest freedom of thought, such an opening of the floodgates has to be quickly reversed. The non-violent spontaneity of the mind is forcibly suppressed, nor, of course, can there be freedom of political action, of assembly, of partisan activity.

The situation of scientific research and technology differs slightly. Totalitarianism breeds its technicians much as an ant society breeds the lice that feed it. They are given all advantages and provided with extraordinary means. But only the usefulness of their achievement counts; their freedom does not extend to the basic concepts of science, and emphatically not to their defense in free intellectual debate.

Against the decision by force, checked at the moment by the existence of the atom bomb, stands the power of men who wish to understand and to get along with one another. Truth alone can unite. If we want to communicate with each other, seriously and under all circumstances, we presume that there is some common ground, to be found only in truth. And we are confident that truth is a meeting ground for man as such — even for enemies locked in a life-or-death struggle.

Language is the means of such union. We can understand one another only in a valid medium, in agreed meanings. There we can understand that our views differ; we can expound and finally, perhaps, overcome the difference; we can recognize for the moment that we are not of one mind, can agree to disagree. We can also lie by means of language, knowingly say what is false. In that case we deceive others, though not ourselves, and are misusing language. But we can go a step further. Constant lying can make the liar believe his lies, can make the line between truth and falsehood disappear. Language then becomes arbitrary. In every key, in each manner of argument or way of thinking, under changing standards and ideals, one will talk — always as a matter of course, and always forgetting what was said before. Falsehood, presented with the vigor of an actor failing to see through his own acting, runs all the way from the shameless, instantly recognizable lie to utterly confusing self-deception. The liar has become entangled in his own mendacious world. Words have lost their constant meaning. Now they mean what the opponent means by them, now they mean the opposite. And a dialectics carried to the point of sophistry will justify this volatility of meaning as truth.

This condition, essential to impersonal machinery, is reached under total rule, whether National Socialist, Communist, or any other. An abyss has opened; speech continues over it but can no longer unite. The question is whether there is a boundary here that turns speech itself into deception, where conversation means only that each participant befogs and deceives the other and, in the final analysis, himself. Intellectuals in totalitarian countries place themselves at the service of the great lie that founds and permeates everything. Men who are capable of constantly voicing a constantly modified untruth are a valuable asset. Once they have fully renounced their liberty and integrity, they are materially favored and attain a high standard of living.

Yet the construction of a principle never exhausts the living individuals who have become its bearers. It does not follow, therefore, from our understanding of the principle that our relations with the individuals must be broken off. To stop talking is politically unjustifiable even if the opponent does not use language to seek a meeting of minds; for talk among men always offers a chance of finally meeting in truth. It is an ineradicable premise that every living human being has a chance for good, though he may seem to have succumbed to evil.

The terrible problem suggested here cannot be taken lightly. Universally, the lie has many faces. Even truth, as I have pointed out elsewhere, bears falsehood within itself. What is specific in totalitarianism is the basic tendency and its extreme form: the lie is a cardinal principle of totalitarian doctrine.

We can obtain a clear picture only from construction. Reality blurs the picture, because in both the free and the totalitarian worlds opposing forces also come into play. In spite of everything, totalitarianism cannot transform people into mere functions. They remain human and require zones of freedom. Thus valves are opened, closed again when danger signals appear, and reopened elsewhere. In the free world, on the other hand, men go astray; rudimentary totalitarian tendencies constantly tempt them to evade the tasks of freedom.

Both worlds have their superiorities. The totalitarian world is superior by virtue of unified direction. Planning enables it to dispose of all the forces of its population. It can conceal its political actions while observing nearly everything done or proposed in the free world. Its silence is not broken by any publicity. Apart from its own credible disclosures, its purposes of the moment remain secret.

The strength of the free world is its freedom. For freedom leads to deeper insights, including fundamentally new scientific discoveries. It leaves room for spontaneity in every field. It achieves its inner security by the rule of law, implemented by reliable institutions. It recognizes mutual controls. It lives in public, with free discussion and competition serving to stimulate all the faculties of individuals. Political action also must be publicly justified.

The totalitarian world is weak at home and strong abroad. At home it can maintain its rule only by terror, but abroad, on the soil of the free world, it can utilize the rules of this world to carry on propaganda and to form subversive organizations with immense resources by centrally planned and directed totalitarian methods. The free world can meet this propaganda only with its own spiritual power, with the ethos of its principle, which will eventually let the propaganda machine idle without effect. With subversive organizations — that incipient formation of a totalitarian state within the free state — it must cope by vigilance and police action under law. It must not resort to totalitarian methods, for if it did, it would destroy its own essence.

The free world is strong at home and weak abroad. Its inner strength rests on the free consent and co-operation of its people; its outward weakness lies in the rifts among the free states and in the failure of each single one to concentrate all its forces. Any attack from outside will find the free world initially inferior, because it is not unified, armed, and ready for battle. It needs time to mobilize its superior potential. Without this time it might be lost.

The East is superior in whatever strength will flow from uniformity achieved by censorship and control of information, by instruction in general public dialectics, by the abolition of free speech and free thought. It knows no other ways of thinking except those shown to it in caricatures of obsolete, reactionary, anachronistic, criminal thinking. But this strength is threatened by the human faculty of critical thought that can be destroyed only when man himself is destroyed — a faculty stimulated even by a caricatured opposition.

The West is superior insofar as unfettered ways of life and thought open the road to experiment, promote freshness and daring, and enhance individual energies. This strength turns into weakness if diversity stops being nourished by a serious faith, if its determining power is lost in rootless frivolity, and if the iron mechanics of technology will then reduce it to mere trimming and finally cast it off. But the regenerative force of freedom works against such a course.

The East has an ideology; the West has none, having many. The East enforces one as the only true ideology; the West leaves all of them free to show themselves, to contest under law, as provided by political freedom. They compete in ideas and achievements, in conceptions, pictures, symbols, and in the theory and practice of their special ways of human life. The East has the Communist ideology, but the West does not have a capitalist one — it only allows Marxist thinking to persuade it that it has the ideology of "capitalism."

Does the lack of a ruling ideology mean strength or weakness? Without ideology, is there an effective faith — which does not have to be tied to doctrinal creeds? This is the fateful question for man and his freedom. No theory can answer it, no knowledge, only man and his freedom. Every individual will answer it to himself, by resolving where he will stand, what he will live and fight for. It is not an answer if men of little faith call plaintively for a strong Western faith to meet the Communist faith of the East. Where are we to get it? Should we invent or resuscitate a faith as a means to an end? A vain endeavor. There is nothing to be "done" here, and nothing to be planned. The possibilities of action will be the subject of Part Three of this book.

The two worlds contend on two levels: in the minds of men, and by main force.

Their intellectual conflict is limited to the free world area; in the area of totalitarianism it is forbidden. Yet insofar as news does get through the iron curtains, as every totalitarian subject who is allowed to go abroad gathers experiences, as finally the rest of the world is neither free nor totalitarian, the struggle can be waged in the form of competition between ways of life.

We might think that the way of life providing more happiness and less constraint for all, along with material well-being, the way that is superior in productive and inventive power and permits diversity of human thought, life, and beauty, would please and induce others to follow the same road. In this intellectual conflict, testimony on behalf of freedom is given by its imprint on the individual. Every individual in the free world who appears unconvincing to the other, who displays the seamy side of misused freedom in lawlessness, arrogance, and greed, inflicts a defeat upon freedom by his very existence. The free world can be saved only if its members prove its value. Yet even by so doing they may intensify the hate of those in the other world, and in their own, who feel inferior and would like to destroy what they deem beyond their grasp.

The totalitarian intellectual offensive in the free world is dangerous because of certain motives which tend to favor totalitarianism everywhere. There is the spell of a paradise that exists only for those who are not living in it and allow fantasies and promises to satisfy their wishful dreams. The content of such dreams seizes men like a social religion; in the very sense in which Marx viewed religion as "opium for the people," he created a new opium. The mere sight of the power machinery has an effect upon those who, obedient and violent at once, would like to participate in it to enhance their sense of existence. To others, totalitarianism appeals by its very negativity. It says "no" to almost all there is and ever was; it is in league with all malcontents, rebels, and desperadoes in the world; the hatred hidden in men comes to the fore, as a boundless, total will to destroy. The magic of Eden, the lure of violence, and nihilistic hatred — such are the ingredients that have gone into the potion drunk by many in the free world. Thus they prepare for the mad act of plunging into the abyss. Of course, the flaws without which totalitarianism would have no propagandistic appeal are in ourselves. Yet this danger is part of a free world. It must be risked and met; it must not be curtailed if man is to find himself in the free world and to bear witness to its title.

Once total rule has been established in a great power, a change takes place in the methods of violence within and without. Internally there will be "peace," with conflict replaced by the unilateral application of the system's overwhelming force, all the way to the methodical extermination of parts of its own population. Outwardly, totalitarianism wages a "cold war" disguised as coexistence. All over the world it will create and direct organizations preparing for the violent overthrow of the existing order. It will lull free nations into security, seek to augment their differences, exploit all weaknesses, insincerities, lassitudes, and vested interests for its totalitarian purpose. Besides, with the highly gifted Russians representing its simple yet apparently mysterious principle, it demonstrates superior intelligence. Skilfully and ruthlessly adapting to new situations, it works with a consistency that fascinates the mere observer.

One method is feigned co-operation. The opponent is tricked — most successfully — into believing that one might work together. It is amazing to watch how the most obvious and crude acts of violence will not dispel this illusion for more than a moment.

The free world usually refuses to face the hard fact that there exist two mutually exclusive principles for the form of political government that permeates our life. Not two opposing principles on the same level, for there is no common meaning that would still somehow connect them. They are not different viewpoints from which one can reason together. Nor are they religions — all of which, no matter how far apart and embattled, have some common link against the emptiness and savagery of irreligion. The issue between these two principles is humanity itself, which each denies to the other. To be or not to be, that is the question between freedom and totalitarianism.

An action based upon the principle of total rule is always bad. It can only seem to agree with desired objectives. "There is some good in it," or, "good things are being done" — such views are delusions. Here, where the principle of life itself is at stake, we must say "no" radically, without compromise. We must see through the satanic illusion of good — or we have fallen for the principle of evil.

It is the strength of totalitarianism that it knows this incompatibility at all times, that it will openly state it only to screen it again and to exploit the opposite view, the reliance on communication and understanding, as the adversary's weakness. The uncompromising purpose of totalitarianism is to maintain state power exclusively by force as such — an end to which it pretends to use all ideologies, all national and human libertarian drives, so as to destroy them in fact.

The technological age is universal, and the conquest of the immense joylessness which technology brings into the world is the common task of all men in this age. What distinguishes nations is their approach to this problem, the premise on which they solve it. There are two diametrically opposed possibilities of meeting this age. Either we meet it so as to save human freedom, with man and his greatness the dominant idea, or we meet it so as to use technology for intensifying thralldom under the will-o'-the-wisps of some redeeming sham greatness, as in National Socialism and Communism.

This contrast generally goes by the misleading names of capitalism and Marxism rather than by its proper ones: freedom and total rule. If we identify the two contrasts we obscure what is now happening. The central tenet of Marxism is the concept that private ownership of the means of production is evil and its abolition is salvation. The concept of private ownership serves to conceal all the horrors of the technological age, all the consequences which the productive and economic structure of this age brings to everyday life, putting an end to all past ways of existence. The world is duped by Marxist thinking; the primary question is not one of private ownership of the means of production at all. The free world strives to protect freedom against monopolies resulting from private ownership, while the totalitarian world abolishes them, along with private ownership, in favor of a single state monopoly and then annihilates all freedom in the name of public ownership. The primary question is how work is organized in fact, and who has the power to dispose of it in fact. Without formal private ownership this power is greater than any economic power in a free system.

Two standards are usually applied in appraising modern social systems. The first is productivity, which can be determined objectively, quantitatively and qualitatively, and approximates the statistically expressed competition between Russia and America. The second standard is the relative satisfaction of human life in the two social systems, and their potential value to human substance, human dignity, and freedom. These qualitative differences are not as comparable and objectively measurable as statistical data.

The Westerners — Europe, America, and, partly following in their footsteps, Czarist Russia and Japan — have brought forth their own technological economy. Not so the rest of the world. Among us, the mass of skilled workers, technicians, and entrepreneurs (now transformed into managers) came along with the development of industry; other countries have yet to acquire it. They have to conquer illiteracy and to achieve the educational prerequisites for training industrial workers. This, at the same time, awakens them to intellectual freedom. The man who learns to read and write learns new ways of thinking, and thinking men suffer differently and acquire new impulses.

We can observe three ways of appropriating Western technology: (1) actual adoption followed by development of one's own skill, as in Japan; (2) industrialization under totalitarian compulsion, as in China; (3) being kept alive by constant aid, as in the "underdeveloped countries."

If we hear that non-Western nations must either win their national independence by totalitarian compulsory modernization or remain actually dependent on Western guidance and aid, Japan is proof to the contrary. In the last decades of the nineteeth century, at an early stage of the technological era, Japan began learning and then, independently, evolving a still nascent technology. She became a modern industrial power, maintained her full independence, but developed a free economy like the West's.

Today it seems too late for other countries to travel this road; they must catch up suddenly with the whole industrial revolution. Modern technology as it is today can no longer flower on preindustrial soil on the initiative of freely competing individuals. The required undertakings are of a scope that can be planned and executed only by state power. The problem is how an entire nation can do all the following things at once: conquer illiteracy, reach an educational level that will enable it to produce an industrial labor force, overcome the powerful obstacles to industrialization that arise from a body of social and religious traditions, and accomplish great technological undertakings in the living framework of a community that must be simultaneously rebuilt on new foundations.

National independence today is bound to technology. This seems to have been the Chinese leaders' choice: for the sake of technology, they chose totalitarianism along with the Marxist-Communist doctrine. If we look at it this way, we see behind the façade of this doctrine a China entering the technological age, appropriating technology as a whole, without limitation, so as to regain her independence and greatness. For the China policy of the West, in the nineteenth century above all, had been superlatively arbitrary and ruthless, a series of humiliations going from bad to worse, and finally a state of foreign exploitation facilitated by extorted privileges.

Chiang Kai-shek remained dependent on America, became a Christian, and failed to extricate himself from the corruption that had permeated leading Chinese circles in their dealings with the foreigners. Chinese communism is the successful independence movement of this great people, terminating decades of civil warfare, able for the first time to re-establish its old territorial limits, and now accelerating its entrance into the technological age with the sole, and rather hesitant, aid of Russia. China today is totalitarian but not Russian; she may, in the spirit of some leaders of the regime, be not as basically totalitarian as Hitler or Stalin, or at least differently totalitarian. It could be that China is taking this road only provisionally, to regain the independence she lost in the colonial age and to accomplish her modern technological reconstruction.

For thousands of years this most populous nation on earth has lived a concept of humanity as sublime as the West's, though different from it. Her successfully claimed independence can be compared only superficially to Tito's, whose claim is bound to fail in the long run. If China, because of a world-political situation which America wanted, is a Russian ally for the time being, she is by no means a Russian satellite.

Though no longer a practical issue, it is not without historical interest to ask whether American policy might possibly have backed the Chinese Communists. Could America, by supporting China's totalitarian technological development, have won a great ally in world politics? What Russia has done could perhaps have been done more extensively and better by America: to send no soldiers but many technicians, to claim no advantages to China's detriment, to foster technological progress by extending massive credit. Was it dogmatic political prejudice that stood in the way? Or would China not have trusted the Americans in any case?

Even if Marxist totalitarian thought should be only a façade for the national regeneration of six hundred million people as a technological world power, this façade is not a matter of indifference. What it means in the schools, and thus for coming generations, is impregnation with Marxist thinking; for the time being, all of the Confucian, Taoist, and Buddhist cultural traditions opposed to the industrial age will be dismantled.

Something tremendous is going on in China, going far beyond the disintegration of Western religious, philosophical, artistic, and social traditions in the scientifically based age of technology. As late as 1918, the Sinologist De Groot wrote about the beginnings of modernization in China: "The conservative party doubtless knows that change is suicide, but will it be able to demonstrate that the cosmic and human *Tao* can indeed be shaken but not destroyed? If it be destined that the cruel work of disruption take its course, that the days of China's old cosmic culture be numbered — then may at least its last day not also doom a nation of millions plunged into misery by foreign influences."

What has suddenly come over China, after long resistance, is the very problem facing all nations, East and West. De Groot's statement that, in the event of a rebirth by modern science and technology, "China would no longer be China, the Chinese no longer Chinese," applies to all nations on earth. Is their end in the age of technology the beginning of their new existence? We, too, need what De Groot wished for China. China is now doing forcibly what we have done slowly, by concealed force, and are about to carry still further.

The Chinese act out of an immemorial past; they are irreplaceable and unexcelled in high philosophy, religion, and art, in a deeply implanted humanism of measure and balance. They have so great a history that we may have faith in their substance. We are akin to them, from the roots of true humanity. They are admirable and lovable. A peaceful understanding with them would be the most natural thing in the world.

Despite the Marxist doctrine now being talked there, it is entirely possible for China to find a way back to herself out of her age-old substance and then to realize the truth of her ancient tradition in new forms. After such a past, we may hope that in the age of technology China will produce her own new form of freedom. For the moment she is obviously living in the consciousness of growing strength; the conflict of freedom and totalitarianism is not yet acute in the population at large, though already creating constant unrest among the leaders and intellectuals. In this conflict China is not neutral, but it has hardly touched her. In foreign policy she is now allied with Russia, without being at one with bolshevism. That in this alliance she co-operates with Russia and has no qualms about approving and praising the rape of such European nations as Hungary may shock us, but perhaps this hardly affects what she is doing at home. If she stands today with totalitarianism against Western freedom, this might in the long run be a misconception of herself that can be overcome.

If Mao Tse-tung is typical of Chinese leaders, the quality of his mind would seem to indicate that in China totalitarianism is not following its ultimate nihilistic trend. None of the Russian or German totalitarians could have written poetry as beautiful as his, modern in content but of ancient culture. It may not yet be the time for China to make her decision in the world conflict of political freedom and totalitarianism. Yet the situation may develop rapidly. In power politics, China is only beginning to develop the industrial potential of her vast territory and immeasurable resources; but technological development, once started, can move apace, and then there will be six hundred million Chinese next to two hundred million Russians. Siberia might become the first objective of Chinese population pressure. But if her present form of total rule should then lead China really to permanent totalitarianism, the result would be a world catastrophe and atomic extinction.

The consequences of aid to underdeveloped countries are still unclear. It seems scarcely possible for them to emulate Japan; a repetition of the Chinese course seems very possible. Today the main example of this alternative is India. India still lives by retained traditions of the British Empire. Her industrialization is progressing, but not so fast as under the British, and not at the pace of China's. India needs help and receives it from both Russia and the West. The bulk of her vast population of many races and tongues is vegetating. A narrow stratum of Western-educated intellectuals governs, is elected, and for the time being sets the course. Communism is on the rise, without as yet constituting a present danger. There is freedom, without being lived or realized. In the nature of things there is competition between China and India. Can India find a way of her own in freedom — as Japan found it — or will there be bloody confusion, disintegration, and a final victory of totalitarianism?

At the moment, India and China are still without decisive military power. Yet they do have a voice. India is neutralist, with strong leanings toward Russia; China is allied with Russia. But something else is important: both have a powerful sense of security in their newly won independence, due simply to the size of their territories that are tantamount to continents, to the mass of their populations, which with their dependencies make out half of mankind, and to the age-old foundation of their history. They anticipate an indestructible duration for their peoples, which have survived all catastrophes for so long. They feel they have time. But in view of the hydrogen bomb this has become an error. Like the whole surface of the globe, their countries are exposed to the fatal disaster, even though no foreign soldier should set foot upon their soil on the day of mankind's doom. It is in China's and India's own interest, no less than in that of others, to co-operate in thought and action in the rescue of mankind at large, and thus in their own.

In the long run, China will, if man survives, surely become a world power of the first rank. In the short run, America and Russia are the only two decisive powers. Today, therefore, we must think chiefly of them in regard to the danger of world war and destruction.

8

RUSSIA,
THE WEST,
AND THE QUESTION
OF NEUTRALITY

Totalitarianism and *freedom* are conflicting principles, *Russia* and the *West* are conflicting historical realities. In the long run, the two conflicts need not coincide. Nations are not principles. The Russians, like the Germans, have potentials other than totalitarianism. Both principles — of political freedom and totalitarianism — undergo changes and can appear as functions of the deeper, enduring substance of great nations. The Russians are not one with totalitarianism.

No honest compromise is possible between the principles of total rule and freedom, but nations can meet one another even when they are governed by conflicting principles. For nations, like individual human beings, are always the reality in which principles are only partly embodied. An uncompromising stand against a principle cannot, therefore, be sensibly equated with total enmity to a nation. Any "crusade" against a nation will disparage it. It rests on a fiction which must backfire, because it would annihilate the opponent in his entirety.

The Russian people — strong of soul, unhappy after a history of enslavement by either Mongols or coercive despotisms of their own, vital, original, vigorous, touching in their religious devotion and sacrifice — have today succumbed to totalitarianism. Broadly speaking, Russia belongs to the West; the Russians are white people, molded by Byzantine Christianity. Yet Russia is Western and Asian at the same time. She is not a part of the Latin-Germanic West with its thousand-year history in the framework of the Catholic church and the later Protestant religions. This history alone has founded the modern world and the technological age. Russia never knew the political liberty of the West; the liberty of medieval cities, which appeared in western Russia also, remained an ineffectual exception. She knew neither our medieval struggles between emperors and popes nor the Crusades nor medieval cathedrals and poems nor the Renaissance nor the Reformation nor the evolution of philosophy and science. Only since the seventeenth and eighteenth centuries has she, as an apt pupil, appropriated many results of this Western development, especially in technology; has produced important scientists and historians and, under Western influence, great writers of her own who belong to world literature; has yielded to German philosophy, finally to Marxism.

Russia's colonial activity differed from that of Europe. She took no part in world conquest but kept pressing slowly, steadily eastward, conquering adjacent regions of Asia until, across the whole vast continent, she reached the Pacific. Because she halted before the great civilized nations, India and China, and her huge colonial conquests affected only primitive peoples without a strong self-awareness founded in their own cultures, they did not give her the appearance of a colonial power — no more than America's similar westward expansion, which annihilated the red Indians all the way to the Pacific, gave this appearance to the United States.

In Germany, the total rule of National Socialism grew on the soil of a morally and politically degenerate democracy, after a lost war followed by impossible peace terms; in Russia it grew on the soil of a despotism uninterrupted for centuries. To understand the world situation, we must see the Russian point of departure in despotism, without confusing despotism with totalitarian rule.

In 1835, De Tocqueville published these brief, matchlessly prophetic words, which have only now become famous:

There are two great nations on earth moving from different points to the same goal: the Russians and the Americans of English origin.

Both became great in obscurity, and while men's eyes were focused on other things, they suddenly placed themselves in the front rank of nations, so that the world learned almost at the same time of their existence and of their greatness.

All other nations seem about to have reached their natural boundaries and must now maintain themselves therein, but these two are still growing. . . . They alone march easily on a path whose limits are not yet in sight.

The American fights only against encumbering nature, the Russian more against men. The first fights the wilderness and savagery, the second is charged with attacking civilization in its full armory. The American conquers mostly by the plow, the Russian, outside his present boundaries, by the swords of his soldiers.

To achieve his purpose, the American relies on personal self-interest and lets the strength and reason of individuals act, without directing them. The Russian, on the other hand, unites the whole power of the state in the autocrat he is disposed to revere. The American works primarily through freedom, the Russian through slavery.

They have different points of departure and different paths, yet each seems destined by some still secret providence to hold half the globe in his hand.

Now that the Big Two have risen to this overwhelming power, the military world situation is paradoxical: Each is anxious not to go to war with the other, dares everything in derogatory words and forecasts of the other's doom, but halts at the brink of a warlike clash between them. When this limit approaches, they are considerate — as America was during the rape of Hungary — for both bear the responsibility for a possible destruction of mankind. Their decisions lie on a plane different from those of all the small nations waging their wars.

Yet the conflict of these two presently greatest organizations of force entails the possibility of a sudden outbreak and a decision whether mankind will live or die. In the Hungarian crisis, when the Russian people — their students, at least — got restless under the breath of possible freedom, as of newly germinating life; when the rulers, seeing themselves menaced and fearing the power of the free spirit embodied in the West, promptly tightened the reins; when the hearts of all Western peoples beat for Hungary — then, in November, 1956, at a dinner for Gomulka, Khrushchev told the Western diplomats, "You don't like us; we will bury you."

Something usually hidden stood revealed. In that lapse of personal excitement, at the very moment of Bulganin's threat to atom-bomb London and Paris, one felt that this was not Marxism speaking, not a mere system of government and social religion, and least of all the magnanimity of the Russian people. Rather, it might be something elemental infused into part of the Russian people under Mongol rule, an Asian hatred, a feeling of being despised. At that moment, this hatred burst out ruthlessly. It was not the spirit of Ivan the Terrible nor that of Lenin — it was the spirit of Genghis Khan that seemed to speak then, ready to subjugate nations by any means whatever, even at the cost of exterminating them and destroying their countries. Such a will to brute force prefers a wilderness round itself to any toleration of other independent life. But it would be a mistake to identify even Khrushchev as a human being, much less the Russian people, with the spirit manifested at that moment. Every individual can be spoken to — the more so if, at a decisive point in history, he becomes conscious of his greatest possible task.

Europe no longer stands on her own feet; no power in Europe can pursue independent world policies, neither France nor England nor a league of all the European states. Moreover, Europe can last only thanks to America. Without America, the Russians would have reached the Atlantic long ago. What would happen if Russian totalitarianism set out to conquer Europe at an opportune moment?

Since World War II, and particularly in the defense of Berlin, America has proved herself magnificently. In Germany, as throughout Europe, she has thus created feelings of security in which we still prosper. But can we rely on America's protection in all instances, especially if blind folly stirs anti-American feelings in almost all the European nations? Thus far, America has lived with a will to peace at almost any price, unless her own existence was directly threatened. She has been inclined to hold aloof from Europe until acts of violence, committed against herself, led her people to approve what her statesmen could not do earlier — as in 1917, after the German declaration of unrestricted submarine warfare, and in 1941, after Pearl Harbor. We cannot take it for granted that America will go on considering herself directly and fatally threatened by a possible loss of Europe, even though she has done so in the past decades.

If only Russia and America did not come to blows, wars without nuclear weapons could attain huge proportions. In a European war waged without hydrogen bombs, and thus without danger to mankind as a whole, only an army able to resist with conventional weapons could cope with the Red Army. If at the chosen moment America did not intervene, the chances are that even now Europe would be quickly conquered without atom bombs; after 1945, when all free nations disarmed but Russia did not, this would have been easy if America had not protected us by her atomic monopoly of those days. Where could we put our trust if the Americans became so blind to their own fate as to refuse to fight outside their own continent, and if the Russians then unleashed their soldiers and their supply of conventional weapons on Europe and acted here as they did in Hungary, without starting a hydrogen war?

This basic political fact — that Europe can no longer help herself and is lost if she relies on herself alone — should be kept in mind in all political actions that Europeans take. To recognize it, as Adenauer unfailingly does, is the premise of a peaceful political world order in our time.

Western solidarity presupposes a common awareness of the terrible threat to all and a general sense of communion in a single, age-old European world — a world that appears in a variety of forms but is grounded in Greek Antiquity, in both the Old and New Testaments of the Jewish Bible, and in Roman practical order, the three joint sources of the Christian tradition and the grandiose development of philosophy, science, art, literature, and political liberty in recent centuries.

Solidarity demands today the unconditional coalition of all free European countries with America. We want such a coalition, but we fail to get it, and we constantly act against it. The Continental countries tend to lean upon Great Britain — what a to-do everywhere when she undertook to keep a few divisions on the Continent, and what disappointment when she revised her defense plans and broke her promise! But Britain plays empire politics and, in case of conflict, puts the interests of the empire ahead of Europe's. And Britain, in turn, leans upon America; but when she neglected the obligations of hegemonic loyalty and proceeded on her own in the Suez case, she had to suffer humiliation at America's hands and see America put her own policy first.

The political order of the Western nations is a rudiment of world order. If these nations, which pursue freedom at home, cannot act freely in reliable concert, they will all lose their free existence by the laxness of their own order. Only he who knows how to use freedom well deserves to be free. Freedom can endure only if it can accomplish what total rule achieves by iron compulsion. Its order is the first step to a world order, its failure the death of all hopes for any world order.

The nonexistence of a Western order was exemplified in the events of 1956. Egypt forcibly and lawlessly seized the Suez Canal; America refused any serious help in restoring legality. After some months, France and Britain used force against Egypt to restore the canal to its rightful owners, and America joined Russia in opposing common Western interests — at the very time when she deserted the Hungarians in their lawful struggle for freedom from foreign occupation. Israel, faced with a growing Egyptian might fostered by Russian arms shipments and expressly designed for her destruction, was allied with France in the Suez operation, and allied and yet not allied with Britain. Israel, this Western nation, was denied an American guarantee of her borders while America called for her withdrawal and denounced her plainly defensive act as aggression.

The whole confusion of the Western consciousness shows in this catalogue. There is no Western political order, and there will be none as long as all Western states keep up their old policies of self-interest with the old motives, claims, and means. We need new policies — but these can arise only on ethical-political premises, only from a change in Western man.

Once there is solidarity, another question will arise: how to institutionalize this basic attitude for mutual consultation and control, to what extent relations would have to be hegemonic, and which decisions could be made by majority vote — not of a majority of states, but of a majority of the free men living in the free states.

A third question is which states should belong to this Western alliance. Certainly it can include only those who join voluntarily and those entitled to join by historical background and present reality. Original and tested freedom must coincide. Not the existence of a state suffices, only the reliability of its popular ethos, of its political and economic practice. Nations not originally Western may join; Islam, for instance, itself founded on the biblical world view, should not bar a people from admission.

It ought to be clear that membership in this fateful brotherhood must not depend upon power-political, military, or geographical reasons. It can only depend on ideology, on the time-tested, continuous ways of life and thinking, and on the resultant direct understanding between populations. No simple act of state, performed by some government of the moment, will suffice; the premise is continuity — the historic human being and the nature of his freedom, and the common bond of origin and fate and having lived together. By way of example, let me present some judgments based on the conception of the West:

Spain lives under a dictatorship but is not totalitarian; her history, her present spiritual reality, her knowledge of individual liberty and dignity unquestionably rank her with the West.

Germany was under a dictatorship for twelve years, and for seven of those she was totalitarian; yet she, too, belongs to the West.

The hard facts of the atomic world situation prevent Western nations presently subject to Russian totalitarianism — Hungary, East Germany, Poland, Romania, Czechoslovakia, Bulgaria — from being liberated by force; but the Western mind should not be closed to them.

Tito's Yugoslavia is not totalitarian, but she is a Communist dictatorship, leans toward totalitarian Russia, and, with regard to Hungary, favored the suppression of freedom. In this form she cannot possibly belong to the Western alliance; but her people are Westerners by inclination and essential nature — as are indeed the Russian people themselves, although their present regime has become the opposite pole.

Israel, a state for ten years only, established by Jews, is recognized by the West as well as by Russia, India, and others, and holds membership in the United Nations. But she is not recognized by the surrounding Arab states, and neither America nor any other great power has guaranteed her boundaries and her existence. Israel was founded as a Jewish homeland, on the strength of solemn British promises, and became a state when the British, in 1948, relinquished their mandate and withdrew from Palestine without providing for order after their departure. The Jews in Palestine had no choice but to create their own political order; but on the very same day all the surrounding Arab states fell upon them to wipe them out. It was a life-or-death struggle for all the Jews in Palestine, and their self-preservation by force against force established their state in reality. The fact of Israel is here. Legal reflections can point out only that the Jews had settled without force, that they had bought their land legally, piece by piece, without fraud or sharp practice, that it was astounding what they achieved by hard work and enterprise, that before 1948 there could never be a question of conquest — but a situation created by war can never be justified or condemned as a matter of right. It exists, and it is now the premise of new rights. That this situation is so unfavorable for the Israelis — and must remain so, since their frontiers could be widened only by force — is a result of British intervention: the threat of the Royal Air Force compelled the Jews, who were winning, to accept an armistice, but it failed to bring the peace which a victorious Israel would doubtlessly have managed to establish. The consequences of this armistice have been the unwillingness of the Arab states to make peace, their economic boycott, and their ever intensified threat to Israel's existence.

Why has all this happened? It was a consequence of a guilt shared by all of Christendom, which again and again put the Jews in danger of life and limb, robbed, exiled, and killed them. After the murder of six million Jews by Hitler's Germany, the rescue of the survivors became a necessity in an uncertain future, in which the same might happen elsewhere.

It was this German guilt, shared by the big Western nations, including America, which in 1948 led inevitably to the self-preservation of the abandoned and still mortally threatened Jews — and this in turn now places an obligation upon the West at large. In 1956, Israel had to react to constant attacks by murderous guerrillas, to an all-Arab boycott, to a refusal to let her ships use the Suez Canal, and, above all, to Egypt's extensive, Russian-sponsored military preparations on the Sinai Peninsula, frankly aimed at destroying Israel as a state and wiping out the Jewish population. No power on earth helped the Israelis at this crucial juncture. None guaranteed their borders; none compelled a peace. They had to act if they would not give up the ghost without a struggle. Disaster was imminent. And so, in conjunction with British and French special interests, Israel's militarily superior and politically prudent action faced the world with the obvious and urgent question: Will Israel be given peace instead of a deceptive armistice, and will the Western powers, including America, underwrite this peace?

Why is this question so momentous for the West, although concerning only a tiny nation? Both the Jews everywhere and the state of Israel are uniquely Western. By biblical religion, the Jews once opened Western eyes to the depths from which we have been able to live despite all evil, from which the assurance of God has made human dignity impervious. It is the Jew in his overwhelming power of suffering and love, his indomitable absoluteness, his assurance of God, who speaks out of Jesus even on the cross, with the psalmist's words, "My God, my God, why hast thou forsaken me?" With the Old Testament and with the New, which is almost entirely their work, the Jews brought Christianity into the world, joining the Greeks and Romans in laying the foundation of the West — the firmest and deepest part of the foundation, which carries the whole. Jesus and the original community still considered themselves Jewish, in the faith which for the Jews had long acquired the universal meaning of the sole truth; the Jews of today are the descendants of those who did not take the next step to Pauline Christianity. They are thus in the incomparable and unique position of being both the founders of and the exceptions to Christianity.

By their uncomfortable presence which keeps raising doubts about Christian dogma; by the greatness of their suffering and sacrifice, in which the fate of Jesus seems really to repeat itself as it first appeared to them in Isaiah's servant of God; by their lack of illusions, which does not try to talk evil out of existence with false comfort or stoical rigidity — by all of this, the Jews may yet become the saving thorn in the Western soul. Here lives something of Christianity's origins, something often veiled and incapacitated in formal Christianity. The Jews' existence in reality reminds us, lest we founder.

To other faiths, other historic vessels of the one truth, Jewish ritualism and talmudism are as absurd as the God-man and the Trinity. Such things belong in the denominational area, which is encompassed and animated by one common ground: the reality of God himself, as the Jewish Bible of both Testaments conceived and turned it into the foundation of the West. This common ground, symbolized in the covenant with God, is betrayed when the Jews are betrayed.

Whoever thinks as a Westerner knows that Israel is part and parcel of the West, by tradition and by reality. We have a unique obligation to include the Jews, and now their state of Israel, in the alliance of Western self-preservation. An attack upon Israel would have to be regarded as an attack upon the West itself and to entail the consequences of such an attack. Since Israel's political existence in the Near East is uncomfortable, all sorts of reasons are found for holding aloof; but in this case vacillation and indecision are symptoms of a moral and political condition of the West which, if it were to persist, would ruin us all. The West cannot abandon Israel without abandoning itself. If the West has no solidarity in this case, it has no reliable solidarity at all and will perish. If Israel falls, so does the West — not because of losing a tiny power-position and a few million people, but because of moral-political depravity.

World peace requires that territorial borders be clear and that the actual division of the globe be thus acknowledged. Border revisions would then be possible only by agreement, without the threat of force. We cannot see as yet how this might be brought about, but there can be no doubt that if the cold war over the boundaries of spheres of influence is not terminated by an acceptance of present boundaries, it will one day become a hot war with atom bombs falling.

In the present state of the world, in which there are ravished satellite states, military bases on both Western and non-Western territories, and economic interests unscrupulously violating all sense of political order, a boundary might conceivably be drawn between the existing Russian and American spheres of interest, leaving the rest of the world free from infiltration by both sides. This alone would mean coexistence in some definable sense, but it is utterly improbable. For conflict will not cease as long as the principles of totalitarianism and of freedom stand against each other.

The colonial age taught us that the globe was newly divided only by new settlements; it was thus that Russia and America expanded to the Pacific, one eastward, the other westward. The British founded Western states with Western populations in Canada, Australia, and New Zealand. Besides, independent states also arose in those days by racial mixture, as in Latin America. But wherever merely colonial rule was established, it has now been shaken off, and the factual rule of the natives by a small minority of settlers has led to untenable conditions which after a period of atrocities and violence will end in the independence of the natives — as in South Africa and the North African countries.

There are still vast, nearly uninhabited regions, deserts, and steppes. If oil is found in these regions, they are suddenly highly important. Where there are sandy and icy wastes, the world is not yet finally divided, for modern technology may turn such regions into inhabited countries. The Sahara projects demonstrate this. And for such enterprises, whether exploiting oil or reclaiming wasteland, there is a lesson to be learned from the experiences of the colonial age: wherever the means for exploiting natural resources are installed and the work is done by native labor under Western direction, there comes into being a new native class which — despite, or perhaps in consequence of, its prosperity — will arouse anti-foreign instincts. One day the installations will be "nationalized," that is to say expropriated.

Let us apply this to the example of Saharan oil. Its exploitation by the West can probably succeed only on three conditions. First, it must be carried on by colonies of settlers under joint Western protection. Only if the entire work force, without exception, comes from the countries that use the oil can the legitimately acquired desert possession endure.

Second, the undertaking must be Western, that is to say, it must be jointly started by European nations and America. If national privileges and monopolistic trends play a part, it will diminish not only the strength of building the enterprise but the power to protect it from subsequent attack. Third, the lines of communication to the sea must not run through countries that lay claim to sovereignty without being reliably Western in kind. From the Sahara, these lines can only run all the way to the Atlantic and must be serviced and protected all along the way by Western settlements. Otherwise, the resulting enclave would some day be dependent upon the will of the territories crossed by its lines of communication.

Such settling requires self-sacrifice on the part of those who undertake it — a spirit like that of the pioneers who built America. If the West no longer has such people in sufficient numbers, the whole project will be futile in the long run. What would be built with money and foreign labor would be in jeopardy from the start and liable to be expropriated soon by the sovereign states of North Africa. If it is not jointly based on Western solidarity, the enterprise will not be jointly and reliably safeguarded either.

The Sahara as the land of a glorious French future is a delusion. France is not strong enough. Rather, the Sahara offers a great opportunity to the West, which only as a whole possesses the strength that would allow France, too, to flower and grow wealthy.

There are European national policies, British empire policies, and American world policies. For Western self-preservation by an incipient world order, the three must coincide. This they can do only by confining themselves: the national policies of the European states must be subordinated to the general interests of the West on either side of the Atlantic, the empire policies of Britain to her European interests, and American world policies to Western self-preservation as a whole. In fact, each of the three still views itself as absolute.

To *Europe* a maxim might apply which Max Weber once coined for Germany: that her mission was to save freedom between the Russian stick and Anglo-Saxon conventions. This can be true in the sense of a self-imposed task, never in that of salvation through independent, sovereign political power. Our solidarity with America is absolute; we know we are lost if it falters.

The unification of Europe, if it is to mean freedom from America, lies in the European spirit, in the individual freedom which the European can draw from the inexhaustible environment of his pervasive, thousand-year-old past. This freedom does deviate in living practice from the American way of life, but it can never be used against America. The Americans themselves are Europeans and have a loving ear for all that reaches them from Europe, if it is good and alive rather than an arrogant, stupid assertion of unrealities. European self-confidence grows narrow when it turns against America. For what would Europe be, if America — Western by European descent — did not join Europe to make up the West?

From the point of view of world history, the self-preservation of Europe might be a primary question if the freedom of men as such were lost with Europe's fall; it might be a secondary question if America alone were able to save freedom — a political and spiritual improbability. To ourselves, as Europeans, Europe is closest. Insofar as freedom is a principle of politics, the self-preservation of Europe is to us that of the free human being. So, it cannot be directed against America. America herself wants Europe to be politically united; she does not fear the strength of a competitor but seeks the strength of her only reliable — because essentially related — ally. World freedom at the price of Europe's destruction is not only improbable but strikes us as impossible.

Britain is a part of Europe and the leading power of an empire. In the past two centuries she has pursued a policy of imperialism; as late as a half-century ago she was indeed the controlling world power, able until the advent of submarines and atom bombs to feel protected by her insular position and to think in detachment from the Continent, where her policy always opposed the most powerful state of the moment and favored the rest.

All this has changed radically. The Commonwealth is no more than a league of English-speaking colonial settlements, not a world empire. Insularity has ceased to protect. In fact, Britain has become entirely a part of Europe, lost if Europe falls, able to exist only along with Europe.

Today her policies are still perilously equivocal. She lives with ghosts of the past, just as France and Germany live with theirs. She keeps trying to survive as a world power, and by producing her own hydrogen bombs she has cloaked this vain effort in a semblance of possibility. She seeks safety in America by herself, not in solidarity with Europe, and humbles herself in the process. She treats the Continental countries in her old fashion as pawns on her chess board. Thus she keeps stepping out of line and is the least reliable of the European members. There is a gulf between the private ethos of an Englishman, so convincing and attractive to others, and the policy which has earned England the name of "perfidious Albion" — a policy of secretly despising other nations as foreigners, thinking to deal cleverly with them by bringing them rights and liberties, and yet merely using them for British ends. Britain's obtuse Near Eastern policy, now adopted by the Americans since they have displaced the British, is a symptom of clinging to utterly obsolete concepts.

America has never sought to conquer the world. She was busy enough taking possession of her own vast continent. She was drawn into both world wars belatedly, reluctantly, and without intentions of conquest. In the First World War it was the threat to her rights posed by German unrestricted submarine warfare that made America go to war — which she probably would have done anyway, only later, if England had been mortally imperiled. For England's destruction would have jeopardized America's existence. In World War II the situation was quite similar: France fell before Hitler and so, on the Continent, did England; then England armed with all her might and stood like a rock on the brink of defeat, undismayed by the "blood, sweat, and tears" of holding free Europe's last bastion, under Churchill's leadership — and still, beside England, it was only America with her courageously handled technology, and even America only in league with Russia and her infinitely patient, obedient, suffering, and dying masses, that overcame Hitler's Germany. Twice the delay could be made up by great sacrifices; a third time, in view of modern weapons technology, it would not be possible to make it up. Hence it is now a fateful question for mankind whether America, involuntarily placed at the hub of world politics and burdened with the decisive responsibility for the entire course of history, will play her part permanently and reliably or will follow her old tendency to isolationist policies carried on purely in defense of American interests.

The rudiments of a free world order lie today in American world policy, but only if it is no mere gesture on the part of a shortsighted American self-interest. There is always the danger that America may do no more, thinking that if only she will assure her own power by weapons technology, strategic bases, and purchases of poor states ("help to underdeveloped countries") and refrain from interfering otherwise, freedom everywhere will come along by itself, according to human nature. This line of thought is so much worse when it permits the simultaneous pursuit of one's own economic interests, with policy formally detached, but actually subservient to those interests — an emphatic kind of interference without responsibility for the whole, dazzled and lulled by false and abstract ideas. On the other hand, America today may set herself to the task that fell to her in the world-historical situation, the task of serving freedom. She may realize her best chance of self-preservation in the *de facto* confederation of free nations; she may regard Europe as part of herself and take the lead in a world policy of freedom, in the actual liberation of all previously colonial nations and states. Then she cannot, for the sake of her oil interests, play politics with feudal lords, desert kings, and slave-traders rather than with the people themselves; she cannot offer the world the spectacle of having her president ceremoniously receive such creatures while refusing to talk to the prime minister of Great Britain.

American world policy would have to coincide with the self-preservation of the West. No British empire policy, no colonial policy of any European nation, no other special foreign-political interest of individual nations should be able to divert it.

For a few more decades the two great powers of the world may be two Western nations, America and Russia — America as the main power of the feeble alliance of free Western nations, Russia with her subjugated satellites. The world order Russia seeks is so far recognizable only as order by coercion. From the beginning of the bolshevist state we have seen its steadily increasing power. Russia attacks whenever the situation permits, as when she attacked Finland and conquered the Baltic states, breaking treaties and deporting a large portion of their populations. She tries blackmail and threatens attacks that she fails to carry out. Nowhere has her vastly growing might been used to further world peace; on the contrary, she has fomented unrest, disorder, and wars — as in Korea and Indochina — in her search for ways to broaden her own power.

The principle of her policy is the same everywhere, but different methods are applied to those who have succumbed, to the European countries, to America, and to the so-called vacuum in the rest of the world.

What Russia does in her own realm has been demonstrated in the unhappy existence of the Hungarians, Poles, Czechs, etc. With the rest of Europe she deals through communist parties designed to conquer the states. Against America she resorts to military, political, and economic world strategy. In the vacuum she teams up with all impulses of discontent, with anti-colonialism, nationalism, economic misery — and then with the love of technology, order, and obedience. The people there have never known inner political freedom; they admire the strength and vigor of even despotic government; they have an elemental feeling for their racial identity. They feel closer to the Russians than to other Westerners, and the Russians do their best to gull them into taking the plunge of submission to total rule. It is a fact that many non-Western, formerly colonial nations or their ruling classes regard communism as an ideal condition, never suspecting the nature of the limbo that will appear in place of the imagined paradise.

The discussions of German reunification provide an example (hard on us Germans!) of Russian totalitarian policy, both as it is and as the West widely misunderstands it. We hear that Germany could only be reunited if Central Europe were so ordered as to threaten neither Russia nor the West. This is quite true, but also pointless — for there can be no such order, unless the two great powers should cease to appear menacing to each other. While they are in conflict, any change in the confines of power will threaten both. A demilitarized zone, an atom-free zone, a neutral zone, a vacuum — both sides would judge all these only by the dangers and advantages they would entail for each.

The basis for these dangers may change. Military bases, now important, may be deprived of significance by new developments in weapons technology. The European area may lose its meaning for world strategy, so that Russia might trade disadvantages there for advantages elsewhere — though this possibility is hardly in sight as yet.

A neutral zone can be advantageous to both sides, but neutrality would be credible only in a power capable of self-defense. A reunited Germany could never be truly neutral; she would only be demilitarized and thus, in case of war, at the mercy of the side that could get there first. Moreover, being spiritually part of the West, she would be suspect to the Russians. German non-participation in either bloc is a formula that Russia can never believe in — though America can, since Germany would, in fact, belong to Western freedom, as Poland, Hungary, and Czechoslovakia do potentially. Neutral Finland and Austria do not disprove this argument, for Russia has agreed to their neutrality because they are border states, because their neutrality affords her actual military advantages, because she can seize them quickly at any time, and, finally, because her policy in these secondary areas may serve her as an alibi for masking major acts of violence elsewhere.

The reunification of Germany will probably remain impossible until either the warlike tension between Russia and the West subsides or future developments put Russia under so much Chinese pressure that she will seek an alliance with the West. For Germany this is a terrible perspective. We are bound to fear that the East Germans will not hold out so long. If their state could become free without reunification, everything would be well; what matters is not reunification but the spiritual and moral destruction of millions of Germans who, in the course of generations, may cease to be Germans. The Western world, at least, must constantly know what goes on here, and must say and say again that it is as unbearable as the fate of the Hungarians.

We shall always misjudge Russian totalitarian policies if we think only in line with the rules of international power politics. The Russians have not abolished these rules; indeed, they have perfected brilliant techniques of their use. But they subject them to an absolute that makes particular political actions incalculable by the rules alone. Only the facts of Russian policy over decades can instruct us. Political argument can go on forever if the simple basic lines of over-all totalitarian policy are not kept in mind all the time.

Totalitarian Russia wants only one kind of world order: world conquest with the goal of total rule as the universal solution. In other words, she wants no world order at all; she is the power which, for the time being, would destroy every Western-inspired world order of free states. She confronts us with a necessity that may be salutary. She makes it impossible for the West to preserve itself unless an act of self-regeneration places it purely and truthfully upon the road that would enable all to have world order in freedom.

Neutrality has more than one meaning. One may hold aloof from conflict so as to remain unaffected. Or one may save one's strength, so that at last, when the others have exhausted themselves, one will retain the superiority of a world arbiter — this was Stalin's dream in 1939. Both types of neutrality belong to the large arsenal of stratagems and tricks and are really no more than temporary expedients.

Neutrality with the serious idea of self-preservation without expansion is quite a different matter. It endangers no one, will not stab even the vanquished in the back, and will resort to force only against incursions upon its own territory. Such neutrality is not an evasion of sacrifice. It makes every effort to arm for defense. It is firmly resolved, in case of need, to die rather than to surrender. But it considers non-violence the proper human condition and wants to establish and maintain it by negotiation and agreement. It thus realizes a specific ethos the concepts of which differ from those of ordinary politics. Its political responsibility is different, for it does not take the world's fate upon its shoulders; its honor is different, for it dispenses with the prestige and the accompanying pride of power; its sovereignty is different, for it wants not to rule but to be free, even in its own community; and its diplomacy is different, for it wants to negotiate openly, not on the sly. This neutrality is an essentially unhistorical moral-political attitude. The question is how, and under what conditions, it appears in history.

If a small state with the will to self-preservation comes into conflict with great powers, it perceives its impotence in world politics. It withdraws upon itself and develops an ethos that will enable it to preserve itself in its smallness. Neutrality was first a premise of maintaining political liberty; the ethos of neutrality on principle was stimulated but not engendered by this necessity.

This type of neutrality is possible only in a nation such as Switzerland, where national freedom is earned together with the freedom of each individual and constantly reinforced in ceaseless perils. For neutrality is worth the sacrifice only so long as the individual earns his own freedom through the freedom of the state. The fact that the utmost individual liberty prevails in small countries is not a free gift but the result of a trustworthy joint spirit of sacrifice. This sacrifice is as necessary in free individual self-restraint as in the national self-restraint of a neutrality policy, for the freedom of all entails the danger that in the context of great world-historic movements the neutral nation will split as her people side with opposing powers of their era — in Swiss history, for instance, Catholicism and Protestantism, Austria and France, or Germany and France. The ethos of the state demands that its people never carry such conflict among them to the point of trying to capture the state — possibly with foreign aid — and then to lead it back into large-scale history. The neutrality of free self-preservation can last only as long as both the individual and the community have the power of self-restraint. A free, neutral people trusts in constant self-education.

It is the strength of this self-education that the freely chosen moderation of the individuals is superior to ideological passions. If the community is based on freedom, the compelling institution as such cannot be the court of last resort in each instance. Here the slogan, "Anything but civil war!" which prevails in organized power states is not absolutely valid. To the power state, civil war is fatal and therefore prevented by force and ideological terror; for the free neutral state it remains a possibility—a terrible danger, but allowed for just the same, since freedom itself would otherwise be threatened. If the small self-governing communities are left so much freedom that—in education, for example, or in religious organization—its arbitrary use might thwart the spirit of the whole, and if the outsider, pointing to this as an absurdity of freedom, asks what would happen then, he is told, "Well, then there will be civil war."

It remains a last resort if the state as a whole rests on ideological freedom, and if ever it is resorted to the community spirit will still be maintained from the ingrained ethos. Civil wars have been the cruelest of all only in unfree countries such as Spain—or among nations that had not yet achieved their inner spiritual freedom but remained tied to ideological absolutes in politics, to moral disparagement of the opponent, and to crusading moods in battle, as America during her Civil War. But an inwardly free people wages civil war from the outset with the goal of peace.

Moral-political neutrality, as opposed to neutrality chosen as a mere temporary expedient, must grow and prove itself historically. Its bearer is a people that has grown along with it, not a paragraph in an international agreement. Only a neutrality that has thus grown and become substantial, so to speak, can command the confidence of other powers. It cannot suddenly be reasoned out and introduced as a state principle.

There are strengths and weaknesses in neutrality. The small neutral state grants its individual citizens the greatest freedom, but the material advantages of neutrality may tempt them into a smug life of trade and profit. The spirit of sacrifice may be lost in philistinism. Insight into the abysses of political action may be obscured by the self-satisfied belief in a possible harmony and universal propriety if only people were like oneself.

These aberrations are not the essence of such neutrality. Its true essence is a high-minded seriousness corresponding to a great power's knowledge of its responsibility for the course of history—a sense of being responsible, by virtue of individual freedom, for the example of self-sacrificing courage, for the unaggressive will to stand on one s own small but fully committed strength, to perish rather than to submit, and in any case to remain a beacon of freedom. And corresponding to the responsibility of the great powers is yet another one of neutrality: to serve humanity by maintaining a place where combatants can meet and talk in the midst of combat; to keep non-violent humanity visible and pure; to make as many sacrifices to the idea of help as the combatants make to the idea of struggle.

Political neutrality must not be confused with neutralism. Political neutrality is related to violent conflict and rests on a moral resolution, while neutralism makes allowances for everything, holds aloof, and results from noncommittal, aesthetic watching. Political neutrality, therefore, does not extend to individual judgment. Since it can only be strong in union with its ethos, it would be lost if its bearers were to become neutralists. For neutralism is a softening of character; but within the neutral state — which presupposes resolute, not neutralist citizens — all possibilities of our human world are being fought out in intellectual struggle.

There is much talk in the world today about a neutrality that should not let itself be drawn into the antithesis of freedom and totalitarianism as an antithesis of America and Russia. On the one hand, one would like to escape from the disaster of a future world war; on the other, to obtain present advantages from a neutral position. An example is the seesaw politics of Tito. He would like to avoid ties with either side. He would like to be courted by both, to accept gifts in freedom. He would like, as a tiny power, to play the great ones against each other. Though he has succeeded for a while, there is a time limit to such neutrality. When neither great power will trust him any longer, he will have to choose between adapting his own, not really totalitarian, party despotism to the Russian pattern — in which he would be wiped out — or converting it into the way of free democratic forms envisioned by some of his former close associates who are now in prison, thus making Yugoslavia a weak but safe member of the West.

The large remainder of the world is either aware of, and in accord with, Western policy — as Japan; or a timelessly and vaguely brooding mass — as India; or a multitude of nations in ferment, knowing only what they do not want. In the long run, they cannot preserve their neutrality. Their interests are more or less closely bound up with the great powers. They are a pliable but explosive mass. Only insofar as they express a state of real freedom among their peoples, in viable forms, will they be able to participate in an as yet unconstituted league of nations which the West would have to form.

The idea of neutrality plays its confusing role for Germany, for a Central European zone, or for all Europe. The crucial point is that in the present world situation, as in all past history, the homegrown neutrality we were discussing, which goes beyond mere political skill, is the exclusive privilege of very small states. They alone, because they are tiny, can be relieved of the responsibility for the violent course of history and thus fulfil the positive sense of neutrality.

Today we think at times of a united Europe that would be strong enough for self-preservation and able to stay neutral in a Russo-American conflict. In manpower and industrial potential it might have that chance if England were included. The premise, however, would be adequate rearmament — a sacrifice that could not be less than that of the two great powers and might have to be greater. But Europe wants her high standards of living, her leisure, her present good life; she fails to do freely what Russia can do by compulsion. Nor does she possess the raw materials and immensely developed industries of America.

Even if Europe did everything in her power, if she buried all her old rivalries and cast off her dominant relics of the past, this would be splendid, but only to enhance her value as America's ally. European neutrality would still be irresponsible; it would prevent the self-preservation of the West, which will endure only as a whole, not in parts. If totalitarianism should attack America, Europe could not stay neutral without grave danger to herself. Only in the event that, in the future, an aggressive will to world conquest or a restless impatience at the presence of totalitarianism should come to the fore in America, might the threat of European neutrality have a braking effect on Europe's sole and indispensable friend — and even then she could not stay neutral in fact. For, if America were militarily destroyed, Europe would follow.

In one single contingency — if America herself should succumb to such totalitarian tendencies as the free world was shocked to perceive in the success, however fleeting, of McCarthy — Europe would have the task of risking the self-preservation of Western freedom alone, at any cost, defying every danger. Her friends would then be all those who have achieved freedom at home. No one can tell who they might be, whether Far Easterners, Indians, or Negroes. What would count then would be neither race nor national origin nor religion — nothing would count but freedom.

The turn of our era from European to global existence has consequences for the meaning of political neutrality. In the European framework, wars took place between members of a common civilization with an underlying biblical religion. They respected each other and fought with an eye to the peace to come in a basically unchanged world. Mankind at large was not in danger, so there was no need to take sides. A nation that did not wish to expand could be recognized as neutral. Thus the homegrown neutrality of Switzerland was subsequently confirmed and guaranteed by the European powers.

Today the situation has changed. First, World War II was viewed as a crime from the start; it broke the barriers that had made it possible to respect a guaranteed neutrality. Second, it was no longer a European war, as World War I had been in the beginning. Its import, from the outset, was that of a world war arraying the free world and totalitarian Russia against totalitarian Germany. This world war taught us what we may expect in the future: if the aggressor is totalitarian and thus a traitor to the spirit of Europe and the West, if he stands for a political principle that would destroy the freedom of all mankind, neutrality can no longer retain its old meaning. It cannot be guaranteed by both sides, as before. To the totalitarian side it is irrelevant, to be disregarded at will, depending on the situation — it was purely on grounds of expediency that Hitler, who overran Holland, Belgium, Denmark, and Norway, left Switzerland untouched, and he wavered more than once in this decision. Neutrality means the self-preservation of freedom, and the mere existence of such a political condition irritates totalitarianism: it ought not to exist. The free side, on the other hand, feels as if the neutral were placing himself outside the interests of mankind, for today's world wars are not waged in a ring inclosed by common attitudes, but as wars of extermination. Mankind has split into principles of government more irreconcilable than absolutism and democracy had been in recent centuries.

The question arises: Can political neutrality still be maintained if the alternative between freedom and totalitarianism overshadows all political events and decisions? Will the meaning of neutrality change? At best, it is tolerated by both combatants as an uncomfortable fact, but not really recognized. Hence neutrality is at a disadvantage. The victor, even if he does not destroy the neutral state, will not respect it and may make it pay for its neutrality. Discomfiting the world, neutrality loses its self-assurance.

Yet in this difficult position neutrality still has its old justifications — before itself as a humane order and, before others, by being there to help. The neutral state proves useful to the great powers, although they frown upon its conduct in the catastrophe. If states break relations, it can represent the interests of their citizens in diplomacy. It can assume functions of control, of protection, even of policing, which the combatants will only intrust to a neutral. It provides a meeting place for mortal enemies who still wish to talk to each other.

But this is no longer enough. In our time of transition before the doom of all, neutrality can perhaps signify a new high task in the interest of all. A neutral state might come to symbolize the possibility of peace for all. Maintained today, in an environment that denies it, the historically grounded and proven neutrality of a small nation might have a justified assurance: There shall be a memento amid the disintegration of mankind! If this can be raised, a ray of hope will be left in the world, encouraging all by the mere fact that there still are such people.

The sacrifice that lends neutrality its strength is made by arming for defense. It consists in the readiness to fight so that even a great power would find an attack on it no trifling matter. Whoever dares to snap at this armored neutral being must risk his own teeth. If the great powers believe in the neutral people's readiness to stake lives and fortunes, they will find it harder to attack. In a world war, to be sure, the neutral nation would perish by the consequences of the atom bomb, along with everyone else, for radioactivity respects no borders. If all mankind should be sacrificed, the neutral would die with it.

The neutral state represents the never entirely dormant minimum of universal humanity, a minimum which, if it reawakens in the combatants, must find a place for recognition and encouragement in an atmosphere of peace and freedom. It is essential that even amidst a crusade, where everything seems at stake, there should remain a place, however infinitesimal, where men are seen as human beings, not as specimens of either totalitarianism or certain forms of supposedly perfect freedom. That would be extraordinary and may be all but impossible to achieve; but it is a lofty idea that says: We cannot bear mankind to split into two fighting monsters.

There is no telling whether the existence of neutral freedom is at times not only so useful to others that all favor it but also a magnet for human sympathies from all sides. It can have this effect only if the conduct of the neutral state and its people is impressive enough to arouse admiration and love; and this, in reality, can be done only in the great, inspiring train of the new political task. Since the world has been parceled out, since there are no more distant lands and wars of conquest must lead to extermination, an understanding of the new situation has become vital. What used to be done cannot be done any more.

Our task in this situation resembles the change in the political volition of the smaller nations when they perceived their inability to go on as before — as the Swiss did after the battle of Marignano, and the Swedes after the failure of Charles XII. The source of that earlier neutrality — the perception of a limit — might be repeated and become a source of political volition for all nations. The ethos of true neutrality, which in small nations is realized even in their way of life and in the individual citizen's sense of existence, could point a way to world order, and self-restraint, the element of the small nations' neutrality, would become universal — for once an attempt at world conquest results in the doom of mankind, the great powers are in the same position as the small ones were at the time when their attempts to engage in world politics had to bring about their own destruction.

Yet this idea can be realized only if all great powers are agreed on it; otherwise the great ones, who dispose of power, will remain responsible for the course of the world. If they unanimously chose self-restraint, fundamentally and permanently as the small neutrals once did, all would become "neutral" and wars would cease. As long as this has not happened, the small neutral nation anticipatorily represents the idea to the extent to which it realizes it in fact, in its small realm.

What is to happen now? What can happen?

No program can outline the requisites of the idea of peace — synonymous today with the survival of mankind. No one has a position of world leadership. The nations, through their representatives, will act on the basis of their diverse origins and situations. There are material and moral motives involved, blind selfishness and self-sacrificing courage, trends of force and trends of co-operation. The greatest power cannot control events, and yet each one, and every individual, exerts some influence.

The great question is whether and what chances still exist today, under the threat of total doom, despite all reasons to the contrary. In the following, we will discuss two opposite possibilities of the contemporary situation: first, the attempt to achieve world peace through the United Nations and, second, the alternative that may face us in the future, of choosing between the surrender of freedom to totalitarianism and the defense of freedom at the risk of total doom, of a self-sacrifice of mankind.

If the result of this discussion will seem oppressive at first, it must all the more emphatically raise the question of a new politics. Could there be a new level of thought, different from all past ways of thinking? If there is no compromise between total rule and freedom, the pressure of the world situation may yet work a change in the nations that live under these principles but amount to more than principles. If all will be doomed by an ideological war, it may be possible to see man as more than a bearer of ideologies. The West may see that, far from realizing the common human will to freedom, it has widely perverted it. The East may recall what it has given up; it may see that the principle has turned out quite differently from the first impulses of its revolution and has led it up a blind alley. East and West may change. In both, human beings may be made more human than ever by experience and insight, by the will to change that is needed in both worlds, in which both may meet.

9

THE
UNITED
NATIONS

The principles laid down in the Preamble of the United Nations Charter are magnificent. Now, one would think, peace must really begin. A state of mind is expressed there: faith in fundamental human rights, in the dignity and worth of the human person, in the equal right of men and women and of nations large and small. Justice is mentioned, respect for the obligations arising from treaties, the will to practice tolerance and live together in peace, as good neighbors. The aim of the charter is to save succeeding generations from the scourge of war — first, by the acceptance of these principles and, second, by the institution of methods precluding the use of armed force, save in the common interest.

Disappointment sets in with further study of the charter and increases with an examination of the reality of the organization created thus far. It culminates in the insight that the principle of falsehood, which has been the essence and the evil of all past politics, has come to prevail more ruthlessly than ever.

The charter talks more about recommendations than about actions of the UN, and the upshot of its procedure is an inability to reach decisions affecting the interests of one of the great powers. That a Security Council resolution requires seven out of eleven votes sounds all right, but then we read that among the seven must be the concurring votes of the five permanent members — China, France, Russia, Great Britain, and the United States. In other words, these five states, and they alone, have the power of veto. Apart from this, the organization is based on the "sovereign equality of all its members," meaning that the numerous obligations expressed in the charter shall not abrogate the sovereignty of any state. It is up to each state to decide whether and when the obligations apply to it.

To proceed from recommendations to actions, we find if we read on, that provision is made, first, for sanctions not involving the use of armed force, then for demonstrations by armed forces, and finally for "other operations" by such forces. Yet none of these actions can be carried out by the United Nations directly, only by such member states as the UN may call upon to do so. The actual decision rests with these, not with the UN, unmasking the fiction that right, legally recognized by an established institution, exists in the absence of executive power. For although the member states are obliged under the charter to make armed forces available to the Security Council, on its call, their compliance still depends on their good will. It cannot be commanded and compelled. But it is obvious that force condemned by the UN cannot be countered by a right that does not dispose of force superior to all other force.

A further weakness, compounded with dishonesty, lies in the express refusal to authorize the United Nations "to intervene in matters which are essentially within the domestic jurisdiction of any state." Members are not obliged to submit such matters to the principles of the charter. But how does this jibe with the other provision that limits membership to states which are able and willing to recognize these principles? Only states that recognize the principles of the charter, not for a moment and in words only, but in practice and in constant ways of thought and argument, could live in peace with one another on that basis.

A complete change in the spirit of the language occurs as the charter moves from principles to institutions. They are numerous, complicated, full of reservations. They seem to be set up so as to cripple themselves by their own activity.

There are arguments against this disappointment in studying the charter. The UN is not a legal but a political institution; only within its organization it has established, among other things, a court for the decision of legal issues. The charter expressly distinguishes "legal disputes," which should be referred to the International Court of Justice, from political questions. But these, too, are to be settled by the UN without using force. The explicit purpose of the institution is "to take effective collective measures for the suppression of acts of aggression or other breaches of the peace, and to bring about by peaceful means, and in conformity with the principles of justice and international law, adjustment or settlement of international disputes." How? The charter states that parties to any dispute "shall, first of all, seek a solution by negotiation, inquiry, mediation, conciliation, arbitration." But then it envisions the means of using force against force by calling on the members, as if this conveyed upon the UN itself the power of enforcing its decisions.

On the whole, then, is this a legal or a political process? Either the majority vote of the international community, taken after hearing and weighing questions in the scales of justice, is really meant to be a legal decision, or else there are negotiations leading to a compromise on which the parties agree, as has always been done when political questions were not regarded as vital, or when it seemed opportune to put off the use of force. For such a compromise one would need only the interested parties, not a full body of eighty sovereign states. Obviously, however, more is wanted than the political settlement of conflicts by a deal among the interested parties — though less than a legal process for the peaceful resolution of disputes. Politics is, on the one hand, to become a legal process that eliminates force from its arsenal; on the other hand, it cannot become such a process, since sovereignty and the veto stand in the way. What does this ambiguity, this illusory vagueness at the bottom of the institution, accomplish in fact?

Let us review what the past decade has shown.

Executive power depends, not on the United Nations, but solely on the policies of the sovereign powers. The UN presses for decisions on legal grounds, to exclude war. It seeks executive power to enforce its decisions. But there can be neither sanctions nor military intervention unless UN resolutions happen to coincide with the sovereign decisions of the great powers — as in the Suez case, for example, with America's and Russia's.

A UN police force made up of contingents from individual states does not provide the UN with executive power. Each contingent actually remains under the orders of its state and can be recalled at any time. It serves the UN only so long as its state desires. Such a force has no combat strength; it is a mere symbol of UN presence. Resistance to it might have consequences in the judgment of world opinion — the part that happens to agree with the UN in a particular case — or it might persuade a great power to put its full force behind the UN. The situation has not yet been put to the test, and UN forces, therefore, are now largely but not wholly delusive.

Resolutions of the United Nations are not carried out. The resolution
against Egyptian interference with Israel's use of the Suez Canal was
ignored by Egypt and not enforced by the UN. The resolution for a
British and French cease-fire and troop withdrawal was obeyed — chron-
ologically, at least — only after Russia's threat to drop atom bombs on
Paris and London and send "volunteers" to Egypt. If the UN does seem
to act, on the other hand, it is not really the UN that is acting. When
America came to the aid of the South Koreans, it was America's will
which the UN legalized (being enabled to do so by a Russian walkout)
and embroidered with small, militarily insignificant units from other
states.

*States that disagree with the aims of the United Nations use it in
behalf of their own policies.* For those who neither wish nor expect any
of the UN's grandly proclaimed aims to succeed, the institution has become a deceptive instrument, consciously used to serve their own political ends. The UN provides them with an opportunity to talk and obtain
information, and with a sounding board for propaganda. They do not
really care for its opinion, but they use it more or less deliberately, more
or less skilfully, more or less unscrupulously as a tool of old-line power
politics. Yet they seek and find this detour only because the legal vindication of their actions before world opinion — the traditional content of
political public pronouncements — does not strike them as a matter of
indifference.

The atmosphere is one of propaganda, not of law. In its principles,
the UN is a manifestation of respect for law. It shows that there is a con
sciousness of law in the world and a demand for justice; that men regard
it as not altogether futile to pay homage to the right. Leaders want to
make their cause convincing, as legally well founded. They want to put
their opponents in the wrong and to justify themselves before their own
people and before world opinion.

But what is thus being played with the moral concept of right is a
tricky game. One deceives one's own people and the world in order to
dupe the representatives of opposing powers. Actual events in the UN
show that its principle of replacing force with law is not only narrowed
but abandoned, save as an illusion to satisfy men's cry for justice.

Public opinion itself has power only in free, legally governed countries. The totalitarian or despotic or predominantly illiterate ones care
little about world opinion, but they do care about public opinion in the
free ones. Thus the UN is used as a means of weakening the free coun-

tries — for, unlike them, the rest of the world knows no spontaneous opinion arising from the motives of freedom and justice that unite all men. We have seen this in the lack of a reaction to the infinitely violent and utterly ruthless injustice perpetrated by the Russians against the Hungarian people. Chou En-lai, speaking in Moscow, in Poland, and in Hungary itself, demonstratively espoused the Russian cause as just; Nehru edged away from it only very late and hesitantly, getting his reward when Russia vetoed a Security Council resolution on Kashmir that was unfavorable to Nehru.

Since the UN does no more than play politics with the concept of law, the concept is discredited. A cynical mood develops, an awareness of swindling all around. Uncomfortable facts are shamelessly swept under the rug; uncomfortable questions meet with silence. Unfavorable facts and reasons are not even listened to, and weighed only for their usefulness to one's political ends. In UN organs, each member feels bound exclusively by the political directives of his state. UN debates lack the earnestness in which men approach inquiries supposed to find the right in disinterested objectivity — although now and then this is achieved by committees such as the one that produced the magnificent UN report on Hungary, a year after the event. As a rule, the proceedings are governed by brazen falsehood, or by more refined legal sophistry.

A lawyer can use his legal mind in two ways: he can be a moral personality working for justice, out of a firm sense of right and with the power of his intellect, the keenness of his conceptual definitions, and the clarity of his constructions; or he can become a sophist who uses the same, now formalized methods and intellectual constructions so as to deceive. The second type is unprincipled, at the service of changing employers and powers. As a matter of course, he will serve interests which he does not examine and does not really care about. He represents them with all the arguments he can find, with redefinitions and suggestive distinctions that veil the true state of affairs, with shifting interpretations, and finally with an appeal to sentiment as a mendacious substitute for the clear, sober sense of right. He can turn right into wrong and wrong into right, "make the worse appear the better reason" and vice versa.

Until now, in the UN, we have seen more of the second than of the first type of lawyer. The legal penetration of human relations, which is the high achievement of jurists, is also the ground on which the achievement may be sacrificed to sophistical fraud. It is the transfer of politics to the realm that should surmount politics. The political lawyer is the dominant figure in a UN activity by which the world would like to be befogged, to find peace of mind in reliance on a rule of law. True, it keeps being shocked when the lie becomes apparent, but it is always ready to forget again and to believe that somehow justice must be underneath it all.

The United Nations is thwarted by injustice — by the injustice it adopts as well as by the injustice it fails to resist in the world. The charter limits membership to states that, in the judgment of the organization, are able and willing to carry out its obligations. But there are voting UN members whose populations are largely illiterate, in whose territory the slave trade flourishes and human rights are trampled underfoot. The UN includes states that are not even independent — such as the Ukraine — but it does not include Communist China with her six hundred million inhabitants. Russia and other totalitarian members are actually built upon principles contradicting those of the charter. From the outset, the UN was set up so that America and Russia with their basically different concepts of law might get along as if they agreed on these concepts.

Thus the formal equality of UN membership covers the most diverse and, in the sense of the charter, dubious states. It is evident that neither at the time of founding nor in the new admissions in subsequent years were the qualifications judged in the light of actual circumstances and by the standards of the charter. From the outset, a policy indifferent to the right prevailed in the choice of members — a choice made in line with political conditions, not with the principles of the charter.

One result is that some vote invariably for the Russian position, while others vote, not so reliably, for the American one. Free, independent judgment is rare. The claim of equal rights for nations large and small is unmasked in practice.

The dominance of political rather than legal concepts leads to glaring contradictions. America will not have Communist China admitted to the UN, because China's Communist constitution was established illegally, by force, and the Formosan remnant of the old China continues only under American protection. In the Near East, however, America wants to recognize violent domestic upheavals as accomplished facts — a distinction that can be justified only politically, not by any legal concept.

Nor can the UN, which absorbs so much wrong into its own thoughts and actions, prevent the wrong that is happening in the world. It is a general condition of human order that if both international and domestic relations are to be placed on a basis of law, the measure of remaining wrongs must not exceed certain limits. If it exceeds them, the injured will resort to force, because legality, as applied to themselves, is obviously nothing but a form of fatal, lawless force. Then the road is opened for self-sacrificing rebellion on behalf of truth and justice, but at the same time, inseparably, for arbitrary action and a lust in violence. Abused, the right arouses force — which is indeed always wrong but stems now from a source that wants the right, and at the same time from a source that wants rather to replace the right with its own force. The UN has not altered this fundamental condition, which is the cause of wars. It has not come to uphold the world's existing legal orders; it cannot restrain its injustices. Anyone crushed by injustice and calling for justice will knock in vain at the doors of the UN; he can succeed only if his claim is backed by the interests of great powers.

The authority of the United Nations serves as a means of evading responsibility. The powers clothe it with authority for their political manipulations, but it has no genuine authority.

America sees the free world in all sorts of trouble, with free nations — though not herself as yet — suffering treaties to be broken on a grand scale or being fatally threatened by their neighbors. America, whose power makes her responsible for the free world before history, reacts in one of two ways: by appealing to the UN or by reserving the use of force.

First — because action seems too risky, or undesirable from the point of view of domestic or foreign policy — she may do nothing and dodge the responsibility for action against deadly wrong by interposing the impotent UN. She may appeal to higher authority, utilizing the already conventional illusion that such an authority without executive power could remove force from the world without resorting to force. But the real responsibility before history belongs to him who has the power and can dispose of force — not to an unreal, utterly dependent, constantly manipulated authority.

Decision and daring are dodged with a gesture of lofty legality. Inaction is justified as obedience to the legality of a mock tribunal. The things whose prevention real justice demands are thus allowed to happen.

Why do statesmen and nations refuse to live up to the historic responsibility which is theirs by virtue of their power? There has been a desire for rest in the Western world since 1919, a will to enjoy prosperity.

We do not want to know what we know only too well. Nations keep fooling themselves, screening the real horizon with stage props they want to believe in, to grasp a bliss that is already consumed in the rush of acquisition and pleasure. Thus, in 1919, they believed in the peace and the reparations of Versailles. Thus, again and again, they clung to paper securities and coercive treaties. Step by step, they let happen what was bound to lead to disaster if it was not promptly recognized and fought with the courage of sacrifice: Manchuria, Ethiopia, the Rhineland, Hitler's rearmament. They compromised, not wanting even a small, virtually riskless war. They wanted no arms burden. When things looked dangerous, they gave in — all the way to Munich. They yielded to blackmail, unwilling to face the possible alternative of war; they would have no alternative. It is the same now, with one difference: now there are atom bombs. The evasion of responsibility is unchanged.

America's second reaction is to reserve the use of force in case she considers her own interests directly affected. The decisive moment uncovers the fact that human existence is ultimately based on force — proving at the same time that the shift of responsibility to the UN was not meant seriously, either. Indeed, no responsibility is ever met by clinging to abstract principles and unreal authorities, only by accepting historic reality.

One allows wrong to be done as long as one does not feel threatened. One remains shortsighted in the face of evil that must ultimately turn against oneself. One will not use one's judgment to see in the bud what will, matured, become the most montrous peril.

One straw we cling to is the concept of "aggression." The League of Nations used it in the past, and today it is again the criterion of the violence against which the UN shall act to preserve world peace. But endless discussions have not yet brought forth a useful definition of aggression.

The most likely source of such a magic formula seems to be territorial inviolability, as in defining an aggressor state as "the first to engage in military, naval, or air operations outside its own borders." It has been suggested that this concept, if incorporated into the United Nations Charter, would actually end all force. The UN itself would only have to decide without resorting to force, especially if the peace protestations of all states were taken at face value and used to make all agree that members of the armed forces of any state committing aggression, as defined, would no longer be bound by their soldier's oath.

Now let us examine what the effect of introducing the concept would be at this time.

First, the precise definition of aggression would have the hoped-for significance only if there were an authority that could be trusted to apply it in every case, and we have learned that there is no such authority. Whenever the UN has operated with the concept, it has done so in partisan fashion. To counter our wishful thinking, we cannot too often recall the events of October and November, 1956 — when Russia and Israel alike were classified as aggressors, and when Nehru outdid everyone in righteous indignation, only to have Krishna Menon tell the UN with regard to the Kashmir question, on February 21, 1957: "My government feels bound only by resolutions in which it has concurred." By creating twofold, manifold justice, the UN repeals all justice.

Second, the limitation of the concept of force to the act of border-crossing raises another question: Is it not aggressive force if a state, on its own territory, sends its police into a business office and expropriates the business? Does it matter whether it does so to its own citizens or to foreigners carrying on their business under a treaty? Or does aggression start only when this lawless domestic police action is met by military action — which in turn, in the nature of things, will call itself "police action"? It has been claimed that localized force is not aggressive, that atrocities, terror, violations of foreign rights within territories recognized as sovereign do not affect world peace. What a mistake! It means to permit the growth on foreign territory — as in Hitler's Germany or Nasser's Egypt — of realities and attitudes bound to lead some day to external aggression. By restricting our own use of force we would breed another, threatening force, protecting its borders until it was ready to cross them.

Third, what constitutes a territorial violation by force? Is it not such a violation if a state masses troops and piles up war materials at the border, stating at the same time that the neighbor state has no right to exist and must disappear? Is there no violation when the border is constantly crossed by bands of murderers and saboteurs — only when larger bodies of troops go into action? How large a number of troops must be involved to turn a border incident into aggression? Is it not aggression against another country to interfere with its commerce by a state-directed boycott or by forcibly keeping its ships out of international waterways? Is it aggression or self-defense if a small state that is thus menaced, injured, obviously facing attack by massed armed forces, breaks out of its encirclement at the last moment? Is it aggression if it seeks to avoid destruction, especially after years of experience have shown that neither the UN nor anyone else will protect it?

Fourth, to apply the concept of aggression, territorial boundaries would have to be free from doubt. Are these boundaries to be drawn by *de facto* power — as by the presence of Russian troops in Hungary, or of Indian troops in Kashmir — or only by the independent will of the people who inhabit these small areas? Are the so-called armistice lines territorial boundaries — even if, as in the Egyptian-held Gaza strip, the occupied area has never belonged to the occupying power? Does East Germany belong to Russia? Do the satellite states? Is intervention uncalled for if Russia slaughters the Hungarian people — as previously the Lithuanians, Estonians, and so on — using some natives as puppets and deporting and enslaving others? Is this simply a domestic affair of the totalitarian Russian complex of states? Does such monstrously wrong violence not affect world peace? How shall we draw the lines whose crossing would be aggression?

Fifth, we cannot assume that a clear definition of aggression would, as claimed, result in unanimity about a particular case. In recent wars, we are told, there could be no doubt who was the aggressor according to the definition: Mussolini in Ethiopia, Hitler in all of his wars, Japan at Pearl Harbor, and the North Koreans at the 38th Parallel in June, 1950. This is certainly true — but in none of these cases did the aggressor plead guilty. Each time, it was only the others who called his act aggression. All aggressors operate "in self-defense," and Russia, China, and North Korea maintain to this day that the North Korean attack in 1950 was a defensive measure.

The basic mistake is to think that the reality of force can be removed from the world by hypostatizing a concept, such as "aggression." Such concepts can be made to serve practical action; they cannot guide it. No rational apparatus can replace the ethos of the acting human beings. We cannot build upon empty abstractions what can emerge only from the reality of mankind.

Untruth is unbearable to human beings. They want truth even when they betray it. This is why we claim to tell the truth even when we are lying.

Lying to gain advantages is conscious and no mean "achievement." To succeed, it requires, first, a masterly application of the principle that what counts is not whether a thing is true but whether it seems to be true and, second, in the face of contradictory realities, an inventive presence of mind to maintain the lie. Much more frequent, therefore, is untruth that involves self-deception along with the deception of others. A man is then not only lying but lying to himself, because he stops trying to distinguish between truth and falsehood. He talks himself into something and out of it; he is not lying in the clear knowledge of truth, but in a state of untruthfulness. He hides from himself what he does not want to see. But this kind of liar lives in unreal notions; if he is suddenly faced with a reality that refutes his notions, he may be unable to evade it for the moment, but he will promptly forget it and lapse into a new, untruthful version of his concrete lie.

Let us apply this to politics. Any struggle by force demands cunning, deception, surprise. Therefore, as long as politics is carried on with a view to possible force and not transformed into a legal process, falsehood will be a political principle.

The political way of life is "diplomacy." Behind it stands the defiant self-assertion of any existence equipped with the necessary power. Existence also asserts itself in villainy, in hating what is better and despising what is worse, in demanding, first equality, then domination.

But the forms of diplomacy are manifold. It is played, by silent agreement, according to rules that hide the vulgar reality. Under a code of honor, mutual consideration is shown in the pursuit of silently acknowledged self-interest, served with maximum skill. The social forms of courtesy, cordiality, and familiarity conceal the potentially violent struggle behind each word. One argues, persuades, refers to truth and to jointly recognized laws, but in so doing one uses the methods of sophistry and does not hear the crux of the matter if it speaks against one. One diverts attention like a cardsharp. One changes the subject, unnoticeably misinterprets words, defends positions that are not under attack at all. The purpose of language is not simply to say what one thinks and wants; it is also to conceal both in a mixture of what is said in candor and in seeming candor.

The diplomatic methods of totalitarianism, Hitlerism as well as Stalinism, are mere variants of the same. They deceived, at first, by debunking the elegant rules of the old diplomatic game, and thus achieved a temporary superiority. In fact, they only did more bluntly and unscrupulously what had always been done. They chose methods fit for a mass society, after the aristocracy of birth and culture had vanished. They moved from the veiled lie, employed among people with a common spirit, to the patent lie. They took the step from the lie controlled by rules of the game, from the conditional and accordingly restricted lie, to the uninhibited, masterly, total lie. And they worked out the theory of this lie: simple slogans — or the masses cannot be won! The crudest, most transparent lie is the most effective; it will be most easily believed! Thoughts that become thoughtless devices will stick in the mind, if only they are constantly repeated!

But one thing is remarkable and encouraging: in all instances, even here, the lie operates with the truth. It wants to seem true. It bears further witness to the fact that man, in contrast to his actual conduct, wants the truth.

Of this new form of political falsehood under total rule we can say, first, that the simplicity of the slogans that are hammered home and have demagogic success is not the simplicity of symbols imprinted in a way of life. Consequently, when a totalitarian state breaks down, there is suddenly nothing left, and the masses are a helpless sand pile. The failure of a power in which people were living with real symbols leaves these people behind as creatures of an encompassing primal will — a will that is incradicably present as long as they live and can become the source of new growth in a communion of faith.

Second, in totalitarianism, all of the talking and lying is merely superficial, a device to soften up opponents and to hone adherents into a fine edge of mechanical thought. Behind this stands the true reality, the organization of men into vigorous striking forces. A state within the state sets itself to take over the old state. The open propaganda that is allowed in the free world is used to strengthen this movement in disciplined organizations. The propaganda can melt people down, so to speak; the organization can prepare them for the planned acts of violence and use the existing cadres for the prompt establishment of total rule over the entire population.

Third, totalitarianism's conscious and unlimited lying is superior in striking power to the dissembling, partly self-deceptive dishonesty found in the free world. The free world will be weak until it achieves full truthfulness according to its own principle. Real truth would make it superior, for the unscrupulous lies of the totalitarians must eventually entangle them in their own notions. Then total rule will become blind to the very realities of freedom, which its own theories — needed in its realm as whetstones for the public jargon — block off from it like stage props.

Lying is no easily removable fault. Exposure will not do away with it, for untruthfulness lies at the root of humanity. "The lie — from the Father of Lies, who brought all evil into the world — is the real rotten spot in human nature," said Kant. It can only be conquered by constantly turning back to the truth. The free world will survive only if it does so decisively, and if every individual repeats it day after day. Truth and freedom go together as much as falsehood and force. Veracity alone can unite the free world; it is lost without veracity, for freedom and falsehood are mutually exclusive. The free world, which alone can achieve peace, must give up its futile efforts to fight lies with lies. Every untruthful act is a step toward totalitarianism.

Getting back to the United Nations, we note a fatal ambiguity in the very origin of the charter. The UN wants to banish force as a tool of politics, but it must depend on the military power of the member states which are to enforce UN verdicts when all other means have failed. The new politics is to be played on a stage of law, which alone disposes of force — but in fact, this force is not at the disposal of the law but remains at the beck and call of many sovereign states. War is supposed to become a police action serving the law, but it remains war all the same.

In practice, this ambiguity reverses the principles of the charter. They are not only abused but used mendaciously. What happens is what has always happened: negotiation, attempts at understanding and compromise on the one hand and, on the other, pressures of self-interest at the risk of using force. Legal process would presuppose that force will not be used under any circumstances and that the judgment of constituted judicial authority will be accepted. Open negotiations would presuppose that a compromise is wanted under all circumstances, that both sides are ready to yield and refuse to admit that questions of vital interest may be insoluble. Neither premise exists; the will of the sovereign states has precedence in fact, and the UN turns into a mere element of the negotiating game that begins outside the organization, extends to it, and always has to do with possible force. The UN is not what it claims to be. It represents a basic untruth.

This untruth would probably be seen more clearly if we knew just how the charter was drawn up. It seems to have been essentially a game between America and Russia. Neither great power wanted to give up any of its sovereignty, though both deemed the project useful. From the start, the will to world peace — which on each side included an expectation of peaceful world conquest by its own political principles — was shot through with concrete political tendencies. The American drafters had to phrase the charter so as to avoid another rejection by Congress, like Wilson's failure with the League of Nations; the Russians had to phrase it so as not to be caught in the principles of the charter, diametrically opposed to their own. On both sides, though from different motives, there were coinciding tendencies to frame a charter whose limitations and reservations and exceptions would exclude a genuine alliance, a charter whose wording would always leave a way open for the opposite argument. The charter resulted neither from a single mind's conception of a comprehensive, logically clear, and consistent structure nor from any unanimous good will. Its ambiguities veil an original incompatibility of aims.

Viewed as a whole, the UN resembles a stage on which an incidental interlude is presented between the great powers' real actions. It is the sham communication in which they hide their purposes by placing themselves among some eighty major and minor states and recognizing the equality of all. The states use this stage to put on a façade for public opinion and to outwit their antagonists. It is a game, a screen behind which each does as he pleases if he has the power and the chance. The votes that are taken after endless speech-making have consequences only for those who see their advantage in them or are small enough to be forced to comply. Thus the UN is a managed organ of the powers, though not always calculably manageable; it is used by them all, though its resolutions can be evaded by almost all but the small ones not protected by a great power. Entirely free from UN compulsion are only the great ones, and those others who might, in practice, be difficult to compel.

At this writing the situation appears as follows: America wants to use the UN to pursue and cover her policies. She always needs a majority for this and must, therefore, woo the others. There are blocs which always vote together, but as neither the Russian nor the American bloc has a majority, the decisions lie with the fluctuating mass of the others — except when Russia and America vote together, as may happen when some luckless country without either power or protection has to foot the bill.

Behind the UN, old-style diplomacy keeps conferring back and forth.

Secret agreements may seem to be reached on matters not to be mentioned in public, and people are quick to talk of deals they will not recognize. During the Suez crisis, for instance, Eisenhower wrote to Ben Gurion that Israel would not regret withdrawing; America, he explained, felt sure that Egypt would not keep Israeli shipping out of the Suez Canal and the Gulf of Aqaba. Israel's statements were more definite: if her ships were attacked in the Gulf of Aqaba, she would feel free to exercise her right of self-defense under Article 51 of the charter—but, said Ben Gurion, the words of the President of the United States meant more to him than treaties. America claimed to have given no moral assurances, while Israel stressed that her withdrawal was made on the strength of such assurances. All these were publicly vague, very general, if not equivocal, statements — reassuring on a basis of friendship, but mere noncommittal pretenses in case of indifference. The Egyptian dictator, meanwhile, did as he pleased; as a Russian puppet, he could count on Russian help in any event.

As long as America views the UN as the principal tool of her own policies, she will be tied to unreason and seem paralyzed. It is a ghostly sight, this so-called world authority operating on the brink of doom with fictions that everyone sees through and yet goes along with. The UN seems on the road to the total lie of its existence.

The question remains whether this kind of soil might yield a new form of political thought and action, with justice done, not only pondered. Criticism such as ours is easy, but it must not let us forget the extraordinary efforts of good will that have been made. Even here, not everything need be a swindle. From the founding act on, we note a will to achieve something that might save peace. It takes the courage and patience of honest statesmanship to hold to this purpose, against the tides of the will to power manifested in the various sovereignties and against suffocating untruthfulness.

We should listen to the active statesmen. After the Suez crisis of 1956, Belgium's Spaak wrote in *Foreign Affairs* that the United Nations, while preventing war up to a point, had not, he feared, fostered justice. He called for charter revision, emphasizing the well-known main points: abolition of the veto; decisions by majority vote; expulsion of offenders against international law; establishment of a UN military striking force; subordination of trivia to essentials in UN resolutions.

But such unequivocally positive proposals must be considered in the light of their immediate effect. The suggested procedure would make the UN a community of free states, with Russia barred. If Russia, in November, 1956, for instance, had been obliged to choose between withdrawal from Hungary and expulsion from the UN, she would in all likelihood have chosen expulsion. The world would have split into two camps, with the UN no longer the same, and a UN army the army of one side only, facing the huge Red Army of the other side. But the UN was set up, after all, to make one world of the powers. However slight, however untruthful, this unity — while it exists, the job is to try to strengthen it and to enhance its truthfulness. Truthfulness includes recognition that a UN without Russia would no longer be the UN, and that without China it will not remain the UN. Can the will to be truthful absorb recognition of untruthfulness?

It could do so only in an effort to see how far this would take us on the road to a better truth. In the UN case: if, to keep the world one, there can be no charter revision without Russo-American agreement, we must expect no reform of practical UN activities without the change in our moral-political consciousness that would lead to the indispensable charter revision. This change might occur at many places on earth, flaring up from tiny sparks. Only then, as a ready framework for the fulfilment of inspiring impulses, could the UN really insure the peace. The readiness of such a framework may have its value.

The UN shows us more than the diplomacy of its members. An organ of mankind, however wretched, appears to mankind. The powerful ideas of peace and world unity are manifested, sham and political falsehood exposed — down to the reality of falsehood in the UN itself. We may ask whether the failure of the present institution and the public, world-wide discussion of the causes of this failure, the arguments driving legality from one-sided abuse toward universal justice, even the wrongs committed by the UN — whether all this might not indirectly contribute to the education of mankind. Some good might be stirred up, if not created, by our unhappy experiences with the UN. What used to remain ineffective individual cerebration has become a public issue and proving ground. Our concern for the great goal might be intensified. It could bring about the change in man.

We may still doubt that the UN can be rebuilt at all. Is it not destined to follow the League of Nations? Did the way of its founding not carry the seed of its decay? Can something conceived in falsehood be put upon the road to truth? It may not be entirely out of the question, for one sole reason: that the initial motives included good will. The true idea had to accept concealment in institutions that almost canceled it out. Almost, but not quite — for the very lie, by disguising itself as truth, paid homage to the truth.

We must not stifle our doubts, our resentments, our indignation — and yet we have to ask ourselves: What is to happen if the UN founders? Another new foundation, with a clear, truthful purpose on the part of all participants? This would mean a fission of the world into two or more blocs, into several UN's instead of the one. Its reconstruction would still be possible only by Russo-American agreement, like that of the original foundation. At this time, a new politics can be made only in the form of this foundation that keeps playing the old politics — but if the form became substance, if it ceased to be a mere form, the predominance of Russia and America, by whose grace the UN exists today, would recede.

Short of achieving its real goal of world peace, the UN might still help to extend the breathing spell of our present peace. There is no telling, of course, whether the interposition of the UN really checks war or merely expresses the fact that no great power wants war at this time. Nor can we tell whether the will to force, once it perceives its opportunity, will not simply ignore the UN as a form without substance. It certainly does not yet give us a trustworthy check on the outbreak of force and total destruction. Still, the UN institution — which is the only one we have — gives us a small chance.

True, the UN would be dangerous to the free world if we shut our eyes to the facts. The free world might cling to the UN and fail to do what needs to be done; it might come to rely upon unreliability. Therefore, the constant exposure of UN failures by the world press must continue. Our affirmation of its existence can be salutary only if we do not fool ourselves about the UN.

To break up the United Nations, as the League of Nations was broken up in its time, would be easy. It will happen if one of the great powers manifests a definitive will to force and deems it expedient to display it; or it may happen if the abstract truthfulness of the free nations turns irresponsible: if they will no longer put up with the constant deception practiced at the UN, without being able to put anything in its place.

Today, the UN cannot be replaced. It can be broken up at any moment by the backstage reality of the hostile great powers and by the illusory nature of its artificial existence — and then, we hear, there will be chaos.

No, there is chaos now. The UN of today is the ambiguous structure that promotes chaos and wants to bring order out of it at the same time.

The UN is more than nothing. There being no chance at the moment of an instantaneous change of heart that would make the powers, large and small, act for peace, the UN, however badly functioning, is a tool to serve peace in unpredictable fashion. For all its senselessness, there is some sense to the UN. It gives rise to grotesque deceptions, yet it does work against these deceptions — for the passage from the world-wide state of fear, that dubious basis of peace, to a state of law, its true basis, is at least postulated in the UN. We cannot see yet how the unstable peace of fear is to turn into a stable peace of organized law; but the UN provides a framework for the day when a trend to justice may take mankind by storm.

10

TOTAL RULE
OR ATOM
BOMB

Since it would entail the probable destruction of mankind, a great-power war today is shunned at almost any price — another "almost," for the question remains at what point, when, and by whom resort will be had to self-preservation by force.

The free world would like to discharge its immense responsibility by meeting force with legal action as long as the force is not fatal to freedom itself. Where America feels that Russia might intervene, she seems paralyzed; endlessly yielding to dictators and desert kings who cannot be reasoned with, she becomes unjust to free countries. The totalitarian world also is touched with concern for the existence of mankind. Where Russia feels that she herself might come to blows with America, she pulls back. Both sides show extreme sensibility, yet both — tacitly agreed on peace, as it were — keep trying how far they can get by threats. It is a peace on a volcano that may erupt at any moment and bury us all. Neither great power can say that she would not want world war under any circumstances, for this would render her helpless before the other's growing power. Each must threaten to stop yielding somewhere. Where this limit lies is uncertain — a situation in which an unscrupulous leader may want to bluff, be called, and be unable to back out.

In this peril we ask imploringly: Is it not impossible for men to decide to use the bomb? The answer is now all too obvious. Both great powers make atom bombs and refuse to abolish them unconditionally. This means, in fact, that while the bombs are said to be deterrents only, circumstances may arise any day that would lead to their use.

Shall this be our answer? Or should we reject the bomb as such, unilaterally, even without mutual controls; should we, in this case, rather refuse to meet threat with threat and relinquish possession of the bomb, since the issue is no longer war but the doom of mankind? Or is a third answer possible, indeed inevitable?

Rationally the question is insoluble, but for our whole political consciousness it is necessary to envision the possible answers clearly, and in line with the political situation. The question would have a basically different meaning if it were to be answered among free nations alone: whether Americans, Frenchmen, Britons, Italians, or Germans were ruling, none of them would or could destroy the others' national substance and humanity. But today the question is bound up with the alternatives of freedom or totalitarianism. It is a question of preserving the possibility of politics itself, and this is the possibility of human dignity. For politics is not only related to force but essentially to freedom; its aim in dealing with force is to achieve freedom from force, by the greatest possible transformation of all human relations into legal relations. Politics could cease only in one of two ways: if force were abolished or if force held full sway, depriving man of his humanity in the centrally planned and directed engine of terror. If man shall not only stay human but become better and more human, the possibility of politics must be preserved.

In today's grand conflict, the atomic powers, Russia and America, shy clear from war with each other. Yet both do their utmost to increase the destructive power of their mass-produced nuclear arms. At the time this is written, America seems to be retaining a substantial lead in bombs and to have fallen behind in missiles for their delivery. Russia can use her missiles to hurl aimed bombs at America from her own territory; America can reach her targets only with missiles of limited range, from bases closer to Russia, or with manned aircraft.

Russia has a huge army equipped with conventional weapons, America only a small one. In a war without atom bombs, Russia would outmatch the rest of the world by the size of her armies and her unconcern for her own soldiers' lives. What would happen if Russian totalitarianism and America got into a hot war? Its expenditure of life would give totalitarianism the advantage over all its neighbors, in addition to the previous advantage of having exploited its own population in the technological preparation for war. America, on the other hand, wants to protect her people; to expose them as little as possible to the dangers of war, she tends to give up the old weapons required by mass armies, to become relatively defenseless in this respect, and to make the issue one of purely technical superiority, in reliance on the atom bomb. The soldierly realities and needs are sidetracked for technical know-how and its total brutality, in the hope that threats will suffice and no war will break out.

This trust in technology has now been dealt its worst blow, when the Americans realized that the Russian missiles can devastate America's big cities and industrial centers while the Russian industries are far more dispersed over a giant continent. True, for the present it is only European countries and others bordering on Russia that are threatened by Russian mass armies, but a Russian victory in these areas would subsequently result in America's destruction. The armament of a huge nation with all old and new means of weapons technology, produced under the compulsion of a low standard of living, is a fact. It cannot be talked away.

The situation grows more dreadful by the month. Will the threat inherent in steadily increasing nuclear arms production never become a reality? Will Russian mass armies wage a world war in Europe and Asia without atom bombs being used? Neither is likely. Staring us in the face is a world war that will again be fought with all possible weapons, from the revolver to the superbomb — and then the extinction of this conflict itself in the radioactive doom of all.

It would be fatal to comfort ourselves with the notion that these are mere threats. He who would not use the bomb under any circumstances need not manufacture it; he would have surrendered already, to anyone who was prepared to use it. A belief in a balance of mere threats is a delusion, for a threat that is not meant seriously is not a threat.

All countries wonder — in the light of their geographical position, their actual power, and their alliances — how to minimize their own peril from war and the bomb. These reflections are manifold and changeable, depending on weapons technology and on the practical politics of the day. The combinations of future possibilities are all but inexhaustible, and so one speculates about the motives of the great powers and of other powers, and about how they might change. One discusses, in principle, whether before a colossus there might perhaps be more safety in weakness than in strength, or the other way round. One reflects on the chances that a demilitarized or actually neutral zone through Central Europe might offer for this zone, or for world peace, or for both. Such ideas are inevitable, but they cannot be right if they make us even for a moment oblivious to the total situation, the strategic picture, the policies of the dominant powers, and, above all, to Russian totalitarianism that is so hard for Westerners to understand.

The strategic picture of Europe depends upon the standpoint. To America, Europe is strategically a glacis. It is important for missile bases, to get as close as possible to Russia — a consideration that may become immaterial with further missile development. It is an industrial potential that must not fall into enemy hands. It is a group of allies whose fate concerns America, for her own roots, to which she feels an obligation, lie in Europe. But Europe, after all, is not America herself. The Americans will find it easier to conceive, perhaps, of a simultaneous withdrawal from Europe by American and Russian armies, to believe in a militarily neutral zone, and finally, failing to comprehend the radical nature of the totalitarian principle, in fact to let Russia seize Europe at her convenience.

To Russia, Europe is a place on her perimeter where she feels threatened by American bases. It is also a region of formidable industrial power, dangerous as an enemy and apt to double Russian strength as a subject. To Russia, Europe would be better destroyed than hostile.

To Europe herself, Russia is next door. Europe is exposed to sudden Russian attack even without atom bombs. Hence, she wants security from local military violence as well as from the atom bombs of a world war.

While this basic situation remains, the particular situations and possibilities change constantly. A truly united Europe might play a powerful part, both in self-protection and as a brake against the outbreak of a world war. Today, in terms of world strategy, her populations, her industries, her intellectuals, her traditions, are an impotent aggregate of rivalries, selfish interests, and distrust without the co-operation that makes for power. Her armament, adding up all that of the individual nations, is infinitesimal compared to Russia's, besides being scattered over Algeria and the remnants of the British empire. It is only at the sacrifice of many of her trivialities, her high standards of living, her national sovereignties, her vampirical ghosts of the past, that Europe could once more become a factor in history and save herself as well.

Now there is an idea, spreading all over the world today, that strikes many as salvation: the demand for a cessation of H-bomb tests. This, people think, would be a first step. It would be possible without controls, since such tests can be detected outside the country that conducts them. Russia has offered such a mutual test suspension; America has refused it.

Adlai Stevenson called for it in the 1956 presidential campaign, but Mr. Eisenhower replied that he would agree only within the framework of general disarmament with mutual controls, since America would lose her headstart if the tests were discontinued. We can safely say that it was not humanitarianism but the desire for a technical advantage that elicited this offer from the Russians, who on their part turned down all of Eisenhower's proposals for controlled disarmament, even mere mutual aerial inspection.

What seems so simple, at first glance, can still be properly judged only in conjunction with all other steps and risks. If a single step, though it may look like disarmament and reduction of the nuclear danger, would actually impair the military power of one side more than the other's, the demand is either hypocritical (on the part of the power that would benefit) or stupid (on the unthinking spectator's part). It may be that the question of benefits cannot be unequivocally answered, and then a discussion may make sense; but in any case the question is, in fact, a deceptive distraction from the real problem. The nuclear danger would not be actually lessened by suspending these tests in peacetime; we should only be lulled into ignoring it.

Still more distracting is the challenge that one great power, on its own initiative, should announce a one-year suspension and resume testing only if during that period the other had not followed suit. The whole matter is put on a moral plane: the good will we demonstrate by an overt act — perhaps an act that would redound to our own advantage — shall trump our opponent's act. This is the fatal method of using evidence of virtue as a weapon in a struggle that is anything but virtuous. It is also the method of fixing the attention of the masses on an apparently simple point, to blind them to the realities of the total situation.

The human task of getting rid of the bombs would thus be reduced to a deceptively simple solution. Instead of being changed, which is the premise of salvation, men would live as before. We greedily snatch at every chance of eliminating the bomb without having to transform our lives — but in vain, for what the present situation asks of mankind is infinitely more than to be freed from fear and to leave everything else as it was.

The evil cannot be exorcised if the heart of the matter is not constantly kept in mind. We are not on the road to salvation until war itself becomes impossible and total disarmament takes place under total control. But the only way to achieve this is a transformation of the human way of life, and truthfulness — the premise of this transformation — is precisely what any such distraction prevents. The terms of the peace are what matters. Until these are seen and realized as a whole, picking out a single act is fraudulent and futile, resulting either from blind fear that clutches at the nearest straw or from self-seeking trickery.

Before we have entered upon a new way of life, a suspension of bomb tests will not affect the basic issue and can be expected only when it would be no more detrimental to one power than to the other. Of course, although not a step toward peace as such, suspension would be most desirable as a public health measure — only for the prevention of total doom it would mean next to nothing. And let us not misconceive the order of importance: what would the death of thousands from bone cancer, or the birth of thousands of monsters, mean in comparison with the extermination of mankind and all life on earth?

Finally, the course of renouncing the bomb altogether is approached in two ways, one roundabout, one forthright. The roundabout approach does not really want to use atom bombs but will not give them up, either. This is a surrender to totalitarianism without admitting it to oneself, an invitation to such blackmail as Hitler once practiced on the West. First, treaty violations would be ignored and violence yielded to, though only outside one's own territory, for the time being. Next — still not directly affected — one would allow the power of total rule to expand by acts of violence against other free countries. In the end, with its preparations completed, it would surge over the borders of the powers it had thus far been careful to respect.

What happens then? Either the masses are ready to lose their freedom, because totalitarianism has taken root in the spirits of the free world as well and is now hailed by many even though coming from without; or, in extremity, they may resolve to resist by all means and to stake everything on the battle — but now, unlike 1939, the effort will be in vain even though the atom bomb is used. Modern weapons technology grants no more periods of grace like the last time. Blackmail will have succeeded for too long.

The forthright renunciation is another matter. It says: The atom bomb must never fall; neither I nor my country will have a hand in it. Whoever makes this decision has already given up resistance to total rule; the attempt to avoid that effect by keeping the absolute renunciation to oneself, as a tacit resolution, is ridiculous.

What is the situation today?

Every chance has been missed: there has been no abolition of the atom bomb, with mutual controls; the free world does not have a shield of conventional weapons, which would require a militarily trained population and economic sacrifices for armament; there is no organized solidarity of the free nations, politically trustworthy and based upon the common spirit of the West. And now — probably suddenly — the moment may come when the decision on the use of the atom bomb must be made by the men whom the mechanisms of political advancement have placed at the helm. Then it will be too late for other alternatives.

What are the pros and cons of the decision?

The thesis that the atom bomb must not be used under any circumstances is backed up by an impressive argument. If all men and life as such were to be destroyed, it says, there must be no nuclear war. For every meaningful action presupposes the continuance of life — not of my life, not of my people's life, but of human life. Hence it is better to submit even to totalitarianism than to risk a nuclear war.

To contradict this thesis seems antihuman, for it implies a lack of confidence that man will always find ways to make life worth living. To love man is to believe that his chances cannot be destroyed as long as he lives. Man's potentialities are endless. The only thing one must not do is to cut off these potentialities along with life itself.

Individuals — so the argument continues — could risk their lives for freedom; they died for the freedom of the survivors. But men cannot have the right to draw all their unwilling fellow men into the risk of perdition. Men have kindled nations with such cries as "Give me liberty or give me death," though the masses may have been unwilling; they did not drop their fight to spare those preferring to live, but viewed their own self-sacrificing courage as controlling for all. But this has changed now that the risk throws the lives of all men into the balance. "Give me liberty or give me death" no longer applies even in the face of total rule, if the death would be the extinction of mankind. A man may think, I will kill myself if totalitarianism conquers; I would die rather than have to live a total lie — but I will never admit that one may drop atom bombs.

We hear the further argument that men fighting for freedom must not kill those who renounce force, who will live at any price and have a right to live in slavery; that he who sacrifices himself for freedom may no longer claim precedence for his cause if the others, who will live at any price, represent the cause of life as such. Granted that in all wars many people were unnecessarily killed; granted that in the saturation bombings of the last war one could not spare Allied prisoners and Germans secretly sympathizing with the Allies, that no choice could be made — but when the inevitable victims would include the whole human race, this new situation calls for a new decision: to renounce combat entirely.

There are answers to these arguments. Before insisting on the survival of mankind at any price, one must know the totalitarianism we have experienced and described: a transformation of human existence to the point where men cease to be human. The peace of totalitarianism is a desert constantly laid waste again by force against rebellious human claims. A totalitarian world state would use the atom bomb — which it alone would control — in limited doses and without endangering the life of mankind as a whole. It would use it in a gradation of terror, for purposes of extermination or simply to put down a revolt in short order. What could be expected under total rule baffles the imagination, because its nature seems humanly impossible and is accordingly not believed in reality.

If we want to defend ourselves against totalitarianism at the risk of putting an end to mankind, we may be told that all of us must accept humiliations or may come into humiliating situations; that it is proud, antihuman arrogance to reject rather than to incorporate them into the permissible self-assurance of man. The answer to this is that a humiliation that dehumanizes all of existence, every hour in the lives of all, is another matter. Whoever thinks that life may be worth living in a world that has been turned into a concentration camp must consider that confidence in man is justified only insofar as scope remains for freedom. This scope is the premise of man's potential. Mere life as such, under consummate total rule, would not be the life of animals in the abundance of nature; it would be an artifical horror of being totally consumed by man's own technological genius.

In all these arguments for and against the final risk, it must not be forgotten that both parties reckon with certainties that do not exist: with the total extinction of mankind by the superbombs or with the total corruption of humanity under total rule. Neither decision is *sure* to destroy either human life or a life that is worth living. No situation is absolutely hopeless.

On the one hand, we see as yet no technical possibility of destroying all life. We can imagine a day when someone will stand by a lever that would, if pulled, obliterate the planet or reduce its surface to a state of lifeless matter. But that day is far off. Anyone compelled to take the extreme risk now would do so in the hope of avoiding extremity. The danger would be enormous, but nobody can know for certain whether the first H-bomb drop would really result in further drops until mankind had perished — after all, the last bomb-thrower must be alive to finish the job. It is only if a single act could affect the whole surface of the globe that its destruction could be accomplished by one man, who would be destroying himself at the same time. If many bombs have to add up to achieve total destruction, the question remains at what point the doom of mankind would become inevitable. Perhaps, a remnant would survive. There might be life in some places, and from them might come new beginnings that we cannot concretely imagine. In decades or centuries, the global surface might be cleansed of radioactivity and accessible once again.

On the other hand, no one can be certain that totalitarianism would finally annihilate man's essence along with his freedom. Totalitarianism might change and disintegrate from within. Human existence might take a new grip on freedom and thus on its potential.

On both sides — final destruction of human existence by the atom bomb, and final destruction of the human essence by totalitarianism — the course to real finality is incalculable. We have to make our choice without knowing all, on the basis of all that we know within our perspective. We cannot figure it out. Perhaps we should, at the risk of dooming life itself, try to prevent what strikes us as the doom of freedom — what we hear then, on our human plane, is a challenge not to give in to total coercion but to join in defense against it, at any risk, but with a chance of success to the end. But perhaps, since the bombs exist, we should submit to total rule — and what we hear then, on our plane, is the demand to endure all, even dehumanization in a concentration-camp state, because human life shall continue at all costs, in the expectation that even in men suffering beyond all measure, in a functionalized, falsified mankind, human dignity will rise again. Both choices dare all, on the ground that hope springs eternal.

My own thought, in view of these twin uncertainties, is that man, unlike the animals, is always free to take any risk for his freedom. If he should throw the life of mankind into the scales for liberty, he would not be taking this risk in order to die, but in order to live in freedom. If this seemed impossible, the makers of constructive history have thus far prized liberty more than life. Should things have changed? Should the present situation have brought man to his deepest fall, to the surrender of his freedom? Should that be what he considers the fulfilment of his task? If so, he would no longer be what we used to call human. Or should the ultimate yardstick now, as ever before, be not a respect for life as such, but respect for a life that is worth living insofar as human freedom can make it so?

This phrasing must not be misunderstood: the risk of life in a struggle with all-violating force differs radically from any act against life in eugenic folly, racist mania, or medical error. Respect for the potential and the value of each single human life bars tampering with any supposedly unworthy individual lives.

Man is born to be free, and the free life that he tries to save by all possible means is more than mere life. Hence, life in the sense of existence — individual life as well as all life — can be staked and sacrificed for the sake of the life that is worth living.

A moment of dread decision may arise. No one can anticipate it in mere thought; no argument can compel a decision one way or another — for more is done here than can be deduced from general principles.

The question can only be answered by the consciences of those who will act or refrain from acting at the decisive moment. At that moment the decision will lie with a few individuals, perhaps with a single one. No one can tell what sort of men these will be, in what patterns their minds will move, who will be their friends and advisers. But the thought of this contingency cannot but make everyone profoundly serious about supporting political leaders, voting for them, and trusting them. These actions carry weight even in the smallest circles that seem far removed from world politics. Everyone shares the responsibility, without knowing anything about the course of political careers and the accidents that place men in key positions. Everywhere it is the state of society that determines which individuals will have their ways made straight. What happens on a small scale is not only indicative of events at large; unforeseen circumstances may make it the cause of bringing rascals or true statesmen to the top. Whom the individual joins, which contemporaries he respects, learns from, imperceptibly models himself upon — this is a basic reality and the responsibility of everyone. This is the source that finally decides what kind of political leaders will come to power.

The moment of decision, and the situation from which it will arise, cannot be foreseen either, but the question of conscience can be sensibly clarified by tentative decisions in hypothetical extremities. We do not want to get into them blindly. The anticipation of possibilities has consequences for the decision itself: dishonest, deceptively soothing notions will be swept away, and extremity will be manifest in all its rigor. Reality itself will pose the question that finite thought cannot solve.

It is a perturbing question. Is an act that may lead to the extinction of mankind intrinsically evil? Is there a limit to the permissible risk of life? Should the atom bomb be renounced unconditionally? Or can there be a recurrence of the sense of Einstein's decision to advise making the bomb when the world was threatened by Hitler's totalitarianism? That decision was still unaware of the principle. Can it face us again, in a new and conscious form?

We get back to a situation leading beyond politics and mere ethics, to a new seriousness of the idea of sacrifice. Throughout past history, there have been recurring moments when words would give way to the arbitrament of force — when, as one used to say, men had come to an end and heaven must speak. Today, this manner of decision has changed fundamentally. The premise on which it used to be sought — that the victor, as a matter of course, would survive — is now invalid.

However suddenly it may confront us, the moment of decision will be determined by all that has gone before. Our reflections can only clarify and keep it from occurring as a thoughtless, unwanted accident. That the decision, when it comes, should at least spring from the highest awareness is the challenge and the achievement of philosophy.

Let us here consider only a few real possibilities. If a world war should break out in a situation like the present one, the chances are that one power would drop super bombs at once — fully expecting the enemy to retaliate but hoping to bring him to his knees by the first surprise blow.

Or the tension may keep building up. Each would expect the other to strike; at some point, the decision would be a matter of hours, with the outbreak and the first acts of war taking place under the enormous pressure of immediately, fatally threatening enemy action. The men at the helm would not feel free any more. Each would feel forced by the other to act against his will. The one to set off the disaster, in that terrible moment, would think he was acting because the other was about to act. Neither would want it, and yet it would happen.

The moment may come about in several ways. If totalitarianism threatens, blackmails, and tries to reach its goal without war, as it so often does, the free world may stop yielding at some point, and the threatening totalitarian leaders may feel unable to bear their failure before their collaborators and their people. Against their previous intentions, they would then feel obliged to carry out their threats as a matter of political survival. The free world would resist, because this time the threats would seem to be the first step to final subjection. Both would feel forced to let the process of destruction run its course, and each would declare the other as the aggressor.

Or moods may press for violent release. The West may lose patience. The constant tension and the arms race may become unbearable and explode in passion, especially if the horror of war has paled in the minds of future generations lacking the actual experience. In the East it might be dangers from within or without that would drive the tyrants to launch their huge military machine on a course of nihilistic self-preservation.

If the fighting begins without atom bombs but subsequently turns into a struggle for existence, the one fearing to lose will use the bomb at any risk, to give himself a last chance or, at the worst, to drag the enemy down with him. It will be self-preservation — whether of freedom or of totalitarianism — or else the doom of all.

Finally, peaceful force can be as merciless as martial force. The fact that it proceeds quietly, slowly, and gradually, to a point where the opponent is not physically destroyed but robbed of his means of subsistence and exposed to starvation, does not make the final effect more tolerable to the individual. Hence, physical force may always erupt against unjust, apparently hopeless peaceful strangulation. This kind of desperate uprising might even come from small countries.

Whatever happens, the decision will be made clearly and conscionably only if the alternative between freedom and totalitarianism is really inescapable. There, none can be neutral; no one aware of responsibility can refuse to share in the decision — no one but a "saint" who lives without a claim upon the world, is not responsible for it, does not fight or meet force with force, suffers evil in silence, and is ready at any time to be tortured and killed without complaining.

Physical conflict is marked by the risk and sacrifice of life. Without sacrifice there is no human existence. Today we have two choices: either the sacrifice — unwanted by the overwhelming majority, accomplished by the daring minority — is *the existence* of mankind itself, doomed because man cannot be free; or mankind sacrifices *the means of force* in gaining its ends in a struggle. But that would mean a change in man, not in his inheritable constitution, but in his historic appearance, in the steadily imperiled balance of his being.

We may ask: Must man be able to risk everything, even the existence of mankind, to become serious enough to change? Is a new humankind to spring from the awareness of this possibly total risk and from the readiness for it? Or, if the change does not take place, shall all be doomed? Shall mankind perish if it finds no way to realize justice in a moral-political community? And if no such way is found, does the substance of humanity then lie where failure is no longer an objection — where indeed man's ultimately real, truly serious purpose is his doom?

We can raise that question, but no one can answer it. We have only mythical answers from prehistoric times, as when God sent the Flood. When the wickedness of men waxed too great, he resolved to let them perish as no longer fit to live. We have had the Flood, but we also have had Noah's rescue. And in the end, God promised never to repeat it.

Goethe said of the dawning modern age: "Mankind will grow more astute and more perceptive, but not better, happier, or more vigorous — not permanently, at least. I see a time coming when God will not enjoy it any more, when he will have to smash everything once again, to rejuvenate his creation. I feel sure that everything tends in that direction, and that the starting time and hour of the rejuvenation period are already appointed in the distant future. But there will be plenty of time yet."

These mythical notions have acts of God in mind, but today the issue is not a cosmic disaster but an act accomplished by the technical skills of men. If their doings would result in self-extermination, only their doings can avoid it. In any event, the gate to the future is sacrifice — either the sacrifice of all human existence or the sacrifice of human existential interests, offered to let mankind become truly human.

If now, after all the lives that men have sacrificed in history, the total sacrifice of mankind appears possible, there remains one ambiguity: would it be an act of despair? Despair turns the man who is ready to die daring, in quest of a better life, into one who seeks death because he is tired of living. The philanthropic will to dare turns into a misanthropic will to destroy.

Or would it be an act of necessity, arising from the unfathomable source of all things? It could be necessary only as a sacrifice made for the sake of eternity. As in the reality of love, God speaks in the courage of daring all — for no adequate worldly cause, but never without such a cause. Hence, this sacrifice does not lie in adventure, only in a will to realization that bows to Transcendence if it fails. The sacrifice does not lie in magic; it means building enduringly in time. But when everything seems to be passing away like magic, it feels safe in eternity.

Because there is truth in serious, unconditional resistance to the abasement of life, the chance of sacrifice — not adequately justifiable by any purpose in the world, but based upon reason by a goal in the situation of the world — is part of man. If we must do everything to eliminate the atom bomb, the condition is that it not be done at the cost of eliminating a truly human life. The sacrifice of mankind's existence is avoidable only by a sacrifice of corresponding magnitude: by the surrender of existential entanglements that is required if men are to be changed. This sacrifice alone would be the firm foundation of a life worth living.

11

CHANGING
SITUATIONS

Thus far, our discussion has been premised on the present state and distribution of nuclear armament. This will change; so will technology in general and the economy and population of the world. If we achieve world peace, we shall also face new, difficult, and dangerous problems.

Today, only America and Russia have nuclear stockpiles and are accordingly great powers. It is up to either one of them alone whether or not to unleash total destruction, and at the moment they seem in tacit agreement against such a course. Yet in all likelihood this situation will not long prevail. Great Britain is already producing the bomb; France has tested it. As early as November, 1956, it was announced from London that British scientists had discovered a process of making hydrogen bombs so cheaply that even small nations could stockpile them. "The discovery is labeled top secret," we read at the time, "in view of the enormous security and defense problems it raises." For the present, anyway, the independent production of fissionable material still calls for large expenditures, for the possession of uranium ores, and for technical knowledge and skills of a high order. But once this material has been spread around the world and given to all "for peaceful uses," it can, in principle, also be used to make bombs everywhere, possibly with the help of foreign technicians.

If we reach that stage, the atomic menace will be universal instead of issuing from two powers only. Small nations might risk everything in despair or irresponsible recklessness; the arrogant nihilist rates other people's lives no higher than his own. Then the world will really know what it means to live on a volcano. The present situation, with world war in two hands, seems simple in comparison with a future in which nations everywhere might have the bomb. It would be utterly obscure. Actions would remain human actions, but decisions would be scattered over so many places that atomic destruction might come over us like an ungovernable natural disaster. It is a prospect of frightening probability.

Technological changes will affect working methods and economic and social patterns. Today, for example, we are in the first stages of automation. The economic order cannot remain the same if economies are barred from the expansion they were thriving on for a century and a half.

In concrete situations we have frequently been led astray by experts claiming universal, or temporarily universal, validity for their economic knowledge. "It is economically impossible for the war to last longer than a few months," they told us in 1914. "A totally ruined economy cannot be rebuilt," they told us before 1945. Events have shown how such seeming economic impossibilities may become possible. They involve sacrifices we do not want to make, so we call them impossible; if exacted by necessity, they do not turn out to be catastrophic at all. Every new situation requires change. The change may remain purely economic, to the detriment of man, or it may stir him in the economic medium to general reflection.

I am not competent even to start discussing economic affairs; but an awareness of them is essential to moral-political volition. The experts ought to make the simple basic factors crystal-clear to everyone. Men who know present economic realities and have the analytical power to comprehend them should not bog down in ever increasing complications, neither in statistics that can be multiplied at random nor in technical possibilities that can be contrived and combined at random. We see the same mistake recurring in most sciences: they lose themselves in infinity. Knowledge is the result of seeing things in a reflectively devised connection and simultaneously testing them on reality. There is knowledge only where infinities are mastered, and only such scientists could, by clear abstraction as well as by the concrete results of their analysis of industries, organizations, economic systems, trusts, and banking, lead us to see the moral decisions that are at work, in detail and in the spirit of the whole.

Marxism has made it a commonplace that the material conditions of our existence, our labor and economic systems, determine all human activity — that it is but the superstructure of a material foundation. Not a commonplace, but no less true, is the complementary idea that labor, economic systems, social patterns, are in turn governed by moral-religious and spiritual motives. Max Weber's discoveries about the historic forms of the working ethos have not yet penetrated into the general consciousness. The debate moves between two theses: "All depends on technology; 'can do' — we just have to find the right means" and, "All depends on the ethos; with faith and good will, the technical means will come." And a third says, "Both are necessary, but our ethical development has lagged behind the technological one and must catch up now." Each of the first two positions is inadequate and false because it claims too much; the third is an outright error, because it lumps essentially different categories under the same notion of progress, in the form of things we "can do."

We must realize that neither the economy nor any of its forms are absolutes. The economy is not the standard for all that we are and can be. It is indispensable — as water is to life, which instantly ends without water; but it is not life any more than water is. The economy derives its meaning only from its uneconomic purpose. It is pervaded by the motives it serves; hence there are so many different possible and real patterns for one and the same technique of labor.

Man must bow to economic demands only insofar as they spring from the matter itself and are accordingly inevitable. We cannot do without calculations and balance sheets if an enterprise is to succeed, whether in totalitarian Russia or in capitalist America. The economy is a matter of planning; in the present state of technology, it is one of central planning by larger or smaller economic units. If there is today a struggle of economic systems, it concerns the place and the extent of this planning, and the power that the planners wield. Either there is total planning by the state itself or else a government provides the legal framework for planning on private initiative. In a sense, such legal frameworks constitute planning of what cannot be planned, by drawing limits and setting conditions for the planning activity.

The contrast between the types of order is radical. Each is state-protected, but the one is also state-directed, whereas the other is left free to operate within the law. They are irreconcilable even though there are analogies between giant enterprises in the free world and enterprises under total rule. Freedom and unfreedom in the whole of existence are not extremes but alternatives. Their fundamental contrast affects the practice of work, the psychology of men, and their way of life.

Again, living conditions are not life itself. Life can be submerged in economics if this is viewed as absolute. But then human freedom is lost, under the central planning of total rule as well as in the politically free kind of enterprise that actually approaches totalitarianism.

Another constant, vastly problematic change takes place in the world's population. In 1800 it totaled about 775 million; in 1850, about 1,075 million; in 1900, about 1,560 million; today it approaches 3,000 million. The increase ties in with rising food production and with the increased consumption of energy. We may wonder what the curve implies for the future. The mass of imponderables makes it impossible to give a maximum population which our planet can support, but there is no doubt that there is one. The quiet, momentarily imperceptible, on the whole unwanted, population growth threatens peace by its elemental actuality.

Hitherto, the unequal growth of nations was uncontrolled, depending only on the birthrate. There would be recurring "population pressure" on adjacent areas, relieved by emigration, by influx into less densely settled regions, by colonization, by conquest. "People without space," that well-known complaint of not long ago, already implied a will to war — a demand for space that was inhabited elsewhere by lesser breeds and withheld from the strong, growing people against the eternal natural right of selection. "People without space" became an evil, arrogant, contemptible battle cry.

Today, the global picture of unequal growth shows the Western nations approaching a standstill, while the pace of Asian, African, and Latin-American growth quickens from year to year. The Chinese have increased from 315 million in 1911 to 470 million in 1941 and some 650 million today; the Indians increased by 50 million from 1931 to 1941. The impression of these Indian and East Asian masses — hungry, restless, rising like a tide that may engulf the globe once they are in possession of technology and arms — is overwhelming. These masses may not yet be a menace, but the menace they will be in a few decades must be considered now. Can we provide outlets, build dikes, co-operate in finding a way out?

The rules of the past — when large parts of the globe were actually still free, when the struggle for space and the movement into other spaces were universal processes — have changed fundamentally. Now, if there is to be peace, population growth must take place within limited areas. This freezing of territorial boundaries seems unjust when the rate of growth leads to excessive differences in the density of population. There are peaceful means of dealing with the problem — immigration, permission to make land purchases, legal forms of what used to be done by force — but they can succeed only in isolated instances, when the interests of immigrants and host country coincide. On the whole, these makeshifts will remain insignificant. What can be done?

Hitherto, overpopulation was always local, never world-wide. One used to think that a harsh "law of nature" was maintaining a balance by epidemics, famines, wars. The harshness of this law would lead to ever increasing disasters; once recognized, however, it may be corrected by human planning. If men agree, the will of mankind can achieve an orderly, non-catastrophic development by birth control.

There is no other way out of a global overpopulation that would be bound to explode in war. Some day, birth control will be an indispensable act of peace, just as unrestricted reproduction — now claimed as a natural right everywhere and encouraged by churches and governments — is in itself a potential act of conquest. If the globe were known to be too small, it would already be regarded as an act of violence; that this is not yet the case, that we cannot figure out a limit to the numbers who can live on earth, merely puts the problem off into the future. It is a political problem of the first rank. The necessity of keeping peace, to avoid the doom of all, must at some time lead to the moral-political demand for birth control.

The possibility of birth control in one country has been demonstrated in a past era in Japanese history. To make it universal would require the participation of all countries — or the coercion of a powerless remnant by the misery, hunger, and death that would result from overpopulation within sealed boundaries. International agreements would have to stipulate the mutual obligation to maintain populations at a certain level.

Today it seems almost out of the question that such a plan could be carried out. It is one of the many "impossibilities" that are quite possible — because they depend upon the human will — and will in time become realities. Unless mankind destroys itself first, the choice we face is simple: either totalitarianism will use planned birth control and the extermination of surplus masses to keep the numbers living at a time in check or else birth control will be achieved by free agreements, under effective institutions, and in common recognition of its necessity.

Let us turn to a third problem. What will happen, in a state of world peace, if our future existence rests upon atomic power? The opportunities are immense. While the atom bomb would disappear, atomic power would usher in a new economic era. The worry about our coal and oil reserves, due to be exhausted in the foreseeable future, has already been lifted from us by the step into the atomic age, the greatest of all taken in the age of technology. If the atom does not destroy us, it will put our whole existence on a new basis. Simultaneously, we observe the rapid development of automation. If the age of wars were behind us, a utopian picture of the future would move into the realm of real possibility.

Vast quantities of power would be at the disposal of automatic machinery supplying all human needs with a minimum of labor. Hard physical toil, until now the foundation of human existence, would be reduced to the vanishing point. There might be unemployment problems in the transition period; then all men would be working short hours. Life would not be fulfilled in work but in leisure. What used to be the privilege of an aristocratic minority would be the lot of all. It looks like the prospect of an earthly paradise: the technological control of our terrestial environment would set us free; instead of ruling us, our environment would smooth our paths. There would be no limit to spontaneous and creative leisure activities, partly performed by the medical, clerical, legal, scientific, technical, educational professions. The physician would again become a physician instead of being mired in machinery. The pastor would show us the way to meditation instead of having to lose his own way in the social bustle. All would have time to study, to inform themselves, to keep abreast of events, and to share the responsibility for political action. In part, this freedom would benefit personal inclinations, the contemplation of eternal truth in the inexhaustible abundance of the world, and above all, the family and the education of the children. And all this free, leisure-born work of the spirit would breed a new ethos, a new discipline of human activity. Sloth would vanish along with the burden of toil.

There have been such expectations ever since the beginnings of modern technology. Many minds were aglow with enthusiasm for the glorious life ahead: the imminence of nature mastered, of man relieved of the physical toil that consumed his energies, of his mind and soul freed to unfold their full potentials. Thus far, however, the results of technological progress have been rather different. Many came to feel indignation and rage at a liberation that actually chained them to new, unfamiliar, time-consuming work, that destroyed the traditional ways of work and of life, that brought unforeseen, undreamed-of evil into the world.

Today, too, the expected paradise appears equivocal. It creates unknown problems. First, what will men do with their "free leisure time"? Even in the old aristocracies there were always only a few individuals achieving spontaneous fulfilment in leisure-time activities. Few men, it seems, can occupy themselves alone; the majority can hardly stand an hour's solitude.

Now, if leisure is not to relax us from work, as before, but to fulfil our lives, what then? We may go on as before, with the masses given whatever helps to distract and save them from having to fall back on their own initiative. The pleasures of freedom are already mechanized; pleasure is becoming another kind of work, as in unholy sports, or it becomes the sensation of watching events staged on an ever shifting scene. In this sort of distraction, leisure is no opportunity for man to explore and develop himself; it becomes an empty function, another form of self-estrangement.

To help those who are bewildered by leisure, we can only appeal to them as individuals. We can never fulfil their lives in leisure; we can only awaken their initiative for doing it themselves. No one can be relieved of the responsibility for what becomes of him, what each one makes of himself. Freedom must be consummated by spontaneity in the individual.

If this were not possible in the long run, there would remain only cynicism tending to misanthropy ("The race isn't worth much") and hopelessness about the future. And yet, the same changed way of thinking which alone can make peace possible and avoid total doom would also fill our leisure and realize in it the peaks of humanity. The common spirit in education, in tradition, in the way of life, would draw even the less gifted and those who are running away from themselves into a measure of self-realization. Just as now the vicious circle of blatant vacuity draws people against their will into empty sensations, speeding them along the road to total calamity, so, conversely, the saving circle would close even upon the restive. It is already visible in individuals and very small, still largely exceptional groups.

Then there are the instincts expressed in war, which the abolition of wars would not abolish: the fierce love of adventure, rape, and pillage; the urge to rise above this life, in risking it; the commitment to a cause one would gladly die for; also the elation of triumph and the suffering and patience of defeat; the idea of soldiering, with its comradely mixture of orderliness, obedience, self-sacrifice, valor, and reliability in the face of death.

These instincts cannot be extinguished, so the planners want to provide or maintain harmless outlets for them. Chances taken in sports, in mountaineering, in scientific experiments, might be a safety valve. Aggressions might be worked out in body-contact sports, the need to stand out, in virtuosity; self-sacrifice might take the form of renunciations, and soldierly comradeship that of rational friendship with its loyalty and commitments. But such ideas never touch the core of the matter. They make superficial plans for something beyond knowledge and planning capacity. One can show possibilities, as in laying out a garden; but we are dealing with human beings, not with trees and plants, and no man can set himself up as a gardener of men. This is what limits all educational planning: that human communication cannot be calculated.

It used to be said that lasting peace would make men soft and ruin them in the end. Now the question would be different, for the lasting peace that we are speaking of would not come as a free gift but from the development of motives tantamount to tension and invigoration. Until now, after a period of peace, men would crave war because the calm and boredom and tedium of safety were becoming unbearable. But in a state of world peace this road would be blocked not only by the compulsion of newly constituted law and the fear of infinite horror, but the total situation which this peace would rest upon would be too full of problems and perils for any such calm and boredom to arise.

There will be questions concerning the management of atomic energy. It involves possible concentrations of power that might become as dangerous to freedom as a central police force in a state of world peace. The trend to this absolute power structure derives from the fact that it was the state, not free enterprise, which in wartime drafted scientists and engineers to achieve the control of atomic energy and the production of fissionable material. No private business, however big, could have risked a failure of the huge investment required for research and experimentation. If atomic power becomes the basis of industry, if everything comes to depend on it, there will be dependency also on the states that supply the material, or on some international agency.

Even if the material were bought in a free, competitive market, from several suppliers, centralized state control might re-establish itself in another fashion. The construction and operation of atomic power plants call for unusual precautions against possible explosions that might devastate large areas, and no amount of precautions can guarantee absolute safety. The population in the environment of atomic plants will have to be insured, but no private company could dare to write such insurance. The extent of possible damage would be incalculable. The insurer, therefore, can be only the state itself, which will thus regain control of the plants by means of licensing and supervision.

Although the possibilities are still obscure, one fears a political threat to the freedom of all. Far from ceasing with the end of wars, the danger of total rule would merely shift its source to the reality of control over atomic power. The blessing of peace would exclude neither the slow evolution of such rule nor the violent solution of elemental problems by central decrees, based on statistics and planning. Like total rule today, and by similarly effective measures, such a peaceful dictatorship might rob all men of their freedom. The military conflicts of the past would become economic — but both types make for totalitarian structures as soon as all power is vested in a few hands. The competition of skills and creative achievements would cease and be replaced by the operations whereby some monopolize atomic energy and others try to get a share in what would then be a necessity of life.

All these questions can only be answered in practice. When human nature, as it appears historically on a changeless biological foundation, has received the necessary jolt, the same forces that would master the atom bomb by abolishing war could also cope with these problems. The new horizons might inspire us to live so as to improve our chances for the future. Yet not much can be anticipated in mere thought. Man can never see the whole picture; he sees only a process that is changing before his eyes.

We shall have to free ourselves from our tendency to look for a goal of ultimate perfection. The world cannot be perfect while it keeps moving in time. From this time onward, the danger of mankind perishing by human action will always be with us — it will never vanish again. It will have to be met constantly and surmounted afresh, and it is under this pressure that man can rise to his highest potentialities. The moment he relaxes in the illusion of final success, the extreme menace will once more be real, and he will finally lose his mere existence, after all.

An unwavering earnestness is henceforth required of man; it is on him, too, that the course of events depends; he must always know whatever can be known at the time. Then he will not despair in the face of what seems insoluble. If he is truly fully in earnest, he will find unforeseen help that fails to appear if he passively lets things happen.

Man either grows in freedom, and maintains the tension of this growth, or he forfeits his right to live. If he is not worthy of his life, he will destroy himself.

PART THREE

12

THE SCIENTISTS
AND THE
"NEW WAY
OF THINKING"

Facing us — we must repeat this again and again — is the possible and intellectually probable end of mankind. All of us know that nothing can help but world peace; some of us add that this peace cannot be achieved by laws and treaties alone, that laws and treaties cannot work without a change in man.

In view of the atom bomb, we have seen, it is not enough to discuss the real possibilities and conceivable forms of world peace in general, or the political state of the world in particular. If mankind's existence is in question, man's total essence must be summoned to provide the answer. We become newly conscious of our basic human condition. In ways we cannot overlook, our time manifests what has happened since man burst out of the cycle of natural events — events identically re-iterated for generations, changing only over long periods of time — and broke through to thought, and thus to history.

No single way of thinking will make us aware of this. Everything we discussed in the preceding chapters of this book brought us up against insoluble questions; we felt we were touching a realm other than that of definite rational objectivity. In speaking of this realm, to be sure, each sentence necessarily takes us back into the rational medium as well — otherwise, thinking comprehension would cease. But our objective now is the content of the other, new way of thinking that tells us where we stand, assures us of our ultimate motives, lets us find and foster our state of mind, and gives us calm. Not until then can our previous thoughts have meaning. Not until we have gained some of the calm that is not stolid indifference but basic philosophical clarity shall we be capable of serious, dependable action.

The purely political, merely intellectual thinking that we call "realistic" remains on the surface and does not touch the really decisive motivations of action. It was in the failure of politics that we saw the suprapolitical element — initially in the form of a *moral precept*. This has been expressed and effective since the time of the prophets, but in isolated cases only. Everyone says it is true; but only a few seem to believe in it. The majority seem tired of it. And indeed, it is incapable of realization by itself alone.

Then we considered *sacrifice*. The extreme situations of existence call for dealing with force, whether in self-preservation or in submission, and make sacrifice inevitable. Men sacrifice themselves in risking their lives, nations in venturing to fight for freedom against superior power; or they sacrifice themselves in a non-violence consistently maintained to the point of destruction or enslavement. What we are seeking is the comprehensive space where not the intellect so much as reason — the philosophical thinking that is innate in all men, but buried in most — will establish the only conditions under which ethics and self-sacrifice can complete their meaning and show the way to salvation and unfoldment, for the individual as well as for the political community.

Yet the truth of this higher level of reason rests upon the reality of the preceding levels. No level can be confined to itself, none can be skipped. The thoughts of *Realpolitik*, confined to themselves, lead to nihilism and eventually to total doom. The moral precept, as self-sufficient moralism, leads to abstract logical conclusions and to the rigidity of judging actions by laws. Self-sacrifice becomes the blind sacrifice in which man, while rising above himself, gives up being himself. And reason, in turn, grows empty if it is not embodied in realism, in morals, and in sacrifice.

The proper task of philosophy is to think rationally, to circumscribe the efficacy of reason and to make us feel it in examples. Only by reason do knowledge, morals, and sacrifice retain their reliable meanings. For reason requires intellectual knowledge: to be able to know what we want, we must know what exists. Reason requires morality: without a precept that we have experienced as valid, action has no content. Reason requires sacrifice: without reaching beyond life, our lives can be neither rational nor fulfilled in the present.

What remains for this last part of our discussion is the final step of reflecting on politics under suprapolitical guidance. For the truth of morality and sacrifice depends upon their absorption in encompassing reason, and here we come to what is both easiest and most difficult.

We shall first ask the scientists who brought the new fact into the world, told the public about it, and called for a "new way of thinking." What they have said so far is almost always purposive and intellectual, in line with scientific thinking, and frequently sounds as if they had, or expected to have, a simple prescription that could be understood and followed without trouble. Yet this is not the way forward. The scientists' own thoughts demand the other kind of thinking. The crux of the "new way of thinking" they talk about is the reversal of the old way, a "revolution of thought" — of which, for all their scientific approach, natural scientists and engineers are neither more nor less capable than other human beings.

The scientists and engineers, not the generals and politicians, were the first to speak plainly about the new fact. Thanks to them, everyone can now know what is happening. They have had no hand in concealment; they are deeply alarmed themselves. Their honesty and sobriety — which in research, unfettered by absolute premises, led to such extraordinary results — made them feel obliged to tell the world how matters stood. They deserve our gratitude.

People tend to blame the scientists for the evils that the discovery of atomic energy has loosed upon the world. Having given man the use of atomic energy, some feel, the scientists must teach him what to do with it; the producer must teach the proper use of his product, and he who achieved something so monstrous must know how to control the monster. Hence, many listen to the admired scientists as to great sages, while others consider them incompetent outside the sphere of physics. Let us see who may be right or wrong on this score.

In 1938, in Berlin, Otto Hahn split the nucleus of the uranium atom. In 1942, in Chicago, Enrico Fermi achieved the first man-made chain reaction. In 1945, the atom bomb was finished, tested in the desert of New Mexico, and dropped on Hiroshima. This rapid development was a result of war: the fear that Hitler, drawing on German physicists, might get the atom bomb that was now considered possible, and that it would unfailingly make him the master of the world, caused a half billion dollars to be spent on a dubious project which in peacetime, from purely economic motives, would have been out of the question. The objective took three years to attain, and the project required all the acumen and brilliance of some leading scientists and thousands of their associates.

The progress from uranium fission to the atom bomb was part of the larger evolution of atomic knowledge in France, England, Denmark, and Germany since the turn of the century. In Robert Jungk's book, *Brighter than a Thousand Suns*, we read of the creative excitement of the first decades, in Göttingen, where the foremost mathematicians and physicists attracted students from all over the world, including almost all the subsequent trail blazers of the atom bomb. We read of the dispersal of that great community, owing to the expulsion of the Jews from Hitler's Reich and the new situation of a world menaced by the tyrant and his army. Finally, we read of the quarrels among the physicists themselves after the fission bomb was dropped, with some consistently pushing on to the fusion bomb, some resisting, hesitantly or clearly, and some simply baffled. We see, successively, the free collaboration of scientists in a peaceful world, leading to unheard-of discoveries; then the magnificent, organized common effort in America, with the tension of thought, the devotion of all skills to one purpose, enhanced by the pressure of the Nazi threat; and finally, the disintegrating community of a less and less free, disillusioned, suspicion-filled, controlled industrial operation.

Suggested by Leo Szilard — who subsequently, too, saw the importance of the possibilities in the changing political situation better than most physicists — and set off by Einstein's letter to President Roosevelt, the project was first run by physicists but was soon taken over, more and more, by the army and the state. Begun as a free organization of scientific self-sacrifice committed to human liberty, it turned increasingly into an enterprise under military supervision. It is memorable for its grand achievement as well as for the breakup of the "family" of science.

The turning point was the reality of the bomb drop of 1945; but if we talk of the "basic calamity," we may ask if the atom bomb is not, perhaps, just a symbol. Could the release of atomic energy be a mere incident in a larger train of events — and if so, in which? We may ask, further, whether this basic process itself is rationally intelligible, since everything in it is conceived, construed, and realized by men and thus necessarily comprehensible to them in its logical sequence, at least in retrospect — or is it part of an impervious mystery and open only to a mythical approach?

At first glance, the basic process is the progress of human technology from the first tool and the use of fire to its vast, methodical unfolding on the basis of natural science. There is but one line of progress: that of rationalization. Every other product of creative human efforts is unique, a consequence of revelations of the human essence; the peaks and fulfilments it reaches can never be identically repeated, but they can be understood and concern posterity insofar as they are open to it. They alone are properly historical. But rationalization, once achieved, can be identically repeated and indefinitely expanded. It can be identically adopted by all human beings. It is misleading to shift the idea of progress from this area, where it belongs, to all areas of mental activity and to history at large; for there it applies only insofar as the advances of rationalization furnish means of realization and premises of existence to all other human activities, including the unique, historically creative, and existential.

Technological progress takes place wherever men live. We can trace it back as a slow process of hundreds of thousands of years, clearly recognizable over the last five thousand, and replaced — after a lost rudiment in Antiquity — only four hundred years ago by a fundamentally different kind: by methodical natural science as a tool of technical skill. This new process, after a slow start, has accelerated since the second half of the eighteenth century to an ever faster and finally breathless pace. There is a look of inevitability about the achievements of individual scientists and engineers; they show up whenever the time is ripe for the next step; the individuals seem replaceable. If in the course of this mostly anonymous process a man of genius makes new discoveries before our admiring eyes, the fact remains that it is but a question of time and someone else would have done so. On the whole, the history of science and technology is one great progressive movement, interspersed with setbacks, but always tending ahead.

What happens today in technology is part of this. The age-old process, without which man's way would be unthinkable, has reached another point where man confronts the question of what he wants to do with his technology. It has always served both constructive and destructive ends, and today its potentialities have leaped from scattered destruction to the annihilation of all life on earth.

Fear of this peril has evoked the idea that it might have been better if atomic energy had never been released and no atom bomb had been built — that if we could choose, we ought to do without atomic energy. Rather than this peril, we should accept all difficulties due to the limitation of other available resources. Yet if we think this way, we must consistently say that it would have been better to do without technology from the outset. Once the process has begun, there is no stopping it, let alone turning it back — except by making an end of life and destroying technology along with the technician. A denial of technology's last step is equivalent to a denial of the first.

Everything man produces in the course of technological progress is a new realization of his existential potentialities. Without knowing beforehand where it will lead, without a final goal, without the will to technology as a whole, his technical creation keeps confronting him with new situations, each of which raises the question of what he will make of it, what he will do in it, in what sense he will master it or succumb to it. If we affirm human existence — if we think we are men and know that, while man is not yet what he can and should be, his nature is the chance whose outcome is up to him, at least in part — then we must recognize the way of technology as unavoidable. Without being able to calculate it beforehand, man uses technology to create his own situation — as today his extremity.

Hence his delight in knowledge and invention. He takes a justifiable pride in his presence at it, his share in it, his knowledge of what has been done. Even more, though, the knowledge of infinite, incalculable possibilities evokes the humility characteristic of all great scientists: how minute is all they have done! And a glance at ghastly possibilities evokes the fear that may lead to doubts whether the road, this human road, is right.

Such inner resistance to empirical knowledge and technology is age-old; the ancients looked upon many scientists as wizards and aides of the devil. Now and then, these qualms would overcome the scientists themselves, and it would be interesting to trace them in their biographies over the centuries. In our time, we hear that Carl Bosch — the originator, with Fritz Haber, of the nitrogen synthesis for military use in World War I, without which Germany could not have held out so long — was troubled in his old age by the thought of what he had done.

We read how shaken Otto Hahn was at the news of Hiroshima, as if he had committed the act. He had nothing to do with the bomb, but he was in the unique position of having, as a pure scientist without an inkling of a bomb, made the particular discovery that started it. Before him, the premise was the grand evolution of atomic science by the Curies, Rutherford, Einstein, Bohr, Heisenberg, among others; after him, thoughts promptly turned to the bomb.

These conflicting reactions spring from dark forebodings that have appeared ever since the beginnings of our history. There have always been opposing impulses: seeing the grandeur of human power and seeing the *hubris* and the evil deeds of man. The Taoists in China envisioned a golden age of perfect harmony and sheer bliss: "Ghosts and demons plagued no one; the skies were clear, the ten thousand things flawless, and no creature died before its time. . . . No one did anything, and yet things always happened by themselves." This state of things was upset by purposeful action, inventions, agriculture, order, laws, morals — by everything that is or includes thought. Technology is part of the evil.

We read of a discussion between a disciple of Confucius and an old gardener. The gardener was watering his plot, fetching the water in a bucket which he carried laboriously up and down the steps hewed into the wall of his well. When the Confucian told him of an invention called a draw-well, which made it possible to bring up lots of water very quickly, without much toil, the idea of adopting this easy, effective means moved the gardener to scorn and indignation. "Where there are wicked inventions," he said, "there are wicked uses, and where there are wicked uses, there are wicked hearts. If one's heart is wicked, he has soiled the purity of his soul. I know this invention, but I would be ashamed of using it."

There, in China, centuries before Christ, the idea of man's salvation in his communal state was discussed — the natural, primal state contrasted with the unnatural and distorted. In fact, however, we cannot conceive of a pure, consistent primal state. What is the difference in essence between the gardener's "natural tools" — his bucket or the steps on the wall of his well — and the "wicked inventions"? The jump from a healthy, mastered technology to an unhealthy, violent one lies in every step, and so does the clash between traditional habits and the delight in innovations.

Myths of paradise and golden ages symbolize a state of harmony that men dream about, a lasting, self-contained bliss as against the ceaseless change and irreconcilable discord of our temporal existence. It may turn from a symbol into a real-life program either for the individual, the sage who will go untouched through the world, or for the community that is to be thrown into the bliss of harmony by revolution. Both can be conceived only in contradictory and inconsistent terms, and accomplished in ruinous fashion. The realization of mythical symbols itself is a new, unnecessary evil added to the inexorable evil of advancing in time. In this advance, machine-smashing and machine romanticism are equally irrational.

A question forces itself upon us: Is man's new ability to destroy all life on earth merely the last phase of a technological process that has always been essentially destructive, anyway? Or has this process always been the premise of the unfoldment of human potentialities, so that only the dangers attached to it at all times have now reached their peak?

Technology as such is by no means a process of total destruction. It gives man both chances. We might interpret the problem and the challenge it poses by saying that man is fundamentally incomplete. He is Nietzsche's "still undetermined animal." It is still up to him to decide — by the decisions of countless individuals — what will become of him. Man can know, and so he ought to know — for that is his essence. He can win technological mastery over natural forces, so he ought to do so — for this provides him with a steadily widening foundation of new potentialities. The technology he has produced does not threaten him as such; it is he who threatens himself with it. The situations it confronts him with are challenges for him. To cope with them, he must change. He will either change or he is unworthy of life and will, against his will, destroy himself by his technology.

This risk was present at the very outset of human evolution. Unlike an animal species, man does not live on changelessly for immeasurable periods of time, until natural events cause sudden destructive catastrophes or the slow, inheritable mutations of life. When man embarked upon his yet-to-be-created history, he unwittingly risked his life in a relatively brief span of a few thousand years. Necessity and evil — in whose conquest he rises above himself — drive him on or devour him. In failure, he would not live on like the animals but would destroy himself and all life with him.

We do not know of any universal plan or goal. We speak as if there were one, as if it called for the uplifting of man — or, failing that, for his doom. When we think, each of us chooses between the quest of uplift or the thoughtless bustle in superficialities, with eventual doom. If we want to be ourselves, we must want to take the greatest chance, along with science and technology, and if it turns out badly, man will have proved unworthy of his existence. Though we cannot imagine or realize any over-all plan, we can share the risks as well as the potentialities and successes — we can lift ourselves into the ever brightening unknown or perish in darkness.

No scientist, therefore, can be blamed for discovering and inventing sources of dangers whose very point is the trial and transformation of man. The scientists are links in the chain of those who evoke the potential that man can grasp, for good or ill. They aggravate the situation, so that we may learn what we must want if we are human. This alone can make us more fully conscious of our humanity, its origins and chances, even though it remains vague for us beyond the challenge of the day.

The scientists, being human, also face the situation and the question what the consequences of their actions could and should be, by virtue of our freedom. They were acting, as men have always been acting, unaware of the consequences, and that is what frightens them now. Mankind listens to these men who wish to help avoid the dread results of their discoveries; they are deemed oracles of truth, yet their conduct shows more helplessness than insight. Einstein induced Roosevelt to have the bomb made when he was fearful of Hitler and the German physicists who might be about to make it, to give it to Hitler, and to enable Hitler's Reich to rule the world; after the war, he warned the world of doom if it continued on this way. But once the brains of scientists and engineers have been started churning — especially with the aid of public resources never yet mobilized on such a scale for any scientific purpose — a well-meant word of caution can hardly matter. Scientists by the thousands have turned into a skilled labor force, a tool of the state that wants tools of maximum destructiveness, so as to be constantly superior to the enemy. Many do as they are told, absorbed in their technical tasks, giving no thought to the whole. Some feel vague pangs of conscience, hesitate, and withdraw from work on weapons.

Indeed, we cannot expect the scientists to solve the questions raised by their achievements. For if they speak on those issues, they are no longer scientific authorities but human beings called upon to think like all the rest. The world owes them its knowledge of the technological facts and possibilities, but in their quality as scientists they cannot find the magic formula. What makes people expect it of them is the modern superstition that life might be based upon science and conducted according to science — but the customary way of scientific thinking will not even take us to the questions we must answer, weigh, and resolve in politics and in philosophical living practice. Scientific thinking can provide premises of material information, but the problems themselves arise on a different level, from a different source.

Philosophy is the thinking that enables man to ascertain what exists and what he wants, to grasp his meaning, and to find himself from the source. Politics, for the purpose of bettering human existence, takes its bearings from power — in which, fundamentally, everyone shares, though he may not know it; the only expert knowledge about this concerns ways and means and news of present realities, not motivations and responsibilities. Physics, technology, science, are matters for experts. They require special knowledge and skills for special tasks. This expert knowledge in the sciences proper is difficult to obtain, takes long special study and training, and is certainly not needed by every human being as such. The political and philosophical equivalents of this expert knowledge *are* needed by every human being. To become political and philosophical "experts," we need the experience of life itself and must draw not only upon the intellect but upon the whole of man with his original motives.

Not everyone can be a physicist. But as a matter of principle, each human being shares in politics and in philosophy, and justly claims in these fields the right to be convinced rather than fobbed off with authoritative statements. Everyone desires to know what he really wants. Political and philosophical thought will help him — not decisively, by scientific instruction, but by illuminating what he already knows.

The scientist as such is non-political. The truth of his knowledge has nothing to do with politics; it remains the same, whether the scientist's own leanings are totalitarian or libertarian. But science may have political consequences. The truths it uncovers may be undesirable to a political power and therefore objects of persecution. They may also have practical applications, especially in weapons technology — the sphere that is our subject.

The link of science and politics shocked the world only when the bombs became immensely, incalculably destructive. The scientists were frightened. Many felt that their scientific duty went beyond announcing their results and realizing technological possibilities. But what else could they do? As scientists, it became clear, they could do nothing more, except for informing the public; as men, they had the obligations of all other men. Now, let us see what scientists have said and done.

Two motivations are distinguishable. Either a scientist seeks the knowledge of nature as such, or he seeks it for purposes of its application. The first starts with the idea of pure knowledge, the second with a purpose. In the case of the atom bomb, the scientist seeks atomic knowledge either for its own sake or so as to cope by technological means with the menace of tyrants at the helms of nations.

If a scientist thinks politically and acts as a trail blazer for the production of the strongest weapons — as was done by Szilard, and by Einstein in his famed letter to Roosevelt — the motivation is intensified when the possible enemy, who would destroy all political freedom, can really make the bomb. Then the greatest possible drive for superiority, or at least for a balance, is a political necessity. But once the bomb exists and its efficacy has been realized, the scientists split again.

Some say, in answer to the threat of possible total destruction, that this must not happen under any circumstances. They take active steps to prevent the production of more and more destructive weapons and come close to treason.

Others say they will have nothing to do with it if it happens. These turn to other research and refuse their co-operation — which in free countries they can do without endangering themselves. For only the totalitarians consider science an exclusive servant of the state and condemn a refusal to co-operate as sabotage; in the free world, the meaning of science is suprapolitical and self-sufficient.

A third group of scientists regard the road of weapons technology as unavoidable, for the time being. The way out, say those, is not to cripple bomb production in your own country; it can only be a common political motivation of both opponents. Until such a community is achieved, they will co-operate in the utmost possible development of destructive power, in the hope that this maximum may most effectively compel reflection and, subsequently, peace.

Still others — the majority — serve their own countries as professional scientists and engineers without giving further thought to it, like skilled workers performing their assigned tasks. The responsibility, they feel, is not theirs but the government's; they only want to do the best possible job. This phenomenon, characteristic of our world, has been called a personality split between profession and conscience. As a man follows one, the other is silent. As he carries out orders in his profession, he does not feel responsible, nor does he think of the final objective — it is none of his business. Each individual, in this view, is a cog in the wheel; if the wheel is criminal, it was not he who gave the orders. It is not his choice; if he thinks about it at all, it is a fate from which he could not escape.

During the drama of the atom bomb, all these problems and possibilities were felt, suffered, pondered by the scientists in the United States, the foremost of whom were refugees from Italy, Hungary, and Germany, hunted by murderous tyranny and proscribed among their own people. Their unanimity about making the bomb lasted only as long as Hitler's power was threatening and no one knew how far science and technology would get with the superbombs. The first dilemma arose after the initial test explosion in New Mexico, at a moment when Hitler's Germany was already crushed and only the Japanese war remained to be finished. Truman's advisory council of leading scientists, consulted on the use of the bomb on a Japanese city, favored it. Many others opposed it at once, but their concern provided no alternative. Opinions varied and changed.

As long as Russia did not have the bomb, many believed that the American bomb would secure world peace forever, without ever being used. Others, on the basis of personal experiences and, in particular, of the destruction of Hiroshima and Nagasaki, had no such absolute faith in American policies; they feared that America, free from the threat of retaliation, might brutally use the bomb to establish her own world dominion. We are told that one man, seeing the only salvation in a Russo-American balance of atomic power, turned traitor in an attempt to play Providence, by passing bomb secrets to Russia.

Most scientists, it seems, did not become quite clear in their own minds and thus did not get to the point of experiencing the new extremity. Unstinting honesty alone keeps us from glossing over the reality of this situation, from evading it by some of the loopholes typical of past political actions and habitual perspectives. It is a curious aspect of scientific action and thought that many scientists, frightened by what they have done, think of peace and call for a solution while carrying matters further. These intelligent men want something and do not want it, and while they talk of tragedy, they act like children.

Robert Jungk tells of their reaction to the victory of Edward Teller — who promptly and unreservedly pushed the hydrogen bomb — over the reluctant J. Robert Oppenheimer: "In Teller, they saw not only the betrayer of a colleague but the living example and embodiment of treason against the ideals of science." In this notion, "the ideals of science," lies the whole fogginess and injustice of their condemnation of Teller. Of a former associate of Teller who kept silent, Jungk says, "Perhaps, like many another atomic scientist today, he feels that Teller's very advocacy and unparalleled exacerbation of the armament madness was the instrument of a divine will and an aid to peace." But Oppenheimer, in 1956, told a visitor, "We have done the devil's work. Now we are returning to our real tasks" — meaning an exclusive devotion to science.

The scientists' hope for salvation — most movingly expressed by Einstein — has been placed in the very science that wrought the menace, on the ground that its spirit should be one of truthfulness, reason, and humanity. There is profound truth here, but it applies only to a source of science, not to science itself, and not to modern scientific activity — which, though still advancing in fact, is detached from the source. Let us examine this more closely.

The spirit of philosophy is what gives meaning to science. It wants science to be. It knows the life of knowledge as the dignity of man. This spirit of honesty, and of love for a world asking to be known, is the source of the universal pursuit of knowledge. It warns against being deceived by anything, by any involvement or prejudice. It develops the methods of cogent discovery and constant self-criticism. It is trustworthy. Great scientists serve as examples — Kepler, for instance. The ethos, he said, cannot possibly vanish from the heart of one possessed by science, since the discovery of nature is a repetition of the thoughts of the Creator. The discovery of the celestial movements, the comprehension of eternal orders — not in playful fancy, but in the interaction of mathematical concepts with empirical observations and measurements — molds the discoverer in a certain resemblance to the divine works, tames his unruly desires, and arouses his love of "justice, mildness, honor, and purity." It makes him indifferent to priority: told that his ideas were presented by Galileo as Galileo's own, Kepler refused to stop

Galileo from claiming them. "Let the Garamantes and the Indians hear of these and other secrets of God; let my enemies proclaim them and let my name perish, if only the name of God, the Father of Spirits, be glorified."

Yet what we call science today is no longer this philosophical source that gives meaning to its existence, but the course of modern research that yields cogent discoveries. The truth of these discoveries is detached from the source that went in search of them. The lost source is ignored, because the criteria of truth are independent of it, existing regardless of the impulses that led to the discoveries. The course of research, once in progress, may become mere intellectual bustle without those motives. Discovery comes to mean personal fame; priority is passionately defended; knowledge becomes useful and is sought for the sake of its use.

The philosophical impulse includes truthfulness as a whole, a desire for knowledge wherever possible — for we know that all our life is subject to the warning of Goethe's Mephistopheles: "If reason and knowledge you will despise, the highest force to which man can rise, I'll have you for sure." And yet, although a science detached from this encompassing, meaningful motivation, a science pursued in specialties by the sole criterion of scientific truth or error, does advance knowledge, its bearers cannot be relied upon outside the special field in which their reputations bar deception. A scientist whose research results are true does not have to be truthful in general. There is no integral link between the scientific ethos of reliable truth in research and the ethos of reliable truthfulness on the part of the researcher.

Scientific research as such is not yet the bond of the knowing. In general, it links only the intellect of men — this mere point of over-all consciousness, in which everyone can agree with everyone else on logically or empirically cogent knowledge. Such is the bond of knowing how to make atom bombs, which can then be used for mutual destruction. To advance knowledge, we join even with our worst enemy. Science is no world-uniting power, and scientific communication is no sign of friendship and trust. It is such a sign only where the fundamental drive of science, which alone gives meaning to it, binds men existentially — where their common work makes them friends because the philosophical motive, the spirit of science, remains alive in it. When Peter Kapitza, Lord Rutherford's Russian friend and assistant of many years, went home on a visit and Stalin did not let him out again, Rutherford sent his costly equipment to Russia, so Kapitza might continue his

must change views toward self

research. What did scientists care for politics? Only a science that is more than science will engender this rare, true communion of the idea. A detached science will not do it.

Science — as the progress of the cogent knowledge of nature — cannot understand its own meaning and can never adequately account for its own necessity. Therefore, it cannot show us the way out of doom, either. Today, its bearers frequently lack that high philosophical impulse; they take up science as a sort of brainwork that can yield a livelihood, position, and prestige like any other vocation. Rutherford, Einstein, and many others who are still living are moving exceptions. The detached science that exists in fact, and keeps advancing, is as such neither human nor rational; it is neutral and indifferent to everything except the truth of its findings. There is no necessary link whatever between the motivation of scientific activity and the human source of a genuine desire to know.

And yet, it is the scientists who call for a "new way of thinking." In 1950, Einstein's message to the Italian scientists referred both to the technical possibility of destroying all life on earth — "Everything seems to fit into this fatal course of events" — and to the only possibility of salvation. "The unleashed power of the atom has changed everything but our way of thinking," he wrote. "We need an essentially new way of thinking if mankind is to survive." And what should this be? "Men must radically change their attitudes toward each other and their views of the future." Wherein should the change lie? In the methods. Force, said Einstein, "must no longer be an instrument of politics" — that is to say, war must be abolished. "In the decisive moment — and I see this grave moment before us — I shall raise my voice with all my remaining strength," he concluded.

The "decisive moment" would certainly be too late; to be effective at that moment, the change in the way of thinking would have to spread among mankind, and that takes time. Yet the "new way of thinking" has since become a formula. Many physicists talk of it as if it were something bound to come. Max Born, for example, sees the same way ahead as Einstein: the complete abolition of war and a power-free politics. "Today," he says, "we do not have much time left; it is up to our generation to succeed in thinking differently. If we fail, the days of civilized humanity are numbered."

We hear different language from a scientist like Oppenheimer, whom Jungk quotes as talking of "beauty," of "our faculty of seeing it in remote, strange, unfamiliar places," of paths that "maintain existence in a great, open, windy world. . . . This is the premise of man, and on these terms we can help, because we love one another." In such sentences I can see only an escape into sophisticated aestheticism, into phrases that are existentially confusing, seductive, and soporific in relation to reality. In another direction, Wolfgang Pauli pointed to a long-neglected "inner road to salvation." He regarded "the idea of the goal of a conquest of contradictions, which involves a synthesis encompassing both rational understanding and the mystical experience of unity, as the explicit or implicit mythos of our own present time." The recognition of that inner road to salvation would lead to a "new humility." To me, such concepts do not seem to indicate an existential change; they rather seem like an escape into mysticism. With such aesthetic or mystical statements, these scientists do demonstrate a new awareness of the inadequacy of scientific insight. But what they seek does not lie in their accustomed channels of thought, and so they present it only as an educated knowledge moving detachedly alongside their professional activity.

The phrase "new way of thinking" touches the crucial point, but thus far it may be merely a phrase that the scientists use without knowing what they are really calling for. When they develop the new way itself, they misunderstand the true impulse. But we must see the meaning, the source, the nature, and the consequences of this new way of thinking.

Some scientists tend to believe that mankind might reach agreement on the basis of simple rational conclusions whose cogency every mind would have to admit. If this fails, they yield to hopeless pessimism. They are quite touching in their confidence in rationality, in their belief that they themselves are already so far advanced in their living practice that we would be saved if everyone followed their example. And they are frightening in their despair — which they have so far expressed only in private. Both the confident and the despairing seem to have no notion of the depths to which the change in the way of thinking — the permeation of the intellect with reason — would have to extend. Nothing short of a transformation of life into a life of reason could be the step that would enable our future leaders to make the saving decisions, say the saving words, and do the saving deeds.

The "new way," the "different thinking," does not mean going further along the lines of the old way, neither in the scientific-technological nor in the politically purposive direction. The problems raised by the existence of the atom bomb cannot possibly be solved by the scientific thinking that led to the discovery of nuclear energy; indeed, the bomb is shaking us out of the philosophical slumber of a baselessly optimistic faith in progress. Things are getting serious again — not only because of war, disease, and hunger, as in the past, but because of the real danger that mankind will perish.

Every individual knows that he must die — and lives, perhaps, as if it were not so. Although he cannot really believe in his death, he knows that it is certain. That mankind will perish is not certain; it is possible, even probable, but not unalterable, like an event of nature. It depends on man himself whether or not it will occur. In this perspective, life must become different from what it was in our previous conception of an indefinitely continuing history of man.

But is the new situation really shattering? Do we not get used to danger? Do we not live on as usual, since it is not really imminent yet? Do we not seek distraction in the heedless bustle of day-to-day activities? Is everyone concerned only with his own death, not with the doom of mankind that would mean no more to him than the death he will die anyway?

Whoever answers this question in the affirmative thinks so little of man — and of himself, presumably — that if he were right, there would indeed be no hope left. There would be no impulse to change. Such a man has never met humanity itself in others, in forms which, however beclouded, he could believe; he has not experienced the realities of history, which this present humanity alone renders wholly convincing. To him, everything turns a turbulent gray in which humanity and its potentials cease. If he were right, this would be truly the beginning of the end.

We may be certain that the impulse to the new way of thinking can come only from men who do not lapse into such existential passivity of vital bustle, of working activities within a narrowing horizon — from men who hold fast to the original potential of humanity, who know their roots in the past and heed its challenge, who want to join in building for the future and think of children and grandchildren, literal or otherwise. It can come only from men who know they have a task in the course of things: to stand for those to come and to take good care of what has been intrusted to them.

What can stimulate the new way of thinking today is not its source. The source, from the beginning, lies in the true humanity that each of us is given by Transcendence, in the humanity that is reborn with every child. The present impulse may arouse the new way, but it does not create what in our present situation is merely a new form of the age-old way of thinking that man has always found in being changed.

Does thinking stop when it can no longer show definite objects, when it no longer leads by means of a direct, logical conclusion to a proposal or an action? Or is there a way of thinking that will non-objectively visualize inner actions to come? Is silence indicated where no way can be shown? If thinking has entered into all possible forms of objective knowledge and all possible communications of its objects, if it has reached the limits of tangibility and the limits of all objective determination — does it then cease, nothing lying beyond?

By no means. What follows here is the step from mere intellectual thinking to encompassing rational thinking that transforms man in his entirety. Every time, since the beginnings of philosophy, the "new way of thinking" has been one with the change in man. It has two stages. The first is recognition of the limits of the old, accustomed ways of thinking — which makes it clear that we try in vain to save ourselves by carrying this thinking further on the same level. But the second stage is learning that there is no end to thinking when its past form is transcended — that we must not yield here to the obscurities we like to cite as "feeling" or "instinct" or "tact," but that we can become aware of the encompassing foundation of thought on which even the intellect with its research, its planning, its technology, bases its objectivizing steps. For these need guidance.

This new thinking can say no more to those who want nothing but plans and instructions, but it will aid people perplexed by the ultimate aimlessness of all planned aims. For they have experienced the intellect's inability to guide the life of existence and resolution. Unless they drown their puzzled thoughts in the din of distracted and, therefore, trivial activities, they will be saved by the thought processes of the new way — which are true only when the thinker changes, not when he just thinks of something. Along with the knowledge of things, these processes evoke an inner attitude of vision, of discrimination, of judgment. In the very use of the old intellectual methods of thinking — which cannot be dispensed with for even a moment — the new way works like a protean order of world consciousness.

There are thus two turning points: first from planning, from the definite knowledge of what can possibly happen, to encompassing philosophical thought — and then back again to thinking in that world of knowledge and planning. The first turn in thinking leads to man's change in his thinking, the second to the effect of his change in the world and to the resulting change in the direction of events. One turning point is not possible without the other. Reason presupposes intellect, and an intellect trying to be self-sufficient would remain empty.

All our thinking is inured to the intellect and its end-and-means relations; even when it goes beyond the intellect, it must stay in it as well, at every step. Wherever we meet the reverse, not objectively instructive thinking, we are inclined to ask: What good is it? How can I put it to use? What shall I do? What arrangements are indicated? The habit of purposive, technical thinking wants all practical questions answered in the form of instructions. Even if we should formally succeed in the new thinking, for brief moments, such questions quickly tend to take us back to the old one. We get the courage for the new thinking only from the change within ourselves, not from any demonstrable, external fact or visible achievement.

In actual fact, the intellect never suffices even to those living in its habits. This is why, at times, we can suddenly hear rationalists engage in all sorts of emotional talk, whether nationalistic, Marxist, optimistic, pessimistic, or religious in character. Such talk is either decorative embroidery or an expression of dark pretensions, vindications, and consolations. Although it defines the spot from which help would have to come — in ways quite different from all the planning and programing — this spot is still occupied by new rationalizations, objectivations, incarnations, and illusory "bodies of knowledge" that do not change the way of thinking at all. Relapsing into the old way, they enunciate soothing fantasies in which we deceive ourselves about the situation, miss our chance to change, and benightedly continue on our accustomed path. Having thought something in the process of change, we all tend to talk it back instantly into the realm of planning, intellectual, objectivating thought. To make it tangible, we rob it of its meaning.

The intellectual habits, imperceptibly enhanced into absolutes, are like a barrier blocking our road to reason. These habits resent all that is to take them beyond ourselves, even though they are not asked to give themselves up. "Visionary talk," "daydreaming," "romanticism" — these are some of the defensive classifications thrown out by the intellect. What it cannot grasp it pushes aside ruthlessly, without an attempt at understanding. Thus it may say, in practical questions, "Don't wail; tell us what's to be done! . . . Don't preach; show us the way! . . . No speculative witchcraft; let's be realistic!"

To be sure, in situations that demand a reversal of thinking, men may plunge into irrationality instead of rising to reason. Those warnings of the intellect are wrong only when they identify reason with irrational obscurity. Real "wailing" or "preaching" or "witchcraft" would be the end of reason as well; but reason is the only salvation for the perplexed who have reached the dead end of the intellect and are about to plunge into irrationality. Man is more than intellect. The surplus can either misunderstand itself in the obscurities of irrationality or find itself in the lucidity of reason. The resentment of the transforming new thought really goes back to man's unwillingness to be himself. It is our defense against claims upon our true selves, and an outgrowth of our secretiveness. We do not like to show ourselves, to lay ourselves bare, to commit our true selves.

When our accustomed intellectual road comes to an end and man's intellect counsels silence, human reason is not silenced yet. There is truth in silence only when it is no empty hush but a silence replete with new thought capable of indirect communication. Does silence not enfold the depth of thoughts striving to be born, the proper thoughts for inner action? And is not, therefore, every intentional, lasting silence — above all, the silence before oneself — already untruthful? Is not the utmost candor required to convey the cause of silence as a source of new, original thought and indirect communication?

Man wants to be able to follow instructions without having to commit himself. He wants to remain aloof and not to expose himself. He wants a place where he is untouchable. He wants no claims made upon his true self, no questioning, no jeopardizing of his self-assurance. In other words, he does not want to be himself — for the untouchable, the reserved, the undisclosed secret is precisely the despair of nonentity. Kierkegaard superlatively showed this cycle of self-unconscious despair in the concepts of "wanting-to-be-oneself" and "not-wanting-to-be-oneself."

The resentment against a reversal of thought is resistance to individual responsibility. We do not want it to be true that it is up to every individual himself what will be and what will become of mankind. We do not want to live and act under such pressure. But reason, as the

prophetic
(predictive)

manifestation at the source, is the premise of all good, and secretiveness is the true source of evil.

The intellect places the objects of thinking — things and people — at a distance where the thought no longer involves the thinker. Are we not hiding already when we cling to intellectual tangibility as our last attainable goal? Is not, therefore, a thinking that limits itself to the intellect an untruth, a form of concealment? It is, unless received into a comprehensive way of thinking that begins and ends with the transformation of man.

In our thinking existence, the self-secluding intellect is like a wall that hems us in unawares. We want all that matters objectified, so that we can know and master it. We want everything as technology, but without the foundation that gives support, measure, and meaning to technology. We dislike the thinking that gives not only validity but content to all plans. We do not want thought to be an inner action. We want, so to speak, to detach from ourselves what must be done, even in the source.

We want to know history and to direct it as if it were unrelated to ourselves. We go to psychology, to sociology, to political science in search of means of direction, which will work only in details. But we expect more. We draw up pictures of the whole, on the basis of which we estimate what must be done to direct the whole. With these pictures — which are façades — we want to operate as with realities behind which we can seclude ourselves. We want to "arrange" everything, and if it cannot be arranged, we despair instead of being ourselves and reaching the source which alone gives meaning and guidance to all arrangements.

This throws us into an *existential confusion* in which we stake everything on so-called facts and think we can disregard ourselves. At the same time, we are thrown into *factual confusion* by our uncritical failure to distinguish the methods of cognition. Behind both confusions lurk shadowy impulses: total resignation, despair, the death wish, a state of outrage at all things, of rebellion against existence. There is within us an unconscious urge to fight any contact with our innermost being, which we consider obscure, incalculable, and therefore profound. The intellect, in itself the antithesis of this confused darkness, becomes the very means of protecting its untouchability. Then the intellect will stubbornly hold its ground and deny itself to that untouched obscurity.

But if the intellect realizes its own limitations, it can, in quite different fashion, place its strength at the service of reason. To the intellect, both the untouchable confusion and reason itself seem dark; but it need not let itself be degraded to a tool of secretiveness and respect the darkness while feeding on it and thus turning false to itself. It can willingly subordinate itself to reason and thus accomplish its own free unfoldment. Then the intellect turns out to be an indispensable tool of reason — a tool which reason constantly transcends without ever losing it.

The light of reason and the darkness of the untouchable — these are the great alternatives from which we choose in coming to be ourselves. From this choice comes the "new way of thinking," which is simply the way of a thinking man who is himself. He stops hiding and is fully present as what he is and will be. The new way of thinking makes him manifest, both to himself and to the other, and to all those who will be with him when he is rational — that is to say, identical with his true self.

13

REASON

The new thinking is the age-old one which thus far has not penetrated far enough to form and guide communities of men: it is reason; it is philosophy. Philosophy has to arouse, to encourage, and to realize itself. Are we suggesting, then, that people should study philosophy, perhaps the philosophical activities of our time, as presented in books and periodicals and in the reports of meetings? By no means. Our advice is to engage in the philosophizing that is part of true humanity, that has been embodied through the centuries in great philosophers whose acquaintance we would desire for anyone who has leisure and wants to reflect — and how much free time is available to most of us, excepting managers and fanatics and the exploited victims of despotic regimes! Philosophy alone yields clarity against the perversion of reason. Philosophy alone confirms, broadly and deeply, the human content which everyone harbors within himself, seeks in reflection, and finds in the realization of his existence.

In our present reality, the academic philosophy that boasts of its scientific character is helpless. What we need is not mere specialized knowledge, as in all the sciences, but a change in man, the kind he has become conscious of since Socrates and Plato. Philosophizing does not provide man with new, precise knowledge; it does not add a new science to the rest. It offers no suggestions, plans, or programs. But it can arouse the inner disposition from which these tangibles derive their guiding sense.

What we have to expound now is bound to seem vacuous and unintelligible unless we suspend the question of its utility. We must overcome our tendency always to ask what we can do with a thing, and we must learn to think without a purpose. Humanity demands that purposeless self-determination and undesigning ascertainment should take us to an effective foundation and guidance of all that we do.

Let us see, first, what reason is.

Every concept achieves an abstraction; to this extent, abstraction is a clarifying instrument of the intellect, and thus of reason. Only definite — distinguishing and contrasting — thoughts are clear thoughts. But although there is no clarity without abstractions, sticking to abstractions alienates us from reality. Abstract thinking becomes untrue thinking if a finite definition claims to be an unrelated truth — that is to say, if it is made absolute.

Unlike this abstract thinking of the mere intellect, rational thinking absorbs the abstractions, transcends them, and returns with them to reality. Such concrete thinking has content and visuality. It is not self-sufficient. It uses fruitful abstraction as a means of achieving clarity and a deeper penetration of reality, but it never loses its grip on what it relates to, where it comes from, whence it draws substance and significance: reality itself.

Again and again in this book, we have encountered abstractions that turned into fallacies, in political opinions, proposals, demands. Let me recall some examples.

"Departmental thinking" leads us to view our own limited activity as absolute, to carry it out regardless of the whole — until, despite formal mutual acknowledgment of the departments, it grows like a tumor in the living body, harmful to the spirit of the whole.

We talk of all-determining "interests." But what really matters is what kind of interests they are, how well we are aware of them, how they may change and can be guided as we become aware of them, and how they are represented by the politicians and the masses. To abstraction, an interest, once defined, is absolute, but concrete thinking requires its integration. The representation of interests is always in danger of succumbing to abstractions; isolation hurts the interests themselves.

Even "sacrifice" is called for in abstraction — as for states as they are or for the good of future generations or for a "leader." We think we can calculate sacrifice, manage it, let others make it. To be concrete, however, sacrifice requires, for example, the moral substance that has come down to us from the past, upholds the present, and holds itself responsible for the future. Even such images of past and future are not reasons for sacrifice; they are mere symbols in the consciousness of those who freely, as individuals or as individual members of their community, make the sacrifice to eternity.

There are abstract concepts of the basic course of events. For example, the current formula of moral development having failed to keep pace with technological progress is purely abstract, unvisualized thinking — for what we call development or progress in technology has no parallel in ethical change. The progress of transferable knowledge and skill differs in essence from the inner transformation that has happened to man at all times and in all ages and is strictly individual. There is no comparison between the intellectual labor of progress and the existential establishment of moral man.

And then there are the panaceas, abstractions that ignore all other realities and are supposed to make the problems perfectly easy to solve — like the aggressor concept or the idea of interest-free money or the technique for putting an end to nuclear tests. One nation — no matter whether Russia or America — may say, "We are suspending all tests and expect our opponents to do the same; if they do not, we must reluctantly resume testing after a year's time." By this one act, the nation that performs it is supposed to achieve moral superiority, so that "the conscience of the world" would compel the antagonist to follow suit. The basic error of this abstraction is to argue as if this simple, clear, salutary challenge were posed by the authority of a world already united — as if it were valid independently of all political and military realities — as if there were no need to inquire whether compliance might be more helpful, in terms of power politics, to one side than to the other, and whether political trickery might not thus disguise self-interest under a cloak of ethics. An abstraction of unequivocal, independent validity ignores the reality in which the question is by no means the same for different nations.

Generally, we can say that unscrupulous politics uses this inclination to abstract thinking — especially among those who "think" the least — by trying constantly to separate whatever questions happen to be under negotiation: the military from the political, the political from the economic, the economic from the cultural. Truly rational thinking distinguishes all these along the way, but its decisions are made so as to interrelate all motives.

A final abstraction detaches national policies from the interest of the whole international community. Self-preservation isolates itself when it views the self-preservation of all others as an obstacle rather than as a justified interest on their part. Thus American policy, which concretely represents the entire free world, becomes abstract when it considers the rest not as partners but as a glacis in the battle with Russia. An example of this appeared during the Suez crisis, when Eisenhower boasted that American Near Eastern policy had achieved independence of British and French aims for the first time. The price of this proud, abstract independence was paid by proceeding against Britain in league with Russia.

The power of abstraction serves our concrete insight, but captivity in abstraction shuts us off from reality. Because of the rule of abstractions and the still common lack of education in rational thought, politicians often present a picture of purely superficial activity. With the air of saying something important, of proposing something new, they create more abstractions that becloud the issues and divert attention while delaying real action. They let sleeping dogs lie. They carry on because of the positions they happen to hold, because they stand for something that has nothing behind it as long as there is no idea as the driving force in which reason meets reality. They must say something to the people, to maintain an unstable, easily shaken, and easily restored contentment. The public is content; all it wants is calm and a flourishing economy, a high standard of living and oblivion in pleasure. The politician is content; when he is talked about, seen and heard for a moment, he feels that he exists. There are great expectations of peace and understanding, and illusions of working in that direction. There is movement in raising and smoothing surface ripples, and helplessness before the tidal waves that approach beyond the horizon. Things are not getting serious, not serious enough. They are still as ever — as before 1914, before 1933, and before 1939. One does not want to know. One feels unable to change things, so one lets them take their course.

And rising against this world of indecisive drift are those who claim to have revelations and to know what must be done to set everything right — the schemers and fanatics of some abstraction or other.

Different from both the mass of actors and their isolated antagonists are the individuals who place their trust in reason. Their fundamental experience is that the thinking person himself is still only awakening, not fully awake — it is this kind of thinking that shows up and conquers abstractions, that shakes off soothing syrup, languor, and creature comforts, and combats fanaticism. It seeks to channel the quickly smothered and soon forgotten volcanic outbursts against the surface bustle into proper expressions of the truth hidden in that confusion.

In this book I am striving for such rational thoughts. I have no ready solution and no panacea. I want to be helpful in thinking so as to come closer to reality. I am looking for abstractions insofar as they give a better approach to reality, and I reject them if they become fixed positions that must always be inadequate. I believe that unreserved thinking can produce more than mere makeshifts in a seemingly irresistible march to the abyss, camouflaged as prosperity. I am looking for inner action linked with thought. What matters is the awakening — not only to this fact or that, but to the basic attitude of rational (that is to say, concrete) thinking. I turn to those who do not want to forget. But I know how far I am from my goal.

It is a basic fact of our existence that we are governed by abstractions through which we see. But we can understand that, as Goethe put it, "Every fact is theory" — in other words, that which we call a fact is already seen and cannot help being seen on the conceptual premises of all our perceptions and definitions. Once we realize this, the forms through which we see become means of illuminating reality rather than deceptive spectacles that distort or discolor. Thus we conceive the idea of an open mind, which enables us to master the very prejudices we cannot do without.

False abstractions are the recourse of men who shun the concrete because they do not want to change. They involve themselves in their abstractions as in a trusswork that they think will give them self-assurance. They want to stay as they are, but with outside help. They want to be left alone, not to be carried along in an upsurge to better things, not to make sacrifices. The abstractions of the intellect end in a void, or in fanaticism; the concretions lie in the historicity of our existence. Reason is capable of listening to existence; it manifests itself when it becomes one with the reality of our being.

The next insight required for the new thinking is one that every human being has, generally without knowing it. It is a distinction clarified by Kant, a simple one, yet hard to keep in mind. For our subject, this insight can be stated as follows:

What is the root cause of our trouble? It has been defined in many ways. Psychologically it may be human ferocity, rapaciousness, love of adventure, the lust of feeling superior to life in flinging it away, etc.

Economically it may be the blind selfishness that has lost its sense of values, subordinates everything to the great leveler, money, and alienates man from himself. Technologically it may be the process of intelligent invention, which produces instruments of production and of destruction simultaneously, to the point where both unlimited production and total destruction are possible. Politically it may be a wrongly organized power practice, a way of government that induces the state to act ruinously even against the will of a vast majority of the people. These and other concepts note, on the one hand, an age-old, ever recurring course of events in general terms; on the other, they describe and explain, within the historical process, what is new at a particular time. In these ways, our knowledge of objectively ascertainable phenomena can indeed be indefinitely advanced. There is no limit to research based on the premise that things happen according to cognoscible necessities — or, rather, its only limit is the fact that all this cognition does not reach the root cause itself, only its manifestations in the forms in which they appear to us from our different points of view.

It is a fatal error to *confuse these cognoscible manifestations with being as such.* The cognoscible manifestations are governed by necessity, but being as such is the source of *freedom.* In the world of cognoscibilities, freedom is not to be found and remains incomprehensible, but we assure ourselves of it by our own actions. It is impossible and paradoxical to treat freedom as if it were there for us to know, to deal with, operate with, reckon with, or to restore on the basis of some psychological science, as by psychotherapy. Though committed unconsciously and as a matter of course, this fundamental error perverts our sense of being. If we base our planned actions on it, it becomes disastrous. For freedom shows in the inner actions of the man who comes to be himself — it speaks in communication, from existence to existence — but it is not an object of knowledge.

Even if we have realized that freedom and cognoscibility are disparate, we tend to forget it because, as finite creatures of the senses, we keep being caught in the deceptive prison of our consciousness, which regards cognoscible objects as absolute.

Once we have understood the difference between freedom and cognoscibility, however, we see also that the root cause of the trouble is not a cognoscible process — neither psychological nor economic nor sociopolitical nor historically necessary nor metaphysical — but is, to man, the consequence of his free acts within an encompassing enigma.

All those processes that can be partly and increasingly known are still, as a whole, mere symptoms, manifestations, or consequences of what was originally done or left undone by free choice.

Freedom itself, of course, will shine more brightly and broadly as the fields of research are explored without restraint — but also the more decisively the better we know the limits of such knowledge.

Lest this be misunderstood, let me make clear that we are not talking now of political freedom. Political freedom is the actual condition of the way a state is governed. As such it can be known. What Thucydides or Montesquieu or De Tocqueville or Max Weber meant by political freedom can be defined and observed in the experience of political life. Its many forms are cognoscible realities. But the will to this political freedom is itself an act of existential freedom, and political freedom is not identical with this will. The existential freedom we were talking about exists wherever there are human beings; it is prepolitical and suprapolitical. It is the personal freedom of being oneself and seems possible even in conditions of political unfreedom. It is possible everywhere, as long as there is a truly human being. Political freedom, on the other hand, has appeared only among some Western nations since the Greeks and the Roman republic. Should we, then, not make so much of it? Could it, as an object of political knowledge, be an isolated phenomenon not valid for, and necessary to, all men?

We must not be deceived by the separation of the two freedoms. Political freedom cannot exist without the passion rising from existential freedom; where it is not related to the deeper freedom of true humanity, it will lose its substance and vanish. But existential freedom, too, is menaced in its visible realization and may even become impossible if political unfreedom is such as to enslave all of man, all of the people, and all that they do in their lives. True, the political subservience of almost all human history — except for that narrow, frequently interrupted strand of Western history — failed to result in the subservience of man as such; but it failed only because, under past living conditions, it did leave men a wide range of actual freedom. It was technology, with its communications and other tools of the omnipresent will of the state, that made the total enslavement of all by the state possible. And it is only now, therefore, that what used to be the ever-threatened concern of a few Western nations has become a necessity for the existence of all men. Now, as never before, true humanity requires political liberty to be able to realize itself at all. Subservience no longer allows the old way out into the worldlessness of remote regions, nor does it offer the wide range of a life that is free in fact.

The only safeguard against total rule — which was impossible without the means of modern technology — is political liberty. The great Asian nations, and all the rest, are now adopting this technology, but can they also adopt the forms of political freedom that would protect their people from the consequences of technology? Is political freedom as transferable as technology? We can only answer once more that the reality of cognoscible political freedom depends upon existential freedom, which is not cognoscible. It lies in the humanity of man. If technology threatens its realization, it must seek political freedom everywhere, to save humanity. If the forms of political freedom are not transferable like technological capacities — because the meaning and the actual success of free institutions, those cognoscibilities of freedom, depend upon the incognoscible existential freedom of man — the great, world-wide question today is how to transform a merely formal and, so to speak, technical freedom into real freedom rather than total rule.

Reason can be circumscribed but not defined. It can be aroused but not known. It is not an object of planning, but in its infinite scope it lets us find the way on which we come to ourselves and to the destiny in which, and which, we are.

May we dare to discuss what seems impossible to discuss even though all depends on it? This is exactly what philosophy has always done, and in its greatest manifestations it has at the same time realized the impossibility — not so as to fall silent, but so as to receive the very impossibility into the structure of its thoughts.

And to what end? It was thus that the most profound links between men were established, that the source within us was illuminated, the foundation that upholds us, the root cause of what exists by our means. It is by such thinking that reason takes effect — that in the medium of intellectual determinations, the only ones in which we can think meaningfully, we perceive the realm that is hidden from the intellect and has been the fount of everything good and true and great that men have achieved.

There will always be the objection that such language is vague and indefinite and does not tell us *what* to think and to do. The only answer is, first, that it is impossible here to be as definite as our intellect is about finite things, aims, means, and plans — what we need here is to resolve upon another kind of thinking, without which all finite knowledge, all purposive action, all daily routine, remain rootless and void. And, second, we need another kind of definiteness in the motion and realization of things that are beyond words or theses or deductions. The line of tangible experiences and the connection with the certainty of finite things are indispensable, but they deceive us if we use them as such, not as mere bridges.

The new — and age-old — thinking transcends the finite thought that cleaves to objects. As speculative thought, it goes beyond the intellect to the source of thinking itself. Such speculative thought has a powerful effect on the thinker, and on the listening re-thinker. In concepts and conceptual movements, in images and metaphors, and in the strength of symbols, it has created a language over the centuries. It has many meanings, as if it were done in a room full of mirrors. When it stays pure and honest, it keep all its words in a balance in which its seriousness can become sure of itself. But its existential weight is not recognizable by its content — only along with the content, by the way in which it is done.

If this transcendent thinking is due to the inadequacy of the world, it rises nonetheless from an encompassing, all-encompassing presence. It is not driven by the thing it transcends. It is drawn where it is going.

There is no ascent to this kind of thinking as if it were the consequence of previous steps or premises. On the contrary, it is the source from which the road leads down to the realization that will give it existence and substance in time.

Transcendent thinking occurs in man as man. It may reach conceptual clarity by philosophical methods, but it may have its full, real force in meditation and natural piety as well. True, without the self-assurance of philosophy this kind of thinking is hard put to defend itself in words against the intellect and its negations; but even then its simple certainty may keep it undaunted in life and deeds and words. On its own ground, as practical insight, it will be decisive for the course of events.

Both practical insight and transcendent thinking lie within the scope of reason. To turn back from the accustomed, self-sufficient intellectual way of thinking to the way of reason — that is the change in man on which his future depends.

Reason is independent. You can kill its bearers, but you cannot turn it into a function of worldly powers, whether states or churches. Yet reason may permeate all of those.

This kind of thinking is not a means to the self-preservation of mankind. It would be futile to incorporate it in a plan, which would always spoil it. But its existence may result in a life that would, by virtue of freedom and against the menace of the atom bombs, save mankind's existence as well.

This thinking may come to naught, however, if it turns into vacuous intellectualism or literary aestheticism. As "artistics" it is no more than a vaguely regulated tomfoolery, fascinating because of its noble origin, but as corrupting as erotic license because it keeps man from being himself. It loses the reason that once gave it birth; it softens man by the semblance of profound truth and prepares him for blind obedience. This thinking is as the thinker does. Where it is true, where it is upheld by the earnestness of existential responsibility, it is a free and illuminating game; its content and its movement manifest in symbols what the intellect can never know, although it carries our lives.

Reason is more than the sum of acts of clear thinking. These acts, rather, spring from a life-carrying basic mood, and it is this mood we call reason.

It does not come over us as a gay or somber attitude toward life; it is not subject to the fluctuations of vitality, although they may disturb it. It does not occur as a vital process.

This rational mood is not inborn. It is acquired under favorable conditions, although its meaning is not bound to these premises of its realization. It can grow only in a quiet, ceaseless struggle; it must be constantly wrested anew from unreason.

It is the essential human trait — whatever else is human shines by its light alone. It is the lofty mood of humanity itself.

It is as strong in youth as in old age, but in all phases of life it is in danger of failing. It is never perfected.

It exists only in common. The individual cannot be rational by himself.

Reason lies in the apperception of our environment, in constructive work, in earning for time and posterity, in peaceful competition, in the vision of beauty, in the contemplation of truth, in the fulfilment of one's destiny. Reason trusts in man and in his will to freedom, which receives intangible and incalculable aid from Transcendence.

Arrayed against reason are the self-destructive urge and the ways of thinking and being that lead to it, the indolence of watching, and the breathless, ruinous bustle that becomes incapable of a fulfilled life.

Against reason stands the supposed right of reticence, the unwillingness to be frank that forbids questioning, keeps mute, and withdraws from our neighbors and from ourselves, invoking a discretion that rightly applies to conventional intercourse. But what is done on the most intimate plane to manifest our existential foundation is the premise of all truthfulness and reason in the world.

Against reason stands the desire to forget. We shunt aside what we know only too well. We want to write *finis* under the undesirable past and thus to get rid of it. We do not want to hear about it. "The moral aspect is a matter of course" — why discuss it? Evil has been done — why reopen old wounds? Dreadful facts exist — why name them and say what is known, anyway? Whatever is thus removed from attention is as good as non-existent. We no longer need to let its consequences work within us; we know them, but we live as though we did not know. But reason demands that we should not forget, that all knowledge be kept not only in memory, but in mind. Reason forbids "killing time," with the intoxications of work, business, success, or with the distractions of pleasure.

Reason is essential to politics because it should prepare the ground for the community of all men in the state and in its institutions. At first, however, the community formed by reason is always one of individuals who find each other and — without agreements, without organization, without expression — embody the hidden rational solidarity. This reality is suprapolitical. It must take political action if politics is to become constructive and enduring, but it cannot be drawn into politics itself. It is, and it wants, more than politics even though passionately espousing politics as a cause that founds or destroys the life of all and must, therefore, be the concern of all. All the great philosophers, even the great mystics, were political thinkers.

The existence of a community of men of reason cannot be reckoned with as a political factor. But reason can become such a factor if it leads the planning intellect to confine its activities to the possible, and thus, in its planning, to allow every chance for rational men to meet, to work, and to grow. All institutions should consider this. They should be regulated only insofar as unavoidably necessary for their purpose; beyond this, the risk of tolerable mistakes in practice is better than a curtailment of the space in which individual reason can grow and take effect. It can, of course, grow only if it is present in men. If it is not present, we are setting up a mechanical apparatus of men who have nothing more than intellect, and the whole will function like a machine. It will turn into an inhuman existence and will duly perish along with its inhumanity. If they are to preserve their human character, all human institutions working with human organs must presume that man himself is potentially rational. If we do not expect reason, we shall not find it.

It would be unreal, however, to found an organization on this community of individual men of reason. In founding organizations, we must think of all men. So, we must erect machine-like organizations. But it is encompassing realism to know that the spirit of the whole which the machine serves, the spirit which can cope with constantly arising difficulties, comes only from the rational group. Just as machines have to be repaired when they are damaged, while life can help itself, mechanized institutions must break down unless their animating rational spirit is able to transform their living tissue, to repair their malfunctions, and to assure their self-preservation as a whole. A decline in present achievements may even be a symptom of solid revitalization.

No organization can produce reason and its conscience. They are its premises. Organization as such may become endlessly complicated and thus destructive of reason; organization conceived by and for reason will, for all its rational complexity, always remain simple. Its every institution is designed to listen to the reason of the individuals to which it owes its humanity and lasting significance.

The organizations that are increasing and multiplying today are headed by men, to be sure, but by men who are themselves subjected to the machine and "mechanized." Such structures are doomed. They will either be melted down in revolutionary crises and yield to a new, rationally borne humanity, or, unwillingly but also unresistingly, they will bring about mankind's destruction by the bomb. Hence, all the justified clamor against bureaucracy, machines, and mechanism. Yet they seem only to grow with all our planning, and to kill men like flies in a spider's web. Standing alone against this is what people call "fanciful": the quiet community of reason, starting with a few men and finally taking in all, limiting all mechanisms in their structure and pervading them with a rational spirit. Let us talk of this "fancy," which our insight tells us is the only saving reality of man.

While our common existence rests on the reliability of contracts and enforceable agreements, on promises and their fulfilment, all this is superficial in comparison with the reliability of rational communication. There, candor is boundless. All affirmation makes allowance for encompassing truth; error is permitted because of unlimited readiness to correct it; even insults will not lead to a breach, being recognized and forgiven in the encompassing union. But there, too, we find the greatest perplexity when such communication seems to run into impassable surface barriers, to founder on personal, untouchable taboos — for the only real guarantee of being is found in communication. If we drop out of it, or if communication as such seems to fail, we face a void, or a desert of empty vegetating. We are then still maintaining relations with each other; we still have an order of common existence; but in fact we are completely apart. What is said wrongly is no longer discussed but simply rejected without illumination. Such intercourse leads directly to twin derailments: we either keep an absolute distance or, in the despair of loneliness, we land without rhyme or reason in each other's arms.

In rational communication there is a common authority to be clarified only in communication itself. We cannot appeal to it against each other; we can only find it together. Here there are no statements of intention which then remain untouchable, as in political, economic, or professional negotiations. There are no limitations on what may be brought up, for any limitation, however plausible to the intellect, to conventions, to common sense, to psychology, goes against reason. The stages of discussion lead from the level of finite reasons — which remain an indispensable guide to the last — to the level of sounding existential sources.

Here we do not formulate "final positions." A final position — which I state as such — means the breaking-off of communication or its restriction to what remains possible if these positions are mutually acknowledged. Yet the very adoption of final positions is already irrational.

To abandon logically final positions, as existential absolutes, means to depart from self-will and obstinacy. In returning to conventional intercourse in the broadest sense, I respect another's final positions and accept them as part of the game. In boundless communication, which is the only rational one, we strive — however hard it may be to attain — for unlimited candor, in which anything goes and nothing is incorrigible. Correction itself, as an act of uniting communication, is possible only if the speaker has exposed himself to error, so that now one can see whether or not this has led him onto an illuminating path. It is only where we dare such boundless communication that we can rely on man himself, not merely on his pledges and contracts.

The followers of reason cannot be unfaithful; they can only seem so — in errors of judgment, in emotionality, in the pernicious distrust of others that asks skeptically why a rational unfaithfulness should be impossible. It is impossible because the communicability of reasons and motives is unlimited, and because, once there has been good will, its illumination must lead to agreement wherever, despite the severest differences of superficial opinion, it is essential to those who have once been united in their historic substance. The surfaces remain in motion; they do not become fixed positions, except tentatively for illuminating purposes. No word is irrevocable. Only one thing is immobile and adamant: the premise of a will to reason, to boundless communication, and to the love that potentially links all men.

Division by differences is objectively possible; all of us are prone to err. But where a real meeting in the communication of reason has once taken place, something remains inextinguishable.

Yet the community of reason, for all its reliability, is not static. Among individuals, it is like being variably joined, now nearer, now farther. It is like a constant rising and falling of hidden existential forces that swell and contract the loving communication itself, without ever jeopardizing it — for it can never disappear where it has once been real. But it is useless, out of good will, to kick against the pricks and feel more affection for another only because we are afraid of feeling less. The force that governs here can only be overcome by re-establishing a concord that may differ from what each of the two thought before, and communication will rarely be able to grow without clashes that extend to the brink of disaster. For only the beauty of sympathy is calm and even, not the truth of reason in the life of time.

The basic fluctuation of communication can be expressed in metaphor: we reflect one another, while each at the same time reflects the rest of mankind. Our very appraisals, the responsibility for which rests on a common but quite undefinable and ineffable faith, gain or lose in value. What Giordano Bruno said of love between the sexes — "The affection of my beloved for quite ordinary persons displeased me chiefly because its robs the lover of any hope to be preferred by his beloved for his own superior worth" — holds analogously for all love among human beings.

We are like sparks, now scintillating more brightly, now vanishing to the point of invisibility, constantly changing in the flux of life. The sparks see each other, and each flares up to a brighter glow for seeing others. The love of reason joins all that is aglow, without prearrangement or representation, and where we see a glow decline, the pain simultaneously reduces our own luminosity.

Togetherness as such is an abstraction; the chance in togetherness between any two people is that both their selves may be strengthened in basic humanity. To refuse to give up this chance shows faith in man as man, but to presume the mere chance as already realized shows a self-deception that evades reality. The consequences of such indolence may be fatal: the apparently real unreality can be abused. It can become a trap, finally turning the semblance of communication into an insidious means of the struggle for existence.

How glorious, by contrast, is the other possibility: that today — in this growing need, in the obliviousness of so many, in this torrent of seemingly irresistible disaster, in this world where reliable factual community vanishes and men are increasingly torn from their historic roots, in these nations that unwittingly betray their own traditions — men can meet and join in reason, love, and truth. They can prepare the ground for the incalculable flowering of new worlds. Nietzsche's word, "Truth begins when there are two," is borne out by every community of individuals, especially under totalitarianism, but no less in free countries, where life may become a life of "total conventions." Here is the lastingly possible human substance, the most vigorous, the most reliable.

All freedom lies in the individual. What shall happen freely cannot be shifted to events or institutions or causal and contextual relations open to sociological analysis. Freedom dwells in depths that make all those relations look superficial. It can issue only from the individual, from many individuals who transcend outward communal forms and really meet one another in man-to-man communication.

In structures, works, institutions, laws, and orders, reason acquires a language that stops being language when reason ceases to animate them — for their reality is not due to static existence, only to the conception, the efficacy, the activity of individuals in time. Thus the basis of human affairs is not visible organization, institutional community, but the community of rational men within it, although its truth can be visible only in those realities. The community of reason cannot be organized as such. There is no "legion of decent people." This most essential, because all-supporting, community exists dependably without a contract. Its performance is not actionable in a court of law.

And yet, in line with its meaning, this community which can never be organized must never keep aloof. It should pervade all organizations, all states and churches and associations, for all these live by the men of reason alone. The men of reason are omnipresent, like the invisible church. In their absence, we find an empty bustle, a blind, mechanical course of events, petrification, and destruction.

Hence, the non-contractual but actual community of reason needs to prevail in all forms of human order — in states, parties, churches, schools, unions, and bureaucracies. It cuts across all conflicts, whether religious, partisan, or international. It exists wherever the individual awakens and finds himself in a place where he can see others — isolated still, and scattered — without being able to refer to them; for potentially each human being belongs to this community, and none has a right to claim it for himself. In the here and now, this reality is always tacit, for speech takes place in the factual, tangible, plannable, cognoscible realm.

We must convince ourselves of the inevitable power of all organization, but also of the impotence of organizations in all great, decisive questions. Lacking vision, they cannot make up their minds. The thinking eye and the strength of decision are the privileges of individuals and of their rational brotherhood. An organization becomes helpless when its routine proves inadequate. Then it can only appoint another committee — "the thing to be done when nothing is to be done" and when the illusion of doing something against one's perplexity is desired at the same time.

But what if, beyond all our increasingly dubious organizations and institutions and programs and activities and conventions, the saving alternative cannot be drawn back into this circle along with the old way of thinking, as something else to be arranged and planned? What then? In any event, it is not a new cause for people who spend their lives traveling from meeting to meeting, talking, listening, being sociable, passing resolutions and accomplishing nothing, neither in inner action nor in external activity, because the very thing they may once have sensed and desired is lost in the shuffle. The bustle puts it out of reach, for it is not a matter of knowledge, planning, or arrangement. It is superior to all organization and ought to guide it, but it cannot be fostered, only discredited, by more organization. Organization is there to work on tangible tasks, and how reason can pervade those is our only problem.

We shall see no way to salvation unless the guidance of politics is taken over by the reality that antedates all politics. The political community of all can find the way of reason only where men who can trust each other in communication inspire trust in others. The germ of all public good, too, lies in the meeting of rational men.

The suprapolitics required to put politics in order is not an authority that might be set up objectively. It exists only in the rational community itself, whose own existence defies determination. The kindling of reason occurs from man to man; the individual is struck by the individual, and by the public speaker on concrete tasks. The credibility of men begins in the narrowest circle of rational intimacy; it spreads in public, in conscious resistance to irrationality. Every individual is responsible for what he listens to and works for in the concrete field, but a moral revival cannot be organizationally promoted. To organize it would be to cancel it.

The reality of the rational community cannot be proved, but mankind's fate depends upon its prevalence in the reality of politics. Its success is uncertain. What cannot be done by compulsion, only by the freedom of reason, will still thrive only when this freedom can guide itself.

One element of this reality, an indispensable condition for the expansion of rational community, is the public clash of minds. It cannot be achieved by law or by force, only by freedom as such — by the freedom of all, unhampered in the struggle by any limit of manifestation and disclosure. Let us consider this easily misunderstood subject.

When Plato realized the power of poetry, music, and art to influence the ethos of each human being, he concluded that his ideal state should subject all these to censorship. Homer should be honorably banished from the state for spreading pernicious doctrine about the gods; morally enfeebling music should be forbidden. The premise of this argument is that the rulers should be philosophers living in view of the archetypes of the eternal ideas, omnisciently seeing through all that is and all that happens, and thus superior in insight to all fixed orders and laws. Since there can be no such superhuman philosophers, human beings must take another road.

Men cannot administer the censorship Plato was thinking of, and the censorship that is recurrently sought by ecclesiastical and secular powers must be combated, since the spirit thrives only in freedom. Under pressure of compulsion, it can repeat and vary but not create. Along with the nuisances, censorship would stifle the chance of truth; along with the weeds, it would uproot the grain. Every individual must have the right of free creation.

And yet, the sense of the Platonic precept remains. Not censorship, but responsibility for all that the mind produces, affirms, and denies is the premise of true and salutary mental activity. But if responsibility fails, as it frequently does — if seductive, morally corrupting artistic and intellectual creations pervade and dominate public life — what then can be done without censorship?

We live in a paradoxical situation. It is only in freedom that we can become truly human, but when we are given freedom, we stray into evil paths. To use an improper simile: if God himself stepped in to direct censorship, he would accomplish truth, but simultaneously he would revoke the human freedom he created. In fact, since censorship is applied by men to men, the censors will have the same basic faults as the censored. Being human, both will frequently err. But censorship is an act of force, and in the sense of humanity — which is in this world as the chance of freedom and thus remains a constant challenge — we must choose the path of peril. For this peril is inherent in humanity, and it is less perilous than the destruction of creative human potentialities by human censorship.

Free conflict must reveal what is at work in the output of those who engage in the arts and letters. The seductive, bewitching, masking, enfeebling elements exist and must be accepted. They should be fought, but not by force. Perception of their untruthfulness will add to the clarity and strength of truth and ethos.

Thus, in place of governmental or ecclesiastical direction of the minds by censorship, there must be general responsibility, of which all grow conscious in struggle. This responsibility breeds the community of men of reason. There are others, so-called blood brotherhoods bound by strict rules that members violate on pain of death; they yield irrationally to bewitching magic and blind obedience. While they last, these oath-bound communities have immense power, but when they break up, their original lack of an ethos shows in the bewilderment of the individuals who stay behind. In contrast, there is the "brotherhood of reasonable men" — objectively invisible even to itself, yet of a reliability grounded in the very depths of man. It upholds every individual and will uphold him even as a spectral realm, when he is in need and alone.

In this invisible brotherhood, everyone shares the responsibility for the effects of creative endeavor. Every approach or acceptance, every act of criticism, praise, or blame, indeed, every mere mention has results in fact. Every judgment confirms, intensifies, prepares, shapes, or spoils in the arena of the minds, where the ceaseless battle for reason is waged. Every responsible judgment is thought out in rational community, not according to the whims of taste. Whatever happens in this arena is a moral-political factor. Nothing can be isolated here; the censorship lies in the general struggle, in everyone's "yes" and "no." It is only when this free censorship becomes aware of its responsibility that reason functions. No personal attachments matter here, no circles, no cliques, no leagues — the only free vinculum is the idea of quality and truth.

The battle of minds requires us to be both charitable and strict. In this tension, each side falls prey to its own confusions, from which reason alone can deliver it. Charitableness, averse to any violence, leaning toward humanity in its untold manifestations, sees, loves, and thinks with the Latin poet: "I am human; to me nothing human seems strange." But there is an ambiguity in this. "We are all human" can be misconstrued to mean, "Understand all, and so forgive all" — and what tribunal has the right to grant such forgiveness? Everyone can and may forgive only what has been done to himself. The result of universal forgiveness is a leveling of good and evil, in which we acquiesce while declaiming our protests. Yet the declaration, "We are all human," may also mean that all of us are capable of change, that all of us have the chance to resolve on a fresh start. No one is irrevocably lost. To be charitable, we must put ourselves in everyone else's place — not to agree with everyone, but to understand his meaning and to allow him his due.

On the other side, while strictness is the premise of truth in the rational battle of minds, it is as likely to degenerate as charitableness. Judgment of others may grow cheap: "The observer alone has a conscience." A chronically outraged dissatisfaction turns on evil with a kind of moralizing that serves far more to flatter its own indignation than to bring truth to the fore. True criticism issues from a positive source that seeks links even in conflict. When an object is criticized, the criticized individual should see himself included in common truth. Such criticism wants to stimulate change, not to deny a man's potential.

To be rationally charitable does not mean to be soft. As we seem to understand and affirm all, we actually undergo a relentless, inescapable experience. It demands strictness. Yet rational strictness cannot be set up as a law, for anything reduced to moral or legal knowledge becomes false if it is taken as absolute. Reason does produce such unavoidable canons, but it is in danger of vanishing itself if the canons, instead of aiding in the finite appraisal of finite thoughts and actions, presume to pass judgment on the whole of man. The strictness of reason, therefore, demands in turn that we be boundlessly charitable — not outwardly tolerant, letting everything pass, but inwardly compassionate. Reason never terminates anything; it leads onward, into the motion that among men can become the singular and yet so simple cause of man being himself.

The paradox of reason is to be open and to preserve freedom while binding itself so as to lead to a decision in the concrete historical moment.

Here the brotherhood of reasonable men is menaced by two seemingly self-evident demands: for the freedom of the spirit, and for the separation of public and private life. Both are justified: the spirit has the right to be protected from censorship, and privacy, from sensationalism. Yet both claims to protection turn into temptations. Imperceptibly, the responsibility of reason is diminished by the spirit's claim to unconditional validity and by the claim of private life to be ignored in our appraisal of intellectual activities in public life.

The realm of the spirit demands independence of judgment for both participants and audiences. The protection of this area from such forcible interference as censorship is not only a premise of free creative endeavor but of the political freedom of men in free states. It must be defended, in Kant's word, as "the Palladium of liberty." It is threatened even by measures against obscene writings, against immoral, dissolute, nihilistic works, against insults to such spiritual realities as "religious feelings." To achieve freedom of responsibility in cultural life, we must dare to give freedom to license and to evil. Forcible censorship does not make for a living order but for a managed, fundamentally disordered and chaotic soil.

It is quite a different and very serious matter that cultural freedom can endure only if the free acts of reason itself guide and control the arbitrary cultural pursuits. Freedom of the spirit presupposes individual responsibility. With the tempting communications of an unexistential spirit, of unvanquished evil impulses, moods, and illusions set free as well, salvation can come only from freedom itself, by the responsible guidance in every individual.

We feel a liberating effect when beauty and terror, good and evil, are transplanted in space, so to speak, by cognition or pictorial representation. But this effect is true only if at the same time clarity grows deeper, discrimination more acute, the ethos stronger, and rational existence more decisive. A culture that is nothing but culture — science as an end in itself, arts and letters as a world that is not only different but isolated in an ivory tower, as *l'art pour l'art* — is the real temptation, for all cultural things are ambiguous.

Culture as such is a dangerous delight. There is magic in the words of bards and sages that may divert its captives from reason. Only submission to the conditions of reason makes a delight in culture an aspect of truth — like the love that submits to the conditions of existence and its loyalty.

The creative spirit is what we call genius. It is not the same as reason. Reason belongs to man as such, if he wants it. It can grow in anyone who thinks honestly, patiently, and unselfishly. Genius belongs to a few; it is the admirable source of all the abundance of life, of images, forms, symbols, of the fulfilment of our imagination. It can become one with reason, as in Plato, Shakespeare, Goethe, and other giants, and then it speaks in the exalted tongue that can bring reason alive in any human being. There we find what we must experience if we hope to develop our own potential. But if genius does not yet bear the guiding power of reason within itself, it is ambiguous. Its products may be irreplaceable, or they may be pernicious magic. We must test them for possible poison. Their effect must be placed under the guidance of reason, which we cannot depend upon in genius itself.

If reason were a matter of genius, if our common human existence depended on a steady supply of geniuses, our situation would be hopeless. There is hope because there may be reason in everybody, and because, from this starting point, the capacities of reason may move on to everybody else. For everybody might have acted upon what he heard; all he needs is encouragement, and the language in which reason has been couched by men of genius.

The unanimity of reason is not that of the sciences. The sciences are intelligible and transferable by intellect alone; they belong to all men but link them purely intellectually. Reason also belongs to all men, but it belongs to their whole being and is not merely a special field of comprehension. It links men who may differ completely in all other respects, in their ways of life, their feelings, their desires; it links them more strongly than they are divided by all their diversities.

The alternative to responsible cultural freedom is cultural anarchy.

Reason demands that the spirit be freed so that we may become truly human. It risks the possible consequences of irresponsibility, because it wants the possibilities of the spirit limited by the responsibility of every individual rather than by censorship from outside — in the hope that man is born to become human, not to perish as an unsuccessful experiment.

Man needs freedom, but no one, no institution, can force him to be responsible — this is why freedom itself, if it fails, must eventually produce slavery. And indeed, irresponsible cultural freedom produces — and at the same time expresses — a moral-political condition that cannot endure, for all its magic. Products that weaken, that lead to vague intoxications or awaken evil impulses, prepare us for irresolution, on the one hand, and for blind obedience to force on the other. The very men who are engaged in this irrational magic want violence, not knowing what and how it is. Their own creations are like anticipatory acts of violence. In the end, the irresponsible spirit, along with all that has yielded to it, will be wiped out at one blow by the terror of total rule — which then will manage to make docile tools out of its irresponsible intellectual trail blazers. They will demonstrate their moral-political and existential vacuity by hailing force, submitting their own designs for it, and unscrupulously carrying out its orders. Accustomed to enjoying mere intelligence and cultural production, they will rejoice in the belief that simple obedience has put them on the road of truth — which in fact, now as before, is to them beyond truth and falsehood, a bottomless void.

Like the absolute independence of the spirit, the claim to privacy endangers the community of reasonable men. In civil society, privacy is protected from slander as well as from disclosures that are true but damaging, unless justified by a demonstrable public or material interest. Based upon law and reinforced by convention, the right to a hidden and undisturbed private life is unlimited for all those who do not want to be political or cultural leaders — in other words, who seek no public influence. Those who seek it invite publicity. If a rational man risks a test to his right to public influence, he cannot want to hide what he is.

Likewise, a man who comes before the public with such detachable materialities as scientific or technological findings may rightly contend that these essentially impersonal achievements do not justify personal questions. He can detach his privacy from the subject, because the subject is special and not to be proved by man, only by itself, by its generally demonstrable truth.

But if a man comes before the public in a cause essentially linked with the human personality, with man's being himself — and if he understands the point of what he is doing — he will no longer ask for a separation of public and private spheres. For in his activities no such line can be drawn any more. Where man appears as himself, he appears in his entirety. He is entitled to appear in public only if he is willing to risk publicity and take the consequences.

The more the seriousness of reason enters into the public spirit, into politics, into the professions, the less can our still so self-evident distinction between the two spheres be maintained. A man who wants to be publicly active in politics, in philosophy, in letters and arts, exposes his entirety to the public. What he does would be dishonest as a kind of façade behind which he might remain hidden.

The ideal statesman, for example, is such a unit of person and cause, of private and public activity, that there can be no more talk of him as a merely private person. By keeping faith with the archetype, his life convinces others. His entire existence is a beneficial public reality. The constant abuse we call "dragging into the glare of publicity" cannot faze him; the law of slander is sufficient protection and will rarely have to be invoked if he, just by being himself, is the slander's most convincing refutation.

Atomic doom is not a necessary process that comes over us and has to be accepted. Every step depends on men who take it on the road to disaster: the discovery of natural phenomena as well as their translation into technology, the order to make the bombs as well as the order to drop them and its execution. We must recognize the difference between man's work, which is up to us, and the work of nature, which we can master only to a degree. We must not fail in what is up to us, by submitting to fate from the outset. To fulfil the obligation of our freedom, we must not renounce it by a premature surrender.

Our great "successes" — triumphantly achieved, jubilantly enjoyed, and blind to the consequences — have plunged us into the great guilt of being content with them as sources of material power. But to know this, and to say so, is not enough, either. No amount of realism and disclosure, no perception or expectation or hope will help if man himself does not come to a decision.

The task of our thinking is to visualize the crucial situation. It should illuminate whatever evasions obscure it. But the decision itself should also be thought through: what it consists in and what the results can be. Such thinking is not yet the act itself, but it may be preparatory to inner action.

But, some will object, what fantastic expectations! Think of the reality of armaments! Are these huge efforts, consuming half the labor of the nations, to have been "in vain"? Are their products never to be used? Surely this whole vast output of energy rests on a serious purpose to resort to these weapons.

And yet — if at first only under the growing stress of the fear that grips all men in view of its reality — this very purpose may change direction. From the possession of the most destructive weapons ever known, on the ground of a boundless courage of sacrifice, of daring destruction by these weapons, there may arise a high resolve to discard them and mutually to give peace to mankind. It would mean that the courage of sacrifice itself had turned into a will to make sacrifices — not only to let such enormous works vanish unused but to submit to a transformation of life as a whole, with all the renunciations this involves, but also with new vistas of immeasurable possibilities.

No one can say that man is up to such a transformation. But we may remember our guideposts, both in Asia and in the West, and we may hope that man might be as such vistas would presuppose. There is no other way out, and to call the step impossible is to pronounce a death sentence upon mankind, to be carried out within the next hundred years. The political condition, the rational ethos, in which abolition of the atom bomb would be possible requires all political decisions to be examined and ranked as to importance in the light of the extremity of doom. This extremity must not be obscured for one moment. It should help us prevent selfish, indolent, and wishful obfuscation. Even seemingly trivial decisions are to be weighed in the balance of extremity. The freedom that brings reason to the fore in politics is true and real only if it stands the test in all stages and in all spheres of human activity.

There is a radical difference between particular problems and a change in man. The former can be solved in the annex of the planning human intellect, leaving man himself untouched. The latter demands the commitment of all of man. The change cannot be sought as a purpose. It cannot be planned; the very act of planning would, in our situation, be a choice of the road to perdition. Something else is needed, coming — or failing to come — from the depths of the free human person, from the resolve in which he finds himself changed to a new kind of preparedness that will let him plan but cannot be planned itself.

We hear the objection that a change in man, who is always an individual, is not a change in politics at large. Great powers that have no common ground as forms of political life, not even in language, are facing each other in the present state of the world with the irreconcilability of mutually exclusive faiths. Even if a change occurred in the politics of one circle, it would still be impossible in the world as a whole; because the others are always there too, and vastly powerful, we cannot do without the old kind of politics that gets its bearings from force as a last resort. The reform of politics, this argument concludes, has always been an infinite and hence insoluble task; there are no visible indications that the pressure of the new total danger will compel a solution.

We can only answer that if a change in politics should come, it would not come by any objective sociopolitical process. It would come if the individuals were changed. What will happen to mankind depends on the individuals who will be standing at the helm in crucial moments. In the final analysis it depends on all the individuals; what goes on between them, between any two or more, lays the foundations of political realities to come.

The realist who has raised those objections may reply that political guidance cannot be expected from the individuals. In the vastness of human history, the individual sees himself as an infinitesimally minute atom; history at large is bound to strike him as a natural process that he cannot influence and must simply accept as it passes over him.

Against this, we should keep reminding ourselves that history at large is still the result of action by innumerable individuals. From the outset, there are individuals. In everything he does, the individual shares the responsibility for the whole. He has some power, however little, for he has a hand in events by acting — or failing to act — in his domain. By every small act of commission or omission he helps to prepare the ground on which other individuals, in the seats of power, will take the actions that will be decisive for the whole. What is done is done by human beings, and human beings always are individuals. Even when they act in groups, in nations, in masses, their every action is that of individuals — however much they may feel like tools of superior powers or of a common will. The suprapolitical element resides in man himself, because it is a matter of his freedom.

There is a blight on the roots of man. A glance at history shows him struggling upward only to relapse; most of his high points were paid for in the cruelty and misery that made them possible. But the blight on the roots lies in every individual. We experience it in ourselves, as the "radical evil" that overpowers us if we do not fight it constantly and freely. Fundamentally, salvation and damnation both proceed from freedom.

The hardest task to be performed anew by every individual — a task which no man can shift to another, which none can do for another — has always been to come to himself in extremity, to be changed, and then to be guided in life by the impulses springing from the change. At first, the fact of the bomb can shock only individuals into a reflection radical enough to make them live henceforth in an earnestness commensurate with the two present tasks of mankind: salvation from total rule and salvation from total destruction. And nothing short of this earnestness is adequate to our eternal task of growing truly human.

How do we stand today? The individual as such has always been a rarity; does he not now seem all but nonexistent? Is it not an enormous illusion to keep hoping for the individual? Have we not long reached the stage of collective leveling — conformist in America, totalitarian in Russia, technological and functional wherever there is industry and bureaucracy? Have we not long forgotten what it is for man to be himself, to think and live freely, and to realize himself in his world? Has all this not long been said, forecast, and observed? Is it not laughable to try opposing the steam roller of history with things that are gone forever, like selfhood and reason?

No knowledge, no experience, can compel affirmative answers to these questions. They fall upon a willing soil of despair, yet against their persuasive magnetism stands the will to keep the road open where it is not blocked by truly compelling knowledge.

Today, because of the technological situation, the blight on the roots of humanity must lead to total extinction unless extremity induces man to change — freely, but with an "assist from above" that can be neither calculated nor experienced nor expected, that can only be hoped for if we really do our best, if a supreme tension in our innermost being lets us hear and practice what our best can be.

What the individual — and it will always be up to individuals — will do when he holds the engines of destruction in his hand, when he is to give or to carry out orders for their use, depends on himself. Whether and how the engines will be used depends upon the outcome of his inner actions in the course of his life. The process is the same throughout technology: its use is determined by what man becomes when he is himself. The salutary use of technology does not come from continued technological thinking but from a different source.

14

THE
RATIONAL
STATESMAN

The ground for events at large is prepared in the mass of individuals. Out of this mass grow the politicians. Their roots are in the mass, but the individual in a position of leadership has an experience unknown to the rest. He is under a pressure that seems to demand more than men can bear, for his dealings with force affect nations — today, indeed, all of mankind — for good or ill, to the point of being or not being.

Many politicians are not up to this position; many seem not even aware of it. They are not under pressure, because they do not realize it. The statesman is he who grows under pressure, whom the pressure brings up to his task. Pericles ceased laughing when he became the leader of his city-state, realized his responsibility, and had to fight day after day for the consent of the Athenians. He convinced them by his life and by his words, and he was in constant personal danger of his life if he failed to carry his fellow citizens with him.

The statesman has to live with force. He faces extremity. It is in his hands, and it threatens his own existence. Even in times of apparent calm he must not forget that his neck is at stake. If he does not accept this risk, he has assumed his power irresponsibly, with the anxious placidity — reprehensible in this spot — of a legally trained civil servant, a trade union official, or what you will. If he is not constantly sensitive to the facts in keeping all means of power and force in mind and at hand, if he does not know where he stands, he may end up in the ridiculous position of a chief executive being removed by a handful of men, saving his life but dooming his country with the words, "I yield to force."

The statesman stands at the frontier of humanity, at the place where someone must stand so that all may live. The fate of all is determined by a few statesmen. Their actions set the course of the world, without any one of them having a complete view or control of it.

Because he stands for power and has power, the statesman is the center of public attention. The nation and all the individuals are inwardly related to him in a variety of ways. The majority — in the Western world, too — regards statesmen as creatures bestowed upon the nations from elsewhere. One does not feel responsible for what they are; one is obsequious even to the props and flunkies representing their power. In the eyes of the masses, they become different from what they were before they came to power, seeming to act upon motives that are either not understood or credulously understood to be what they tell to their people and to the world. They do all the acting and thinking; we do none of it. They are our fate, for good or evil. They are taken for granted, worshiped and flattered or damned and shunned, glorified as saviors or blamed for whatever goes wrong. The statesman is saddled with our dissatisfaction with ourselves and the world; we hold him guilty, not of what he does but of what he finds to start with — of the human condition that makes his task necessary.

The rational attitude, as opposed to these irrational ones, is to view the statesman with the respect due to eminence, and at the same time with the concern of sensing our common fate in him. We should view him critically but justly, and our judgment should incline to gratitude wherever there are grounds.

Mankind's fate depends on the extent to which the individuals called to statesmanship appear convincing to the rest — to the majority or to large numbers or even to small groups — so that others will want to think, to live, to act as they do. These few men, not isolated, not deified, but rooted in the real will of those who recognize themselves in them, might come to power because they dominate men by their character from within, not by force from without.

Today we see politicians whose countenance and deportment baffle us. Do they know where they stand, what they are doing? What are they thinking of? Invariably they show us laughing faces. It is as though the world expected them to be cheerful, whether the smiles they hide behind are stiffly impenetrable or jovially merry or good-naturedly contented or surprised, disconcerted grins or other variations. Do their people, do they themselves, want a façade of universal foolishness to cover the dreadful earnestness of all they see, know, and do? Or is there really nothing to hide; is it an utter helplessness that shows, rather — as people caught in a lie or blunder will laugh instead of looking downcast, as if nothing had happened? No, this can only be a façade. We may assume that some responsible leaders are really quite different even today.

We may distinguish the statesman from the politicians.

Politicians of vital élan may achieve and realize their power by extraordinary skill and daring. They seem like tigers in their unshakable presence of mind, inhibited only by the self-discipline imposed by their goal, which is power as such. To them, the people are a mass to be manipulated so that it will obey, work, and keep quiet. The statesman, on the other hand, is guided by moral-political ideas in the framework of a historic situation. His existence convinces and forms a nation. He does not produce imitators but successors.

Mere politicians relish power, enjoy its appearance, and may perhaps unthinkingly content themselves with the seeming grandeur of noisily manifested temporary power. The statesman, on the other hand, wants the power that enables him to perform his great task. He is sensitive to fluctuations of real power, so as to meet any present danger, but he cares nothing for the pomp and panoply of his power; he would rather conceal it. He feels his position of power not as a claim on others but on himself — as a chance to work, not to swagger. He feels a responsibility that seems beyond human strength, though men must bear it. He has no authority above him to refer to, none in this world.

Busy politicians drift along with events, with speeches, notes, writings, that accomplish nothing outside the old routine of raising economic productivity by laws and regulations for the intelligent rationalization of industry, with or without success, depending on conditions. The politician becomes a statesman when he is not content to muddle through the road to catastrophe with endless operations, large or small. The statesman senses, picks, and finds his way in the dark. What he does to meet the needs of the day is pervaded by an ethos that thinks farther and, by the manner of his leadership, helps to transform the very process of evil. The politicians bustle chaotically in ephemera; they write history in quicksand. The statesman works within the continuity of history to found things that will endure.

Today, a statesman is a man who knows that the saving political course is bound up with a change in man. It would, of course, be folly on his part to act as if the change were already accomplished; but in his person the statesman can show us, believably, that he himself is undergoing this change — that his aims are stated, his reasons communicated, and his steps taken on that basis. He will reply to people, to his own people and to everyone else. He will not allow them to perish by thoughtless evasion of the issue. He will be frank, without mental reservations. He will demand that others learn to see. He will not cease drawing their attention to essentials, to the hierarchy of values, to the realities of the situation.

He will know that he dare not wait and see. He dare not think that he can find a way empirically, at a moment's notice. Insofar as he has to, he will expose his thoughts and actions to the light that comes to him from his experience of the present historic situation and from his awareness of the human task.

He will find the words that touch the inner motives of innumerable individuals, that enlighten and awaken them and thus create a public consciousness. In simple language that hits the mark, convinces logically, and interprets visually, he will implant the crucial issue in the hearts of men.

Politics in this sense — the thoughts and actions that bring all-encompassing order into the human community — is not a profession to be learned. Statesmen are not produced by schools of political science. They are not professionals or specialists. They represent the ethos of a people, something that everyone should and could understand. They are not working at a trade but are called to serve the common cause.

But they require the expert knowledge of the economic, military, cultural, ideological, and international specialists. Professionalism becomes their tool. The greatness of a statesman lies in his feeling for the methods of expertness, in his quick grasp of the essentials, in finding experts, listening to them, allowing them to work and to get results — not in being a specialist himself. A successful banker, one who had not learned his business from the bottom of the ladder but had entered it at the top because of his ability and education, admitted in my presence that he had no notion of bookkeeping. The statesman, too, knows where to get the knowledge he may need at any given moment. He is neither a specialist nor omniscient, but he knows his way around in all fields. He lives in the whole, and by the whole.

But statesmen, if they are great, are not isolated phenomena. They attract men of similar stature, let them come to the fore, let them learn by taking part in the business of government. If we want to speak about a school for statesmen, it means personal apprenticeship in the spirit of a community where political thinking is practiced as a kind of universal thinking that cannot be directly taught.

The statesman does not deceive himself about people. He knows to what extent stupidity, passions, habits, illusions, seemingly magical promises still sway the masses. He knows the effect of material conditions, of poverty and despair. But he knows, too, that such judgment can never be final. Every individual in the mass is a human being. The statesman wants to see his own moral-political principles borne by the multitude, in which they lie hidden but ready. The masses may succumb to the lures of political spellbinders, because unreason and antireason are at work in every human being, but a rational statesman, believable and powerful, can arouse counterforces in the very same masses. They are waiting for him to tell them what they really want, and they follow him because he does tell them. This is why he daily turns to these masses, which in the final analysis decide about his success. In the long run, what the masses of men will not hear is politically nonexistent.

The statesman must work with people as they really are, here and now. They make up his world. He cannot tailor them to his specifications. Hitler said he had to work with the people he found, and indeed, for his type of power he needed fanatics, criminals, and irrationalists, but intelligent, active, vigorous, and hard-working ones. Perhaps such irrationalists can be cast in a different mold, if different demands are made upon them. In any case, quite different human types can be brought forth by the same nation, depending on what side of them you appeal to, what you expect of them, what confidence you place in them, what challenges you confront them with, what sort of example you set them, and what you give them to hear.

To be a statesman today, a man must rise by means of parties and elections, over disheartening, humiliating obstacles. He must take the way to power as it exists in his situation, in his time, and in his country. But what individuals or groups of rational friends can do at any time is unpredictable. Success may show to a man of daring what unforeseen opportunities exist in fact, once he breaks through partisan restrictions to appeal to the people. He will always have to ask himself what motives he can appeal to, so as to awaken the people's moral-political reason and to win power at the same time. The realism of psychological and sociological perception and the so-called knowledge of human nature are always right only for aspects of what has already happened — never, by themselves, for what is still to come.

In the free world we consider public opinion, which our elections reflect, as the final authority. But public opinion, as expressed at any given moment, is neither unified nor fixed. It seems both manageable and suggestible — though it can also be the true expression of original insight and at times, quite unpredictably, of profound wisdom.

Politicians and statesmen must appeal to forces that will get them votes. They sense what is stirring in the electorate and appears more or less clearly as public opinion. There are two ways of going about it, however. The politician regards public opinion as a given fact and submits to it, whereas the statesman creates public opinion, seeing through the talk of the day to the hidden will, which he awakens.

The statesman knows that personalities must appear in whom a nation recognizes itself, who tell it what is, what is desirable, and what is to be done. Various individuals do this in various ways, for the people to choose from. Thus every citizen shall learn to inquire and to think politically, to become aware of local and national situations, and to make it clear to himself what he wants. To the statesman, the political struggle for votes is from the outset a process of popular education, an education indispensable to the self-preservation of political freedom itself.

But this situation offers several possibilities. There is education to reason, there is spellbinding for disaster, and there is the leveling lack of leadership in mere formal democracy without popular political education. The statesman is a demagogue either in the good or the bad sense of the word — in the great sense of Pericles, whose counsel educated the Athenians, or in the usual sense of Cleon, who led them into the misfortunes of an ever-ready *hubris*. The demagogue knows that personal effect is essential but incalculable. It depends on the forces in man to which the demagogue appeals, whether to the common and mean that promise a greater chance of immediate success, or to the noble, in supreme tension and uncertainty. The incalculable factor appears not only in devilish stupidity but chiefly in the men who rise by the ethos of great politics. The Pied Piper of Hamelin is the counterpart of the statesman who, like Moses, shows the way in the wilderness.

The statesman's ethos is part of the ethos that bears a people and the individuals in it. We are evading the issue if we separate politics and ethics and shift the making of great decisions away from the common ethos into "just politics," for which others are held responsible — if we despise these others, perhaps, because "politics is crooked." As if a man could live outside of, and without responsibility for, the politics by which he lives in fact! The supposed sanctity of a free private existence and of a world of the spirit distinct from politics seems possible under certain relatively stable political conditions — but it only seems so. For precisely because of its untruthful unconcern with politics, irresponsibility will see the despised politics shatter, destroy, and unmask its existence.

To the rational statesman, politics is an ethos. On the large scale of public life he shows what the individual is and does in the mass. The rational statesman exists by the people's reason, to which the lasting loyalty of the community of reasonable men enables him to give effect.

To him, the unity of politics and ethos is fundamental; only reflection separates them. If we ask what it is that a statesman can never do, cannot acquiesce in under any circumstances, the purely formal answer is that he himself cannot forsake the meaning of his moral-political task. He will reject whatever would destroy this unity of ethos and self-preservation even if situations and mere politicians suggest it. In dealing with unreason, he will follow the guidance of reason. How far, in so doing, he may feel free to go along with unreason cannot be concretely deduced from any maxim.

Reason does not immediately conquer and pervade the world. Political action and thought denote explicitly participation in the world of unreason, of irrationality, of tricks and ruses. But the statesman employs his tricks and ruses in the service of reason. In quest of the self-preservation of his state and nation he simultaneously pursues their ethos, which alone invests their self-preservation with substance and value. Whatever he may say and do, he is always educating his people, for good or evil. He works from the suprapolitical into political self-preservation, and back to the suprapolitical.

People tend to obey a great, confidence-inspiring statesman. They take it for granted that one will be given them, no one knows whence or why, to rid them of their own responsibility. Correspondingly, there are governments whose first moral-political demand is that the people trust them. But the great statesman who is one with his people, their representative and teacher at the same time, does not ask for unconditional trust. He candidly presents the objective possibilities and his own motives and asks for criticism. In no other way can the people come to share the responsibility. He does not think at all that confidence is due to his office as such.

To understand political action fully, we must know what the statesman knows. But in a crisis, in moments of stress, during a struggle that can be won only by secrecy, we cannot be told everything. Then the statesman needs our confidence. He must say, "Trust me, let me act, and obey" — but at the same time he must add, by implication, "And hold me to account when it is all over." The people's confidence in a statesman is responsible, too — first for his rise, and then, in times of decision, for the confidence he has won. The people must remain entitled to know the facts and the reasons — to be told as much as possible at any moment, and everything in the end.

The politician who wants to become a statesman should be critically probed, so to speak, observed and examined for his fitness to take the helm. Criticism should ask why he is trusted in fact, why people vote for him. It should analyze these motives as well as the politician's public personality: his ideas, speeches, gestures, actions, public relations, and dealings with men. It should tolerate no blind or ill-motivated confidence. The confidence the statesman earns should be well-founded, as he himself wants to win it in the storm of publicity. His life must be an open book, because it is the concern of all. There is a touch of the paradigmatic in his nature, for a people that sees itself in him and yet stays critical. He will prevail over criticism of his policies by argument and persuasion, over criticism of his ethos by his own reality.

The criticism, in turn, has its own responsibility. It is evil when it comes from mere love of negation, of "debunking," of sardonic wit — when it is the pointless inanity of intellectual brilliance and literary sensationalism. In partisan conflict it is still hampered. It reaches its peak in the free, self-critical public discussion that seeks nothing but the truth.

If the statesman's life, his actions, his language, his success, have won him respect, love, and gratitude, he must still not be deified. It is part of the rational statesman's makeup to reject hero-worship — not only because he knows that he can be wrong but because such an attitude toward him on the people's part would destroy the very point of his political activity, the expansion of freedom.

All political activity is carried on within a set of concepts and by means of a basic way of thinking. The totalitarian power politician uses the concepts and techniques of thinking to direct and dupe the masses; the party machine is systematically trained in their employment for the dialectical and sophistical justification of whatever is desired. The clearer the totalitarian will, the more this whole system of thought is an operational instrument to be applied at will. The powers that be may want the individual inculcated with a "Marxist faith" or a "racial faith," but the leaders themselves are thinking of the total rule in which they, too, are engulfed as soon as they share it.

The rational statesman is no less in control of the concepts and methods of thinking. He does not let ideologies limit his horizon; they are at the beck and call of his mind, which remains alert to the perception of new possibilities. But he does not operate the ideologies with a will to power as such, as the totalitarians do, but from the substance of free humanity. He thinks out of the depths of his historic truth, which is not finished but must always show itself anew.

To the rational statesman, the import of political and philosophical thought from the Greeks to our own day is precisely the preservation of its diversity, its contrariety, its constant conflict. Disorder and anarchy of thought must be risked for the restoration of original order and unity — for this must happen truthfully, not under compulsion by the breeding of techniques of thought with dogmatically fixed contents. The vitality of free, unlimited thinking is at the disposal of politically free communities; it enables them to find the language in which the statesman can express his will and in which the people, changed by such thinking, can understand their own.

Both totalitarian and free thought are human activities. However deep the gulf between them, it must be bridgeable by their common humanity. The rational statesman will solve the problem of communicating with the totalitarians.

Traditional diplomacy, with its well-mannered rules of the game and its premise of a common ground of interest-determined deals and compromises, is helpless before this problem. The bargaining may take place, with some small success here and there, but on the whole, and in essence, it will not lead to peace. Hence the disappointment of the believers in the old diplomacy. At a loss for a way out, they stake all on the one card of military strength, of peace by mutual intimidation. "How," they ask, "can we speak with someone who keeps using language to deceive rather than to communicate and co-operate? In speaking, he perverts the very meaning of speech. What point can there be in talking to him? He understands only power and force."

This is certainly an error. The totalitarians are people like ourselves — at a minimum, their humanity is attested by the fact that they cloak themselves in the appearance of speech. The rational statesman will find ways to speak so that they will hear him. How? That is the imminent creative challenge, to be anticipated only in abstract phrasings. The statesman will address the totalitarians without replying in kind. He will not return lie for lie, abuse for abuse; rather, his every word will be truthful. He will speak calmly and simply. His words and questions and statements will unmask falsehood without having to call it false in so many words. Thus he will reach the souls of the totalitarian leaders; at first, he may well be the man they hate the most. But he will go on patiently, ceaselessly, and on the strength of an attitude that hides no mental reservations, he will not only open the eyes of more and more free peoples but will get through to the subjects of total rule. It is difficult to speak like this, not once but all the time, and to make such language ring as the irresistible voice of the world. Today we hear it on occasion, like a miraculous note that touches us and quickly fades away; it is anything but the common tongue of politicians in free countries. But if it is to grip men as the harbinger of truth, it must be heard every day.

The rational statesman knows that the struggle between freedom and totalitarianism has a superficial but presently compelling military and political reality. Daily he weighs what must be done for self-preservation. But he also knows that both the basic struggle and the lasting decision are moral and spiritual. In the light of this knowledge he considers education, in which the main organizational effort must be made — on which depend not only the intellectual level of the coming generation but the present decision between freedom and total rule, and, in the final analysis, mankind's existence.

We must not confuse technological training with the awakening of true humanity. Both are needed, but the training for a purpose should remain, or get back, under the guidance of humanity. Today, with weapons technology militarily decisive, the West is shocked to find Russia far ahead in some fields, to see that almost unlimited funds are spent there on research, that work is concentrated in a community of brains, that scientists are prized and privileged and trained in numbers outstripping the West. And while the Russians have been transformed from the largely illiterate subjects of the Czar into the well-schooled Soviet nation, education has deteriorated in the West: in America, the pernicious doctrines of John Dewey have wrought havoc in the school system, until children themselves start to rebel at learning too little and the universities complain of inadequate high school standards. Yet what frightens people is not the insufficiency of basic education, only the quantitative and qualitative shortage of scientific and industrial progeny.

This is where we must start building for the future. This is where governmental failures do not show up immediately but years later, when the men responsible have long been replaced. The original failure is due to the reluctance of politicians who consider their actions only from day to day and in view of the next election. For the more distant future, this sin of omission is as menacing as hardly anything else.

Competition in technology and economic productivity is not a matter of indifference; in the armament field, it could help totalitarianism to win without war. But the issue will be decided by competition in the substance of life, which is founded on education. Total rule wants only technicians; in education beyond that purpose, it provides the Marxist intellectual drill which youth — if reports can be believed — already finds boring; it is not even resisted, merely ignored. But the free world can achieve its transformation only if the substance of education is delivered from the spiritual confines of technological and sectarian narrow-mindedness. In America there are excellent private schools and scattered educational achievements of a high order; all over Germany there are outstanding teachers doing a good job as individuals, despite all. But the elan of the change is missing to this day.

If the rational statesman is the great educator he should be — if, acting in concert with cultural forces and pedagogical talents, he spends many times the sums available today — he will facilitate that slow moving growth of future generations that can lay a new foundation in a time apparently bound for the abyss. There can be no such growth without great rational statesmen borne by a popular will which they have clarified; they are the ones who achieve the slow changes in man rather than the instantly visible "economic miracles." Such changes take time, on the whole, though they may shine visibly in individuals even now. The chances are that the struggle between freedom and total rule will be decided in education, unnoticeably, quietly, and for good.

On the technological level, the issues are economic productivity and military strength; the spiritual issue is the change in man. The first type of competition builds machines and leads to the evil of man's function-alization and to his destruction by the bomb; the second enables him to be changed, to become truly human, and to save his existence — if economic productivity and weapons technology are made to serve man rather than to kill him.

15

SUBSTITUTES

FOR

REASON

Everyone seeks the saving grace we call reason. We talk of "common sense," of political "realism," of "religion." But common sense will suffice only in relatively stable situations; it is not enough. Political realism tells us how to get our bearings in the realm of facts, but it misses the supra-political element that really counts in politics. Religion opens a door that remains open when everything in the world fails — but as church-dom it is a worldly organization, one of many that engage in politics and are unable to guide it.

Common sense, political realism, and formal religion carry truth within themselves and are indispensable to reason; they become true if they are pervaded by reason, if reason realizes itself in them. But they become false if they depart from reason by considering themselves ab-solute. They cannot take the place of reason.

Reason as such is not organized, nor is it a system of thought. It is the freedom of man as man, his way to infinite communication. There is no substitute for it, but it can be present in common sense, in political real-ism, in formal religion — all of which, by themselves, tend to become irrational — and can raise them to their proper height and purity.

Common sense is what one likes to resort to in difficult situations, to find the natural and simple way against the fantastic and complex. It is the grasp of things as they are and of what must be done. It protects us from general principles which, though correct, are destructive in appli-cation, being abstract and blind to reality. Common sense finds what cannot be logically deduced or adequately justified, but will convinc-ingly solve our problems here and now.

In part, common sense is an ethos of undefined rules — of tact — that has become a matter of course in the framework of existing orders and conventions. It is limited by confidence in the existence of such orders, and therefore possible only under stable, accustomed conditions. It offers formulas for the moderation that justifies a host of firm rules by such indefinite maxims as "One shouldn't. . . . That isn't done. . . . This is the thing to do. . . ."

Yet common sense means more — not just the rules of a given society, but something common to mankind. Even then it presupposes an undefined order, a propriety in the nature of things, a valid standard. To recognize this concretely without knowing it in general is what constitutes common sense. As a sense of what is right, possible, and effective it becomes the highest authority.

As such, however, it can take two forms. It may envision itself as complete, as the court of last resort — and then, on its premise of being right, it neglects what does not fit into its orders. It obscures the frontiers, overlooks silent violence, and is blind to realities of our world that are symptoms of what will some day sweep away the order of this fixed common sense. All of us want it, all of us call on it for help in the confusions of existence, but it will fail where the human soul breaks through generalities. In a crisis, more is needed than common sense. When it is suspended by a deeper reality, the suspension cannot be countered from the sphere of common sense alone, only from that of reason.

Common sense does not suffice for our existence, because it opposes what is beyond it, though not beyond man — and yet, it is only the impossible that makes man truly human. In other words, common sense is blind both to the very worst and to the very best. It does not understand a communication that dares everything, because this will ask questions which common sense finds improper and repugnant to its superficial tendencies. The saving decisions in extremity, on a small scale as well as in history at large, come from a depth that common sense cannot attain.

On the other hand, common sense may transform itself from an authority into a path. Then it becomes reason, as in the "common sense maxims" formulated by Kant: "First, think yourself; second, think in every other person's place; and third, always think in agreement with yourself."

Reason is also said to show in politics as *political realism*. We have the nature of average human qualities; we have men, with their impulses, their aggressiveness, fear, and cowardice, their love of adventure, their need for security, their untruthfulness; we have the necessities of the sociological situation. To act successfully, we must know the realities and reckon with them. Reason, we are told, is nothing but realism.

In political realism, human motives as such are not taken seriously. One does not ask whether they are true and rightful; they are there, and one asks about their political effect. Thus Machiavelli held that Christian virtues make bad soldiers but reliable citizens. He thought that the Church destroys these virtues: that as people come closer to Rome, they become more faithless, superstitious, and immoral. There is evidence to support such ideas in the comprehension of possible motives, but their agreement with reality will always need empirical research. This alone shows to what extent something we may have correctly understood is real.

In this view, everything that man does becomes politically relevant. It can be known and reckoned with. A psychology of human motives evolves, so does a sociology of situations, interrelationships, social structures, types of power and organization. In this political science and psychology, the suprapolitical element disappears. Everything that we call suprapolitical is then mere human reality, political material, subpolitical, a calculable factor of political thinking. It provides for no guidance of politics by anything that is not itself political. Politics becomes the absolute human reality. "Politics," as Napoleon said, "is destiny."

The most consistent and ruthless political doctrine we know is the Hindu theory of *Kautilya*. It considers all the consequences of the fact of force and develops all the paths to victory in a contest of force. On principle, it says, right is whatever succeeds. All moral qualms are discarded; the total lie is good politics if only it succeeds in its deception. It is good politics to refrain from direct action until the opponent has been sufficiently weakened by cunning and trickery and so confused with apparent friendship that the last act of subjection can take place without the risks of combat — as wild beasts are lured into a trap. He who calculates correctly, who does not allow the slightest moral scruple to bother and inhibit him, follows the rule that is valid in politics and inexorable and absolute in this entire sphere. Accordingly, he will win over all the half-hearted who act against this political rule. The Indian thinker develops the means of getting the upper hand in situations of force without reference to ideas, without guidance by any suprapolitical element, to the sole end of power for power's sake.

We may feel reminded of Machiavelli, but unjustly so. In this greatest modern political realist we do find a limit we cannot see beyond; it is the *virtù* of the great statesman who goes his successful way in conflict, leagued with *fortuna*. There is much to be calculated and known, especially in retrospect, but these basic political forces, *virtù* and *fortuna*, are incalculable and thus suprapolitical. We cannot know them as we know natural forces and their causality; they are the very unknowable elements that make up the substance of political reality.

Machiavelli's statesman trusts in the incalculable ability that is born of his *virtù* and in his awareness of destiny that makes him feel befriended by *fortuna*, fickle though she be. The ground on which this political realist stands is outside the circle of his calculations. Machiavelli shows this frontier, describes it, but does not recognize it. But does the frontier itself show no more? Ideas of the foundation and maintenance of the state, of republican liberty and national independence, are essential to Machiavelli, though they do not dominate the structure of his works. We see their broad presence, but they are not made a principle by the great analyst of the will to power as such, who neither indicts nor vindicates what he regards as beyond good and evil.

Now there is no doubt of the extraordinary insights to be acquired by means of political realism. All great political thinkers share this realism; they grasp the importance of personalities, their weaknesses and strengths, as well as sociological causalities and contexts. They construe these in their special phenomena as consequences of certain principles — as Plato, Montesquieu, De Tocqueville have done. No modern political thought can ignore Machiavelli. But this realism is insufficient and becomes false if it is made absolute.

By the standards of such political absolutism, reason itself is viewed as unrealistic and, in the sense of *Realpolitik*, unreasonable. It is then termed idealistic and said to ignore the realities of politics, to be visionary, impotent, destructive. Let us answer this point.

First: The great political thinkers are not content with *virtù* and *fortuna*, this boundary which they do not deny but whose obscurity does not attract them. They want more. What Thucydides has in mind, for all his realism, shows in the speech of Pericles and in his personality that stands before us as a norm like reason itself, indefinable and without any psychology. De Tocqueville has said what he wants in his universal political realism: "I have but one passion — love of liberty and human dignity. All forms of government are to me only more or less perfect means of satisfying this sacred and legitimate human passion." In Thucydides, De Tocqueville, and the rest, the nature of this liberty and of its political significance remains as potent as it is indeterminable. It is suprapolitically based.

Second: What happens empirically belongs to the reality in which a statesman acts. But reality is not the norm of his actions, nor can the norm be derived from reality. The origin of the norm is a new question, not answerable by *virtù* and *fortuna*.

Third: The realists deceive themselves about the actual possibilities and sudden potentialities of political reality. They are always completely surprised by the evil which fear and the pressure of ruthless totalitarian planning can produce in a brittle, stereotyped society — up to the murder of six million Jews in Hitler's Germany — or by the good that can well up from the courage of sacrifice and the appeal to justice when a lying life becomes intolerable, as in the Hungarian uprising of 1956. The suprapolitical element alone can open our eyes to the deepest abysses as well as to the highest potentialities.

Fourth: Does reason travel along two basically unrelated paths — the realistic, turning to tangible facts, and the fictional with its fanciful appeal to freedom? There are, indeed, two levels here. But on the first level reality itself is always inadequately envisioned, while the second is concerned with ideas rather than fictions. This double track would be wrong if it were the same kind of thinking; but it is a matter of intellect versus reason, of cognoscibility as opposed to freedom. Truth grows where real knowledge enters the service of freedom and this in turn alters the world, so that new facts arise, to be understood not by adequate causes but out of the substantial content of freedom itself.

We hear, finally, that the demands of reason really stem from *religion* — that this is the suprapolitical area from which politics is to be guided to salvation. What precedes all worldly things, what cannot be known as they can be known, speaks religiously in revelation, in church, cult, and dogma, in the ethos that God wills and the church interprets. What transcends intellect, and is intangibly present and effective in reason, is thus made tangible: embodied in mysteries, sanctified in certain individuals, images, institutions, places, and times.

But what is thus comprehensible in the world is at the same time man-made. If it becomes absolute, as in cults and churches, and takes God's place in the world, it serves the need for sensuous presence, meets the helpless individual's desire for a real guarantee; but with this very power of supporting the individual it tends to lose the purported Transcendence in a merely "transcendental" reality of all that is holy. Only symbolically does it retain the truth and the power of the ambiguous language of Transcendence: to give man scope in which to find what he really wants in his freedom. For in his obscure and fundamentally unfathomable situation he makes his decisions not only by means of realistic orientation but in the light of symbols of Transcendence. In the consciousness of all that is real he seeks his uncertain way.

The traditional symbols of formal religion are therefore indispensable. The ritual experience and the thinking imagery of dogma are vessels holding a transcendent substance, initiating us as mere children into a reality that we experience even though we do not understand it yet. In images and metaphors, in moods and celebrations, the unthinkable becomes accessible. No lifelong mental labor could grasp it all.

Yet its very ambiguity is a challenge to our freedom, lest we fall into the irrationalities and inhumanities for which the churches and their representatives have to answer in all religions, especially in our own Christianity. And this ambiguity demands that we constantly keep repeating the transformation of our consciousness from dependence on sensuous embodiment to the uncertain freedom of symbolic meanings. God — who said in the language of revelation, "Thou shalt not make unto thyself any graven image" — is nowhere. The responsibility for understanding always rests with the freely created human being himself.

Formal religion is true only insofar as it is pervaded by reason — that silent power that purifies all religion and cleanses its dark, troubled springs. It affects all faiths, creeds, and churches. Reason is indivisible. No one has it; everyone seeks it. It takes shape in the world only by objective embodiment, also in formal religions.

The reason which purifies religion even while feeding on it makes us acquiesce in ignorance while striving for all possible knowledge; it leads to confidence in good will, to an awareness of Transcendence which gives me to myself in my freedom, to the achievement of a basis for trust even in extremity and total failure. What religion calls reason is already philosophy; what it calls more than reason enhances reason and thereby testifies to its own truth. But where religion detaches itself from reason it endangers the course of events.

Let us inquire from the reason of present formal religion and theology what they will have to say to the fact of the atom bomb. "Reason," they say, "is to do God's will" — a symbolic language that might unite us all. But what is God's will? What is his will in regard to the atom bomb? What must men do to do his will?

The theologian answers that God's will has been revealed and can be found in the Bible, as interpreted by church and theologians. They tell us what to do and what not to do. Today, too, churches and theologians take the floor with reference to the authority of divine revelation.

We must say in advance that any search for God's will in the Bible leads to contradictions. The most profound is that between world denial and world affirmation; but there are others — for, instead of one biblical faith, we have many churches, all armed with the Bible but interpreting it differently. Against this welter of contradictions, we have reason. In view of the ambiguity of revelation — which is nothing but the ambiguity of religious symbolism as such — reason preserves the freedom of reading the symbols on its own responsibility, ever anew and ever spontaneously. It will also look behind the revealed symbol of "God's will," which it can experience only in the freedom of its own existence — never definitively, but in timebound, historic motion. It cannot claim to appear in the name of a universally valid, universally communicable will of God.

When churches and theologians take up the question of God's will regarding the atom bomb, they are no more unanimous than on other points of faith, and no more than the rest of the world is on the atomic question. Their horror is the same as everyone else's, and their opposing views are the same as those expressed in secular circles.

Either we hear that atomic armament must go on as long as the other side keeps it up and that the practice of states as they are is justified by the traditional doctrine of original sin as the source of existence, which we must not arbitrarily obviate; or we are told that we must refrain from any participation in nuclear armament, whatever the risk, and must leave the consequences to Providence. This argument holds that the old moral-theological views of state and politics as derived from original sin are invalidated by the complete novelty of extinction by bombs; now the demand is to relinquish politics in favor of a purely reflective unconditionality. The radical "No" to the bomb is voiced unconditionally, without seeing even a chance of removing it from the world. Things are left, on the one hand, to cynical totalitarian strength and, on the other, to a will to political freedom that will brave any danger. This unconditional "No" has so far been voiced only by those whose own impotence guaranteed that their thinking could not affect the course of events; churches whose words might have a world-wide effect — the Vatican, for instance — have been rather more cautious.

The reply to the question of God's will — how we might discover it even in regard to the atom bomb — is inseparable from our conception of God. We are told that man must not thwart Providence by depriving it of its foundation, the existence of life; that the ultimate step would imply a lack of faith in Providence; that man may not choose between freedom and totalitarianism, between two forms of life he considers worth living and not worth living, if his choice of the life he considers worth living would jeopardize the life of mankind as a whole.

Against this argument we may say that its proponent raises himself above Providence. How does he know that divine Providence is limited to the existence of mankind on earth? He wants us to trust in God for the salvation of human possibilities if man submits to total rule; but he has lost his own confidence in God if he thinks he must help God by simply refusing to risk the end of life on earth at any cost. He misses his chance to stand up freely for his God-given freedom, by any means visible to human eyes. The consequences of his acts are "in the hands of God" — he himself can only try to gauge them and is always liable to err. His task is to act in the perspective of his insufficient knowledge; inaction would throw him back into nature, where things merely happen.

If I refrain from action, if I surrender mankind and myself to the functionalization of total rule because I must not endanger life as a whole, I deny myself to Providence. I am to serve it freely, within the horizon of my freedom, since I am born human. To withdraw, on the ground of not wishing to anticipate divine Providence, means to claim anticipatory knowledge of this Providence — and such knowledge would really be only a clinging to life itself as the final authority.

In the biblical faith we find not only the contrast between affirming and denying the world, but the magnificent polarity of realization in the world and indifference to it. To put it in symbolic terms: God made the world, saw that it was good, and wants man to make himself at home in it, to multiply, and to gain mastery over nature — but at the same time God opens his kingdom in another world to the man who grows indifferent to this world and longs to renounce it. Both poles of this symbolism are misleading if man thinks he might recognize God's will generally. Does this will aim at the duration of the world or at its end?

If world affirmation becomes affirmation at any cost, the very faith in God rises to dispute the theologians who claim to know his will: to wit, that man should never use the atom bomb. They deduce this from the Commandment, "Thou shalt not kill," and from the thesis that God wants mankind to live; but in their symbolic language we could say with equal weight that God may want the bombs to fall and to let mankind in its present form destroy itself. God's promise not to send another Flood may have been a false symbol. He may want man to change freely — to live if he does, to die if he does not — because in his present dissolute state he is unworthy of life. And if one cites the few "righteous," for whose sake God would not let all mankind perish, could it not be that none of the righteous have done all they could, so that they, too, are guilty?

And in the second case, if unconcern with the world becomes inaction in the world, renunciation of it for faith, Last Judgment, and eternal salvation, another side of the faith in God will object to the theologians' plaintive but practically indifferent attitude toward the atom bomb, regardless of consequences. Symbolically speaking, God may want men to live and to survive in the world, but not unconditionally. Man is to live in keeping with this survival. He has lasted for immeasurable ages, emerging from mere vegetation by skill and increasing control of nature, by community and order; now he is to last in the new possibility of total self-destruction. We may think, in the symbolism of the divine will, that God has not told man to destroy himself but has given him a choice in time: survival, on condition of changing into a better man, or doom. The redemption from atomic death cannot succeed if everything else about man remains as before.

Such discussions occur in symbolic language, and hence must be kept in suspense. Nobody knows the will of God. If I claim to know it — in our case, to know either that he does not want the atom bomb used or that he wants mankind to perish — I touch upon the very concept of God. This concept contravenes any knowledge of God's will. Any such knowledge would deny our God, the God of the Bible, the "Transcendence" of philosophy.

The Bible has no unequivocal answer to the question of whether God wants mankind to last or to perish. Yet it is the document grown over a thousand years that is most seriously and directly concerned with the possibility of an end to all things.

We can only know what we want in our limited situation, on the basis of the reason given to us; we can only hope that our will may be part of the encompassing, the unimaginable and unthinkable, which we symbolically envision as the will of God. We must not forget: we cannot do without the symbolism, but what we think and imagine in it must always be inadequate.

Among the symbols we have a free, responsible choice. To me, the one equating God's will with the survival of mankind at any cost seems unbiblical and unphilosophical. Survival is not possible under all circumstances, only if man does his best to be changed and, on this basis, to find the right political action. The phrasing, "God gives man a choice," may still be our most appropriate visualization of the symbolism of God's will; but both the choice and the visualized symbol belong to time, which is not absolute reality.

The churches today are still effective organizations. Though their spiritual power has decreased tremendously in the past century, their material power — their influence on education and legislation, for example, or their political patronage — has risen, and their authority is more frequently invoked than in past decades. It would be unrealistic not to recognize their import in the course of affairs. In organizing the power of the faith in God, and thus of philosophy, they remain unique. We cannot tell them what they should do; but we may well inquire what they will and could do.

It is easy to criticize the churches.

They spread a false calm, by promises of mercy in the beyond and by ideas that satisfy in themselves. Theologians will even talk in jurisdictional terms, claiming to be experts in the field of salvation and calling devout faith and obedience to the church sufficient to obtain it.

One possible result is political irresponsibility: their moral-theological thinking leads churches and theologians to special, but politically relevant, judgments whereby, unwillingly and unwittingly, they give actual help to certain political parties, whether Communists, Socialists, or German Christian Democrats.

Since they proclaim dogmatic beliefs and exclude those who hold others, their internecine passions discredit the truth of faith itself. They help their own, always limited, circles rather than mankind at large.

In the past they mostly imperiled science and whatever else they were fighting as new and modern, from the Middle Ages on. Today they imperil reason, the radicalism of which might help in our new situation, for they paralyze it with a dubious confidence in God — in other words, in the Church, which is something finite in the world. They becalm man's reason, diminish his responsibility, and foster passivity with reference to divine Providence.

The churches tend to regard the course of the past five centuries as a single process of decay. Hence, they have so far been unwilling to join in this great, fateful process which includes science and technology. They would resist radical truth and radical freedom. They were the forces of tranquilization, of restriction, of concealment, particularly during the internecine struggles that characterize the biblical religions of both Christianity and Islam.

And today they shrink from radical reason, which knows that more is needed than the ecclesiastic adjustments of thought and action — more than the dogmatisms and blind pseudo-radicalisms of theologians who want to be Gospel Christians but cannot be.

We cannot regard these tendencies as essential features of the churches, for the book they rest upon is the Bible, which bars tranquilization. The seriousness of eschatological thought is ineradicable. Political irresponsibility and a withdrawal upon "jurisdictions" are barred by the biblical concept of history, which involves everything in the grand course of events. Symbolically speaking, this course is either with God or against God. God is the issue, and so it is only in unconditional solidarity, renouncing all claims to supremacy or universal theological truth or catholicity, that the churches can truly bear witness to God and reach the depths in man from which alone salvation might come by Transcendence. In principle, dogmatic phraseology is as flexible as symbolic language. The single truth appears in many forms, not in one solely valid one.

The change in the form of dogmatic beliefs — or, differently put, in the effective meaning of the symbols — calls for renunciations and a new seriousness. Today it may be futile for theologians to cling to the incarnation of God in Christ; to the doctrines of the Trinity; to obligations that have become absurd; to revelations that are specifically Christian, essentially different from Hindu and Chinese ones, claiming precedence over all others. Theologians seem to preserve such features with an all but violent stubbornness; yet they ought to fall by the wayside if, in

fact, they are no longer vitally and existentially believed. Only a renunciation of what is not really believed can resuscitate the vigor of the
biblical faith: the faith in the reality of Jesus, the most revolutionary of
men; in the Ten Commandments and the symbol of Mount Sinai; in all
of the innumerable biblical symbols. In the return to a faith ascertained
in symbols — whether adopting or rejecting them — our existence would
grow unconditional and thus reliable, and the dishonesty which so often
imperceptibly invades our philosophical and theological language would
disappear.

Every chance of the churches lies in the Bible — provided they can,
in awareness of the turning point, make its original voice ring again
today. If the turning point we are facing really involves mankind's end,
the churches, too, have come into our common situation that subjects
our habits, our traditions, our learning to the question of what it means
to the life or death of all. Will they now commit themselves in accordance with the threat of doom and the greatness of the situation? Will
they keep faith with their own origin and do once more what was done
when they arose, in the worst extremity since the time of the prophets?

In today's extremity, the best chance may lie in the churches, insofar
as their members still believe. It cannot be their task any more to justify
wars and exhort men to keep arming, or — in line with modern pacifism —
to outlaw war and forbid the faithful to take part in arming. These
would be superficial simplifications. There can be no easy choice in a
situation that appears so very different to reason. As the Church has
always claimed, it must have a deeper influence, on every individual.
But there its demands must become so serious, so strict, so clear, so unconditional — without adjusting to average frailty and to the evil in men,
without offering facilitating means of grace — that the Church itself will
be in danger of being abandoned by its flock.

This seems to be the great decision facing the churches. Will they,
unlike their predecessors in history, be moved by the unprecedented
challenge to commit themselves and their power in the world — to
hazard their own existence in the name of the God they talk about?

An appeal to the faithful for sacrifices seems certain to fail unless it
involves a risk of sacrifices on the part of the churches themselves. If
they dared to stir the nations out of their churchly calm, if they risked
mass apostasy, the churches would be staking their own existence — and
if they wish to be truthful, they can do no less now, before the possible
end of all that is human. They would be calling on men to give up what

they have found in the Church for centuries. They would warn the faithful not to look to the Church for further help in their desire for finite bliss, in their irrationalities and superstitions, along their own unblest, pernicious path.

If the churches dared thus to put themselves in jeopardy, the Word would be credible everywhere, every day, on the lips of priests and theologians. They would say what exists, what threatens, what impends, what is being done. In a new earnestness, they would repeat the eternal challenge to man: to be changed in his foundations — and in conjunction with his everyday life, with all that men do and think. Before Transcendence, they would manifest what used to be proclaimed on solemn occasions only: freedom and reason and love, and the readiness for sacrifice which these imply.

With this venture, church politics would not vanish — it can never vanish entirely, churches being organizations — but it would move into the background. The churches at large would cease to engage in old-style politics. Their organizational unity would be a matter of indifference, because the one truth would be realized in many communities and in many forms. They would resemble sects of the past, as long as those were in revolt against the political unity of the visible Church, for the supersensory, invisible unity of truth, and did not themselves become churches. They would no longer engage directly in politics but would effectively arouse the seriousness that could then motivate and support the seriousness of politics. All this would not happen on account of politics nor on account of the bomb — though occasioned by it today — but without any purpose, for the sake of God and man. In themselves, the churches would beget the change they are to stimulate in man at large.

The human situation, now as ever, demands a rebirth of man. How it will occur must be left to experience and action. If I see the best chances for it on Protestant soil, this is due only to the Protestant principle which approximates philosophy: no mediator; direct contact with God; universal priesthood — and a corresponding institutional dismemberment of the Church into many creeds and independent congregations.

The churches, the Roman Catholic one above all, still have a vast, inestimable authority. We cannot tell to what extent this is only a last, eagerly sought, but not really convincing refuge in the breakdown of all authority. Be that as it may, a commitment of this authority, so as to make the churches bearers of truth and reason in the faith, might have a powerful, helpful effect. But if they cannot rouse themselves out of their entanglement in worldliness and worldly cunning to an earnest faith in God, they will drift along with the rest, on the road to perdition.

But, one will say, can a professor of philosophy do more to help? He cannot. Philosophical thought can cleanse, prepare, ascertain, but it has no definite advice to give to the question of what men should do now, on this spot, in that position of power. This advice can — prepared, perhaps, by philosophical thought — be found only by the acting, responsible human being himself. The man at the helm, if he is acting in earnest, is himself a philosopher. But the task of philosophizing is to show facts and possibilities in the broadest scope, to say what is and what can be, and to set up yardsticks for testing what does and what does not seem consistent, appropriate, and true.

The future of mankind does not lie with biblical religion and its churches alone. They encompass only a fraction of mankind, and this Western fraction in turn has largely lost faith in the churches. They could do much, but they alone cannot save us.

What is needed with them, not against them, is philosophy — accessible to all men and not bound to revealed religion. We see the difference in the communicative import of preaching and philosophizing.

Preaching is the proclamation of the revealed word of God. It appeals to faith and to the obedience of good will, and bodily communicates a certainty of Transcendence. It indicts sin and demands atonement. It speaks in the name of a higher authority, which the Church derives from God himself.

Philosophizing is more modest but poses another high challenge. In it, man turns to man on the same level, without any authorization but that due to everyone as a potentially rational being. It abides in the human situation. It makes sure of its own good will. It does not demand obedience but leads to reflection, so as to find in itself a claim to possible existence before Transcendence. It wants to alert men, but it leaves every decision and all responsibility with every individual. It has no power to "give," only to awaken what will meet it halfway.

History appears to teach us that philosophy will fail wherever helpless men seek objectively tangible supports and guarantees — wherever masses must be saved from anarchy and despair by the leadership of an authority they do not understand — wherever they cry in bewilderment to be freed from their freedom, to be given orders, to obey. Should we, then, not rather build the future on what the churches proclaim, give, demand in their sermons? Is philosophizing, the constant action of reason, not in vain? The answer is "No"; preaching alone will no longer do. Even though convincing to many, prophets and preachers of penance cannot suffice. It is only if the force they emit were translated into reason that it could have the world-wide effect required. Why is that?

First, since the intellect has provided us with the means of total destruction without being able to produce the means of guiding us in the use of its own achievements, help can come only from the power that set the intellect in motion and made it creative. Where the intellect has brought us to the brink of disaster, the power of reason alone can hold us back.

Second, our only chance today lies in a change of man on a broad scale, affecting first a few, then many, and finally, perhaps, a majority. The atom bomb, war, the claim of absolute sovereignty and all that it implies — these cannot be controlled today by statesmen unless the masses in the East and in the West, moved and enlightened by reason and changed ways of thinking, compel such control.

The real truth in reason and religion is one and the same. We all seek and want the same, and before this sameness, religious symbolisms are of secondary importance. Since we can speak and visualize in symbols only, the thing we have in common remains inexpressible — or only expressible in terms so general that historic fulfilment in particular symbols is needed to give them substance.

Man asks, "What makes life worth living? Where can we put our trust in death? Or in view of a possible end of mankind? Or at the frontier of all things?" Religion answers by couching the question itself in symbolic language. It asks, "What is God's will?" and answers that man should come close to God — that he penetrate to the depths, to the transcendent ground of things — that in all we do, even in the face of mankind's doom, we come to ourselves in the One that is more than the universe. That this truth should not be falsified, should not relieve us of the burden of freedom or tempt us to take it easy and miss our activity in the world — this is the job that reason alone can do.

16

REASON AND IRRATIONALITY IN OUR HISTORIC-POLITICAL KNOWLEDGE OF THE WORLD

Everyone has ideas about human society, its order and disorder, and what it is and ought to be — ideas mostly composed of fragments and split by fixed, contradictory thinking habits. We let public discussion be limited by such ideas, which we unquestioningly take for granted. The works of philosophers, jurists, and historians have brought such thinking into consistent systems.

Our sense of being is determined by our knowledge of our place in history, and our actions are determined by our concept of our historic task. This basic fact has long been stated and examined. People have tried to make certain of premises hitherto accepted as matters of course, to discard prejudices, so as now to achieve truth from the source of reality.

But, we may ask next, is any such attempt more than a clarification of some new prejudice that fails to notice its supposedly self-evident premise? Or, if it is more, does that attempt not end in a bottomless void? Does the totality of all possibilities, the removal of all prejudices, not miss the very reality that always depends on some restriction, some choice, some exclusion of alternatives? It is easy to answer that the one remaining choice lies between nihilism and prejudice, to prefer prejudice and to denounce "objectivity" as destructive. This answer is false.

Reality lies in the movement of reason, which knowingly finds its way into every possibility, remains universally open and unbiased, but will always turn into present historic existence and thus is not universal. Our real existence is visible only in aspects of its historic appearance, and that only in retrospect. We cannot know it in its proper infinity and eternity.

The way of reason demands that we reach out for all possible knowledge. Concepts, whether prevalent or only possible, must be known and tested without submitting to any of them. It is irrational to be overwhelmed by aspects and theories, but they can prepare the ground on which all of them are mere means or possible points of view. If, in this reason, historical, sociological, political, legal consciousness grows neither rigid nor scattered in the endless variety of random chances, it can awaken the source and drive us to the change that must take place if we shall master our situation.

Let us first visualize a basic feature of our cognitive capacities: the difference between faith and knowledge, and the significance of faith in politics.

Philosophical faith is not a content we believe in; it is an activity we believe by. A devout Catholic once told me, "I don't know if God exists, but I feel sheltered in him." This is certainly not good theology, but it is a statement possible in philosophical faith. This faith does not hear God himself, but it hears him in a reality manifested in ambiguous symbols. It does not measure God by reason, nor does it deify reason; it experiences reason as the God-given means to reach the way to Transcendence in infinite motion. Only in lofty moments, fleeting but unforgettable, is it fulfilled.

Philosophical faith knows itself only as historic motion, trusting in the source that tells it to hear and to heed what reason perceives. This is why it refers to no revelation, neither to one recognized by some limited community nor to any of its own. It is marked by discretion even toward itself, in regard to the flatly imperceptible, incomprehensible, unascertainable — to that which needs only to be precisely expressed to become unsure of itself again. No one living in the reality of this faith will cite it in vindication. If he tries to express it, he knows that the attempt is merely a way of reading symbols, not the confession of a dogma which must seem irrational to him in matters of faith.

Hence, philosophical faith must see all creeds as historic symbols that concern it. It is not only tolerant of them — as of matters of indifference

— but open-minded toward all realized contents, because they affect it, too.

There is only one limit to this receptive and responsive tolerance: it must be intolerant of intolerance. Wherever creeds try to prevail in the world by force, it must meet force with force. It has been a basic phenomenon of historic existence that time and again, in powers seeking world dominion, a faith confessed as a creed and taught and trained as the only true faith has had frightful consequences.

Today this happens once more, in a manner characteristic of the age of science and technology. Marxist doctrine, a creed from the start, has spread so widely that its converts now seem to outnumber both Christians and Buddhists. To understand this, we must realize that the substance of Marxism is scientific superstition. It invokes science, abandons it in fact, and makes a fetish of the remnant it retains. It abandons science, for it stops aiming at methodical inquiry, critical examination, and universal validity by intellectually cogent insight; instead, it claims to possess truth as finished, immutable doctrine — as the Catholic Church, for instance, does in Thomas Aquinas, whose spiritual level and wealth are, of course, not comparable. The pseudo-scientific idol exacts its sacrifices in doctrinal unity, in the persecution of deviations, and in the acknowledgment of central direction, as in Mao's submission to Moscow.

In this situation we need now an insight that is inseparable from freedom, scientifically comprehensible, yet realizable only as a moral act of rational man: the insight that philosophical faith is not objective knowledge, that philosophy is not science, but that they are allied. Reason is not intellect, but not for an instant will it lose touch with the intellect. The meaning of these statements has become clearer in the past century; the insight is here, but it does not prevail even in the world of science. Its concrete realization is an unfinished task that will take all of man's moral character and reliable critical judgment.

Reason will not prevail while philosophy pretends to be a science — and thus, today, inevitably leads to scientific superstition. Nor will reason prevail if philosophy slights the sciences, ignores or rejects them. Reason sides firmly with science, wants, backs, moves, and constantly consorts with it.

Rational politics deals with questions of existence, not of faith. It does not want to link the two, for the philosophical faith that unfolds in the movement of reason is not faith in the sense of a creed; rather, it means liberation of whatever does not claim totality by force. Questions of existence, having to do with material interests, are always open to negotiation, to compromise, to agreement. Only the faith that claims totality and the will to power that is not satisfied short of world rule make a joint settlement of existence questions, a politics of particular "interests," impossible.

In this situation we must consider, first, that for a while the confessors of a faith seem overwhelmingly powerful. Everything seems in their favor; they give the impression of an irresistible tide. The measure of courage, the longing for martyrdom, the joys of dying for the cause and self-abandonment in absurd confessions of guilt — all these are so great that increasing numbers are carried away by an earnestness that commands such sacrifices.

In view of such phenomena, many think we must oppose this kind of faith with an equally strong faith. By so doing, we would already give up our faith in reason. To confront one fanatical, cannibalistic creed with another would be to betray our rational form of faith, to exchange it for the form of the dreaded enemy, to descend to his irrational level, though with another creed — for reason is not a faith, not subject to organization, not apt to become a church, a doctrine, a system; it is the ever moving freedom of man himself. Besides, it would be futile to plan and arrange for such a fanatical faith.

The situation calls for something entirely different. The Marxist scientific superstition employs force, deliberately and actually. For self-preservation, force must be met with force — intensified force with a force correspondingly intensified. Nothing in the world, least of all the philosophical faith of reason, can maintain its existence without the courage of sacrifice. This courage, in the honest solidarity of free men, will engender a will not to let the rational faith that has been kindled in the free world go a-glimmer again, but to make it rise, in free moral-spiritual conflict, with new, irresistible force against the powers of corruption. Today, the West has not yet come to this decision in reliable solidarity.

Integrity in politics — confining ourselves to the settlement of material interests and to self-preservation against force — is impossible without faith. Yet this faith, in which no content is absolute but all beliefs are left free, cannot deduce its course of action logically from the theses of a creed; it can only develop a common insight rationally, from the nature of existing material interests. That it is a faith is evident from the readiness for sacrifice — which here, on a mutual basis, achieves its aim of settling questions of existence in the common order in which humanity can unfold and thrive. Yet the same faith shows valor, self-sacrifice, and full commitment if the level of possible rational community is left and naked force breaks out.

The second point to consider was put into words by Max Weber: "You can't reason with warriors for the faith." In other words, politics has a fundamentally different import where there is no place for reason.

Within former conflicts of interest there could be claims of such radical difference that the parties, though still linked by the scope of reason, would let heaven decide — that is to say, they went to war on the premise that both, after the victory of one had settled the issue, would continue to exist. Only where a state power sought expansion as such, strove for world power and finally for world dominion, was war waged with the alternative of total subjection. It was different, too, when world powers fought not for sober temporal interests but in the name of God, to spread their one and only true faith — as in the early wars of Islam, in the Crusades, in the religious wars in Christendom.

Today, the atom bomb has changed the situation in principle. For all the differences in recent causes of war, the alternative today is simple. Either the issue is one of material existence — in which case it cannot become a question of faith between free governments functioning under law; in the present situation it will be peacefully resolved under all circumstances. Or the issue identifies questions of existence with questions of faith, as today the imperialism of totalitarian power — Russia's now, and China's, perhaps, in the future — is identified with the Marxist social religion. In that case, everything differs from conflicts between nations governed by law and enjoying freedom of faith, of science, and of the philosophy of reason.

And yet, as we and this power-hungry alien religion are living in the same world, under the same threat of the atom bomb, the proposition, "You can't reason with warriors for the faith," cannot be the last word if mankind is to survive. Attempts to talk with each other must never be abandoned. The bearers of that faith, who cannot be reasoned with, are still human beings — and if we believe in reason, we must, until the last, seemingly hopeless, moment cling to the question of how it may be possible to reason with them after all.

We delude ourselves and answer the question wishfully and detrimentally if we forget what this struggle for the faith means to our opponents and that they are presently obsessed with it — in other words, that for the time being we must still see, first of all, to our own strength, to be able to meet the force of the religious enemy with at least equal force. Any diminution of this strength results from slothful obliviousness.

The true answer to the question lies in patience — in the patience of searching for the right words, the right arguments, the right and candid actions that will arouse our enemy to the reason which, being human, he must have hidden in him. But all this cannot be accomplished solely by a rational effort to find the right phrasings. It cannot be accomplished until rational man is reborn in the West; for this reasoning with warriors for the faith — which seems impossible, according to past experience — requires the same qualities as communication among individuals: purity of motive, vigor of thought, the ethos of unconditional existence. The statesman's entire approach, his tone, his instantaneous reactions, the word that is his bond, the posture that inspires faith in his lack of expansionist designs, the confidence that he stands for a nation animated largely by his ethos — all this might work miracles.

Nothing less is needed than the transformation we have been discussing all along. The essence of reason would do here what no threat of military power can achieve. The strength of reason lies in the unshakable certainty that its road, with its call for political freedom, is basically the true road of man; but this strength lies also in the restraint, the constant awareness on the part of every individual that he is not on the absolutely right road which needs no correction, but that he must listen to others.

Any talks between the free and totalitarian worlds will occur under the pressure of mutual preparations for violence, with each side blaming the other. The first step toward reason would be a mutual acknowledgment that our opponent cannot give up the force that we retain. Politics still continues as this constant reference to possible force, as bargaining and treaty-making contingent on a status quo, as trickery and cunning. This fact, too, should be acknowledged in any talks, for the time being — for the point of rational communication is not to abuse it for deception in the conflict of force, but to create among men a vinculum that would eventually make this form of conflict impossible. If reason is not unconditional but lets itself be degraded to a means of totalitarian deception or free inertia, it is no longer reason.

Human life does not go on recurring like animal life, immutable for countless generations; it occurs as history, which does not repeat itself. If we have any knowledge of the historic-political process which we have inherited, in which we stand, and to which we are contributing at every moment, we perceive it between two poles. We see rules and patterns of recurring similarities; but we see, too, that there is a limit to all regularities and similarities and analogies in the course of events — that indeed they point to the very thing that does not recur: to the historic essence. This, from a general point of view, is merely the special feature of any case; viewed on the spot, however, it is our existential reality. Both poles are made absolute, the lasting general pattern and the unique historic event. This unique aspect, as opposed to the general, is the entirety in which every specialty is another entirety.

If we want to find out what we ought to do, we should like to know where we stand in the entirety of the historic process. The unique situation of each present time is related to previous and succeeding situations. Knowledge of the process would not only determine our actions, according to general rules valid for recurrent similar cases; if we knew the whole from beginning to end, we would also know what we, in our place, can do successfully because "the time is ripe," because our action would be in harmony with the encompassing process, not idle and futile for running counter to it.

An awareness of history, grown into comprehensive knowledge, can lend wings to the enthusiasm of doing vigorously what must be done, in league with the spirit of history — or it can cast us down into passivity, into thinking, "Whatever I do makes no difference; what must be, must be; I shudder at this necessity and resign myself."

The question is whether we are not fooled in both cases by an enchanting but rationally and politically noxious fiction. Is such universal knowledge of history possible? Is there even an object of such knowledge, assuming ours were immeasurably increased? If there is not, then all human truth and freedom rests on the fact that entirety is not only unknowable but non-existent. The course of events lies open to the free decisions that man makes, knowing the facts. Only a totally different knowledge — a divine one, inconceivable to us and absurd to our finite logic — could see freedom and its actions in the perspective of an existing, infinite, eternal entirety.

Let us repeat this great question that determines our sense of being and the manner of our responsibility. Is there a *basic process* of doom and salvation, objectively existing and cognoscible to the human mind?

Or does the basic process lie in freedom itself? That is to say: does it result from human decisions — decisions which have not yet been finally made? Today we are in danger of hiding our situation behind a faith in a basic process that does not exist. False notions make us fail to do what can be done.

We cannot even suggest here the vast, inexhaustible scope of historical research. It is marked by methodical awareness, by intellectual cogency — and thus, as it justly and successfully claims, by universal validity — and finally, by the exactitude and particularity of the knowledge it can attain. I confine myself to a few points.

Examples alone will illustrate what a *causal* interpretation of history can and cannot do. One of the great, representative achievements of modern historical science is Max Weber's *Protestant Ethics and the Spirit of Capitalism*. There we find the accessible facts, from statistical phenomena to the meaning of sermons, explored from all sides. We find detailed research into minutiae and clarifications of fundamental issues, living historical pictures for our imagination and conceptual questions and answers for methodical thinking. Yet what is the result in generally valid knowledge? An effort of such magnitude instructs by virtue of its historical content; it trains our minds, but what, finally, do we know for certain? "I have shown," Max Weber tells us, in effect, "that the ethics of Calvinist Protestantism was a factor in the evolution of modern capitalism. Just how influential this factor was I cannot say; I *think* it had a great influence." Impassioned research, visualization of the facts, and at the same time critical reserve in weighing certainty and import of the generally valid results — these are the characteristics of this type of intellectual curiosity, as long as it remains a science and does not become a creed.

Equally characteristic are the misunderstandings which this model achievement has caused in our time. What was relative knowledge to Weber was promptly made absolute. Some, refuting things he had never said, pointed to other factors in the origin of capitalism, factors long known and assumed as known by Weber. Others misinterpreted him as having shown the root of our present ills in Protestantism; with the cause revealed, they said, one could get rid of it.

None of this is the point of Weber's work. Any such transformation of knowledge into an absolute, an element of faith, destroys the meaning of scientific research, which springs from an original, unlimited, ever-critical desire to know regardless of the desirability or undesirability of the resulting knowledge. Research is carried on in a constantly renewable atmosphere of neutrality. The urge to share in what can be known is suspended if knowledge comes under a cloud of delusions and evaluations. Yet it remains the impulse for research itself — for mere exactitude, indifferent to the results, would not be able to motivate and maintain the consuming activities of cognition.

Aside from causal, there is *teleological* thinking about history, its interpretation from the ends it seems to serve. In studying organisms, their structure and functions, we cannot help using considerations of purpose, if only to perceive them as living creatures. Their existence seems based on a plan. This plan — in contrast to man-made machines designed for a purpose — is not finitely and measurably, but infinitely, purposive; only a teleological view enables us to ask the specific biological questions which are then answered causally, in physical or chemical terms. The analogous interpretation of history asks what events were good for, what desirable end they achieved, what they prevented. We need not and cannot infer the real existence of a guiding hand in history — this hand, like a hand guiding biological purposes, would seem to human minds both incomprehensibly wise and incomprehensibly stupid, both salutary and destructive, good and bad, merciful and merciless. But a teleological view will clarify relationships which would remain obscure without this type of inquiry.

Teleologically, for example, the definitive collapse of European world dominion may be called the result of the fact that Europe, in the flower of her industrial growth, lost her ethos and brought calamity over the world. But this result may in turn be regarded as the possible starting point of a European renascence — a rebirth that would not lead to a new form of despotism, but to the communication of nations, however different, in a community of peace. Instead of European power, the humanely convincing Western idea of freedom would come to the fore in the world, for it is founded in the roots of man, not adopted from foreign sources. It leaves to every nation the initiative for its historic course.

If the West could be reborn and could prevail by the power of conviction, as in the past it used to prevail by force, the downfall of the rule of force — which Europe, in Hitler's Reich, achieved for a moment and threatened to impose forever — might bring forth a new way of political thinking. It might make a peaceful community of all nations possible, and mankind's doom by the atom bomb impossible. Since Europe's failure in quality does not mean there is better quality elsewhere, the present outbreak of totalitarian evil excepts no people on the globe — but the teleological view wants to discover positive germs in negativity itself. It regards precisely the ultimate danger as apt to make these germs sprout all over. It sees a hidden goal in the course of evil: to develop freedom and truth and substantial humanity, because the universal communication, without which all would perish, can be freely accomplished at the very moment when it is most urgently needed.

Teleologically, totalitarianism may seem necessary to make freedom real. Since the Western world has not been pervaded by freedom, since its freedom failed to assume responsibility for life and lost itself in hypocrisies, one can say that it took the most terrible threat of all time to bring it back to itself, to rally it from deterioration, to make it serious, real, and true.

Only honest freedom can become a model for others wanting to be free. Before the terrible totalitarian menace that would eradicate freedom, everyone must prove himself — outwardly in self-preservation against the force from abroad, inwardly against the totalitarian tendencies that lie in man as such, and today in so many failing Western nations. Teleologically, this decisive inner struggle is governed by the maxim that there can be no dialectical synthesis of freedom and totalitarianism. It is either-or; I cannot be honest, reliable, clear thinking, if in my heart I am facing both ways and seeing both as elements of an encompassing whole. A lasting synthesis, even in the form of peaceful coexistence, is impossible on the side of total rule, which employs the coexistence theme as a means of deception, to conceal the preparatory stages of the fight for world rule.

In both directions — in inner contention and in the outward conduct of international politics — the search for an allegedly possible synthesis is a self-deception practiced by a part of the free world, by its irresponsible neutralist literati. In teleological interpretation, it means that those who do not see the real, present, and manifest extremity of totalitarianism are doomed by their blindness and ill will, but they are given a chance to see and thus to come to the right path of inner living and consequently proper political action.

Thus teleological thinking shows also how the purpose that may lie in a situation can be missed. Today, we hear that a fruitful polarity with Russian bolshevism might be achievable; but such thinking can grow only in the soil of the same moral-political decay which in 1933 led the Western powers and the Vatican to look forward to fruitful co-operation with Nazism. It ignores elementary facts indicating that the premise of a synthesis is lacking — that the existence of a common ground, of mere common rules of combat and communication, is not recognized, only pretended, by the adversary. If we deceive ourselves about the radical either-or of freedom and totalitarianism, we practically give up our own freedom.

By no means, however, should we break political relations for that reason. Negotiations, agreements, and exchanges of information remain, rather, the methods of extending the breathing spell until a change in the situation and in humanity may perhaps turn the breathing spell into a state of peace.

Synthesis cannot be the teleological meaning of the existence of totalitarianism — of its actual existence alongside the free world or its potential existence within this world. Instead, totalitarianism is seen as the goad that uncovers all halfheartedness, smugness, dishonesty, or perversion within the life of the free world and makes a bleeding wound of it. The goad makes it necessary for freedom to educate and transform itself — this is the evil's conceivable teleological import. But the transformation cannot occur in the direction of totalitarianism, not by a union of communism and capitalism, not with the idea of thus combining freedom and justice — in the misconception that, while the free world offers liberty, the totalitarian world offered justice.

Both freedom and justice are possible only in the world that is politically free. They have not yet been attained there, because of dishonesty and premature satisfaction, but under total rule the necessary self-criticism and moral transformation are fundamentally impossible. To be effective, the goad requires public information, which totalitarianism deliberately excludes. In entering the public life of the free world, totalitarianism sharpens the goad, but in its own world it keeps the reverse from happening.

A teleological view of the atom bomb, finally, would regard it as given to two great powers so that neither should have a monopoly with its temptation to conquer the world at will. Would America have done so? Perhaps, with a monopoly on the bomb, America might have coerced the world into a special narrow concept of freedom, in smug, optimistic inability to see to the bottom of things. To prevent this, to keep mankind's path open, it was necessary — from a teleological point of view — for one possible coercion to meet with another possible coercion. It is from the tension of peril, from the threat of doom to all, that truth will grow.

Yet this whole teleological way of thinking, however oddly the possible truth of its thoughts may touch us, is only a game. There is no cogency about teleological relations; they can clarify situations and, above all, can help the free world to sense the challenge it must meet, but they do not enable us to help the conceived purpose along, as it were, by planned action. This would be perverting the relationship of freedom and teleological thinking — for no man knows Providence. Instead of seizing the finite goals and means accessible to human purposive thought, he would yield to the delusion of being able to guide history as a whole.

If an illness, because of its menace, can sometimes be interpreted as salutary for the patient's existential earnestness, it does not follow that we should bring on an illness for this purpose, or that it would have the desired result. The goal lies beyond any human purpose; pursued by such means, it would be missed. If, for example, bomb secrets were given to Russia on such a presumption of knowing Providence, the act, in the human context, was plain treason and can never be justified in providential terms. The philosophical posture of such thinking is wrong, arrogant, and childishly naïve.

Still another approach to history is *ideological* interpretation. Animals fight for existence and so do men, but men fight for more than mere existence: they fight for the existence of a cause or a faith, for a way of life or a conception of life. In conflict, men interpret their aims. Then the conflict becomes at the same time a clash of minds, and this, politically, means evangelizing for one's own convictions.

Sets of political convictions are called ideologies. They do not consist of single arguments; they bear on the basic approach to political action, on concepts of history, and on the view of what matters in life. We shall list a few such ideologies, letting them speak, roughly and selectively, for themselves and adding to each, in parentheses, a critical characterization from a different ideology.

1. The "organic" view of the world: States of human existence, however full of inequalities, are arranged by God and correspond to an eternal, pre-existing world order that can be disturbed or more faithfully adhered to, but not fundamentally questioned. (In fact, such orders correspond to privileged interests.)

2. "Natural law": We must resign ourselves to living in a sinful world; being sinners ourselves, we cannot change it. We must make relative order, as best we can — always unjustly, because always sinfully — according to social doctrines that will permit a coercive rule tempered by the consciousness of sin and by the eternal salvation offered by the institutions of the Church. (In fact, a certain contentment in the consciousness of sin, the assurance of grace, and the coercive order will be the prevailing mood.)

3. Authoritarianism: Domination is a basic fact of human existence. There must be command and obedience, governors and governed. The authorities alone decide and are responsible; as a subject, I must, should, and may simply obey. (As a result, the subject's vision is narrowed and his choice made easy, for he need not inquire whether the authorities' objective is justified or unjustified or criminal — obedience as such is dutiful and meritorious. The consequence for the rulers is unchecked irresponsibility.)

4. Nationalism: My people, their state, and its present interests are paramount in politics. There is nothing above the nation, nothing that should not be subordinated to the nation; everyone can realize his humanity only within his own people. (In fact, our historic consciousness is here narrowed and made objective and absolute, instead of linking the interests of our people with those of mankind and its history.)

5. Humanitarianism: Mankind, its needs, its nature, and its order are paramount. There is a universal rightfulness, whereby all politics is to be judged and guided. (In fact, the sense of history disappears, and remaining are empty phrases.)

6. Anarchism: Conditions are radically wrong, estranging man from himself. The world must be reorganized, and any move in this direction is truth — hence the call for eternal revolution and for the destruction of the so-called organic order that is always discrimination, inequality, injustice. (The source of this view is absolute despair of human existence. The real consequence of such constant regeneration is the terror of absolute force as the sole curb on absolute chaos.)

7. Chiliasm: The present moment in history is unique. It is a turning point to a new age. No norm applies, only newness. (Such eschatological thinking aims at the end that is a beginning; it is refuted by the reality of factual continuity.)

Such ideologies may be developed to justify our own desires and actions, or to interpret the meaning of our enemies' actions — in which case they are designed for attack. In fact, the concept of ideology arose from conflict. We call our opponent's view an ideology and criticize it by showing where it came from. We disclose the false consciousness, the reprehensible aims and interests cloaked in our opponent's ideology. By analyzing his ideology we mean to conquer it, for knowledge is superior to ignorance, awareness to unawareness.

There are two forms of intellectual conflict by ideological interpretation: the fight with lies and the fight for truth. If the definition of ideologies is used in the struggle for existence, the opponent is indicted for a false ideology or pictured as having it. His actions are branded not only as hostile but as the fruits of this false ideology and therefore reprehensible. In this struggle, which is factually devoid of communication, thinking becomes mendacious; it matters not whether a thought is true as long as it is effective.

If, on the other hand, a spiritual struggle for truth is waged in ideologies, the contestants start with a mutual will to communicate with each other. The conflict benefits both of them. Both become more aware; both can correct themselves; both can reach limits where something still un-illuminated but convincing seeks further illumination.

But the question always remains how ideologies are related to reality. Ideologies are products of thought; reality is the realm of action. Thinking itself is reality, though not unequivocally so; it detaches itself from reality, so as to produce two realities: the interpretation and that which is interpreted. In no case is an object of ideological interpretation identical with the reality occupied by its convinced protagonist. No real power and no human being is wholly one with an ideology — which always shows only one side of any phenomenon. The unfathomable historic reality is a struggle of powers, but it is not identical with the struggle of the objects of ideological interpretation. Conflicts are clarified by our thinking, and by our efforts to follow our opponent's thinking, but any over-all view of an ideology — or of the objective entirety of ideologies — is either a front line in battle to the thinker and to those he is thinking about, or it is one of many indifferent typologies that can be multiplied and combined at will.

The fact that we interpret reality and ourselves, and are human only by so doing, confronts us with an abysmal dilemma — for interpretation never comes to an end. Nietzsche put it unanswerably: "Everything," he said in effect, "is interpretation; all interpretations are subject to reinterpretation of their motives and consequences; once I exist as a thinking person, I am interpreting either things or some previous interpretation." There is no halt, except by sticking arbitrarily to one interpretation. Or is there a halt, after all — not a barrier, but an escape from the vortex of indefinitely reversible interpretations? We can find such a halt either in divine revelation, if we believe in it — then the infinite movement of history grows from the interpretation of this revelation, which is the original reality — or we find it in reason, which on the ground of historic existence, in communication with others, enters upon the endless historic movement of intensified communication even with utter strangers.

We must remember that the insight won by understanding interpretation is not a discovery of natural processes. My understanding incalculably changes what I understand — therefore, my responsibility for understanding differs fundamentally from that for perceptions of nature. The very act of understanding makes it a factor in reality, while natural discovery becomes so only by application.

Where, finally, this interpreting is done in the realm of reason, the question is whether there can be any thinking in over-all concepts that is free from ideology. Is any such concept not another ideology? In interpreting ideologies, can we divest ourselves from ideological thought? Can there be a construction of ideologies that is not an ideology itself?

First, the practical answer: we have a meaningful discussion if, in subjecting words and actions to ideological analysis, we ask whether we agree with a particular view, whether we want its consequences, recognize the limits of its meaning, and recognize other motives. Intellectually, there is no end to these debates; practically, they must have an end and a new beginning at every moment that compels us to act — that is, to choose.

As for theoretical insight, we can answer that the constructive analysis of ideologies in objectivized forms is neither deceptive nor ideologically distorted if we know what we are doing. We are putting up consistent constructions — ideal types — not in order to mistake them for realities, but to check the realities against them, to see where the realities fit them and where they do not. We are not seeing actual powers in these ideal types; we use them as tools for understanding. We must try them out, to see whether they will work. Ideologies cease being ideologies and become tools of understanding when reason takes hold and brings each one to the fore in its own special sense.

The sense of being part of infinite historic progress makes us wish to smooth the path by proper planning. We are busy "fixing" things, drawing up future programs. From this view, the meaning of life lies not in the present but in the future — we cannot believe in an end. History strikes us as an ascent through error and suffering.

Reason makes us see the important distinction between indispensable special planning for the moment and fatal total planning for an unattainable entirety — between inspiring free activity in the area open to man and fanaticized activity in a fictitious area.

There is a famous line by Marx: "The philosophers have only reinterpreted the world, but the point is to change it." Now, Western activity has always sought to change and improve things; it has always broken with traditions and customs. The difference is that previously, except for evanescent sectarian projects, all activity used to deal with particular temporal plans, encompassed in an entirety that was to be envisioned in contemplation and suffered in practice. Marx, on the contrary, took the step from mere historic-philosophical contemplation of entirety, like Hegel's, to political activity based on a supposed total knowledge. To him, the historic-philosophical, designedly contemplative insight became supposed cognition and an instrument for making history — as the engineer employs natural science to build his machines. Because he thought he had total knowledge of the process of history, Marx could see a point in total planning, in which the all-embracing activity of man coincides with the supposedly grasped historic necessity.

Yet Marx did not mean to apply total knowledge as technical machinery. His total knowledge is dialectical; it sees the movement of history, in which it is included, as a dialectical force. Therefore, it turns against the mechanical view. It does not see history guided according to a prescription, by the technical application of a fixed knowledge of nature, but by the dialectical movement of this knowledge itself, occurring in the productivity of technological labor and its social consequences. According to Marx, this thinking brings about what is required by the times and represented by the leadership, the knowing vanguard. Hence, the party line is considered identical with the course of history, and deviations from the party line are viewed as revolts against history, the deity from which there is no appeal.

In practice, what was once an idea of philosophical import becomes a debating technique of despotism and its slavish intellectual minions. This technique can vindicate every step, justify every demand — for everything is possible to dialectics, once the method has been accepted without differentiating between extraordinarily varied forms of dialectics and its meaning.

In making a supposed total knowledge of history the basis of total planning, Marx encompasses all of man in his plan. He not only wants to change the world for man; he wants to change man himself — and he expects to do this not by an arbitrary intellectual design, but by the manifest necessity of history which he claims to have discovered.

In Marx's work and influence we have to make a distinction. Marx was the first to understand capitalism comprehensively — and with extraordinary powers of thought and observation — as the economic mutation of the technological age. He was the first to reveal this age as a process of technological labor with consequences for the communal structure and for humanity. This, with his economic analysis of the relationships within capitalism, has added new perceptions — and numerous, but corrigible errors — to our permanent store of knowledge. But Marx's basic attitude is another matter. It is not that of a critical scientist; instead, he is a prophet and agitator for the political manufacture of a new human condition, blind to realities that do not fit his aim and to the founts of true humanity. Marx thinks despotically. He propounds a politics of force. While his perceptions are an irrevocable factor in modern knowledge, his hypostatization of political terrorism has become a factor in present history. Marx's intellectual utopia was born of outrage, hatred, and an abstract zeal for justice; today, with its meaning gone, it is no more than a façade for total rule as such. Marx did not envision the dictatorship of the proletariat as that of a tyrant or a tyrannical clique replacing the proletariat with an *Apparat*, a new privileged class. Nor did this totalitarianism arise, as Marx expected, in the West from the industrial revolution; it is the coercive power used, first by Russia and then by non-industrial Asian countries, to appropriate technology and abolish illiteracy, that obstacle to technological progress. "Socialism," Lenin said, "is Communism plus electrification."

In this ultimate deterioration, Marxist thought is farther than ever from reason. It is the unreason of the absolute intellect linked with unlimited and deliberate violence. This is the form in which it now wields vast power among non-Western peoples and works like a stealthy poison in the Western world.

Unlike the dogmatic, single-minded, pseudo-scientific violence of Marx, there is a scientific attitude that would combine the progress of knowledge with methodical direction of the course of events as a whole. It wants knowledge utilized and realized in free decisions, in the co-operation of many, in the framework of political freedom under law. This sounds simple — and yet, in our age, we see a degree of planning, organizing, and mechanizing that threatens to exceed all bounds, to enmesh, to permeate, and essentially to destroy all human existence.

Our existence depends on intelligent planning. It always has. Thousands of years before Christ, planning for the control of great rivers, the Nile and the Hwang Ho, engaged the organized labor of masses of men and huge bureaucracies. States have been founded and governments established on planning. Such planning, in its proper place of mastering nature for human purposes and hence shaping labor and the organization of labor, rests upon technological, industrial, and economic knowledge and has vastly increased with the growth of knowledge and techniques in the past century. It lies in the nature of things and accordingly coincides in the free and totalitarian worlds. What we call the organization, the entirety of conscious planning, is part of the age of technology; it is the same phenomenon in Russia, America, China, or elsewhere. Yet there are differences.

First, while the mass-ruled world of the industrial revolution leads everywhere to a potential functionalization of man, there is a fork in the road. Totalitarianism uses its organization as a tool; the free world allows various organizations to develop. Under total rule there is but one, delegating powers to subordinate organizations but retaining full control; there is no freedom, because all are subject to one total planning — because the *Apparat* is the state. In the free world, organizations have their own responsibilities, standing alongside or in competition with each other. As a result, they do not seize all of man; while limiting individual freedom of choice in fact — by the imposition of unpleasant material consequences — they do not destroy it. There are struggles within organizations, over management or profits or employment policies, and though their size may give them substantial political influence, they are never one with the state. The single totalitarian organization stifles human freedom; the multiple organizations made inevitable by technology threaten man but leave him free to fight for the shape he wants to give them.

Second, the belief that everything can be "fixed" is apt to mislead us. In the end, we want to "fix" man himself, to make him over according to plan, by breeding or by environmental compulsion. In practice, attempts at such planning can only be disastrous, in view of our limited knowledge and capacity. For all apparent fluctuations, no essential change in man's biological and psychological makeup can be expected within a few generations, not even within a few thousand years. Any attempt to plan such a change on the basis of experiences with animal breeding must fail, since our inadequate knowledge tells us only about objective hereditary characteristics, about physical traits or such constitutional features as memory or resistance to fatigue, as if we wished to produce useful human work animals. It does not tell us what man is as man, in the freedom of his existence. Besides, the procedure is an outright slap at human dignity and individual freedom. It jeopardizes life and limb. Man would "fix" man, to be "fixed" in turn. The question would be "Who fixes whom?"

Third, there is no sharp line between things that cannot be planned and things which, on principle, might be planned if we knew enough about them. Whatever the individual does in freedom is beyond planning, but there might be conditions more favorable than others to human spontaneity. Conceivably, we might plan for the unplannable by giving scope to free potentialities. All living things can be nurtured, not merely bred. For man, there is education — but this can be substantially realized only by personalities who will educate themselves, who will find the way without rules, in human contacts, in devotion and attention, in a severity governed by the idea of the faith they are to kindle, by all means of instruction and training within the confines of tradition. The limits of pedagogical planning are narrow, and the result of exceeding them is either formal drill or the chaos of polymathy which precisely fails to educate man as such.

Yet the means of conveying cultural traditions offer one of the great challenges to pedagogical and political leadership. Here we are concerned with things beyond planning. We would like, in the final analysis, to plan so as to prevent the results of our planning from exceeding the bounds of planning — but this brings us to the boundary line where our objectives are in danger of being voided by their very achievement.

Planning is an activity of the intellect; reason guides its meaning — which is not exhausted by any particular goal — and recognizes its limits. Meaningless planning is destructive; planning cannot take the place of reason. There is too little planning if things we can control are left to chance; there is too much if the whole of human affairs is to be subjected to our designs and made over.

Finally, there is modern technological thinking which aspires to turn the course of things in a desirable direction on grounds of scientific research in history, sociology, statistics, mass psychology, etc. — not, as Marx would, by any total knowledge. Here we think we are discovering laws of human behavior and of history that will enable us to guide the course of events like a natural process. We hope to extend our knowledge of psychological and sociological factors and expect the spread of such knowledge to facilitate its application. What began in the areas of working hygiene and labor rationalization, what is being done with aptitude tests, by plant psychologists, by social workers, what is attempted in marriage counseling — all this leads up to the concept of a supposedly coming scientific guidance of all things.

There is an amazing confusion here, of scientific research, scientific superstition, personal helpfulness and good sense in human intercourse, and fanciful illusions. In the end, the errors rising from an uncritical distortion of rudiments match the Marxist ones. The two kinds meet and join.

The intellect that is behind all planning claims too much if it tries to direct the decisions of freedom, which are acts of reason. The trouble starts when overplanning puts a supposedly scientific guidance in place of a change to rational freedom. Man can only change as an individual and then, perhaps, arouse the freedom of others, but the slightest touch of coercion would destroy what counts. The state of the world is changed by the achievement of reason within its circle, of the individual within his sphere. The most private action is such as to oblige rational man to ask himself — as Kant put it — whether he wants a world in which his action would be repeated time and again, would become exemplary and normal. It is as if every action of the individual helped to create a world where such actions would be the rule.

If, on the other hand, man thinks he knows all and wants to run the world by planning all, if he wants to put history, and himself as its interpreter, in the deity's place, he may indeed coerce mankind by political terror; he may even force the intellect to serve him to the limit of its propagandistic, disputatious, conceptual, technological faculties — but he will kill reason. The germinal forces, the originality of new cognition, the feeling for the true nature of cognition, the creative life of the spirit — all this will disappear, unless it continues underground, in hidden resistance. If man tries to "dictate freedom," to impress a supposedly absolute truth upon mankind by repetition, drill, or threats — whether in the name of a proletarian dictatorship or in that of a master race — truth itself ceases.

A misconceived freedom will have similar disastrous effects if free science, in a seemingly more critical spirit, uses its technically applicable knowledge to pervade a docile society steeped in scientific superstitions with constant planning of an uncritical sort. Over-all salvation does not come from any science. Where the purportedly political sciences overstate their case, they divert us from the root of the matter: from the basic freedom of reason, which cannot be planned but is the source, and the guide, of all planning that will make sense.

Total planning, which transforms all human existence into a structure of mass organization — a planning always confined to the finite horizons of the human intellect — voids humanity as such; but a planning which in the end, in manifold fashion, entangles our existence in needless and pointless necessities will become just as unbearable. Failing to limit itself to what really can and must be planned, it makes freedom vanish.

There are limits to prediction as well as to planning. No one can foretell with any degree of certainty what men will do, what will happen due to human action. We can envision possibilities and probabilities and impossibilities, but experience tells us that the impossible can happen, that the probable may never happen, and above all, that new, completely unthought-of realities may appear.

The intellect always predicts the negative only. It knows what is doomed. In biology, finding some species extinguished, it partly understands why, but it never finds a way to recreate them. The same is true of human affairs. There are developments — the time, for instance, for which such sources of energy as coal, oil, or water power can be expected to last, or the possibilities of food production on earth and the corresponding maximum population — which the intellect will grasp, though rarely with the precision of calculating planetary movements. But creativity is unpredictable. Man adds something new to the world, something not adequately comprehensible in terms of what went before, not even in retrospect. Nobody can foresee what men are capable of — whether, for instance, scientists in the spirit of Newton or Einstein will manage once more to bring a cognoscible order (along with its chance of new, unexpected discoveries) out of the chaos of today's physical facts, or whether we face the end of the progress of knowledge. Nor can we foresee whether new prophets will rise and guide us by their revelations on some divinely oriented course of rational action, or whether there will be moral-political rebirths to determine ways of life, to draw boundaries, to teach moderation, and to uplift human nature. Man's potential is inexhaustible. Nothing great, nothing fundamental has ever been foretold, nor have its origins been understood in retrospect. We can state conditions it would not have happened without, not the causes that made it happen.

These possibilities cannot be counted on, but they cannot be discounted, either. The intellect can, I repeat, predict the negative only — except for what it may be able to "fix" itself — and so it always sees only disaster ahead. The thought of man's positive chances remains void, for to conceive and predict them would be to realize them. But the indefinite thought of these chances is inspiring, although it gives us nothing to lean upon. It holds the way open, and it keeps the intellect from casting us into despair with its negativity.

Action, however, must be prepared from all intellectually predictable perspectives. Physical and political knowledge can suggest timely measures that will not leave us defenseless in the face of surprise attack — measures that may be unnecessary but may also prove decisive, as did the sacrifices which Themistocles, ten years before Salamis, exacted from the Athenians to build the fleet that enabled them to win victory when the Persian hordes swept like a deluge of destruction over the free West.

The significance of anticipatory thinking lies in the illumination of possibilities, not in prediction, and much less in knowledge of the future. We must guard against taking anticipatory thoughts for certainties. If simple, perceptible basic lines for the future seem obvious, if there are decisive guideposts for our planning, the responsible human being is still free to perceive new facts that can make everything look different. But the more open the mind that has perceived the facts, the more it has weighed them, the more profoundly will it approach the last, incalculable choice. Then it will be as impossible to cut the knot blindly, with unscrupulous brutality, as to give up the decision and to lapse into helpless inaction.

We can think of situations and moments when individuals will decide, but this thinking fails in attempts to prophesy. Preparatory thinking is not prophetical thinking, for the original human decision cannot be foreseen.

It is men who make events. They are in the inescapable situation of having to act or not to act and bearing the responsibility in both cases — also for what happens if they fail to do what they might have done. Every individual, whether active or passive, is a factor in events that he cannot see in their entirety.

But what he does or fails to do becomes detached from him and his intentions. Every act has unintended and unthought-of consequences. True, the individual, be he the mightiest and wisest, is all but powerless before the process as a whole; it seems to happen like an event in nature — and yet, it is no such inescapable event. What the individual cannot do, individuals can do together. What man has made can be controlled by the community of men.

Everything depends on whether and how this community comes into being. There, too, we have always given way too much to optimistic expectations. We have refused to recognize threats of disaster, have clung to possessions, failed to make the sacrifices needed for salvation, and let the worst come to pass. But until now, political disaster, though always aggravated by omissions, was limited in scope; if today's clear danger does not radically change the basic attitude of men, the doom of all is sealed.

A good example of quite properly envisioned possibilities turning into deceptive expectations is an analogous error to which both the Marxists and the free world have succumbed. The Marxists, on the ground of their supposed knowledge, expect the inevitable collapse of capitalism; they wait patiently, ready for Communist world conquest at the moment of catastrophe. The free world, on the ground of its supposed insight into human nature, expects the totalitarian regimes to fall; it waits patiently, ready to aid universal freedom at the moment of catastrophe.

But possibilities must not be taken for realities. Action based on such delusions is bound to go wrong. The prophecies of Marx have not come true. None of the things he predicted occurred in the Western areas where living conditions were so radically changed by the industrial revolution. But in the East — against his thesis — his ideas were adopted as a cover for catching up quickly, by totalitarian means, with the technological revolution.

The expectations of the free West are no more certain. The notion of a cognoscible human nature, dooming unnatural political forms by a a reliable will to freedom, may be wrong. Humanity, no doubt, is one from many points of view — as in its common understanding of technology and science and other intellectual realities — but beside these common traits there may be innate differences large enough to cast doubt on not only rational but human communication. We assume that what we want is possible; we believe in a hidden nature of God's creature, man. Our hopes feed on it. But we do not know, and we should be transgressing against reason if we claimed as a human reality what is at best a human possibility.

Thus, while in the long run it may be no mistake to expect Russian or Chinese totalitarianism to change or collapse, it would be irresponsible to base any present action on such expectations: to underestimate the menace, to relax in self-preservation, and to yield to the illusion that rational communication already exists and that populations under total rule are already moving toward freedom.

Predictions about the atom bomb are equally futile. We should like to know, of course, whether mankind will be extinct in a hundred years or less, or whether the bomb will vanish and nuclear energy will be domesticated, to serve man rather than to threaten him with doom. But today, in our situation, such questions are unanswerable. Today the human task is to examine possibilities and probabilities without mistaking even the greatest probability for a certainty. It is to do what we can to find ways of existing under unfathomable conditions. It is to realize that our intellect can conceive of negative possibilities, can predict death and destruction even as probabilities, but cannot forecast the great human impulses — and that, in incalculable fashion, everything done here and now by every individual may become a factor in shaping the future.

Only in awareness of our ignorance can discussions of the possible choice between the atom bomb and totalitarianism be properly understood. In such discussions we can neither anticipate the decision in principle — in either direction — nor can we be sure that the alternative will arise. The concrete possibilities are too involved for anyone's preparatory thinking. No one knows the situations that will face us eventually. But when they arise, the question will be clear, and the free man who makes the decision will find it one of suprapolitical necessity.

No thought of ours can anticipate the solution. Henceforth, human life will always remain under the cloud of the atom bomb, even if a great change should minimize the menace. No resolve of ours can anticipate the resolve of future generations. Because of the real, serious, irrevocable situation created by the bomb, man will need to be changed over and over again.

Today, between desperate vistas and a superficial optimism, we are once more impressed with the age-old question of mankind's end. The test of reason is to be aware of the methods and limits of our historic-political knowledge of the world, to expose ourselves to all facts and possibilities, and yet to shun the all but compelling hopelessness and the ensuing indifference and cynicism.

The empirical aspects of decline in modern history have often been pointed out. Men of high quality come to be rarer and rarer. There is a dearth of great personalities, in the style of past centuries; creative works of art, letters, and philosophy cannot be compared with the level of the past. The vast strides of natural science have been made by men who, for all their excellence, seem like officials of an inventive intelligence linked with a stirring scientific movement. The great statesmen of our time — Churchill, for one — are in fact no longer creative but representative of things past, terminal figures, sadly knowing in their valiant stand. There are highly cultured individuals of broad, magnificent spirituality, but what marks them today is the fact that they, despite occasional efforts to the contrary, inwardly reject the whole scientific-technological revolution. They will have no part of it and despise it even in its use.

Throughout past history, death, in a sense, was voided for the individual. He was sure of survival — whether in the children to whom, half-consciously, he handed down traditions or in the substance of the permanent community to which he belonged or in the trees he planted for his posterity or in the anonymous after-effects of the good he thought and did. Now, this continuity is severed for more and more people all over the globe. They are uprooted; their native communities grow feebler, more accidental; they are detached from the soil in which their forebears lie buried.

For a century and half, it has been stated and restated that we are living on the brink of an abyss that will swallow, first, political freedom, then culture, then humanity, then human life itself. The forecasts of decline have been made vastly impressive by partial concrete confirmation. This self-analysis is a symptom of our time; but its perceptions and prophecies are age-old, going back almost to the beginnings of recorded history. Still, today they enter into the general consciousness.

We like to think of the terminal process as that of the past four centuries. According to one view, it was the luciferous course of cognition, that seeming, grandly deceptive ascent and progress, that marked the turn toward the abyss.

Indeed, this age — compared with mere rudiments in Greek Antiquity — has borne the new science and technology. The fact astounds us. Why only now? Why only here in the West? Why, after slow initial steps, at so furious a pace that we now feel like passengers in a runaway carriage? Historical research and interpretation can show many premises of this development, but the fact as such remains opaque. And the process is duplicated in political life by the trend to centralization, organization, bureaucracy — begun in the states of absolutist government, continued and intensified by the French Revolution and Napoleon, and exceeding all bounds in the totalitarianism of our time.

The turn from special to total planning and organization was accomplished politically in the French Revolution. Its grand beginning — not yet implying this turn — was swamped by forces that would use terror to obtain control of man himself, so as to change him according to a total plan. Napoleon terminated this movement for the time being, by means of another, more limited dictatorship; but Marx, on new premises, carried the principle further, and Russian bolshevism drew the practical conclusions by bursting the initial idealistic shell. The grim, increasingly anonymous will to power of erupting totalitarianism has a single, not clearly conscious aim: to change man himself, by a total planning that includes world conquest — for nothing else would block all escape. In the *Apparat* of one absolute rule, human existence would be leveled down to mere functions. Fed by biological fertility, this existence could go on destroying itself by functionalization or mass murder, indifferent to all individuals and nations. History would end, though existence would continue. The atom bomb and total rule are the two terminal forms of destruction.

This aspect of the modern age seems to grow more compelling if we note how many developments are converging upon the same terminal goal. There is the completed division of the earth, the end of colonial expansion, the liberation of peoples from European rule. There is the dissolution, centuries-old but accelerated and spread to all mankind since 1914, of traditional ways of life, of belief, of thinking. There is the destruction of thought by its own power — a phenomenon occurring among the great Greek Sophists and in some Indian, notably Buddhist philosophies, but never yet as decisively, as radically, as in Nietzsche,

Kierkegaard, and other Western thinkers. There is the constant acceleration of technological development, the incipient new industrial revolution by nuclear energy and automation, whose completion could not but change man's entire existence. There is the man-made but unforeseen situation created by the unceasing forward thrust of the West, while all others — especially the great civilized nations of China and India — clung to tradition and became intellectually impoverished and morally corrupt. Lastly, there is the evolutionary line on which all eyes are now focused: the technical, economic, political entanglement of human existence in a process leading to slavery and organized dehumanization.

The evolutions seem to coincide. Everywhere man has reached the limits of his past forms of existence — as if his enormous capacities had actually rendered him helpless. And this moment brings to him both the political process of destroying himself in totalitarianism and the technological implement for wiping himself off the face of the earth.

In one view of history, this road was taken from the start: the making of fire in the Promethean age is seen there as the first step in a march that has now taken us to the simultaneous arrival of unimaginable opportunities and the possibility, if not the probability, of destroying ourselves and all other life. In this view, human history — the few thousand years that we know of and the tens of thousands before — may seem like a passing moment in the planet's history, with the germ of the new, total destructiveness carried in humanity from its very beginning.

Yet though the end, man's destruction of himself and all life, may thus appear as a natural outcome, the appearance is deceptive. For the process is not one of nature. From the beginning, and now more than ever, man had a choice. He will have it to the end. If we withdraw from our freedom of choice, we give up our humanity — today, for the first time, with the result that all existence will perish.

The expectation of total doom has been strongly reinforced by mythical thoughts and images outlining total views of history and of the process of being. Basically, such views are ancient. In eschatological thinking — Gnostic, Christian, or Hindu — they relate to eternity: the world's end opens the kingdom of God or Nirvana or the inconceivable source of being to which all things return. The end is the beginning, and the world a phenomenon within a cosmic-metaphysical process.

The historic reason for man's nature, his struggles, his experiences of uplift and apostasy, has been mythically conceived by the Jews, in the Fall, and by the Greeks in the deed of Prometheus. Later, Gnostic thinking imagined mythical-daemonic processes: the fight between the primeval powers of light and darkness, between God and the devil; the fall of angels wanting to be God; the one great doom that created the world and guides its ills and will be completed in its destruction. Differing in substance but alike in the turn of mind, such terminal thinking has gone through the ages. Without a devil or other evil enemy of life, Nietzsche envisioned the cognitive process as one of human self-destruction: truth itself is death. And H. G. Wells, that progressive, optimistic world historian, reversed himself startlingly, almost despairingly, at the end of his life: without changing his rationalistic approach, he suddenly found the imminent end of man and all life unavoidable. He sought a word for the "unknown power" that once created being and now had apparently turned against it; though disliking the implication of positive hostility, he finally called it "the antagonist" — the power that is setting out to extinguish life.

This "antagonist" is the devil in a new guise — although Wells not only avoids the term but drops all elements of guilt and evil, while believing with clearly unshakable conviction in the diabolic factors corresponding to his own approach. But there is no devil, and there are no demons. As St. Augustine already noted, they have a fictitious existence only if man will be duped by the notion of their reality. The responsibility is man's; he tries in vain to shift it to such powers. By so doing, he facilitates his task and furthers the evil — which, after all, is due to his own will, to his own unreason and antireason. He talks of the devil when he should be blaming himself.

The basic process at the evil's source is the irrationality of man, the surrender of his freedom.

It is part of the irrationality to make a basic process the subject of some assumed knowledge — whether conceived in progressive optimism or Marxistically as a historic process of labor that rescues man from self-estrangement or Gnostically conjured as an act of the devil. All these notions tempt us to avoid the one properly human possibility: freely and responsibly to venture upon an uncertain future. Entering into this freedom means taking upon ourselves what the notions of total knowledge shunt off upon an objective process. Man shall find the way to his salvation where the decision is up to him — to each one, to many, to all. He shall see through all the forms of his false urge to be relieved. He will perish if he does not assume his responsibility, consciously and clearly.

The idea of a process independent of man is a fiction: without him, there is no basic process of history. Nor is there an unilluminable but mythically visible daemonic process inescapably compelling him by his own inner necessities. Instead, man's task is to master what he has made. The sorcerer's apprentice cannot get rid of the spirits he conjured up with the master's magic formula, because he lacks the master's formula for making them vanish. But man is not to call for any magic formula. It would be futile. He lives on one condition: that he is the master. He needs no formula — neither to produce science and technology by his intellect nor to control their production and their products by his reason. Man can see what matters, can reflect, can change, and can act. What happens if he does not is his fault, not blind fate.

17

REASON

AND

DEMOCRACY

It would be folly to expect the world to be put right by a few reasonable men. To become effective and durable, reason must pervade the nations. This is why we need democracy, the system in which the people — and peoples — are supposed to "reason together."

What we hear today about democracy is paradoxical. All governments, whether totalitarian or free, cite the will of the people and call themselves democratic. All of them present the people as their sovereign, at least in mass meetings, national celebrations, and memorial orations. As a word, "democracy" has become publicly sacrosanct, an idol of our time.

In print, however, democracy is rejected by a large body of opinion. It is described as unable to put reason into practice and thus, in fact, resulting in the worst tyranny, either by the majority or by total rule. Human nature is said to be unreasonable, making democracy madness.

Against this antithesis of idol and devil, the real meaning of democracy can be established only by reason itself. Then, instead of glorifying or damning it, we shall examine its reality in all its ramifications and see it as our hard, stony, but only possible road. All the basic ideas about the risks of democracy have been with us since De Tocqueville and Max Weber, but in these men we find a pained, indeed a shocked awareness of its possibilities combined with an ineradicable faith in man and his freedom. The ruthlessly critical view of these political thinkers is not directed against democracy but toward its self-improvement; for they realize that the actual course of social history and the necessity of reason itself make democracy indispensable. The human task is to surmount its risks in the unforeseeable course of history, by intense, patient effort and practical, effective self-criticism.

Churchill is said to have called democracy the worst form of government, except for all others. His sense of humor found a word for the fundamental disorder of human affairs, in which democracy seems the least noxious form of government, being the only visible or conceivable way to provide opportunities for incalculable improvement by the growth of reason in the people themselves.

Only in small states, under favorable circumstances, can the love of home and country become one with democratic thinking. In large nations, the human ruthlessness of politics and the terrors and dangers of democracy are felt more strongly than the beauty of challenge. Shortly before the First World War, I was present at a conversation between a Swiss jurist and Max Weber, the great German political thinker. Both men were profoundly democratic. "We must love the state," said the Swiss. "What?" replied Weber, "the monster wants love, too?"

So, what is democracy? There are many conflicting concepts of it, but only one idea. Let us try to state it in a few theses.

1. Reason can prevail reliably only if it guides the people along with their leaders, not just a few lone, aloof individuals. This is impossible unless every individual has a chance to think and to act with the rest. Democracy, therefore, requires the whole people to be educated so as to develop everyone's thought and judgment to the limits of his natural capacity. It calls for publicity of thought, especially of news, discussions, propositions, and plans.

2. Reason is not a property but a vehicle. It can move only by way of universal education for democracy as common thought and action. It follows that democracy is never final but keeps changing its shape, and from this, in turn, follows the requirement of self-criticism. Democracy will last only if it keeps improving.

3. In principle, reason belongs to every human being. Hence, every individual has absolute value and must never be a mere tool. No individual is replaceable. The objective is that everyone, according to his lights, should be able to realize man's innate essence, his freedom. Hence, democracy aims at equality; it seeks to give everyone equal rights, in the sense of equal opportunities. This goal, insofar as it is possible at all, can only be attained under a government of laws. The actions of all, including the heads of the government, must be tied to

laws that have been legally enacted and can be legally amended. New conditions call for new laws; the injustice that always remains requires constant improvement by legislation.

4. Reason works by persuasion, not by force. But as force is actually present in human action, rational self-preservation must meet force with force. Democracy, therefore, employs police powers against law-breakers, but only as authorized by law or in judicial proceedings. Thus everyone is protected from arbitrary and illegal violence by the state, secure in life and limb.

5. As a state of mind, reason has precedence over all specific laws and institutions. Recognized above any laws are human rights that both bind and free all men and are not subject to legislation, flexible as this must be. Before any judgment, evaluation, and regulation of the manifold actions and qualities of men comes a liberal allowance for all human potentialities; before the conception, adoption, and enforcement of any law comes sensitivity to injustice and to wrong as such. Democracy finds wordings for the rights of man and tries to safeguard them against future encroachments. It protects individuals and minorities from majority coercion. It lives by the active solicitude that makes a wrong done to one a matter of concern to all.

6. Politically, reason never forgets that it is men who govern. Like the governed, they are creatures with human failings and prone to err. At some time, government even by the best of men needs checking up on. But this control, carried out by human beings, must be mutual: in the intellectual battle of opinions, in the distribution of offices, in the accounting rendered to the voters.

Democracy aims at a government of reason, through government by the people. Yet how can the people govern before they are rational?

This is a question of the means of making the popular will clear, public, and a fact. These means are the press, the assembly of the people — in very small democracies an actual meeting of all citizens, in large ones a popular vote on previously published and extensively debated issues — and the representation of the people in elected parliamentary bodies. But what if these tools of the democratic idea turn against it? If, for instance, a parliamentary majority violates its own principles, as in the German Reichstag's suicidal enabling act of 1933? And if a plebiscite decides, by majority vote, to do away with the government of laws — as happened also in the Germany of 1933, when National Socialists, German Nationalists, and Communists agreed on this objective? What if the people freely resolve to have no more freedom? Has the majority the right to say that it will not prevail in the future? Has it the right to abolish democracy, to wipe out human rights, to coerce minorities? Can it be right and lawful for a majority decision to destroy all justice and legality?

Here lies the Gordian knot that can become inextricable for democracies at any time, in any crisis. No democratic form of government can guarantee the democratic idea. And where is the authority to cut the knot?

The trouble is that democracy, which is to make the people rational, presupposes a rational people. Irrational force will not vanish until all are rational. But what if reason deserts the people?

We can distinguish between the will of a temporary majority and the people's basic, permanently ingrained, rational will. The temporary will may go astray, and a minority, perhaps only a few, may be representing the true, basic will. But in reality there is no organ of government to speak for that basic will; every institution — the head of the state and its smallest governing body, the legislature, the judiciary, the plebiscite — can fail and succumb to irrationality. We depend upon real authorities. In a democracy we depend upon majorities, on the assumption that their decisions, if proved wrong, can be corrected later. But what if the decision abolishes correction and effects destruction?

No device can be sure of preventing the abuse by democratic institutions of democratic principles; the only guarantee is an enduringly rational turn of mind in those who use the institutions. The danger lies at the point where a rational minority submits to coercion by a majority that would resort to force to kill all reason. By such submission, the minority opens the floodgates and allows the deluge of force to burst — as in the Second World War, whose outcome, by sheer luck, restored half a chance for freedom; next time, nuclear warfare would finish everything. Or reason, now embodied only in great statesmen followed, perhaps, by tiny minorities, may in its turn resort first to skilful maneuvering within the law, but finally, at the crucial moment, to force against majority coercion. Such resistance to acts of a formally legal majority — even though it would destroy the law — is illegal, not justifiable by any institution.

Democracy, in short, can endure as a reality only if it masters the purely rationalistic institutional consequences of its libertarian laws — in other words, if its idea is vigorous enough to curb suicidal votes. But this is possible only by the acts of those who are at the helm, or take the helm, in a crisis. The same legal institutions can be used to save democracy and to destroy it. No law, no order, can anticipate what will happen at such moments; the rationalism of jurisprudence, the balance of departments, the traditions of officialdom — all these can fail. It is the great statesman who appears — or fails to appear — at such moments, proving himself by his ability to carry his allies in key positions with him for the cause of reason, and by the lasting significance of his success.

Democracy is tolerant of all possibilities, but it must be able to become intolerant of intolerance itself. It is against force but must oppose force with force. It permits all intellectual, social, and political movements, but where their organizations and actions jeopardize the course of democratic reason, the state power must be capable of restraining them. All too often, politicians and officials unworthy of democracy are tied into legal knots by the shrewd men who would do away with all legality. Unable to disentangle themselves, they conceal their failure by talking, negotiating in all directions, and doing nothing. The democratic idea is lost in the hands of mere politicians who will let it die in pseudo-democratic emotionalism.

Yet all this goes to show only that democracy is built on volcanic soil and cannot be maintained by legal guarantees alone.

Democracy is as hazardous as life itself. The moments of crisis in the great powers of any age are decisive for world history, and at such moments democracy cannot survive just by patient bargaining, making sensible compromises, and splitting the difference. It may do so in periods of calm, but even then the breath of evil must be felt and kept in mind — even then, vigilance must be constant if the men of democracy, instead of being paralyzed with fright in times of peril, are to make bold decisions and to stick to them, moving and convincing others.

Democracy is an idea. This means that it cannot be perfect anywhere, that indeed its ideal form is beyond visualization. Man's reason tells him that no good, perfectible order exists in the world. The awareness of human imperfectibility is a corollary of the democratic idea.

As an idea, however, it is not weak or skeptical. It has the thoughtfulness of reason, its powerful impulse, its inspiring enthusiasm. The idea is before our eyes — never grasped, ever present yet ever elusive, and always guiding. To the realist it seems fantastic, and if we were to take its mere pattern for a practical program, and our awareness of the impulse for real achievement, he would be right. He is wrong if he fails to perceive that any real, more than fleetingly successful achievement is bound up with an idea, although it takes broad horizons, extensive knowledge, and competent action to make the idea strong.

The word "democracy" is used today in vindication by all states, yet the concept defies any simple definition. We must distinguish, first, between the idea of democracy and its institutions of the moment — which are endlessly variable, filled with the idea only to a degree, and apt to turn into fixtures destructive of the idea. The idea lives on the substance of a historic tradition extending to the popular ethos of everyday life. Idolized as a specific constitution, democracy may be swallowed whole, like a nostrum, or it may be imposed upon nations, supposedly for their own benefit. The idea, therefore, has a long history, running from Antiquity over the guild systems and Mediterranean city-states to its modern forms, which have achieved a measure of historically grounded stability only in countries that have long known freedom, such as Britain, the United States, the Netherlands, and Switzerland. Since the French Revolution, it has had another modern history which distorted the idea into abstract principles, with the logical result of institutions and actions that have kept destroying freedom and democracy.

Second, we must distinguish between a form of government and a manner of government. Democracy may mean one of the several state forms — democracy, aristocracy, monarchy — known since Antiquity. Or it may mean a manner of government — what Kant calls the "republican manner of government," which has no opposite but despotism. Both democratic and despotic rule may occur in all three forms of government.

Third, we must distinguish the idea of democracy from the notion of popular sovereignty. Identical at first, the two diverge and become opposites if the path of reason is given up for the premise of an existing absolute wisdom in the people as they are. The objects of idolatry, in this case, are not institutions but the people themselves, by means of their institutions. The sovereign people are sanctified, so to speak, as absolute princes used to be: "The people's voice is God's voice."

The only true, all-wise popular sovereign demands obedience, and there is no more appeal from the people's will than there ever was from that of a sovereign prince in the age of absolutism. The only question is how to determine their will. Who expresses it? There are two answers: either the majority, as shown by votes, or the minority of a vanguard that claims to know the true popular will as distinct from the confused, vacillating, and manipulable masses. It is men, always, who claim to rule in the name of the sovereign people, and since the sovereign people's will is absolute, the result is either coercion of minorities by rulers chosen by the majority, or coercion of all by a minority. From the supposed existence of a popular will, which the rulers claim to represent, they further deduce the right to exterminate their opponents as rebels against the sovereign people. An absolute, institutionalized popular sovereignty will reject all deviation as falsehood and ill will, and the organs and leaders embodying it will put an end to discussion.

The democratic idea stands against such idolatry. It knows no reigning and governing sovereign, but it knows a will that must constantly evolve anew in a process of self-education, in institutions which, for all their firmness and despite all checks and safeguards, remain modifiable. It requires solidarity of the most diverse members of the rationally oriented and directed community. It requires, on the one hand, a liberal approach, and on the other, the inviolability of existing law. The ruling individuals are always bound by law, in line with the democratic idea, while the individuals embodying popular sovereignty can, if need be, rule by decree, in sovereign disregard of both the law and their decrees.

The way of the democratic idea is an incessant common struggle for truth. Everything is subject to unlimited public debate, though not based upon debate but on decisions. Whatever truth is found at any time must be decided under pressure of the situation. In case of disagreement, provisional agreement on actions that are deemed necessary is achieved by majority vote, with the minority suspending its divergent views, knowing that in the future, in new situations, it will have another chance to put them to the test and make them prevail. Complying loyally with what are now common decisions, the minority in turn enjoys the protection of the laws and of a solidarity founded upon the common democratic idea.

The idea of democracy is sober, clear, and inspiring; the claim of absolute popular sovereignty is wild, murky, and fanaticized.

Should we avoid the word "democracy" because it invites so many interpretations and is open to so much abuse? Would not its abolition be all the more justified since the doctrine of Antiquity coined the concept as that of a form of government, alongside monarchy and aristocracy? But the abolition would be pointless and futile, for the word does mean the people — all the people of a state. All of them shall get to exercise their right of thinking and acting in concert.

The only stark contrast is between democratic and despotic rule. When we say "democracy," we mean Kant's "republican manner of government." For this, democracy is the best name we have.

Wherever a government claims to be democratic — as all of them do nowadays — we face the question of the alternative: of that which is not democratic. We reject everything "undemocratic" and accuse one another of being ruled by minorities rather than by the people. Here, we hear, monopoly capital is in the saddle, there a party clique. Here men are subject to capitalistic exploitation, there to despotic exploitation.

Yet these alternatives are propagandistic arguments that take details for the whole. They refer to tangible, specific aspects. Against them, there is one sole and radical alternative that determines all we want and do, and this can only be infinitely circumscribed, not closely defined — for its primary characteristic is that it is not an alternative of antithetical doctrines. It is an alternative of basic ways of life. The way of reason knows doctrines as special means to special ends, but it never turns into a doctrine and thus cannot have a doctrine for its antithesis. It resists any doctrinization — any type of confinement in definitive rigidities, in absolute embodiments, or in the turntables of a dialectical movement.

As a way of reason, democracy refuses to be hypostatized. If it is based on reason, it cannot help seeing that, while reason ought to prevail, while we hope it will prevail, it is actually neither all-pervasive nor certain to last indefinitely. Yet democracy refuses to conclude from this experience that the rule of irrationality is unchangeable, that unreasonable mankind must be forever ruled by equally unreasonable force.

Democracy does not permit us to assume that rulers are, or could or should be, superhuman. It insists that, in the nature of things, every challenge faces human beings, and it rejects any other authorization — whether by an office, as a direct mandate of God, or by the charisma of a divinely instituted leader. It is aware of the seriousness of official responsibility and of the gifts of great men, and it respects both without idolizing them. It knows that without both of them it cannot thrive.

The alternative to the democratic idea is whatever seeks to dodge the task of humanity. This has always happened and is still happening in grandiose forms, whether claiming divinity or absolute knowledge. All such alternatives may be described, in Kant's term, as states of despotism. At best, they block the path of rational man; today they block the path to the rescue of mankind. In fortunate moments despots are said to have governed well, but such moments were mere accidents on the road to ruin. For it is not thus that the nations awaken: the mass of individuals achieve neither insight nor responsibility; they stay imprisoned in their particular environments — whether wretched or beautiful — under totalitarian direction; they are technically drilled, made into useful, skilful, knowledgeable tools of labor, but removed in all instances from the great, infinite process of human development.

The democratic way, for all its errors and seeming dead ends, provides a chance for a majority of men to grow into thinking, responsible creatures; it does so even though its first result is a leveling that entails the risk of democracy's being perverted into one of the worst dictatorships ever known. The democratic idea rests on the human task of rational self-realization, on the unique, irreplaceable character of every individual, and on the dignity of man as a rational being. Failings in democratic practice are not justified, of course, but put in perspective by the far greater failings of all other present systems. To despair of the democratic idea is to despair of man.

How best to institutionalize the "republican manner of government" — true democracy — is another question. While the idea is one, the institutions that are its instruments are manifold and always subject to the tests of logic and experience. Fundamentally, democracy ties the political state of affairs that makes freedom possible to decisions made by majorities. Free, secret and equal elections are recognized as the institutional center, as the mark, the distinguishing feature, of political liberty. Elections must be secret, first of all, without any threat of a possible violation of this secrecy; the voter must be sure that no one will learn how he voted and that he will be safe from detrimental consequences of his vote. Second, there must be real freedom to form parties and put up candidates, so that the voter may choose between views, impulses, platforms, and personalities emerging from the population and presenting themselves for election. Third, all voters must have the same voice. The organization of this type of elections is in itself a choice between types of the will to freedom.

The dubiousness of democratic elections has often been discussed, with the belief in the voters' political judgment, in their knowledge of what they are doing, revealed as blind optimism. To begin with, elections are always the privilege of some group. They are held in particular countries, not all over the world, whereas mankind as a whole should be deciding on its existence or non-existence. Yet how to find or recognize a majority among nearly three billion people? A majority makes sense only in a group that is in constant touch, a community that has a basis of common knowledge and common views of the possible. Majorities can be determined only by organization. The premise of any election is a closed body of eligible voters.

Besides, majority rule tends to make the mass prevail rather than the personality. It makes no difference, in principle, whether the mass is a ruling clique of a few dozen aristocratic families or the whole faculty of a college or the population of a country — majority rule as such violates the maxim that votes should be weighed, not counted.

Next, elections are governed by propaganda, not by reason. Modern psychology has developed advertising methods that mobilize the unconscious to motivate a purchase; instinctively or deliberately, the same methods are used for political propaganda.

Then, although candidates compete for election, they have been picked for nomination by a party (which depends on the source of its funds) or by the state. These selections are made by comparatively minute groups, and the mass of voters is faced with the proposals of these small groups. The voter may not approve of a single candidate, may consider them all unqualified, but the election compels him to choose someone he does not want, because no one he would want is running. Despite free elections, politicians do not rise from the people, for the people; they come as from another world, to which we must submit willy-nilly, with sympathy or antipathy. A wall separates the small party bureaucracies from the mass of the people. Elections give the illusion of freedom but are in fact a game among the powers that be — this is why we talk of "formal democracy": instead of drawing forth the best energies of a people, this legal institution hands actual control to very different forces, turning democracy into another form of oligarchy and dictatorship.

Moreover, the existence of party bureaucracies makes it inevitable that leadership will fall to men who are willing to make politics their profession and the party their career, doing what such a career requires. Their qualities correspond to their party background; they may not be the worst among the people, but they certainly are not the best.

Yet it is they who finally rise to the positions of supreme power, who will take the helm and guide the nation's destiny.

Finally — and this is the gravest objection — the overwhelming majority of today's voters are uninformed, incapable of political judgment, and uninterested in politics. Today, when everyone is a voter and has a voice in deciding the fate of all, it is alarming for any believer in democracy to hear that a majority of the people in all European and American countries have no idea what their votes are all about. We saw it in Germany, in 1933 and before: how every rational political argument, every mention of obvious fact, will founder on the pig-headedness of emotional excitement; how many kinds of discontent will aggravate each other; how the easygoing will be persuaded that things aren't so bad — just give the totalitarians a chance to show what they can do! — and will build on illusions. But then, when the deluge breaks, how anxiously they will neither believe the worst nor risk too much, will feel borne by a "popular mood" and want to be "in on it" at any cost, fearing nothing so much as to be left out! Whoever has seen a majority of his fellow citizens in all walks of life go out of their minds, so to speak, may well come to doubt man's political qualifications.

But shall we let ourselves be convinced by those whose own conduct seems to bear out their contention that democracy is absurd? Are we to allow them to prove by their baseness and stupidity that men are too base and stupid to be capable of democracy? No. For we must not forget that even in the Germany of 1933 we saw individuals — not a majority, but quite a few: a locksmith here, an electrician there, men in all walks of life, men of reason. Though ineffective at the time, they were undaunted. What individuals are, many or all can be, since reason lies concealed in every human being.

None of these objections is conclusive. They are not wrong, but on the whole they miss the chances of the democratic way. We have been talking of elections and plebiscites: they are indispensable if men shall be free, if the people as a whole shall find the way of reason and participate in freedom. The very fact of elections is an occasion for political self-education; and if as a rule — not always — it has so far failed to produce this result, it may always do so.

Elections and plebiscites are our only instruments for finding out what is wanted at any moment, as thermometers are our instruments for measuring heat. Yet what is measured here is not only changeable like temperature. What is expressed in the number of votes is an aspect of human freedom, whether corrupt, obscure, confused, and empty, or substantial and true. Self-education transforms this aspect into experience and thought. The popular will is not a determinable object; itself in flux, it cannot be objectively measured and expressed. The idea of the true popular will is the idea of reason: it means that the people know what they want, that every individual knows what he wants, but only if reason prevails. We must tell each other what we think we want — that is the communication of democracy, in which we come to know our real will.

Besides, as instruments, elections are modifiable. There is plenty of room for technical improvements in majority rule. Voting procedures may differ according to purpose and scope and electorate, ranging from plebiscites — in which the whole population decides on a specific issue or personality, as in confirming Napoleon III in power or choosing a President of the United States — to the parliamentary election of parties by proportional representation and to corporate elections. The democratic idea is not wedded to any electoral system, not even to a single universal franchise — only to the requirement that every citizen be called upon to share in political thought, action, and responsibility at some essential point that affects the whole.

Voting arrangements and the distribution of elections among groups and in time are vital elements of democratic institutions — therefore, men who feel their responsibility for freedom will never play partisan politics with the electoral system. It is here, rather, that parties show whether they stand together on the common ground of freedom and democracy and reason — whether they envision something that can never be a partisan issue because it touches the foundation without which meaningful parties could not exist. The sense of a democratic electoral system cannot and never could be direct government by all the people, or by their parliamentary representatives. The point, rather, is for elections to determine the individuals who will then have freedom to govern and will bear the full responsibility. They need long terms of office — but terms there must be, lest any individual come to think of identifying himself permanently with power — and they need the greatest possible stability. There are areas of politics, foreign affairs in particular, which can be successfully conducted by only one man at a time, not even by the vote of small committees. This one must be able to act for a limited period and to be called to account. "What is democracy?" General Ludendorff once asked Max Weber, and Weber answered, "You pick a man who says, 'Let me act, follow me, and afterwards you can hang me.'" The general said, "That's a democracy I like" — probably showing by this reply that he had misunderstood the definition and missed its second half: Weber's statement of the terrible seriousness of political action. We are not governed by laws, nor by legislatures or committees, but by men, and at crucial points by single individuals — a necessity that was perverted into the horrible *Führerprinzip*, a tyranny over all, in the order of their subjection. This could happen because the basic necessity had been forgotten in the previous undemocratic democracy without individuals. The urge to have a *Führer* is an escape of the bewildered, the fearful, the weary, the pursuers of happiness. A readiness to take responsibility and a will to give it, conditionally, to others — these are the marks of a feeling for the nature of government, and for the rigor and sobriety of politics.

The revealing analyses of the democratic way are legion. Hitler, for instance, once he was in power, gloried in having "defeated insane democracy by its own insanity" — and indeed, he had used democratic means for a "legal" seizure of the power to crush all legality. If the idea of democracy is the realization of freedom and the constant self-improvement of all, the course of German democracy as realized in the Weimar Republic was a somersault into total rule.

The charges brought against democracy are old, going back to Plato, and the perversion of democracy into its opposite may be considered a form of degeneration, according to the old theory of constitutional cycles. But in modern democracy something new has been added: the technological possibilities; the size of the democratic states; the information shared by all the people; the need to work for a living — there are no more slaves, as in Plato's time — and the complexity of labor and economic relations, and our ever inadequate knowledge of these facts, for all their scientific exploration. Now, the alternative is either nihilistic criticism of democracy, lacking the strength of a will to the idea and actually preparing total rule and the doom of mankind, or self-criticism of our democratic reality, with the strength of a moral-political will rooted in the life of the individual.

We Germans, in the decades before 1933, heard democracy criticized in every possible way, in all modifications and from all motives. There was indictment and total rejection. There was retreat to a supposedly better world of aesthetics and culture and avoidance of reality. There was ruthless and largely justified criticism of the specifically German democratic conditions of the time, and there were the witty, ironic, and gleeful writings of the constitutionally outraged, whose brilliance found a willing echo in the outrage of others. There were the hidden pressures for upheaval everywhere, laying the ground for total rule with the cry for a change — any change. There was open combat, calling on all kinds of malcontents, raising the hopes of all poor wretches, all failures, all criminals, promising to solve all difficulties, painting a spurious but glorious picture of a mighty new Reich to come. And there were the helpless democrats, moral-political failures devoted to vanities and party prejudices and special interests, lacking faith but calling for a "new faith" and "new ideas" and inventing the concept of "authoritarian democracy" and other inanities. They did not know any better. They betrayed the ground under their feet, the democratic idea.

Against this deterioration of a democracy that had arisen from a nation's collapse rather than from the self-sacrificing will to freedom — and against the brilliant, purely negative criticisms of democracy as such — we can cite other authorities. We have the historic experience that the democratic manner of government can succeed, and we have the great literature of the democratic idea, from Montesquieu and Kant to De Tocqueville and Max Weber. But this is not enough. A historical and sociological examination of the democratic process, whether leading to its reversal in total rule or to the realization of its idea, is just a step to get our bearings. The knowledge we gain must awaken our own impulses. The question is what the observer or critic wants, or whether he wants nothing. That most of the pre-1933 critics wanted nothing — except for some who wanted all democracy wiped out — was the crux of their irresponsibility. This criticism of democracy only helped to destroy it. The point is whether the democratic critic, however ruthless, wants democracy to succeed — or what other purpose his revealing analyses of bleak democratic realities are to serve.

One contemporary view of democracy sees the statesman depend on the masses that raise him to power and confirm him day by day. The modern leveling of men results in government by those men who owe their success to specific and by no means admirable qualities. They are actually led by the masses, which are in turn at the mercy of the notions and decisions of those few. It seems impossible for reason to prevail under such circumstances. The incompetent politicians and inert masses

— which respond only to emotional appeals — corrupt each other. They cut the ground from under the men of reason, who can only keep aloof as long as they may. And the leaders depend not only on the great mass whose constant echo they need, but on more limited masses: on vested interests, parties, a bureaucracy that can facilitate or prevent the execution of any project. Men come to power on terms that discriminate against true statesmen.

And yet, the partial truth in such views has proved no bar to great statesmen, nor is it cogent for an evaluation of the mass.

It is true that a man who wants power cannot achieve his objective without considerable adjustment. He must "play the game." He must dress up as whichever average type may be in fashion. He can do this responsibly, maintaining his independence, only if he has the gift of an actor who is not playing but controlling his parts. He can be himself in every part, because his decisions at crucial moments are his own, and because he stays in character by being true to his own self. What this situation demands of men who come to power today is as extraordinary as the challenges met by the heroes of primeval chaos, but it is not superhuman.

And what of the nature of the masses? When intelligence tests came up at the start of this century, we psychiatrists were appalled by the ignorance and lack of judgment that seemed to be average in all strata of the population. Whenever such inquiries are repeated — today in the form of public opinion polls — the results are startling. "Normal means slightly idiotic," we said fifty years ago.

The conclusion we keep hearing is that the masses cannot be democratic, since the majority is neither sufficiently gifted for critical thought nor sufficiently well educated and informed for independent judgment. As a result, we hear, they are inert, aroused for moments only, and then not to political judgment, though their votes give them a fatal political influence. In the main, they live in habitual political lethargy.

But the sad results of intelligence tests, of opinion research and polls, can be deceptive if too much is made of them. Ignorance and misinformation about vital issues, concepts, and plans of the day tell us nothing definite about the motivations and practical critical faculties of those questioned. The most carefully designed intelligence tests may lead us to misjudge the subject. If arbitrary likes and dislikes are inferior to these relatively objective tests, the responsible appraisal of individuals by other individuals is in turn superior to their necessarily deficient objectivity. Performance proves more than tests.

Besides, the inertia of many is no fixed quantity. We cannot tell what may bring them out of it. There is more restlessness in the nations than the inertia thesis will admit, and some very deeply concerned individuals will keep silent and be mistaken for dolts because no one has spoken to them. We do not know what individuals are thinking in their daily lives without being able to put it plainly into words. Many repress their indefinite restlessness in a feeling of impotence, finding no place where they might help. Their dissatisfaction with the whole state of affairs, with political parties in which they never find what they are dimly seeking, remains beneath the surface.

In some cases, however, restlessness combines with unreason. When the individual mistakes his natural assertiveness for reason and the key to universal salvation, the claim to reason becomes irrational. Instead of the stir of reason, we have the excitement of dogmatism.

Stirred by reason, the individual rightly wants to know and to think, to receive instruction and information. He wants to reflect and to be enlightened in conversation. He knows he is not at his goal; he is looking for a way to deeper insight. But where dogmatism claims to be reason, it thinks it owns the truth. The fanaticism of the schemers, the circle-squarers, the inventors of perpetual-motion machines, the discoverers of solutions to the problems of mankind, of universal remedies that will end all our troubles in short order — all these have something in common: the irrational claim of incompetents to have achieved perfect knowledge by abstractions of the erring intellect. They identify themselves with a cause that is a sham. The will to communicate yields to a will to promulgate. The contention that their own supposed knowledge will resolve all difficulties hides a yearning for world leadership.

It is strange to see how a passionate desire for communication may combine truth and falsehood, and how unreason will show in such a misplaced, misdirected urge. There was the man who sent a memorandum to the UN: "I am one of the common people," said his covering letter. "We may offer you the best, and you will not heed it. By refusing to listen, you blackmail the people into holding still for their doom. I ask for discussion. For some comment, at least, to start with. Write me — write whatever you please; I shall not mind. We must talk, after all." What a perversion of truth! We must talk — but must we start with the

United Nations? We feel ignored — does that mean we, as individuals, are "the people" and being blackmailed? We want communication — does that give us the right to communicate with any so-called Very Important Person? Reason demands modesty. Others, not the individual himself, decide on the effectiveness of what he has to say. His neighbors are his natural audience; in their company he shows himself a man of reason. He may write — this is easy nowadays and does not mean much. He must see where it will get him, who will listen to him, with whom and in what cause he can work to make reason prevail. A large part of reason is not to mistake our own thoughts and wishes for reason itself.

If those who call men generally inept are right, we must despair of human existence. This conclusion was most magnificently drawn by some Hindu philosophers, thousands of years ago; but if it is not drawn, the question remains how the few who can follow the road of reason in politics may rise to power — and the only visible way to that end is the democratic one. The notion that some other way, concentrating authoritarian power in a few hands, would offer a better chance is irrational. Instances of able and successful policies being pursued for generations, as in Roman or English history, are not models for the future; though historically admirable, they were unable to start a trend to the realization of reason in their peoples. Their failure was not inevitable, and yet, by the standard of duration in the world, it was the result of fatal flaws in those very policies. What America, with her English and European heritage, can do in this respect is still uncertain.

The only alternative to despair is faith in *man* — not in what he is now, not in men, but in what he can be as a human being. No one who seeks and finds reason can believe that it may be all in vain. On the strength of his own reason, and of the reason encountered in others, he tends to assume that herein lies our chance. Of course, it is not a certainty; it is, once again, the great, fateful question how reason can be given effect in reality. How can truth, which at first will always strike individuals only, reach the public? How — instead of vanishing time after time in the conventions of everyday life, in the deluge of talk, under mountains of print — can it prevail?

If we distrust reason, if we doubt the human susceptibility to reason, we have no faith in man. It means we give up on men, despise them, regard them as beasts to be tamed. We are no longer governed by the idea of man as a rational being; instead, we accept the average, objectivized reality as the norm and see nothing but streaming masses driven by hunger, by envy, by aimless unrest, by fanaticism. We see crowds go out of their minds, those lumps of clay in the hands of hypnotizing demagogues, and consider them characteristic. And we forget that this mass consists of individuals, each of whom, at bottom, does not really want to vanish in the mass like that, but to be truly human.

As one feels toward his fellows, so they appear to him. If he feels contempt, he will see only the contemptible; if he expects nothing, he will find nothing. He who takes gestures, idioms, etiquette for the human being will not get to know the human being. Nothing is more superficial and at the same time inhuman than misanthropy — though disdain for mankind may at times seem all but compelling. Nothing is cheaper than to demand that men live up to our own ideal, to use this dubious yardstick to reject them, and to forget our own failings. Reason rests on the expectation of reason in man. It is patient. About to lose hope, it blames itself.

Democracy's greatest critics — men like De Tocqueville and Weber whose observations, ideas, and visions the merely negative critics feed upon — believed in man and therefore in democracy's ability to lead to freedom. They took care not to proclaim as knowledge what no one can know, but all their criticism served their libertarian purpose. They were democratic without loving democracy — for the goal is not democracy but human freedom; democracy is a hard, inescapable necessity, our only chance to save freedom in the transformation of society necessitated by the technological age. But at the root of this will to democracy lies the biblical concept of God: since man is created in the divine image, every man must have human rights. Human equality — that much-abused and usually perverted political idea of the French Revolution — is a fundamental and inviolable moral demand.

Democracy is not a fiction of the sovereign people as a personal ruler — an authority whose supreme wisdom is charged with the sole responsibility by all individuals, who then feel free of responsibility themselves. Democracy is every individual. Everyone himself is responsible for the way he lives, thinks, and works, for the actions he decides to take, and for the way he does all this in common with his neighbors.

To feel free of this responsibility is the basic perversion of democracy — to refuse to admit our personal liability for what was done and what happened, to reduce rather than to increase our obligations, to shut our minds to the idea of constant self-education. Once it was the rulers whose sins were visited upon the people; now the culprit is to be the sovereign people. But we are the sovereign people. We all partake of it. If we do not want this, democracy is a fraud in which all are "free" and none participate.

All are equal. If we want democracy, this means that each, by his existence, must help to take care of the whole. He cannot ask to be cared for by a state that he does not care for with all his good will, all his knowledge, all his capacities. In the past, people would accept domination by others like a natural event, impotently, with stolid patience or in blind, desperate rebellion. In democracy alone do men as such want to rule; in democracy alone can and must the responsibility be theirs. But if the basic mood of irresponsibility and inner rebellion against coercion persists in democracy — directed now at coercion by the deified sovereign people that no one wants to be — then this is a denial of democracy.

There is no doubt that we are far from the realization of the democratic idea. The sovereign people are not wise or good, let alone divine. They have yet to grow rational. They are on the way, but it is only if the perversions of democracy are constantly fought and conquered within the individuals that democracy can exist as the basic process of freedom. It grows only in this process; where the proper responsibility is not really assumed by free individuals, it must perish. Hence, democracy is not primarily a claim of men on the state but everybody's claim upon himself, whose fulfilment enables him to participate in democracy — a claim we may consider from three points of view: the sense of responsibility, the love of great men, and self-education.

It depends on the people how and by whom they are ruled — this is the principle of free democratic elections. Objective analysis, to be sure, shows the realities of government largely determined by historical situations, by the power position of a state in the world, by material conditions, by the way of life, the organization of labor, the social structure, and the qualities of the leaders whom such national traits produce. Yet there is always a limit to this sociological view; it never gets to the really crucial point. Crucial are the free decisions that can never be finally known. Crucial is the indeterminable freedom of the people, which exists only as the freedom of every individual. This freedom — along with its renunciation and its abuse — is the premise rather than the result of what happens.

It is an evasion if I shift the responsibility onto a "sovereign people" apart from myself. The collective expresses its will through a majority; if this is acknowledged as sovereign, its responsibility must also be so acknowledged. To let the majority decide but to disclaim responsibility for its decisions is untruthful nonsense. "The nations answer for the deeds of their kings," said the old rule. Today they must accept the consequences of their majority decisions, as if they were their own.

In 1933, still in a free election, we Germans set up total rule and abolished democracy and government under law — all by majority vote. (This was the common objective of an otherwise irreconcilable majority of National Socialists and Communists; that the former group won out was due, aside from its superior voting strength, to the fact that other parties accepted Nazi totalitarianism without civil war, while rejecting Communist totalitarianism.) Subsequently, by an even larger majority, the democratically chosen Reichstag stripped itself of power and gave free rein to total rule. Yet if the people are now held responsible, in line with the meaning of democracy, there is an outcry. I wrote about this in 1946, in my book *The Question of German Guilt*: there is indeed no collective guilt — guilt is always personal — but the political liability for the consequences of democratic decisions rests upon all, and where this is not recognized, democracy is not viable.

Of course, while all must answer politically, all are not equally guilty. The German who voted in March, 1933, for National Socialists, German Nationalists, or Communists is not only politically liable but morally guilty. If I voted differently and want to know to what extent I am guilty beyond my political liability, I must ask myself whether I did everything I could to prevent this outcome — throughout the years before, throughout my life. For democracy can realize its idea only if it constantly illuminates its own past. The basic facts of the past must be taught and explained in the schools, together with the political insights that will make another, differently garbed betrayal more difficult, if not impossible.

The second fateful question of democracy is how the sovereign people can bring their best men to power. Equality means equality of opportunity and equality before the law; it can never mean equality of natural talent and the strength of personal existence, nor equality of moral reliability. The democratic idea requires justice for human variety and for the scale of rank among men, which can never be objectively determined. In the democratic ethos of equality no one is either despised or idolized. The greater and more solid carry weight; self-restraint is practiced for the love of quality, yet no one demands recognition of his own superior quality. Envy is the most dangerous of vices.

A democracy that will endure opposes unjust privilege but fosters its own aristocracy. It appreciates natural gifts, the merits of achievement born of consuming effort, and the moral qualities of judgment and reason — and it does so in free recognition, not in forced subjection. The dislike that most of us feel for those who excel by nature, talent, or merit is overcome by the love of our own inner quality, which is enhanced in the love of greater quality outside ourselves. Respect is part of the democratic ethos.

There are facts which conflict with the idea and are often cited to confound it: the fact that the call for equality leads to leveling; the fact that envy will tear down everything better; the fact that the weight of the average, the common, the special technical skill drags everything down, that whatever selection occurs is not of the best but of specifically gifted "pushers," sly, unscrupulous opportunists who know how to make contacts and how to use them. There are few elites and many pseudo-elites. For good or ill, there has always been what sociologists call "selection," whether planned or unconscious. In past history, only thin upper strata were educated, could read and write, shared in the tradition of great works and historic memories, of statecraft and jurisprudence. There are evident advantages in a background of political education, in the long training of a youth that is around politics before being politically active, in intellectual, rhetorical rivalry before the real rivalry for power. There is evident wisdom and knowledge of human nature in the selections made by a ruler who recognizes people with the faculties he lacks. But today, on the new premises of technology, all education is open to all men, as a matter of principle. The conquest of illiteracy makes education a common link among the whole people.

There has always been selection from the mass — formerly from the mass of the privileged, now from the mass of the entire population. In democracies, the selection has often miscarried. In certain sociological situations, specific qualities come to the fore, while other qualities of possibly far greater human value are discounted. The doors to advancement are opened or shut by institutions, and by the personal decisions made within the institutional frameworks. And it is always up to individual initiative to see and to seize the opportunities offered.

The realization of democracy depends on the selection of the best in all realms of life. Political leaders have a cardinal responsibility for the choice of their collaborators and for the education of their successors. For democracy is education.

If all the justified criticism of democracy were true as it is stated, we should be lost by now. It cannot be the whole truth. But if we fail to heed the partial truths shown in such criticism — if they do not stimulate changes in everyone's inner actions and in the public decisions and institutions of the community — we shall yield to irresponsible tranquillity in the face of threatening doom. What must help here is the very politics that leads to a change, the politics of the democratic idea. Necessity is the mother of any politics that will endure; it gives to politics its suprapolitical guidance. Great politics is communal self-education to reason. On the statesmen's part it is education, by their rational appeal to their countries and by their example.

The rational way of the free world is one of self-enlightenment, self-criticism, self-reproach. It leads, from every individual's way of thinking, to the self-education of nations, and hence to the education of generations to come. For the lasting foundation of this self-educational process, nothing is as vital to democracy as the education of youth — the youth of the entire people. Democracy, freedom, and reason depend on it. This education alone can preserve the historic content of our existence and replenish our lives in the new world situation with creative vigor.

Education requires teachers. We may be taking this too much for granted today — as if our educators already knew all about the right education, about its contents and planning. But it is the teachers themselves who must be educated in the course of the self-education of all men, at all ages. The perversion of education under democracy, along with increased educational activities, points to the cycle of educating and being educated — a fertile cycle if it is replete with the contents of faith, knowledge, and skill. Here, as in every rational evolution, the crux is not a straight causal connection. The idea of an educated teacher passing on his finished education to unfinished children is as absurd, on the whole, as the notion of an educated and accordingly infallible adult population. Only he can teach who is still being taught, who keeps educating himself by means of communication. And only he who is taught such self-education in the medium of strict and disciplined studies is being properly taught.

In the degeneration of the democratic idea we tend to forget what education is. The past century has brought a split between education and the teachings of science. By education we mean the preparation of young people for utility; we respect science if it is economically useful; we cultivate it, and its teaching in our schools, for the sake of this utility, and scientists and teachers cite it to justify their material demands. This utility reaches its peak when the existence of the state depends on science, as happened for the first time when modern technology culminated in atomic weapons. Today, America has been made acutely conscious of it by sudden evidence — and hysterical exaggeration — of Russian superiority. Science, and the scientific training of youth that is becoming necessary in unprecedented volume, grows in status until the most exorbitant material means are willingly placed at its disposal. Nuclear physicists have become the most precious of men — notably in Russia, where they seem to command what material comforts they please and to be living less dangerously than anyone.

This present moment, with its concern about our technological progeny, challenges our vigilance — for the consequences of our alarm are ambiguous. We are now ready to make vast sums available for "education" for our technological, scientific, and military self-preservation. But neither in Russia nor in the West does this mean that we appreciate science, let alone the spirit of science. The sole issue is technology — a special area and faculty of the intellect. Those employed in it become functionalized, highly skilled workers serving certain ends. They have acquired no education. Training in certain knowledges and skills to the point of climactic specialization does not educate a human being. It does not develop scientific ways of thought, does not foster reason, does not stimulate intellectual life at large and participation in the historic but ever newly creative traditions of mankind.

But this other, non-purposive education is the greater task, of more lasting significance to the sole possible basis of mastering all our technological, economic, and military ills. To this end, we need to reflect on the full scope of education. In Russia it is provided by Marxist instruction, which seems on the point of boring Russian youth; in the free world, the non-purposive is the real education, and the future of mankind depends upon its success. It is not nearly enough to ask that the humanities be stressed along with natural science. It is not enough to apply pedagogical, psychological, didactic precepts. The premise of an educational revival would be the emergence of a reservoir of teachers, from college professors down to elementary school teachers, whose meaningful activity, whose devotion to greatness, whose seriousness of living would stand out in the community and gain them respect and influence. Financially, this would take many times the sums expended today, but money alone will not do it. There, too, man himself must be changed.

We cannot even begin to outline the oft-expressed basic ideas on education, but we may mention three points that affect democracy in particular.

First, the strength of freedom rests on democratic recognition of human rank. For instance, we have special classes for backward children and separate schools for morons, but hardly anywhere do we find classes for the gifted, or separate schools for the unusually gifted. Democracy threatens itself if the majority opposes justice to the gifted; it will dig its own grave if it weakens the self-preservation of the whole by failing to let the best come to the fore in all tasks, all walks of life, all human potentialities. That the inevitable selection procedures in our schools always lead to errors and injustices goes without saying, since there are flaws in every human institution. Constant self-criticism and improvement are essential there, too.

Second, besides an introduction to the classic and biblical traditions, a grasp of the basic principles of natural science and technology, and a visualization of the democratic civic ethos, the substance of education should provide youth with an orientation about total rule. The strength of freedom in democratic countries depends on insight into the nature of totalitarianism as a new principle of government possible in a technological age. This principle can today, before coming to power, spread like a fungus disease throughout the free world. The infectious matter is omnipresent, owing to human nature, and the immunity conferred by reason is not absolutely reliable without the clarity of understanding. The disease is cured by free conviction and a rational way of life; it would be a mistake to ask for an antitotalitarian, anti-Marxist turn of mind without clear knowledge. A teacher must be able to hold his own in free discussion. He must not bar any objection. Where Marxism and totalitarianism are fought directly by coercive measures, by persecutions, inquisitions, or mere conformist pressures, they are, in fact, brought forth — for he who fights them by these means is himself a representative of the totalitarian spirit he claims to be opposing. Thus, although enemies, Fascists and Communists not only helped each other in fact but stood as one, for all their enmity, against the spirit of freedom that was loathsome to both. Hitler and Stalin understood and admired each other.

Third, education proper — as distinct from mere specialized training — will be of long-range importance even to technology. Specialized training yields highly useful human tools, but even in natural science it provides no scientific education. It is this education, however, with its wide-open approach to the realities of nature as a whole and to all possibilities of knowledge irrespective of their technological utility, that spurs an original intellectual curiosity to the boundless advancement of knowledge. And without such advancement new discoveries will ultimately cease, with technological inventions alone going on for a while, on ground already gained, until they cease as well.

In the democratic idea, politics itself is education. But unlike the politics and education of the past, which were restricted to privileged classes, ours must be an education of the whole people. Education is the basis of possible politics, and conversely, a rational, suprapolitically guided politics will put its imprint upon education. The consequences affect every individual, permeating both private and public life.

This differs from the concept of the political realists. In their eyes, politics is not education but the competence of a few whose private lives are irrelevant and who are not concerned with the people's private lives, either. Politics, in this view, is a public affair unaffected by whatever happens in the seclusion of the private ethos. Politics is not made by the silent in the land. And so, as far as politics is concerned, the appeal to reason in every individual is utopian.

How much unrealism hides in this "realism"! All politics that is no mere makeshift but establishment and re-establishment of effective continuity — that is to say, all enduring politics — involves the simultaneous education of a people. The foundation of politics is the hidden reality of all those whose nature emerges in political events, if only in elections. The silent in the land are the carriers of the moral spirit on which all politics depends, and their existence is derived from education, first in the family, later on in the schools. If the moral substance fails, *Realpolitik* will sweep all of them over the precipice.

The democratic idea — the idea of reason in the reality of our national and international community life — seems utopian to the critic who regards its perversions as essential rather than as transient phenomena. And not only in politics, but everywhere, is reason deemed utopian: we are told that human nature does not permit us to hope for it, that its own nature condemns it to impotence.

All arguments for this view can be rebutted, but none can be refuted. The simple, seemingly plausible theses face and complement each other. The arguments against reason speak of it as if it were unknown; the arguments for reason cannot deduce it from anything else. Reason is its own premise.

Where there is reason, it supports itself, wants itself, takes effect by itself, and holds out. Failing to achieve its purpose, it asks itself where it may not have been pure; failing altogether, it remains sure of itself, sure that it ought to be.

One thing is certain: there is reason in the world. Men seek it and try to act rationally; what is not rational is the world, the battleground of reason and irrationality. Today, too, in all strata, groups, and occupations, we meet men who are themselves. They still are few. They look for each other without signs or appointments. They seldom prevail. Or might they be making themselves felt already? Are we on the verge of a tremendous reaction of awakening humanity against all present trends? Can we expect a rational rebirth of man? No negative answer to these questions can be conclusive.

I should like to sum up by giving my answers to two questions.

First: Are we to trust in reason, that most sublime faculty that has been a matter for a few philosophers, perhaps, but not for human beings in real life?

Yes, for reason is the essence of true humanity. If the philosopher's thoughts were not everyone's business — if their object could not be awakened in every mind because it is present in every mind — he could not be what he is meant to be: a trail blazer for man, a teacher of what man is and can be, what he is capable of and where he stands in the universe. The fact that reason is rare in reality and always imperfect, even among philosophers, shows that man's way is hard, not that it is impossible.

And if all thinking has been in vain — if there have always been men who knew what ought to be done and attempted it in the spheres of their existence — then it is good that it happened. If mankind should perish, this would vindicate its potential. These thousands of years of thinking would save the honor of man in the insane process of his self-extermination.

And second: Are we to trust in reason, which is unorganized, never had and never can have an organization of its own, while all effective human effectivity rests upon organization?

Yes, for reason can pervade all organizations, strengthening each one and itself as well. It lives in the churches, in government, in the family, in schools and universities, in all social structures within all nations. It turns to those, not to deny their historic reality but to return them to their original truth, but also to put them on its own terms, on the terms of unreserved reason.

18

FEAR
AND
CONFIDENCE

Let us recapitulate the situation once again. In the past, the worst disasters could not kill mankind. Multitudes, whole nations, guilty or not guilty, perished; others survived and forgot. But now our intellect tells us with inescapable logic that soon there will be no more oblivious survivors. No one will be alive. There could be confidence, in the past, because in every disaster some were spared. Life went on. Remnants led to new beginnings. Now, however, man can no longer afford disaster without the consequence of universal doom — an idea so novel, as a real probability, that we hesitate to think it through. It takes an effort just to put it into words.

We should like to be sure what will happen, but such knowledge is not for man. Nothing is sure but the *threat* of total destruction. The situations embodying the threat change rapidly, and the causalities are so involved that any calculation is misleading — as indeed it always was. The conceivable combinations are endless, the possibilities inconceivable. Since there is no generally valid view of history, there is no knowledge of certain perdition either.

The result, on our part, should not be calm but intensified activity. What this can be and do is the great question; the answer is that no plan, no action can succeed without a change in our common will, based on a change in individual thinking. We cannot tell what men will freely do, which side of freedom will be realized, by which decisions, in which situations. But what we cannot know is up to us to bring about, and everybody must begin with himself.

Thoughts of the future are bound to be discouraging if we forget freedom and Transcendence. Mere intellectual thinking removes responsibility along with confidence; it weakens us and leads us to submit passively to disaster. Or it makes us active only in clutching at straws, in vain total planning, in nihilistic thoughts and actions, in savage accord with the total destruction that occurs, in false hopes or in the gratification of defiance.

He who will base his life on rationalistic certainties — who wants to be sure of the future — cannot help despairing. But he who feels the human tasks in the roots of his freedom and in the face of Transcendence will be inspired to do what he can. Once our minds are opened to the depths of Transcendence, we stop asking for certainties.

The letters I received from listeners to a broadcast I made on the subject of this book surprised me by their overwhelming hopelessness. I quote:

What has been designed for a purpose tends to achieve it. No possibility fails to become a reality; so, there must be total destruction by the bomb. . . . From the start, technology implies destruction. The super-bomb only fulfills its meaning. . . . Mankind's existence is coming to an end; that cannot be helped.

Like its opposite, such hopelessness rests on concepts of a total knowledge of history — the kind we have been discussing in a previous chapter — or on faith in a predestined course of events. Against it, we can only say once more that imminent doom is possible but not certain, since it depends upon mankind itself. That it cannot be helped is untrue. It is not a recognizable natural or historic process; if it comes, it will not come of necessity but as a result of human failure. Symbolically speaking, man will be punished for his wickedness. Having turned out to be not worth living, he will be rejected like an unsuccessful experiment. The prophetic words of the Old Testament apply today as they did when they were uttered, and only now have they achieved the seriousness of reality.

Others of my correspondents stress the futility of talking about it, since talk cannot avert calamity. I quote:

Realistically, you cannot tell people anything; they go blindly to their doom. Can you persuade the "experts," the key politicians in particular, however urgently you preach to them? They keep talking of peace and still resolve upon wars. And preaching reason to the common herd is obsolete. What's the use? . . . You ignore what is written in Matth. 24: that the end of the world will come because, despite all, men remain eternally unreasonable. No one man can stem the evil. I have long seen that it is hopeless, and so has the Lord — that is why he will soon end it all!

The hopelessness is couched in phrases based on supposedly known laws of history:

There have always been wars; if in the long run there can be no wars without atom bombs, there is no help. . . . Man does not change. . . . It is and will be as it always was: reason was never heeded and will not be heeded.

Who would not feel hopeless at times? It is the great temptation, and a contributory cause of doom. Rational reflections can always show only that hopelessness is wrong when it claims to be sure. This is important, but it is not enough. Hope springs from another source, which we cannot force into the open. But hope, too, turns false when it feels certain that all will be well.

One might say: in Germany, in our narrow political horizon, I hope for the old, buried, and not yet exhumed source of philosophical insights in the moral and religious foundation of the West. In America — today the area of decision in the world of political reality — I hope for the old, pious, morally radical forces. There, where men have suddenly come to change and reflect before, the world situation may make everyone feel the unprecedented responsibility for the course of mankind — the breath of history and the unique task within it. A great transforming impulse might jolt the Americans out of superficial optimism, out of moral pharisaism, out of the rationalism of know-how, and awaken them to their own selves. A nation that constituted its government wisely and successfully, that produced great statesmen, poets, and theologians, the nation of Emerson and James, a Western nation, yet more open-minded than the rest because of its emigrant roots and ingenuous beginnings — such a nation may yet do the extraordinary which the life or death of mankind now depends upon.

But voicing such concrete hopes is puerile and pointless. To get to the bottom of our confidence and lend effect to it, we must destroy all false confidence. Our tranquillity in the years before 1914 and 1933 was delusive — will the series continue? Only the unthinking can build their lives on the premise that catastrophe will not occur — or that, if it does, a way out will appear in extremity.

Can we have confidence in technological escape routes from the technological menace? In space, perhaps? No — such ideas belong to the *hubris* of technological omnipotence. Besides, wherever man goes, he will take along his destructive as well as his constructive tools.

Can we trust in the discovery of a kind of antidote to the bane of radioactivity, as defenses have thus far been developed against every offense? Nothing suggests a possibility of effective protection. It is most unlikely that means will be found to counter the total transformation of the condition now permitting life on earth — a very strange and, as far as we know, unique condition — into one of the "normal" cosmic states that preclude life.

There remains the idea of a new Noah's Ark: the artificial reconstruction of our living conditions in huge subterranean shelters that would have to contain everything required for prolonged subsistence. A remnant of mankind might survive there for decades or generations, until the atmosphere would cease being fatal to the living, and plants, animals, and men could spread once more. If some Jules Verne thought up a way to do this, critical and inventive engineers, biologists, and physicians would have to test its practicability, and then the politicians would have to decide on the immense expenditures which such preparations for the survival of a few would take. And what then? What would the many do who could not be included in this rescue operation?

Or, we may imagine a political way out and deny that man is doomed unless he changes. Just because experience shows that man does not change, we may reason, there will be no total doom. Things will go on as before, but without world wars. It is quite possible, even probable, to have the constant threat of war without the reality. Fear of the bombs will prevent it: their use is known to be useless, since both would perish and neither would win, and their growing destructiveness only makes a reckless move less likely. Men will get used to living in a state of undischarged high tension. Why should the balance of terror not last? There will be lasting peace — not due to righteousness, not because the conditions of eternal peace will be met, but because war will be impossible. There will indeed be a new world situation, but not a new man. The old, unchangeable Adam will renounce war in fact, because he must, if not because he ought to. Fear, and the minimum of intelligence it takes to grasp the folly of collective suicide, is motivation enough. How this will affect the present enmity of the totalitarian and free worlds — whether total rule will slowly dissolve from within or be transformed by free breezes — these are matters of political development; whatever happens, they will not affect the exclusion of great-power war from the arsenal of politics. The powers will not acknowledge this exclusion by disarming, for the balance of terror is as indispensable to it as the renunciation of war: the less terror, the more danger of war. Let us just keep going, wait and see, seize our opportunities, act as ever, in our ever limited interests and perspectives. Mankind will not commit suicide.

I keep hearing such talk, and it has a plausible ring. Of all justifications of confidence, this seems the least illusory. It is common sense speaking, arguing from the immutability of human nature and from basically simple causal determinants in the infinite complexity of surface events.

I admit that this way of thinking comes over me now and then. But as other insights contradict its tranquillizing consequences, I resist it like a temptation, on the ground that nothing is impossible if the captains — against common sense, against reason, against the moral qualms that inhibit even criminals — decide to drag everyone down with them. When Hitler saw he was doomed, he plainly wanted to doom the German people, too, while he had the power. Collective suicide is not out of the question if leaders meet in loathing or indifference or blind destructiveness, or if but one of them feels that way. They may slide into the abyss as they slid into war in 1914. All this is uncertain.

Fear alone cannot bring lasting peace. Is it not illusory to build a world on fear, on negotiations and agreements resting on fear alone? The way out of evil is not that cheap. This is too short a view; it sees what is going on and what is imminent, but no durable order.

Our natural sense of existence also tells us that mankind cannot perish. It says: I cannot believe in this man-made doom in the near future. Something will stop it. Fearful misery, suffering, and death are possible, probable, certain — but the total doom of mankind is another matter. I do not believe it.

And again I admit that it is only for moments that I myself can make my heart believe what my mind finds so cogently probable. I must shake myself out of a tendency to forget. Inside us, an original vitality resists and make us live in fact as if that doom could not be. We like to go back to the joy of affirmative existence; we do not relinquish it even when we tear ourselves away and see the shadows.

But against all tranquillity stands a basic experience shared by all those who are now old: that more than once in our lifetime the impossible has happened. True, we may have thought of it, but as of something in the distant future and of no concern to us — until it burst upon our present reality. There was the First World War that removed Europe from the world's center. There was National Socialism that murdered six million Jews. When we first heard of atomic energy, in the twenties, it was theory. We learned of amazing discoveries of great interest to our conceptions of matter; practically, they seemed to have no importance. Today they are facts of life.

So, if tranquillity will again lull us into feeling that a thing is impossible because it is monstrous, beyond the horizon of "normal" concepts, we must recall the known facts and ask ourselves why it should be impossible for mankind to perish, and to perish soon? Would it be more monstrous than the fact that man himself is bringing cosmic forces, the sun's own energies, to earth by freeing them from its hitherto tranquil matter?

Aghast, we want to draw back from extremity. It cannot be. It must not be. No panic! we cry. We want calm. In an atmosphere of calm, we think, this can be handled.

Yet it could be that only if extremity remains in view and the failure of all direct ways to salvation is realized — that only then will men be so deeply shaken that they will be changed, with consequences unattainable as the direct objectives of purposive action.

Or, finally, can we look forward to new prophets and divine revelations? No — for even if they seemed possible, they would be inconceivable. We cannot act meaningfully in the expectation of things beyond our ken. Under a spell of self-made illusions we would fail to do what can be done.

An unequivocal, effective proclamation of universal truth seems impossible nowadays. Everywhere people are learning to read and to write, and thus to think intellectually. Wherever the intellect stakes out its claim to independent understanding, there are but two possibilities: to sacrifice this intellect in unthinking obedience — as revelations actually demand today — or to develop it together with its rational limitations. Sacrificing the intellect is unworthy of man; it means that we let other men, not God, think for us and give us orders. It is not only futile but dangerous today to look forward to prophets, for the prophet's place is quickly taken by the *"Führer,"* the Pied Piper whom the nations hail as a redeemer. No *Führer* can help now; men can only help themselves together. The way of reason is the only one left to those who would be truly human — that is, to all — and effective reason still lives in the terseness of philosophy and in the old piety that hides in individuals everywhere. To await prophets and leaders is false confidence.

Neither hopelessness nor confidence can be proved by rational knowledge. The arguments for despair, deducing inevitabilities from total knowledge, are as inadequate as the arguments that trust in the victory of common sense. Despair and confidence are moods, not insights. We call them pessimism and optimism. Neither one is open to persuasion; each finds infinite arguments and overlooks the counterarguments.

The pessimist today sees only total doom. He used to expect an endless, inhuman, antlike existence, but this is old-fashioned now that all life threatens to end. Triumphantly and stoically he sees his worst predictions surpassed. He remains passive, leaving the course of events to chance, and mankind a prey to the violent. He regards times of freedom as brief interruptions of despotism.

The optimist resents all calamitous forecasts. But it always remains to be seen whether his positive outlook can cope with the realities of the future, whether he will even see them or simply evade them. What will happen once his delusions are no longer borne out by a seemingly impregnable political position and prosperity? He will keep fooling himself, since in all events he will see that which will save him.

Optimism and pessimism are equally unfounded and inadequate. As knowledge they are delusive; in practice they distract from the task of man. They do not lead to the high road of humanity. Do not calamity and opportunity both lie in the course of events? Is it not only when man does his best and is ready for whatever happens, beyond optimism and pessimism, that he is rational and truly human?

The man who knows what he wants and what he should do has confidence. Hence the plea of those lacking in it: Tell me my job — my possible contribution — what I shall do here and now! They want a tangible prescription they can follow. I quote again from letters received after my broadcast:

You stressed that salvation can come only from reason, from the rational attitude of every individual. What exactly do you expect? How could a creature like myself help, for instance? What is my rational action? I beg for directions, for a word to me about my attitude, my reason, in this ultimate peril. . . . It is still not clear to me how we and others with the right inner posture and reason can exert a positive influence on world events. How should that work? What could we change? We think it is not enough to be good, decent, and faithful to achieve what you may have in mind.

It is true that the whole world will not change if I change. But the change in myself is the premise of the greater change.

It is true that no man and no people can direct the world's course. But in a crisis, a people — or a man — may destroy it.

It is true that direct political activity must be pursued wherever possible, for freedom and democracy presuppose the individual's will and duty to take personal responsibility for political events. But the direct way is not the only one. My general conduct in the community has political significance.

Not infrequently, though, that very natural question, "What shall I do here and now?" rests on false premises. As their tacit expression, it casts doubt upon the questioner's basic approach. The first of these false premises is the desire for some specifiable, purposive action that I might take without changing myself. I want to stay untouched and untouchable in the background, doing only what can be planned on the surface and designed for an end. I want to be told what to do, but I myself, as a moral being, do not want to be involved.

There is also the self-righteous feeling of being now what the individual ought to become. There is the notion that thinking as such, without the responsibility of inner action, has value. There is the contention that my private life, the ethos of my personal activities, has nothing to do with politics: I deny the causal connection between actions in my individual environment and political events at large. But with the whole of man called for, this is evasive thinking.

All these false premises have one common motive. I want to live on as before, in the pervasive dishonesty of my ambiguous emotions and half-baked thoughts; in the enjoyment of well-being and status; in a variety of erotic distractions; in the discontinuity of my life; in distinctive conventions, whether aristocratic, proletarian, bureaucratic, academic, or bohemian; in the appearance of actually non-committal, superficial reflection.

I flee from the inner voice that is heard only in serious meditation.

I flee from the relentless demand to change my very will — the demand I would outshout or cloak in silence. Not until this flight ends and the change comes shall I be myself, emerging from the solitude in which the change occurred and must recur, over and over. Then the solitude will become one of two poles, and the other, of open communication, will be the purer for it.

To the question, "What am I to do?" no practical instructions are available, only answers that will illuminate demands which everyone must make upon himself.

First, I am to inform myself all around, to be able to make well-founded decisions. I am to take notice of facts, but to do so critically. I am to think the possibilities through, to make room for knowing my own will.

Second, I am to try to come from the false consciousness of what is and what I am — from the consciousness in which I find myself now — to a true consciousness. To discover acts of self-deception, truthfulness calls for distrust, but for a distrust arising from trust in the possibility of freedom.

Third, I am to change my life. Without this change I shall not be worthy of trust and capable of unreserved communication. Without this change in countless individuals, mankind cannot be saved either.

Fourth, wherever I stand, I am to make my own choices. What must be done is not to be set in motion by general precepts; it needs a substantial foundation in the historic existence of every individual. He who criticizes government policy ought to ask himself first how he is living and acting, and whether his own motivations and conduct have not helped to bring such politicians to power.

Fifth, I am to realize that my purpose — saving the life of mankind — cannot be attained as a purpose, only as a result. If those who determine the course of events have changed their lives to accord with encompassing reason, their activities in the world — in pursuing material interests, in personal intercourse, in everyday living — will preclude actions that lead to general ruin and will facilitate actions that make for a common human ground.

The first premise of political action is that everyone knows what is going on. Our situation might arouse us as no previous one has; the palpable jeopardy of man's very existence might awaken slumbering human depths. But have there not been similar situations on the eve of threatening disaster, before some horror that men felt in their bones? "My contemporaries," Heinrich von Kleist wrote in a manifesto,

happy or hapless contemporaries — what shall I call you? . . . What marvelous blindness ignores the proximity of monstrous, unheard-of events, the ripening of things of which our great-grandchildren will still speak with horror! What changes are due! What changes are you in the midst of, unseeing, thinking that trivia are happening in your trivial void! . . . This prophecy — yes, more than once have I heard these words chided as exaggerations. They are said to induce a certain false shock that weakens rather than excites the minds. People are said to look back to see if the end is really yawning beneath their feet; if they see the towers and gables of houses still standing, they breathe again as though awakening from a bad dream.

Kleist was writing of the Napoleonic menace. It sounds as if it had been said today, and yet it referred to a limited threat — not, as now, to a total one affecting all mankind. Today, fear has become a political reality. We have peace today because of fear on both sides, due to the atomic balance of terror. But this in itself is not a peace to rely on.

What matters is where the fear takes us, whether we repress it in blind obliviousness or let it sink in to clear our rational vision. Fear may cause us to recall the roots of humanity and to grow aware of our task: to prepare the ground, by changing the individual and thus the general political ethos, for dissolving the state of fear into a state of legality upheld by self-sacrifice and reason. Yet this task can be fulfilled only together with our other task: to make life worth living, by the same self-sacrifice and reason. Fear for life, and for the foundation of all life, need not pass everywhere into the blind fear that simply wants to prevent war at any cost — that will not arm when others arm, will not prepare for defense when others prepare for attack — a fear that vaguely tends to submit to force peacefully, step by step, without bloodshed, and to endure slavery if only life remains.

The first step today is to increase the fear — though perhaps not among the political leaders who know it, and live in it, if they are responsible. What needs increasing is the fear of the people; this should grow to overpowering force, not of blind submissiveness, but of a bright, transforming ethos that will bring forth appropriate statesmen and support their actions.

For fear is ambiguous. As sheer fear it merely cries for help at any cost and is in vain. It must turn into a power that compels men to save themselves in the sphere of reason; then it can evoke the will that grasps its meaning before Transcendence, transforms man, and makes him true. The great fear of mankind can be a creative fear, and then it will work like a catalyst for the emergence of freedom.

To this end, all must know and be affected — not a few individuals, but the people of the nations. They must be reminded constantly, publicly, of our situation, of the facts and possibilities; from distraction they must be brought to attention by ceaseless repetition of the crucial point in new wordings and convincing mental pictures. Only thus can the point be brought home to all men. It must be said, argued, shouted daily. The matter must not be allowed to rest, neither in public nor in the mind and heart of any individual.

This demand is resisted by our desire for quiet and conventionality. We want to forget. We make moral taboos of our illusions; whoever disturbs them is rebuked for undermining our morale, for cutting the ground from under us, or for spreading panic. Panic, we hear, is always bad. But the cry, "Above all, no panic!" is misleading. We are not talking of the moment of crisis, when disaster is upon us and panic adds to the confusion. We are talking of the lasting, urging fear that may make us save ourselves.

The warning, "Above all, no panic," corresponds to the German slogan of 1933, "Above all, no civil war!" It voices the self-deceiving will to avoid an evil at the cost of getting into the worst of evils. You wait for a solution, for things to take a better turn "by themselves." A desire for quiet that ventures nothing is mere blind fear disguised as pseudo-reason.

Others object to alarming people as futile, since a vast majority would react quite differently from our expectations. They would be too dull to hear the facts and too unimaginative to envision them; repetition would only deafen them further; at bottom, they would not believe us. Or they would refuse to give any thought to mankind's doom, fearing only their own death, and that only when it is imminent. Or they would react passively, because "there is nothing to be done about it, anyway." They would live blithely from day to day: "We're here now, and the morrow will take care of itself — it won't be so bad." Or they might comfort themselves with international agreements, call for negotiations, and believe in the effectiveness of any accord, on the theory that things will get well "step by step."

A final objection points out that fear will cause panic wherever and whenever things are to be done that make the danger immediately sensible. People dread the construction of nuclear power piles, for instance. Or, if an army is to be equipped with atomic weapons, there is a frightened reaction: "We'll be safer if this hellish thing is elsewhere but not right here; let's renounce it, so we'll be spared." The consequence is a tendency to yield to any blackmailing atomic power. This sort of panic shuts our eyes to the over-all world situation, to world strategy, to the possibilities of atom bomb use, and to the conditions of world peace. It paralyzes any comprehensive reflection on the true premises of security.

All these objections show the perils of half-knowledge and the possible results of fear. Are we to conclude that it is better to keep silent, to conceal things, and to calm people? No — for as human beings we have no way but that of knowledge and fear. It is too little knowledge that shows in the panicky fear; we must see to it that the relevant facts are known in their entirety. Senseless fear produces abstract, inadequate, purely intellectual reactions, illusory hopes, silly blunders. Such fear should be clarified so as to lead to rational vision rather than blind panic. If panicky fear drives us into irrationality, enlightened fear frees us for reason. We must take the unlimited risks of knowledge and fear if we want to remain truly human.

The risks of a false reaction to fear do not mean that there are no chances. We may reason this way: it is in talking of the terrible threat that the challenge posed by man's true nature is illuminated. About the existence of this challenge there can be no doubt; and if it exists, we may hope that it can be heard and heeded. Not to share this hope means to have lost all confidence in man. Though shaken by no matter how many facts, this confidence can be restored from the depths in which every honest, thinking individual hears the challenge. If I have no confidence in man, I have no confidence in the foundation of man's existence.

Can one live without any confidence? There seems to be such a living pattern — which may be cited as a final objection to confidence itself. In the last analysis, confidence must prevail without the support of any rational proof.

A sense of stability marked most historical ages. There were great events, dangers, adventures, but in a changeless, valid world order that kept men safe. Today we feel caught up in an all-consuming motion to which we contribute, unintentionally or intentionally, by what we do and what we are. As the pace quickens, everyone is swept along willy-nilly. We keep trying for temporary stabilizations, but an absolute one is futile. In the past, the movement of history was dispersed and unconscious; now it has become one global, conscious process of mankind.

Three basic political approaches to this movement have emerged and failed.

The first says: I will have no part in the course of calamity. I want to keep myself pure, and I can do so only by excluding myself, ready to bear what the course of events may bring, and to perish in it. There have been such ways of life since time immemorial. Ascetics live in the world that tolerates them, feeds them, wants them at times, but does not concern them; they do not intervene in it, ask nothing, suffer everything — they live as if the world did not exist. Today, however, such a life is hardly possible. Wherever modern civilization penetrates, man is compelled to work, to assume some function in the totality of labor. There is little room for the contemplative life. On the other hand, this life of "count me out" is actually quick to turn impure, inconsistent, and contemptible. It becomes either skeptical indifference or outraged acceptance in a still uninjured personal position. This leads to the confusion of condemning what I live by — and wanted to hold aloof from. It should not concern me, yet I am entangled in it by my life and judgment.

The second approach says: I want to be in on it. This is a world process; what does not go along is annulled or annihilated by irresistible fate. I can be either nothing or part of the substance of things, so whatever enters with the iron tread of necessity will lead me. I am not only with it — I am it, if I hear and obey. My fate is one with the world's; I see and welcome the wave of the future. I become a Nazi; I become a Communist; I obediently apply the force I share in to those who resist or who do not belong, to those of ill will or to those naturally unfit for what I know to be truth as well as reality. Whatever cruelty, seeming injustice, and coercion is committed by the force I live by, the force that carries me, is the destined course of salvation. This force does only what must happen in any case. I know the world spirit, the course of history — the why and how of the struggle of classes or races, for instance — and I do what I have come to know. My sense of existence is powerfully enhanced, proving that I am on the right track. And if things go wrong, I mull over the dark destiny of being; I extract, experience, excogitate that there is such a thing, that it was hidden and will appear, and I stand ready to follow. . . . It is this pliant thinking that makes men ready to go along with each new despotism, without any faith but that in their own knowledge of historic destiny.

The third approach is that of defiant independence. I cannot be indifferent to this chaotic world, this conglomeration of stupidity and malice, for I am outraged. There is no other world; but this one, as it is, is not for me. My reality is negation — in general, and consequently in every particular. I defy this nonsense. I take what personal happiness comes my way, against the general trend, and I perish senselessly, but in possession of my inner independence.

Yet in so doing I involve myself in contradictions. I am outraged, but I cannot remain guiltless. Under the Nazis, life in negation was still carried on in Nazi terms; I was, in fact, living by the Nazis and sharing their guilt if my "No" did not extend to the instant risk and sacrifice of my life. So it is with every negation of things at large. The man who says "No" — whether audibly, as in the free world where any nonsense may be uttered, or inaudibly — still goes on living. He thinks he is being different in this life, an exception, a case of resistance on the smallest scale, a private individual, an outsider. Yet everything tends to entangle him in the reality he rejects.

All three approaches — worldlessness, complicity, defiance — are inadequate to the problem. Each time, the solution seems clear but is unclear and biased in practice, in relation to the whole. All three miss the existential situation. They lose sight of the measure of man; they miss the human opportunities of reason. The ascetic is ineffectual; he seems to vanish in his solitude. The joiner surrenders to the evil of violence. The stubborn independent does not get beyond saying "No" to an evil for which he, too, bears the guilt. These three approaches do not tell us what to do; they show only what does not help.

The basic question is what makes life worth living.

To achieve a life that is worthy of him, man must survive — but he will survive only if he achieves that life. This is a circle that we cannot break out of merely to stay alive. Now, at the brink, mere life depends on worthy living. This alone leads to the actions that would bar atomic doom.

For such a life it cannot suffice to be safe, peaceful, and prosperous. There are ambiguities in praising, respecting, worshipping life as such.

The faith in life is truthful when it explores the mystery of living; it is truthful when it protects the human body — even a legally imprisoned criminal's — from physical violation by the state; it is still truthful when it shudders to kill in war. But it is not the last thing. It becomes untruthful, untrue, and ruinous when life as such is made the sole, the absolutely highest good. Then man takes the place of Transcendence, expressing an actual lack of faith.

Besides, it is a vain endeavor to stem the march to the abyss by proclaiming the sanctity of life, for this kindles only inconsequential emotions, not a revival of the ethos itself.

The life worship becomes untrue wherever it forgets that man is superior to his life. He can sanctify it only by fulfilling his task. The conditions of a life worthy of man, the premises of finding the road to salvation, are the risk and the sacrifice of life — not in themselves, but as moments of human reason and love.

The questions are always the same. What makes life worth living? What do I want in the face of extremity? What will I do, what will I be, how will I live in awareness of my humanity and our common peril? Is there a truth that makes the ultimate effort and, if it fails, lets us meet the end without fear?

This is where ends and means and plans and achievements cease. What makes life worth living has consequences in action and in the conduct of life, but it cannot be willed — for it is the source of our will. Man's present reality must show what is, and what he is, but it can show this only on the premise and in the fulfilment of his way of life. I live in order to manifest it, and this kind of life is already the manifestation.

The threat of doom will not be banished by measures confined to the atom bomb, nor by measures designed merely to prevent a new war; what is required is that all particular actions, purposes, plans, agreement, or institutions issue from the entirety of human life. What is done in any of these directions will be lastingly, constructively successful only if all of them, without exception, work together. The result would be a new politics.

At first, the new politics would have to move in the tracks of the old politics that is still with us but must be overcome. What the change in individuals can sometimes accomplish cannot be done at once in the community of all. Attempts at instant reformation would quickly produce total anarchy and despotism. The political change must let the

use the postal system

new grow in the framework of the old; it must fill the old track with new meanings, until it can be left for a new track. Individual decisions make this a common process, with large areas still in darkness as the light starts shining here and there.

The old politics acts on the principles of present enmity and future war; the new politics will act on the principle that there can be honest, rational communication and peace. What matters in the old politics is neither to be fooled by your opponent nor to fool yourself; each jeopardizes self-preservation. But what matters further, to make the new politics possible, is to drum the reality and the meaning of all those activities into the general consciousness, to strip the camouflage from what goes on not only among our enemies but among ourselves — for it is only then that man can come out of his drifting, that ethos, reason, and self-sacrifice can awaken and find both the valor of self-preservation and the turn to a true will to peace in a new politics. The old politics sees everything in the reality of friend and foe, with reference to war. The new politics will search in this reality for the premises of peace.

To the old politics, which ultimately relates all things to the Cold War and the impending hot one, all spheres of life turn into "theaters of war." In present world strategy we find not only a military theater, but economic, cultural, ideological, religious theaters of war — effects upon all of which are carefully considered and psychologically calculated in the propaganda effort to sway opinions, motives, ways of action. Our time will make the choice between this refinement of the old politics and its transformation. If the change occurs, the question will be not only where violent struggle shall cease, but where and how struggles that are not naturally violent shall be divorced from violence and retained. Every step toward pure, non-violent struggle is a step in the conquest of war.

While the threat of war exists, reason would be weakened if a statesman, or a nation, abolished all indirect, war-related methods at one stroke. But everyone today can know about these methods and be aware of the unnatural, poisonous, ruinous abuse they constitute. The question now is when it will be politically possible to venture into the new politics — to stop the abuse of economics as a political weapon, for instance, because the inner self-preservation of the Western world (as discussed in our chapter on the end of colonialism) has developed far enough to permit it.

The old politics does not recognize any act that does not benefit its own state power. Even "cultural policy" is part of power politics. When it communicates its own national spirit, its language, its works, its way of life, it is thinking of national prestige, not of humanity — except, perhaps, when it fancies its nation as humanity's perfect embodiment, a model of human excellence which all the rest should join for their own salvation.

The new politics will be able to proceed with candor, because its self-preservation is strictly defensive and without expansionist aims. It gives up any claims to totality; it grants freedom; it allows ideas to be communicated regardless of their political consequences. It dares to promote its own way as a common way for all, by relinquishing the power potentials of the old politics. It frankly shows both its self-interest, if any, and its disinterestedness. Thus it can stimulate forces that agree with it.

The passage from the old politics to the new would be the passage from falsehood to truth. Today, the old "sophistical maxims" are still as effective as when Kant exposed them. *Fac et excusa* — do it when you have the chance, and explain later; the very brazenness of the deed lends it a certain glow of inner conviction, because success is the best advocate. *Si fecisti, nega* — if you did it, deny that you are at fault; blame others or human nature. *Divide et impera* — set the rulers against the people or against each other; by seeming to side with the underdog you will subject them all, one by one. Kant says that these maxims, being generally known, do not fool anyone, and that no one is ashamed of being found out, only of having failed — for aggrandizement of power, however accomplished, is the only honor in politics.

The new politics would make men ashamed of following these maxims. They would no longer win appreciative smiles from the knowing and unsmiling applause from masses that do not believe in man because they do not believe in themselves. Not until men are changed can they frankly resolve to discard the sophistical maxims, the principle of falsehood in politics, in word and deed.

The old politics culminates, on the one hand, in the frankly ruthless will to power that exterminates the enemy who does not submit and, on the other hand, in the disingenuous, deceiving, and self-deceiving vindication of war by the sole guilt of the enemy, whom the victor calls to account. In the case of naked force there is the chance of mercy; in the case of hypocritical justification, the chance of merciless exploitation of victory by imposing intolerable burdens upon the vanquished.

The new politics, resting on the political ethos that regards peace as the now definitive premise of any human existence, will press for firm moral judgments, but the essence of evil, in its eyes, is the lie — above all, the hypocritical lie — including the grain of falsehood in a true ac-cusation. It will end the most diabolical, though seemingly unbloody, type of combat: the tallying-up of one another's guilt by every means at hand. Instead, like a rational individual, it seeks to preserve itself by finding its own faults first. Where the fault lies with the other side, where a principle (and not, therefore, its every human representative!) seems morally and politically evil, the new politics will show concretely what is going on, will analyze, illuminate, expose the noxious principle — but it will do so, first, without abandoning its own truthfulness at any point of the exposure, and second, without censoriousness, intending, rather, to convince.

This struggle never ceases. To let it go on in the light of full publicity is the beginning of peace. In this true battle of minds — which today, in the framework of the old politics, is often so obscured as to be imper-ceptible — the point is to know the facts and to impart ideas. It is to cut to the root of the matter, to find the simplest forms in which men can absorb ideas and be convinced — not to falsify truth and conviction with suggestive slogans that will substitute for understanding. We cannot elaborate here, but ahead of us lies a great new world of intellectual struggle, distinguished by breadth, abundance, and precision, and in-spired by the ethos of a true polemics that no longer wants to hoodwink men with sophisms but will seek truth together.

Violent war will cease once the battle of minds has shown it up, with all its premises, as a thing we cannot want any more. War will cease when men are no longer fooled, when they sense the power of con-viction in their own thinking, and when they understand that they themselves are responsible for the evil if they promote it by their un-truthfulness.

In foolishly idealistic politics we act as if the condition we want had been attained already. In foolishly realistic politics we act as if it were unattainable. Both ways are irresponsible. The responsible way is to foster each rudiment, to nurture each germ, to take up each good im-pulse, to see the chances of the future in the facts of the present and to think and act with these chances in mind. This is not a middle way be-tween extremes; it is the high road above the two abysmal benightments that we call idealism and realism.

What we are asking here may seem too much. It is possible, but dishearteningly unlikely. Yet hopelessness is the anticipation of defeat; man is not entitled to it as long as he can act — and this appears to be his only way of acting so as to come to himself and at the same time save his temporal existence.

The course of human events has not been purely calamitous: there was, and is, the reality of reason. The development of reason is the story of philosophy, that truly human trait which runs through mankind but has never ruled it yet. Now, our salvation hangs upon the rule of reason. If reason as a whole is ineffective, if its power fails, doom seems bound to follow — and yet, to the very moment of doom, it is not certain. Until that moment, the chance of rational action leaves room for hope. If our faith in reason is shaken by the experience of many irrational moments in ourselves, and by the rule of unreason in the world, experience still tells us also how reason has been awakened and how it may grow. If we cannot count on meeting reason, we still see that everything good is done in the confidence of meeting reasonable men.

If I grow despondent in view of extremity, reason tells me that it is the coward who comes to conclusions about the end, about inevitable doom. The man of courage, no matter how much he knows, does what he can and keeps hoping as long as he lives.

Philosophy, too, is ossified rather than brave if it merely makes us wait stoically to be buried by the expected disaster. Courageous philosophy stirs us in our innermost depths and lets us learn what extremity reveals.

We have the sight of the glorious world left to us, and the loving union with others for the time it is granted. Left to us is the assurance of an eternal source in our temporal love. Left, on this foundation, is the aim of living in this world by reason — not just by the finite intellect — and the rational direction of our thoughts, our impulses, our efforts from everyday life on, toward staving off the imminent final catastrophe.

When we, when all come to reason — when some come to it, not in spots, but in their entire lives, when this reason, once kindled among a few, spreads like a purifying flame — then only may we hope confidently that disaster will be averted.

The confidence that tells us that what seems utopian is not impossible — that miracles may happen — is not founded in this world. We receive it, if we fulfil it by our potentialities, from a source that encompasses this world. Yet if the moment of total perdition should come, this would show in the horizon of our knowledge that our reason, too, has been a temporal, transient phenomenon. We do not know its purpose; we are conscious only of the need for it, conscious that it would be better to perish knowingly, as rational beings, than to live blindly through the years and to plunge to our doom irrationally, first hastening it, then overwhelmed by fear.

Reason gives us lasting confidence even if it should vanish in time, along with human existence. What sort of confidence? In the world, reason is the ultimate of our possible foundations. But it is not the ultimate itself, for temporal existence is not ultimate reality. Of that reality we cannot speak as we do of things in the world, of objects or ideas that are tangible or conceivable, as speech requires. And yet, even if all temporal existence in our human categories comes to an end, we still ask: Whither? It is not nothing, if reason was heeded in freedom.

If we halt at the limits of the world and judge from its perspective, we are taking what is called the modern point of view. From this viewpoint, the present vista of doom — man's, not the world's — has not arisen from religious motives; it is the real, technological situation alone that compels us to recognize the total menace. It becomes the pivot of our lives. And in all honesty, confidence cannot be absolute in the world: the peril remains; we can only be confident that men *should* follow the dictates of reason. To this end, to live and act confidently in such utter uncertainty, we need a more profound confidence that is not of this world, nor born of reason alone.

It was a dreadful thought for cultured men of former generations to want no children rather than see them exposed to the villainies of coming mob rule — or for others to wonder whether it would not be sensible and desirable for mankind to commit suicide by refusing to procreate. Today, some may be even more strongly tempted to want no children, lest they fall a prey to the inevitable horror of atomic death.

Indeed, if man is not driven by thoughtless vitality, nothing short of *transcendent reality* will encourage him to continue in an increasingly menacing world and to risk himself in his children. Nowhere else can he look for guidance that may show them the way to belong to those who will, perhaps, avert disaster.

Would the doom of reason be the revelation of nothingness? No, for its own existence assures reason that it is not void. To have striven for it is worthy of man — and possible for man, because his own self was given to him in the gift of reason, he knows not whence. Because it is sure of itself only if it is conscious of being a demand from elsewhere, reason has an unknown, unknowable reality in the eternal.

In eternity, our idea of God has its only fixed point. What other particular form it assumes is secondary, for any form is inadequate. To the Westerner, the idea of God in the terminal situation of failure is historically founded on the Bible: the prophets spoke of total doom, of the Day of Yahweh when everything would be destroyed; the early Christians spoke of the imminent end of the world. When state and nation and even the faith of the Jews broke down and the remnants were sacrificing to Isis, Jeremiah told Baruch, his despairing disciple, "The Lord saith thus: Behold, that which I have built will I break down, and that which I have planted I will pluck up, even this whole land. And seekest thou great things for thyself? Seek them not; for behold, I will bring evil upon all flesh." Suffice it that God be, is Jeremiah's meaning.

This is the final horizon, from which all things are seen in the proper perspective. In this horizon, courage grows from a confidence that no temporal failure can quench, not even that of reason. This confidence gives us the will to pursue reason as long as men exist, to dare and to build even if we cannot know how long our building will stand.

The reality of God's existence is not irrational, no triumph of a phantom; it is suprarational and includes and encompasses reason. It is this reality which asks us to be rational. Reason is its gift to man, to be freely, creatively developed and held fast. The cause of all things is not reason but the incomprehensible reality above us, the symbolic term for which is God.

God is unthinkable. Thoughts and concepts of God are symbols, misleading if taken by themselves. We may call God "almighty," transcending all reason but encompassing reason — yet if this symbol is conceived after the fashion of temporal might, it becomes sacrilegious nonsense. The suprarational deity becomes irrational and arbitrary; the Almighty turns into a tyrant. Or we may call God "personal." This concept, too, is a symbol, expressing a sense of being linked with the first cause, trusting in spite of all, as we trust a person. But "personal" is an inappropriate word for the deity, which is more than personal — being, rather, the "cause" of personality as it appears in man. Thus the deity is being thought and conceived in manifold, ever inadequate symbols — most adequately, perhaps, where the idea has no worldly content any more and seems to vanish as a mere form in the void. For it is still from that void that we are upheld by the full force of the true reality.

Confidence is placed in the hidden deity. The besmirching of the idea of God by Gnostic legends, by speculations and images entangled with gods and demons, turns our free trust into an unfree certainty. If the deity is present, immutable, and real, the mists and will-o'-the-wisps and sorceries of thought and conception disappear. Before the deity, all worldly things become trivial and yet infinitely significant to finite rational creatures, as manifestations of their pledge of eternity. Here alone is true confidence.

What Jeremiah said on the final horizon may be enough. Job put it into words: "The Lord hath given, the Lord hath taken away, blessed be the name of the Lord." This is the selfless thought: suffice it that God be; I cannot know his will, but it is mine. Any prayer of praise and thanksgiving expresses this human selflessness that has no interest but one: the reality of God. It must despair if this reality fails, for existence is nothing. No argument can assure it of temporal realities; even if it lives with them — and how unsteadily in time! — it knows this is not its own doing. Hence the praise and thanks to the incomprehensible.

May we ask more? Personal immortality, eternal bliss, or "grace"? Must we see more: "the eternal punishments of hell"?

If our consciousness of immortality is real, it does not need any guarantee. To the philosophical human being, any "promise" is man-made, in fact; the churchly belief that it is God's word can be neither affirmed nor denied by philosophy. This faith, which localizes God's direct revelation in the world, in time and place, must be left alone and known by its fruits in the world, in its sometimes ambiguous reality. The word of men carries weight if the speakers are trustworthy. Though it brings no assurance, no promise, no revelation to our philosophizing, it does give us an irreplaceable association with men who have come to themselves in a situation like ours, who have asked their questions and lived their answers.

Our sense of immortality lies in conscience. It lies decisively in love, that wondrous reality — we are mortal when we are loveless, immortal when we love. Our love for the dead would be faithless if it lost its sense of eternity.

But whether and how we know that we and our loved ones are immortal does not depend on actual knowledge — there is none — but on ourselves. There is no natural process of immortality, alike for all, as birth and death are. Immortality does not happen by itself. I gain it if I am loving and good, but I disintegrate if my life is loveless and jumbled. Loving, I see the immortality of those who are bound to me in love.

We symbolize our sense of immortality as a future community of beloved spirits, of all spirits. This symbol does not mean a physical existence, as we experience it in time and space; it limns a picture of eternity, as of a future in time. It is an illusion to take the symbol for existential reality. An immortality in the sense of future existence would cease being immortality; it would be an infinitely prolonged and — as Lessing put in — infinitely dull existence. Immortality is the eternity that encompasses all time, but it is not time.

One whose life is fulfilled in the present — "immortal" — bears the future in time. One whose present life is empty bears no future. To live for the moment, in an attitude of *après moi le déluge*, it not to enjoy even the moment.

Taken as a reality, the symbol of immortality tempts us to take things easy in the world. If I am assured of my place in heaven, I grow more indifferent to the world. If a concrete revelation promises me a concrete immortality, I am distracted from whatever, to my last moment in time, must remain essential if I am to do my job in the world and thus to experience the true immortality which symbols merely illuminate. If, on the other hand, I have no sense of immortality at all — if I am certain that there is no eternity, nothing but the reality experienced by my senses — then all seriousness comes to an end. I lapse into hapless doings and driftings without a goal, a prisoner of abstractions. Things lose their transparency. No symbols speak to me, though their traditional language purls on in conventions, and my feeling of their brittleness frees me from all restraint: nothing is true; everything is permitted. I vegetate in callous indifference or go on a rampage of my new nihilistic experience.

"Not famine, not pestilence, not war will bring back seriousness," Kierkegaard said. "It is not till the eternal punishments of hell regain their reality that man will turn serious." Indeed it would seem so. The man who doubts hell without living by the strength of philosophical thinking is lost; there is more reason in the idea of hell than in the pseudo-certainty of being able to indulge myself unpunished because death will end everything. Yet the threat of punishment is no more appropriate than the promise of eternal bliss; both would divide the indivisible, the eternity in time. Evil carries hell within it now, as virtue is its own reward.

What the fear of hell-fire used to accomplish can now be done by philosophical thinking, if it is not just a mental operation but reflects on existence. The reality of the meaning behind the concept of hell is as certain to philosophical insight as the concept's symbolic nature. What is at work, in purified form, in the truth of philosophizing is the same power that used to work on man's concrete fears by the image of a supposedly real hell. Only he can claim truth who is sure enough of the eternity of present love and conscience to live in it more firmly than he could have in the concrete fear of hell. He can afford using symbols as long as he does not consider them more than they are. Kierkegaard's phrase is ambiguous: bad if it means a faith that is actually superstition, good if it rouses the seriousness of eternity in human doings.

We are received by the real, unforeseeable future as long as the eternal manifests itself; we are no longer received by a real future when we experience its doom. Both times, the eternal is real to us only if it includes ourselves.

What is the present that is eternal? It is the clairvoyant love of humans sharing their destinies in rational union; it is the consciousness of doing right; it is the strength of advancing on the path of reason; it is the resistance that checks my self-will, my drifting, my untruthfulness, my anger, my arrogance, like the flaming sword of an angel parrying whatever would revolt in my existence; it is what happens in the deepest recesses of my being, by myself and not by myself alone; it is what guides my outward actions.

Measured by the yardstick of the deity, what I do — and what mankind, through the men for whose leadership it must answer, decides about itself — is nothing. But in this nullity it is infinitely important to man as what is left to his freedom, what is up to him.

The eternal present, immortality, is not a mock future dangled before the glorious and terrible urge to live that is never sated and always wants only to go on living — the urge that seizes all of us, to our good fortune and to our ruin. Let us not slander its beauty. Being deceptive as well as bountiful, however, it is not our salvation. We could not live without it; but with this alone we remain fatally deficient.

The vista of doom enhances the felicities of love, of proximity, of all that is surely ephemeral in time — not because we should drown and forget our sorrows in quick enjoyment ("Let us eat and drink, for tomorrow we die"), but because this dark present background brightens the shining certainty of the unimaginable and unthinkable in space and time.

The course of things does not involve the entire individual. It does involve his whole physical and political existence and all his concepts and thoughts — but not, in all this, his entire potential existence, which cuts across time, is superior to time, is really present.

This present is not an eternity that was or will be; but in time it is both remembrance — meaning repetition — and hope, meaning expectation. Repetition and expectation are mere temporal aspects, if the eternal present becomes manifestly conscious in time and space and, by these symbols, in categories of thought. In understanding them, eternity stays with itself.

It is the shortcoming of temporality that in it remembrance and hope must constantly supplement what could be abundant and self-sufficient only as eternity itself. At sublime moments, man may have an overpowering experience of the eternal present: in the act of sacrifice, in the unquestioning, all-illuminating power of love, in contemplative insight, in the confidence of reason. But the moment vanishes, extinguishing time. It only endures, for all time, as ground for hope.

Unfathomable remembrance reveals the eternal present but will never lose a touch of infinite longing. The all-encompassing breadth of hope lets us bear the evanescent temporality but finds no fit expression, since its content is not a future in this world.

Jesus told his disciples: "Behold, the kingdom of God is within you" — it is here. So it is to philosophical thinking: what counts is the reality of the eternal, the way of life and action, as encompassing immortality.

This presence of eternity may result in mankind's rescue from suicide. And in this presence, even if reason and existence fail, hope will remain.